RECOLLECTIONS AND OPINIONS OF AN OLD PIONEER

By Peter H. Burnett
The First Governor of the State of California

THE NARRATIVE PRESS
TRUE FIRST-PERSON HISTORICAL ACCOUNTS

To Col. Alexander W. Doniphan, The Xenophon Of The Mexican War, The Able And Eloquent Advocate, The Man Of Undoubted Integrity, This Work Is Dedicated, As Evidence Of The Admiration And Esteem Of His Old Friend,

The Author

.

This edition is a reproduction of an early original copy published and printed in 1880 by D. Appleton And Company, 1, 3, and 5 Bond Street: New York.

The Narrative Press
P.O. Box 2487, Santa Barbara, California 93120 U.S.A.
Telephone: (800) 315-9005 Web: www.narrativepress.com

ISBN 1-58976-256-8 (Paperback)

Produced in the United States of America

CONTENTS

Preface.

In the month of October, 1860, I began to write out my recollections and opinions, intending to leave the manuscript to my children, as I thought that a true account of my opinions, and long and diversified experience, might be of benefit to them and their posterity, though of less importance to others. But I had not progressed very far before I was interrupted by several causes.

Since November, 1860, I had not further prosecuted my design until the month of March, 1878. In the month of December, 1877, a learned and distinguished historian, then and now engaged in writing a general history of the Pacific coast, called upon me, and kindly requested me to furnish him with such historical data as I possessed. Having already reduced to writing a considerable portion of my recollections and opinions, I determined to finish the work I had undertaken, and to permit him to take a copy of all, or such portions as he might desire, for his use in preparing his own history.

I had lived so long and seen so much, and my experience had been so varied, that the task grew upon my hands as I proceeded, and has swollen into a volume almost double the size first anticipated. Until the month of October, 1879, and until after I had separately submitted the manuscript to the examination of two learned and able men, I had not decided to publish it. Circumstances have induced me to do so; and, as the work has been so largely written from memory alone, its publication during my life will enable me to correct any serious mistakes I may have made. The narrative ends with September 26, 1878.

The work, having been originally intended for my children, contains much personal and family history, more interesting to my relatives than to the general reader. Yet, as my own history is connected to some extent with that of the Western and Pacific States, I think there are some facts stated of general importance, which have not been, perhaps, so fully recorded by others.

I was born a pioneer, as Nashville at the date of my birth was but a small village, and Tennessee a border-State, but thinly populated. I have been a pioneer most of my life; and whenever, since my arrival in California, I have seen a party of immigrants, with their ox-teams and white-sheeted wagons, I have been excited, have felt younger, and was for the moment anxious to make another trip. If the theory of Symmes had been proven by time to be true, and had a fine and accessible country been discovered at the north or south pole before I attained the age of sixty, I should have been strongly tempted to organize a party of emigrants for that distant region.

While the settlement of a new country is full of perils, hardships, and privations, it is still exceedingly interesting. The first settlers find nature in a state of grand repose; but this repose is soon followed by great activity and most satisfactory progress. In some five or six years the orchards begin to bear their fruits, smiling villages, pleasant homes, and happy families are seen on all sides, and "the wilderness begins to blossom as the rose."

Chapter I.

I am the eldest son of George and Dorothy Burnet, and was born in Nashville, Tennessee, November 15, 1807. My father was born in Pittsylvania County, Virginia, September 26, 1770, and died in Clay County, Missouri, February 22, 1838. The family all spelled the name with a single t. When I was about nineteen, I added another t, and my example has been followed by all my brothers. My reason for the change was the opinion that the name would be more complete and emphatic when spelled Burnett.

My mother was the daughter of Thomas Hardeman, and was born in Davidson County, Tennessee, May 15, 1786, and died in Platte County, Missouri, March 17, 1843. My grandfather Hardeman was born in Virginia, January 8, 1750; and his brother, whom I never saw, settled in Georgia. My grandfather Hardeman was among the first settlers of Tennessee, and participated in the Indian wars of that country. He was a stout man, possessed a very fine constitution, a determined will, and *naturally* a splendid intellect. His education was originally very limited, but by study he became a man of distinction. He was the neighbor and warm friend of General Andrew Jackson, and was, with the General, a member of the first Constitutional Convention of Tennessee. He was a farmer and made a fortune, living to the age of seventy-two. He reared eight sons and three daughters: Nicholas Perkins, Nancy, John, Constant, Eleazar, Peter, Dorothy, Thomas Jones, Blackstone, Elizabeth, and Baily. All these married, and all reared families, except my aunt Elizabeth.

My grandfather Hardeman was twice married, his two wives being sisters, but all his children were the issue of his first marriage. He brought up his sons to his own business, except John and Baily, to whom he gave fine educations. They were intended for the bar, but never practiced. Both were men of fine mental capacity, especially uncle John, who was one of the most accomplished literary men of the Western States.

My grandfather Hardeman taught certain maxims to his children that have come down to his grandchildren, and have had a great influence over his posterity:

First. Pay your honest debts.

Second. Never disgrace the family.

Third. Help the honest and industrious kin.

My father came to Nashville when it was a small village, and was married to my mother in 1802, in Davidson County, Tennessee. He had several brothers and sisters, some of whom I remember to have seen. They nearly all lived and died in Kentucky. I never saw my grandfather Burnet. My father was a carpenter and farmer, uncle William was a blacksmith, uncle John a school-teacher, uncle James a farmer, and uncle Henry a cabinet-maker. All my father's brothers and sisters were married, and all reared families. All my uncles and aunts on both sides are gone. Many of them lived to be old people. I remember well when I belonged to the younger members of the family. Now I stand among the eldest.There was a great difference between my father's and mother's families. The Hardemans were fond of pleasure, and were generally extravagant when young. Most of them, especially my male cousins, when setting out in life, wasted their patrimony, not in dissipation of any kind, but in fashionable life; and afterward set earnestly to work, most of them making good livings, and some of them fortunes. The Hardemans were generally men of the world, first fond of fashionable pleasures, dress, and show, and afterward seekers of fortune. But, though wild when young men, I have yet to hear of the first instance in which they were ever accused of any criminal offense, great or small. They sometimes had fisticuff fights (though very rarely), but I never knew one of them to fight a duel. With very rare exceptions, they all paid their debts. They were generally good business men, and good traders in such property as lands and stock, and were punctual in keeping their promises, and firm in telling the truth. All of the name were very proud of the family; and, though they might have disputes among themselves, they would not permit others to speak ill even of those they themselves blamed. They were very generous in aiding their relatives in starting in business, generally by good advice to the young, and often by loans of money. They were especially kind to the unfortunate. They were generally quick-tempered and downright in the expression of their opinions. My grandfather Hardeman and most of his sons seemed to think it a conscientious duty, when they saw any one do what they clearly considered a mean act, to tell him what they thought of him in plain terms. They were candid and resolute men, and you always knew how you stood with them. If they disliked you, they would tell you so. There were many marriages between cousins, especially in the Perkins family, who were related through my grandmother Hardeman, whose maiden name was Perkins. The Perkins family came from North Carolina.

On the contrary, my father's family were not seekers of fortune, Uncle James being the only one who ever acquired any considerable amount of property. They were men of peace, very just, industrious, sober, and piously disposed. They cared very little for riches, being content with a fair living; but they possessed fine literary abilities. My father was raised very poor, and never went to school but three months in his life. He emigrated West while a young man, and spent his time mostly at hard work; and, although he had never studied English grammar, he wrote and spoke the language with substantial accuracy. He possessed an extraordinary mathematical talent, so that he could solve in a few moments very difficult problems. I remember an instance, which occurred after I was grown. I saw a problem published in a newspaper in Tennessee when I was about twenty-two, and it took me some three days to arrive at a correct solution. Upon a visit to my father in 1830, I proposed the same question to him, and it did not take him more than half an hour, and he did not make half as many figures as I had done. The rules by which he solved most questions were his own. He understood the *reason* of the science.

My uncle, John Burnet, had a fine talent for general science, and several of my cousins on my father's side have been lawyers of ability. One of my father's cousins, of whom I remember to have heard him often speak, and whose opportunities had been very limited, rose to distinction at the bar and on the bench. I remember my father often referred to this relative as a fit example for me to follow.

My father was very industrious, understood his trade as a carpenter well, and made a pretty good farmer; but he had no capacity for trading, and was often cheated. I never knew but one of the Hardemans who was dissipated, and that was Uncle Perkins; but that which was a cause of surprise was that, during the dissipated part of his life, he made a good living, and when he died left his family in comfortable circumstances. Of the Burnets, all the old set were examples of sobriety, peace, kindness, and honesty; and among the younger class, including cousins and half cousins, I never knew of but three who were confirmed drunkards; and I never heard of any one of the blood committing any crime, great or small.

My father and mother reared eight children, five sons and three daughters: Constantia Dudley, Peter Hardeman, Glen Owen, George William, Elizabeth Ann, James White, Mary Henry Jones, and Thomas Smith. Sister Constantia was twice married, and died in Liberty, Missouri, in 1846. Sister Mary married Dr. Benjamin S. Long in 1838, and died in Clay County, Missouri, in 1843. Sister Elizabeth has been twice married, and now lives a widow in Mendocino County, California, and has ten living children. Glen, Thomas, and myself reside in California, and my brother White in Oregon. My brother William lived in Oregon from the fall of 1846 until his death, December 25, 1877.

Our family are much divided in religion. Glen and White are Disciples, or Campbellites, as they are sometimes called; Sister Elizabeth is a Baptist; Thomas is a Southern Methodist; and I am Catholic. Brothers Glen and Thomas are preachers, Brother White is a farmer, and I am a banker. Brother Thomas is now living with his second wife. Glen and myself married sisters, the only daughters of Peter Rogers, who died in Clay County, Missouri, in 1858, aged about seventy.

We reared six children — three sons and three daughters:

Dwight J. Burnett, born in Hardeman County, Tennessee, May 23, 1829, and married to Miss Mary Wilcox in Sacramento City, January, 1850.

Martha L. Burnett, born in Liberty, Clay County, Missouri, April 29, 1833, and married to C. T. Ryland in Alviso, Santa Clara County, California, January 23, 1851.

Romeetta J. Burnett, born in Liberty, Missouri, February 14, 1836, and married to W. T. Wallace in Alviso, California, March 30, 1853.

John M. Burnett, born in Liberty, Missouri, February 4, 1838, and married to Miss Ellen Casey in San Francisco, April 27, 1863.

Armstead L. Burnett, born in Liberty, Missouri, October 7, 1839, married to Miss Flora Johnson in San José, California, November 21, 1860, and died in San José, May 26, 1862.

Sallie C. Burnett, born in Platte City, Platte County, Missouri, September 27, 1841, married to Francis Poe in San José, November 21, 1860, and died in Sacramento City, May 24, 1861.

REMOVALS: TO THE FARM — TO MISSOURI.

My father built several of the first log and frame buildings in Nashville, and one frame building for himself. My earliest recollections are connected with Nashville. I remember my father's house, and that he punished me one evening for running away from home; a circumstance well calculated, in its nature, to make a lasting impression. About 1811 he moved upon a farm in Williamson County, about four miles south of Franklin, and on the main road to Columbia, the county seat of Maury County. My grandfather Hardeman having removed to Howard County, Missouri, about 1816, my father went to look at that locality in the summer of 1817, and moved there in the fall of that year. We spent the first winter in a large camp with a dirt floor, boarded up on the sides with clapboards, and covered with the same, leaving a hole in the center of the roof for the escape of the smoke. All the family lived together in the same room, the whites on one side and the blacks on the other. In the fall of 1819, or spring of 1820, we removed to Franklin in the same county, then a most flourishing place, where my father worked at his trade and also kept a boarding-house, until the town began to decline; when, in the fall of 1820, we returned to the farm four miles above Franklin. The Missouri bottoms were exceedingly sickly in 1820-'21; so much so, that the larger portion of the inhabitants removed to the hills. In these years my father's family suffered very much from fever and ague. I remember that all of the family, fourteen in number, were sick at the same time, except a little negro boy about six years old. I suffered from fever and ague two falls and winters in succession, when I was twelve and thirteen years of age.

The location of my father's farm, in the Missouri bottom, being so unhealthy, we removed to Clay County in the spring of 1822, my father having entered a tract of 160 acres at the Land Office, at $1.25 per acre. Here we had to begin again to clear off the timber and build houses. The first steamboats I ever saw were at Franklin in 1820. They were the first steamers on the Missouri River, with one exception. A short time before, a single steamer, as I am informed, had passed a short distance above Franklin, and was snagged and sunk. The steamers that I saw were three in number, and were sent by Colonel Richard M. Johnson, contractor for supplies at Council Bluffs, at which point the United States Government then had a military post. I remember that one of these vessels was propelled by a stern-wheel, and had a large wooden figurehead, representing the head and neck of an immense snake, through the mouth of which the steam escaped. This boat made quite a grand appearance, and caused much speculation among the people. Some were of the opinion that all the steam machinery (which they called "works") was in the belly of this snake. I remember seeing these boats start up the river from the landing. They crossed over to the Booneville side, and in crossing were barely able to keep from falling below the point they left. This was in the summer, when the water was high and the current rapid. Now, however, a steamer on that river will stem the current at any stage of the water with ease. The boat alluded to was called "the Western Engineer." There were no regular steamboats on the river until some five years later.

The early settlers in Missouri had a very hard time of it, especially those who could not hunt the wild game successfully, which was at that time abundant. When we moved from Howard to Clay County (a distance of some two hundred and fifty miles by water), our supplies and household furniture were sent up the river in a flatboat, which had to be towed up most of the way by men, who walked upon the bank of the stream, pulling a long rope attached to the boat, and cutting down the willows along the bank in many places, so as to open a foot-path. The water was low, and it required some forty days to make the trip. All the supplies of merchandise were transported at that time from St. Louis to Liberty Landing in keel-boats. For this reason freight was high and prices in proportion: coffee, 50 cts. per pound; sugar, 25 to 37 1/2 cts.; calico, 37 1/2 to 50 cts. per yard; and brown cotton, from 25 to 37 1/2 cts. Iron and salt, two most necessary articles, were high, and it was difficult for farmers to pay for them.

It so happened that, although when we settled in Howard and Clay Counties provisions were scarce and high, when we had succeeded in raising produce for sale, the demand had diminished, the supply had increased, and prices declined to a low figure. Indian corn was 10 cts. a bushel, wheat 50 cts., pork $1.25 per hundred pounds, and other things in proportion. As everything the farmers had for sale was very *low*, and all they purchased very *high*, they were able to purchase very little, and that of the plainest description. A sack or two of coffee and a barrel of brown sugar would last a merchant some time. Many persons supplied themselves with maple sugar. This was the case with my father. I remember that "sugar-making time" was always a season of hard work, but of festivity with the young people, especially when the sugar was "stirred off." At this time what was called a "sugar-stick" was in great demand. After the sugar was molded into cakes or grained, it was carefully deposited in the black-walnut "sugar-chest," and put under lock and key. The ants were very fond of sugar, and would find their way into the chest. To keep them out, each of the four legs was put into a small, hollow, square block of wood, filled with tar. This Stygian pool these insignificant little pests would never cross.

MODE OF LIVING — MANNERS AND CUSTOMS

Our manner of living was very simple. For some years the only mills in the country were propelled by horses, each customer furnishing his own team, and taking his proper turn to grind his grain. At times when the mills were thronged (and this was generally so in winter), they had to wait from one to two days. During this time the mill-boys mostly lived on parched corn. The manner of sending to mill was to put a bag, some three feet long, and containing from two and a half to three bushels of grain, across the back of a gentle horse, the bag being well balanced by having the same quantity in each end, and then putting a man or boy upon the top to keep it on, and to guide the horse. It often happened that both bag and boy tumbled off, and then there was trouble, not so much because the boy was a little hurt (for he would soon recover), but because it was difficult to get the bag on again. When any one could shoulder a bag of corn, he was considered a man; and to stand in a half-bushel measure, and shoulder a bag containing two and a half to three bushels, was considered quite a feat. I heard of a woman who could do so, but never saw her, and can not say that the statement was true.

For some years very little wheat was grown, Indian corn being the only grain raised; and, when wheat was produced, there were no good flour-mills for some time. If, during those times, we had a biscuit and a cup of coffee every Sunday morning we were fortunate. As a substitute for coffee, we often used rye or corn meal parched;

and instead of "store tea" we used the root of the sassafras. Our clothing was "homespun," made by our mothers and sisters — jeans and linsey for the males, and linsey and striped cotton for the females. Hunting-shirts and pants of dressed buckskin were very common, and in some very rare cases females were clad in dressed buckskin. In summer the boys and girls went barefoot, and young and married women often. Moccasins were often worn instead of shoes. I have seen young women, in going to public places, stop a short distance before reaching the place, take off their coarse shoes, and put on their "Sunday shoes." Such a thing as a fine carriage was never seen. Some very few had what was then called a "Dearborn," being a small vehicle for one horse, and without any top to it. Our linsey and jeans for every-day use were usually colored with hickory or walnut bark, that of a finer quality with indigo. A suit of blue jeans was considered a fine dress. I remember that in Clay County, about 1824-'25, there were only three or four men who could boast of a suit of broadcloth. A young man who had been in the service of the United States as a soldier came to Liberty, Clay County, about that time, and dressed himself in a new suit of blue broadcloth, surmounted by an elegant new fur hat of his own workmanship (he was a hatter), and he used to strut up and down the only street in the place, to the great astonishment of others. At that time there must have been about three hundred voters in the county.

The principal trade at that date was in skins, honey, and beeswax, all wild productions. When Missouri was first settled, cotton was cultivated for domestic use. The seeds were picked out by hand, or by a small gin consisting of two wooden rollers, three quarters of an inch in diameter and a foot long, to one of which a crank and handle were attached. The operator sat across a bench, upon which the rollers on the top of a piece of timber were securely fastened, and turned the crank with his right and applied the cotton with his left hand. The rollers were placed together, so that turning one would turn the other; and, while the cotton, in thin slices, would pass between them, the seed could not. It was, however, a slow process.

What were called "cotton pickings" were then very common. The young people of the neighborhood assembled about dark, divided themselves into two equal parties, placed the quantity of cotton to be picked in two large piles before a big fire, and then commenced a race to see which party would get through first. The cotton picked more easily when warmed, and this was the reason for placing it before the fire. Much cheating was done by hiding away portions of the unpicked cotton. The object was to accomplish the task as early as possible, and then to enter into the dance, or the various plays then common, such as "Old Jake," "Pleased or displeased?" "Tired of your company?" "Bishop of Winchester has lost his crown," and "We are marching along toward Quebeck." I remember that, when I was about fourteen years of age, I attended a cotton-picking in Howard County, at the house of a widow. I had never danced any, and, though naturally diffident, I determined I would break the ice. There was present an old maid, Miss Milly A., with whom I was well acquainted — a large, corpulent woman, low, thick-set, and weighing about two hundred pounds. With her I danced some seven sets (most of them Virginia reels), without a rest. Though so large, she moved over the puncheon floor with ease and grace, and was amply able, I found to my sorrow, to tire me out; for the next day I was so sore that I could scarcely walk. This rash experiment cured me of dancing for some years.

At my father's house I never saw a cotton-picking. It was usual in the fall and winter to pick the cotton at night, in which task all of us participated who were able to work. The young ladies spun and wove, and often made a beautiful article of stiped and checked cotton cloth, out of which they made themselves dresses. Hemp and flax, especially the latter, were used in the manufacture of summer clothing for children and men. My sister Constantia was very fond of reading, was well educated for that day, and was the most talented of the family. I remember to have heard my mother laughingly complain that my sister would stop the loom any time to read a book. The weaving of the family was generally done by the white women, and mainly by the unmarried daughters.

It required great industry, rigid economy, and wise foresight to make a plain living in those times. I have often thought of the severe struggles of my parents and their children to live. The leather for our winter shoes was tanned at home, and the shoes for the family were made by my father and myself, after I was large enough to assist him. Peg-work was not then understood, and it required some little art to make and bristle "an end," as they called the waxed thread with which the shoes were sewed.

The climate of Missouri is cold and changeable, requiring stock to be fed some five or six months in the year. In the early settlement of the State, the people suffered much from sickness caused by exposure, bad food (as the corn from which the bread was made was often frost-bitten), and the decay of such masses of timber as were left dead in the fields.

Log-rolling was also one of the laborious amusements of those days. To clear away the dense forests for cultivation was a work of some years. The underbrush was grubbed up, the small trees (saplings) were cut down and burned, and the large trees belted around with the axe, by cutting through the sap of the trees, which process was called "deadening." The trees belted would soon die, and their tops first fall off, and afterward the trunks would fall down, often breaking the rail fences and crushing the growing corn, and in the winter time occasionally killing the cattle running in the stalk-fields. Sometimes a human being would be killed by a falling limb, or by a stroke of lightning. My sister Constantia's first husband, James M. Miller, was killed by lightning on the bank of the Missouri river at Booneville about 1821; and my wife only escaped death from a similar cause at Liberty, Missouri, in 1833, by accidentally leaving the fireplace where she was sitting, and retiring to the adjoining room, only just one moment before the lightning struck the stone chimney, throwing down the top, and melting together the blades of a pair of large scissors hanging below the mantel-piece against the chimney.

The early settlers of the West were greatly aided by the wild game, fruits, and honey, which were most abundant. There were walnuts, hickory-nuts, hazel-nuts, pecans, raspberries, blackberries, wild plums, summer, fall, and winter grapes; of game, the squirrel, rabbit, opossum, coon, deer, and black bear; and of fowls, the quail, wild duck, goose, swan, prairie chicken, and wild turkey, the noblest game-fowl among them all. For some years no tame turkeys were raised, as the wild were abundant and just as good. Domestication may change the color of the plumage, but not the quality or the color of the flesh of the turkey. One turkey hen would usually rear a flock of from ten to fifteen each year. We had dogs well trained to hunt the turkeys by trailing them up and forcing them to take refuge in the timber, the dogs standing below the turkey on the tree, and keeping up an incessant barking, so as to keep his attention fixed upon the dogs, while the skillful hunter approached unobserved within rifle-shot. The dogs used were the ordinary curs.

I remember a circumstance which occurred in Clay County when I was about seventeen, and my brother Glen fifteen. I had left my father's house, and was living with my sister Constantia's second husband, Major William L. Smith, then a merchant of Liberty. Two or three days before Christmas I went to visit my parents, and to spend the Christmas holidays at home. The well-trained dogs, Major, Captain, and Cue, had not forgotten me. My mother requested Glen and myself to kill some wild turkeys for the Christmas dinner, and directed us to shoot them in the head, so as not to tear the body. Fully confident in our marksmanship, we promised her we would do so. Taking the faithful and keen-scented dogs and the trusty old rifle, with its black-walnut stock and flint-lock, we started into the hills toward the Missouri bottoms, and soon found a flock of gobblers, one of which alighted in a tall red-oak tree, near the top. Being older than my brother and a guest, it was my privilege to have the first shot. I approached as near as I could venture to do (as I saw the turkey was very wild, from the high head he held), and determined that I would, as requested, shoot him in the head; but when I endeavored to take aim, the distance was so great and the object so small that I despaired of hitting his head; and so taking, as I thought, good aim at his body, I fired and he fell. From his much fluttering, I feared I had not given him a fatal shot, and that the dogs, in their efforts to kill him, would tear his flesh; so I told my brother to run to the turkey, while I remained to load my rifle, the custom of the hunter being to load his gun the first thing, and on the spot from which he fires his shot. When I had loaded and went to the turkey, I found I had shot him through the neck just below the head, the ball breaking his neck-bone. We then proceeded, and soon started up a flock of hens (as the hens and gobblers go in separate flocks in winter, and pair in spring), one of which alighted in the fork of a hackberry tree. I requested my brother to shoot, but he declined, thinking no doubt that I was a superior shot. So I determined, as before, that I would shoot the turkey in the head; but when taking aim I despaired of success, and taking, as I again thought, good aim at the body of the bird, I fired and she fell. When I came to examine her, I found my ball had just knocked off the top of her head, entering the skull to the depth of half an inch.

With these two turkeys we went home in triumph, and, as I did not then disclose the fact of having taken aim at the body, I was considered the best shot in the neighborhood. It was a singular circumstance that my mother should have first directed us to shoot the birds in the head, and that I should have accidentally done so twice in succession. The explanation is that I had simply overshot, owing perhaps to an overcharge of powder.

BEE-HUNT — FISTICUFF FIGHTS — LAZY BILL.

Before I went to live with Major Smith, a circumstance occurred that deeply distressed our family. In the fall of 1823 I went in company with an uncle on a bee-hunt. We took a negro man ("Uncle Hal") and my father's good wagon and team, and a number of kegs and one barrel to hold the honey which we expected to find. We crossed the State line into the Indian country, keeping the open prairie until we had passed several miles beyond the frontier, when we left our wagon in the edge of the prairie, and, with the horses, guns, blankets, and a few kegs, took to the timber. We traveled through the forest one day, and looked diligently for bees as we rode along on our horses. I remember that I found two bee-trees that day. I was very proud of my success, as no others were found, and my uncle was a veteran bee-hunter. We hunted three or four days before we returned to the wagon. Bees were generally hunted in the fall or winter, as the hives were then full of honey. In the fall the hunter would find the hive by seeing the bees coming in and going out; but in the winter he would discover the bee-tree by finding the dead bees on the snow at the foot of the tree. When a bee dies in a hive the living cast out his dead body, which falls to the ground. This is done during the few warm clear days in winter.

When we left the wagon in the edge of the prairie, it was early in October. The tall prairie grass was green, and there was no apparent danger of fire; but the second night out there fell a severe frost, and as we approached the prairie we smelt the smoke, and at once feared our wagon was gone. The prairie had been set on fire, I suppose, by the Indians, to drive all the game into the timber. The fire extended into the thick underbrush that skirted the prairie, and cooked the ripe summer grapes on the vines that bound the hazel thickets together. We had some difficulty in finding the place where we left the wagon; but, when we did at length find it, there was none of its wood-work left but the hubs, and they were still burning. I remember the most sorrowful looks of my uncle and of the negro man. The latter was a faithful slave, about forty years old; he had always driven the team, and was proud of it. He was so much distressed that he wept. I was greatly distressed myself, for I knew what a heavy loss it would be to the family. My father was not able to purchase another, and afterward for some time had to get along with a cart, which he made himself.

In reference to the simple mode of dress then common among the people of Western Missouri, I will state an illustrative circumstance. I was not present, but had the facts from the gentleman himself. He was a man of education, of strictly temperate habits, and, although not a professor of religion, remarkable for his general good conduct. He was a merchant of Liberty, and on one occasion he attended preaching in the country not far from town. He was one of the very few who dressed in broadcloth, which he wore on this occasion. The preacher was an old man well known; and during his sermon he referred to this gentleman, not by name, but as the smooth-faced young man in fine apparel, and severely condemned his style of dress, as being contrary to the spirit of the gospel. The behavior of the gentleman was orderly and respectful.

In those primitive times fisticuff fights were very common, especially at our militia trainings. After the military exercises (which were not remarkable for accuracy) were over, some bully would mount a stump, imitate the clapping and crowing of a cock, and declare aloud that he could whip any man in that crowd except his friends. Those who were not his professed friends were thus challenged to fight. If the challenge was accepted, the two combatants selected their seconds, and repaired to some place where the crowd could witness the contest, the seconds keeping back the throng outside the limits designated, and knocking down any one who attempted to interfere. When a hero was conquered, he made it known by a low cry of "'Nuff!'" After washing their faces, the combatants usually took a friendly drink together; and, if the vanquished was not satisfied, he went away determined upon another trial at some future time.

These contests were governed by certain rules, according to which they were generally conducted. They arose, not from hatred or animosity as a general rule, but from pride and love of fame. It was simply a very severe trial of manhood, perseverance, and skill. I have known men on such occasions to lose part of the ear or nose, and sometimes an eye. In most cases both parties were severely bruised, bitten, and gouged, and would be weeks in recovering. It was a brutal, but not fatal mode of combat. I never knew one to terminate fatally. The custom of stabbing and shooting came into use after this. The conqueror took great, and the conquered little, pleasure in relating the incidents of the fight. The description of one was diffuse, of the other concise. Most generally the defeated hero had some complaint to make of foul play, or some plausible excuse to give, like an unsuccessful candidate for office.

Among our neighbors in Clay County, there was a tall, long-legged, lazy man, of the name of William Fox, called "lazy Bill." He did very little work, and yet managed well, had a good farm, made a good living, and was a good stock-raiser. Among his cattle he had a very fine, blooded male calf, running in his blue-grass pasture, on the side of a considerable ridge. One warm day Fox caught the calf (then six months old) by the tail, and the animal at once started on a run down hill, increasing his speed at every successive jump. At first Fox's steps were of reasonable length, but soon they became awfully long, and Fox saw that he could not possibly continue such a rate of speed. In passing near a sapling, he ran around on the other side from the calf, still holding on to the tail. The result was a sudden fetch-up and fall of both Fox and the calf. The calf went off apparently unhurt, but next morning Fox found him dead. Upon examination, he found that the calf's back was disjointed a short distance above the root of the tail. It was not so long a race as that of John Gilpin, but more fatal.

It was among these simple backwoods people that I grew up to manhood. When my father settled in Howard County, that point was upon the frontier; and when he moved to Clay he was still upon the confines of civilization. Clay was one of the most western counties of one of the most western States; all the country west of that to the shore of the great Pacific Ocean being wild Indian country, in which white men were not permitted to reside, except the traders licensed by the United States, and the officers and soldiers stationed at the military posts. The means of education did not then exist, except to a very limited extent; and we had too much hard work to admit of attending school, except at intervals during the summer. At school I learned to spell, read, write, and cipher so far as the rule of supposition, and studied English grammar so as to be able to parse and punctuate with tolerable accuracy. This was the sum total of my school education.

PRAIRIES — THEIR ORIGIN.

Much speculation has been indulged in, as to the origin of those beautiful grassy plains in the West called prairies. From my own observation, I take this theory to be true: Before the country was inhabited by Indians, those now bare spaces were covered with timber, and this timber, in places, was first prostrated by hurricanes, and, when dry, was set on fire by the Indians. So intense were the fires caused by such a mass of dry fuel that the young growth of timber was entirely destroyed, and the coarse prairie grass came up in the vacant spaces, it being the only grass that will grow well in the hot sun, and for this reason soon subdued the other wild grasses usually found intermixed with the timber. The timber being entirely destroyed over a considerable space, the fires of each succeeding fall encroached more and more upon the timbered portions of the country. I have observed that the surface of the prairies of the West was generally either level or gently undulating, permitting the wind to sweep freely over every part of it. As we approach the hilly country skirting the Missouri bottoms, we nearly always find dense forests of timber, till we ascend the river west to the dry region, where timber never grows. The Indians, living solely upon the wild game, found the fallen timber in their way of travel and impeding their success in hunting; and they therefore set the dry wood on fire. They also found in due time that it was far more difficult to hunt the deer in the prairie than in the timber; and they accordingly fired the prairies in the early fall, so as to force the game into the timber for food.

Some have supposed that the origin of the prairies was due to drought. This I think can not be correct, for the reason that the soil of the prairies is naturally rich, and more moist than the soil of the timbered land. The drought would of course more affect the hilly land than that which was level or gently undulating. Besides, the underbrush, especially the hazel (which loves a rich soil and grows very thickly upon the ground), is found in much greater abundance on level and gently undulating land, and is easily killed by fire in the fall immediately after frost, and before the leaves fall. I know this was the case when my father's wagon was burned. The fire on that occasion extended some distance into the timber, killing but not consuming the green underbrush, especially the hazel. The young hazel that would next year grow from the roots, being intermixed with the old and dry brush, would be killed by the fire the succeeding fall. This process of burning would entirely destroy the roots in time, thus enlarging the prairie until the increase in size would be stopped by the hilly country or other obstructions.

The reason why there were no prairies in Tennessee and Kentucky was the fact that the predominant timber in those States is the beech and poplar, which are not easily killed by fire. The beech seldom or never forks, but sends out its numerous small limbs from a few feet above the ground to its top, making so dense a shade that little or no shrubbery can grow in a beech forest. However much the beech timber may be crowded, the trees will still send out their limbs horizontally, and will not grow tall, like most other timber (especially the pine family) when crowded. Even when there was an undergrowth in those States, it was mostly the cane, which is an evergreen and will not burn in a forest, though it grows as thick as hemp. On the contrary, there was no beech, poplar, or cane in the vicinity of the prairies; but the timber was mainly oak, elm, hickory, walnut, hackberry, and wild cherry, all of which grow tall and slender when crowded, and have no horizontal limbs near the ground. There was therefore room beneath for a thick undergrowth, and the soil, being exceedingly rich, could well support the large and small growths upon the same space. It is also a well-known fact that hurricanes often occur in the West, and that they are so severe as to prostrate all the standing timber, throwing all the trees in the same direction. I remember to have seen two spots over which these terrible tempests had passed. One was in Howard and the other in Jackson County, Missouri; and the fallen timber lay so thick upon the ground that it was difficult to pass through it on horseback. According to my recollection, hurricanes were very rare in Tennessee and Kentucky. These destructive storms are usually about half a mile in width and several miles in length.

RETURN TO TENNESSEE — EMPLOYED AS CLERK IN AN HOTEL.

I remained with my brother-in-law, William L. Smith, some fifteen months, and then returned to my father's house. In the fall of 1826, when I was in my nineteenth year, Uncle Constant Hardeman and wife came to visit us from their home in Rutherford County, Tennessee; and, after due consideration, it was determined that I should accompany them on their return. My father gave me a horse three years old the preceding spring, a saddle and bridle, a new camlet cloak, and twenty-six dollars in money; and my mother furnished me with a good suit of jeans. We usually traveled about thirty-three miles a day. My young horse stood the trip well at the beginning, but gradually became exhausted, so that by the time we reached Nashville it was all I could do to get along. My pride was much wounded by my situation. Before leaving home, I had not often seen the inside of an hotel; and I was therefore very green, which became painfully more evident as we approached the older settlements. I was naturally diffident when young; and, when I arrived in Tennessee among my rich kin, I at once recognized my comparative poverty and ignorance. I remember that the first time that I ever saw Pope's translation of the Iliad was at the house of Uncle Constant Hardeman, soon after my arrival there; and, had it been gold or precious stones, the pleasure would not have equaled that which I enjoyed. I was very fond of reading, and eagerly devoured everything that fell in my way. But when I saw that my relatives were rich, and valued riches more than knowledge, I determined that I would employ my energies in the accumulation of a fortune. Conscious of my own poverty, ignorance, and homely dress, I fancied that I was sometimes slighted by my relatives. I, however, said nothing, made no complaints, but laid it up in my heart that I would some day equal if not surpass them.

After spending a few weeks with my uncle Constant and other relatives near him, I visited my Uncle Blackstone Hardeman, who then lived in Maury County, Tennessee, and who was upon the eve of removing to the Western District, a new portion of that State, to which the Indian title had been but lately extinguished, and which was settling up rapidly by emigrants, mainly from the older localities of that State. As I was out of business, I decided to go with him and assist him to make the journey. It was in November, and we had heavy cold rains on the way, making it a hard trip. When we arrived at his new farm near Bolivar, Hardeman County, my suit of jeans was pretty well gone, the elbows of my coat being worn out. My uncle Blackstone succeeded in procuring me a situation as clerk at the hotel in Bolivar, kept by an old man, Duguid Mims. It was a large frame building covered in, the floors laid, the outside weatherboarded up, and the outside doors hung; but the inside work was unfinished. The country was new, and men at a hotel or on a steamboat will generally act out their true characters. I had, therefore, a good school of human nature, and found a great deal of it in mankind.

My salary was one hundred dollars per annum, and my duty was to wait on the guests at the table, keep the books, and collect the bills. The only decent articles of dress that I had were my fur hat and camlet cloak. My term of service commenced on the day before Christmas, and there was a great frolic among the guests at the hotel. Among other freaks committed by them, they cut up into narrow strips all the hats they could find; and as mine, with others, was placed on a large work-bench in the main hall, it fared as the rest did. I was exceedingly green and awkward, as may well be supposed; and my imperfections were the more remarked from the fact that I succeeded a young man, of the name of Outlaw, who understood the duties of the position well. My kind old employer had never seen me but twice before, and the only money I had was in the hands of my uncle, who lived six or seven miles from town. It was a busy time, and I had no immediate opportunity to communicate with him; and, as I was ashamed to ask Mr. Mims or any one else to credit me, I was compelled to go bare-headed for a week. I was the subject of much jesting, was badly quizzed and greatly mortified; but I worked on resolutely, said nothing, and was always at my post of duty. In about a week my uncle came to town, and I stated to him my situation, and through his influence I procured another hat.

By assiduity and attention I soon learned the duties of my new position; and in about three months I procured a new suit of clothes, the first suit of broadcloth I ever wore. I remember overhearing the remarks that were made when I first put it on. "Do you see Burnett? He is coming out."

My employer had a daughter of his own, and two grown-up step-daughters, who were very pretty girls; but they considered themselves as my superiors, and I never kept their company.

I remained with Mr. Mims five or six months. In the spring the business of the hotel was dull, and the inside work of the building had to be finished. The old man was very enterprising, dipping into almost everything that offered, and going into debt pretty freely; but he was very industrious and honest. As there was so little travel at this season, and as Mr. Mims was extensively engaged in brick-making, he would take the negro boy who was the hostler to the brickyard. When any guests arrived, I first waited on them, then took their horses to the stable, fed and curried them, and saddled them up in the morning; and, when there was nothing else to do, I took the paint-brush and went to painting the hotel building. I knew nothing of the business at first, as it was little known in my former locality; but I soon, in this way, learned to do plain painting well.

SAMUEL HOUSTON — NEWTON CANNON — ANDREW MARTIN — DAVID CROCKETT — ADAM HUNTSMAN.

One day, while engaged very busily in painting the ceiling overhead, the Rev. W. Blount Peck, who was about to open a store on Clear Creek, some ten miles from Bolivar, came to see me, and said that he wished to employ me to take charge of the entire businessof selling the goods, keeping the books, and collecting the debts, and he himself would purchase the goods. He offered me two hundred dollars per annum, he paying for my washing, board, and lodging. I said that I was engaged to serve Mr. Mims for one year, and could not violate my engagement, but would lay the matter before him, and if he consented I would take charge of the store upon the terms stated. Accordingly, I conferred with Mr. Mims, and he kindly gave me permission to quit his service, saying that he would not stand in the way of my promotion.

When I set out in life, I was fully conscious of my want of information, and I at first decided in my own mind to say very little, but listen and learn, and in this way avoid exposure. But I found, from practical experience, that the best way to correct errors was to make them known, and then some friend would kindly correct them for you; and, if no friend should do so, your enemies would. I found that patient and intelligent perseverance almost always won.

While at the hotel, I saw General Samuel Houston, David Crockett, Adam Huntsman, Newton Cannon, Andrew Martin, and other leading men of Tennessee; and I heard Houston, Crockett, and Cannon speak. Houston, then in the prime of life, was a tall, noble Virginian, possessing a most commanding figure and voice, with a bold, flowery, and eloquent style of oratory. He had a great command of language, and spoke slowly, emphatically, and distinctly, so that all could hear him, and all wished to hear him. Newton Cannon was a very plain, earnest, forcible, and rapid speaker, a strict logician, but not a popular orator. While Houston and Cannon were speaking, no one ever laughed, as they never dealt in amusing anecdotes. General Houston never succeeded at the bar. His mind was not of a legal cast. Cannon possessed as much if not more legal ability, and was fully Houston's equal in statesmanship; but he could not command the admiration of the masses, as Houston did.

David Crockett was a man of another cast of mind and manner. He possessed a fine natural intellect, good memory, and great good nature. He had treasured up all the good anecdotes he had ever heard, and could readily relate many striking incidents of his own career. He was deficient in education, and had no practical knowledge of statesmanship; but he was willing and able to learn, and had the patience to bear ridicule and reproach for the time being. He was an off-hand speaker, full of anecdotes, and kept a crowd greatly amused. His comparisons and illustrations were new and simple, but strong and pointed. Few public speakers could get any advantage of David Crockett before a crowd of backwoods people. His good-natured, honest, jolly face would remind one of Dryden's description

"Of Bacchus — ever fair and ever young."

I knew in Hardeman County a Baptist preacher of the name of Casey, one of Nature's orators, who murdered the King's English in every sentence and mispronounced half his words. Yet he was so eloquent that one forgot these defects, and they almost became graces, as they were peculiarities with him. It was very much so with David Crockett. Any one hearing either of these speakers would wish to hear him again.

W. B. PECK — JOHN Y. COCKRAM — PETER MINNER.

So soon as Parson Peck, as he was familiarly called, had finished his storehouse (which was a log-cabin about eighteen by twenty feet, with chinked cracks, clapboard roof, and puncheon floor), I took my leave of Bolivar. The stock was not large, and Parson Peck usually made his purchases upon time in New Orleans. He did a general credit business, the debts becoming due about Christmas, and payable in cotton, which was generally delivered in the seed at the cotton-gin near the store, a receipt taken for so many pounds, and the receipt transferred to us. Parson Peck was a Methodist, and resided about ten miles from the store, and the labor and responsibility of conducting the business necessarily fell upon me. He was from East Tennessee, and was a brother of Judge Peck of the Supreme Court of Tennessee, and of Judge Peck of the United States District Court for Missouri. It was a talented family, and Parson Peck was a man of fine literary ability. His wife before her marriage was a Miss Rivers, a sister of Dr. Rivers, and daughter of a wealthy planter of Hardeman County. I remember him and his lady with sentiments of gratitude.

The mercantile business, especially in a new country, where the credit system prevails, and especially where the merchant has but little capital, is certain to prove a failure. As my employer had very little capital, he was unsuccessful; and, as I had managed the business in selling and collecting, he blamed me to some extent, though I did not wrong him at all. I did my duty faithfully to the utmost of my ability. In turn, I censured him because he had twice pledged the same debt to two different creditors of his. These mutual charges led to a partial estrangement, which continued until I left the State. I have deeply regretted the circumstance. Upon more mature reflection I became satisfied that the act of pledging the same book account to two different creditors was purely a mistake, and that he was entirely honest in his intentions. After I became satisfied of my mistake I inquired for him, and, learning that he was probably in Philadelphia, I wrote a kind explanation to him directed to that city. I desired to do him all the justice in my power, and to renew to him the assurances of my esteem and gratitude. Whether he received my letter or not I never knew.

While I was doing business as a clerk for Parson Peck in the winter of 1827-'28, a circumstance occurred that made a lasting impression upon my memory. It was one of the happy incidents of my life.

There were two farmers, both Methodists, who were in partnership in a cotton-gin situated near the store. John Y. Cockram, aged about forty-five, was the owner of six or eight slaves, and cultivated a plantation of considerable size; while Peter Minner, aged about thirty-three, was not the owner of any slaves, but had a small farm, and was in very moderate circumstances. John Y. Cockram was a native of New Madrid County, Missouri, and was a peculiar man, possessed of a fine intellect, pretty well improved. I never met any one who was blessed with a more engaging manner. He was a noble man, and possessed the rare power of governing others without the use of force. He assured me that he had never struck one of his children a blow in his life, and never but one of his slaves, and that a little negro girl. His seven or eight children, and all of his slaves, were exceedingly dutiful, and devotedly attached to him.

Peter Minner was a man of plain good sense, remarkable for his kind and humble demeanor, but did not possess the natural intellect or literary cultivation of Cockram. Minner resided near the gin, and Cockram some distance from it. When the gin had been completed Minner received the cotton from the customers and superintended the business generally, Cockram giving his main attention to his plantation.

After they had been doing business some time, and had received and ginned a large amount of cotton for various persons, Cockram came one day and said to me, in confidence, that he feared there was something wrong in Minner's accounts. He exhibited to me the partnership books, kept by Minner, and we examined them together to ascertain the true state of the case. I was myself familiar with many of the transactions, as I was very intimate with both partners, and boarded at Minner's house. For my life I could not see how Minner could ever explain the errors apparent upon the face of the books, or justify himself. It seemed to be as clear a case of fraud as facts and figures could make.

Cockram asked me what he ought to do. I told him to see Minner at once, state to him plainly his fears, and ask for an investigation. He accordingly called upon Minner, who heard his statement with kindness and patience, and at once consented to refer the matter to two arbitrators, chosen by the consent of both parties. I was one of the arbitrators, and I remember the manner of Minner during the investigation, for I observed him closely. He kept his eyes fixed upon the floor, except at intervals, when returning an answer to a point made by Cockram. He would then raise his large, meek, black eye, look me full in the face, and give his explanation. I watched his eye, and could read his very soul, and there was no guilt there. The mild and pure expression of that gentle eye went to my inmost heart. It was all I could do to restrain my tears; and I can never think of that most beautiful scene without emotion. Oh, if there be on this earth one object more beautiful than all others, it is the sweet expression of the eye of a just man.

The arbitrators had no decision to make. Minner's explanations were so clear and satisfactory, that the noble Cockram, without waiting to hear any expression of opinion from the arbitrators, sprang to his feet and exclaimed, "Gentlemen, I am satisfied."

This incident was of great benefit to me in afterlife. It taught me a beautiful lesson. I had rather look for men's virtues than for their vices, rather err upon the side of charity than against it, and prefer to hear *both* sides before I come to any conclusion.

The two men remained friends, and both died of fever three or four years afterward, each leaving a widow and several children. Cockram became the sole owner of the gin; and, after his crop of cotton had been gathered one fall, the gin was destroyed by fire, and his whole crop with it. When informed of the disaster, he simply replied, "These hands can raise more."

COURTSHIP AND MARRIAGE.

It was during the time that I acted as clerk for Parson Peck that I became acquainted with the lady who afterward became my wife. There are two very important epochs in one's life: when he gets married himself, and when he gives away his first daughter. To give away the second is not so trying. When you rear a son, knowing as you do all his traits and habits, you can form some probable conclusion as to his future course in life; but, as a *general* rule, you never know your son-in-law well until some time after his marriage.

My wife's father, Peter Rogers, formerly lived in Wilson County, Tennessee, where his children were born. The fall after I commenced business for Parson Peck, Mr. Rogers removed to a farm in the immediate neighborhood. His brother, Dr. John Rogers, had been living and practicing his profession in that vicinity for one or two years. I knew the doctor well, and he was often at the store. The eldest son of Mr. Rogers, Hardin J., was a finely educated young man, and the first time I ever saw him I loved him — why, I could not tell, but I loved him. He was a noble young man, with a fine face and beautiful black eye, my favorite. Mr. Rogers had two daughters, Harriet W. and Sarah M., the first sixteen and the other fourteen years of age. I often heard the young men of the vicinity speak of the two sisters, and especially a young friend of mine, Calvin Stevens, who frequently waited upon Miss Harriet. He was a very pleasant fellow, and was very fond of the society of the ladies. I had not the slightest idea of marriage myself, but I determined, from a mere mischievous freak, to cut out Calvin. I was satisfied that he had no serious intention of marrying any one. He had a very fine tall figure, handsome face, and engaging manners. In these respects I considered him my superior, but I thought I could out-talk him; and so I did. But, when I had succeeded in cutting out Calvin, I found myself caught. The girl had won my heart. She was a little above the medium height, with a trim, neat figure, sparkling black eye, handsome face, low, sweet voice, and gentle manners. Her father and mother were admirable people. I have met few if any better people than Mother Rogers. Mr. Rogers was a man of fine common sense, had a kind, generous heart, good habits, and a most determined will. He had served under General Jackson in the Creek war; and, though possessed of great good nature, when fully roused he was as brave as a lion. Himself, wife, and Miss Harriet were Methodists. Their home was the abode of industry, integrity, and peace. I liked the family. They were good livers, but not rich. Mr. Rogers was an indulgent father and master, and a good neighbor. It was almost impossible to involve Mr. and Mrs. Rogers in neighborhood quarrels, those pests of society. They were alike esteemed by all, both rich and poor. I never saw Mr. Rogers shed a tear, though he lost his wife and several grown children. It was not his nature to weep either for joy or sorrow.

I was not for some time aware of the fact that I was in love with the girl. I accompanied her home one Saturday; and after dinner we were engaged in conversation for some two or three hours. At last it suddenly occurred to me that it was time I should go home. I hastily bade her good evening, and rushed into the yard, and happened to meet her father passing through it. I looked around for the sun, and was amazed to find that it was gone. In a confused manner, I inquired of Mr. Rogers what had become of the sun. He politely replied, "It has gone down, Mr. Burnett." I knew then that I was in love. It was a *plain* case.

When I found myself deeply in love, I considered the matter carefully. I remember well that, on the night of that same Saturday, I laid myself down upon the hard counter (the place where I usually slept) with a blanket under me, and a roll of flannel for a pillow, and spent the whole night without sleep, debating with myself whether I should go the next day and make a serious speech to Miss Harriet. I was a poor clerk, with nothing to depend upon for a living but my own exertions. This was a powerful objection; but my heart won the day, and the heart is sometimes as right as the head. The matter was decided; and it is my nature to act promptly when I have once determined to do a thing. Let me only be fully satisfied as to the course to be pursued, and I at once go straight to a point. The next day I went to see Miss Harriet. I was not abrupt, but earnest and candid. I introduced the subject discreetly, made the best speech I could, and secured her consent and that of her parents. This was early in June, and we were married on the 20th of August, 1828. The day was dark and rainy until about an hour before sunset, when it cleared off beautifully, and the sun set in smiles. I hope my sun of life may set as tranquilly as the sun of that day. If it should (and I have faith to believe it will), my wedding-day will have been a fit emblem of my life.

I was of the opinion that I could go through the ceremony without trepidation, and I felt none until I passed over the steps across the yard fence, when I suddenly felt so weak that I could scarcely stand. The guests had most of them arrived, and were in the yard looking at me as I approached the house. But I made my way hastily through the crowd, and my acquaintances each rushed forward, saying, "How are you?" I was so confused that I simply held out my right hand for each one to shake; and when my cousin Mary Hardeman spoke to me, though I was as well acquainted with her as I was with any one, I did not know her. But, this excitement having passed away, I was myself again, and was not confused when my friend Parson Peck performed the ceremony. When married, I was nearly twenty-one and my wife nearly seventeen.

I owe much of my success in life to her. Had I not married early, I do not know what might have been my course in life. I might have fallen into vicious habits. Though I was not religious myself, I loved a religious girl — there is something in piety so becoming a gentle woman. My wife was never noisy, fanatical, or widly enthusiastic in her religious feelings; but she was *very firm*. For many years after our marriage she had a hard time of it as to her religion. I was full of mischief, fond of jokes, and loved festive occasions; and I used to urge her to go with me to dances, but she always firmly yet mildly refused. She has always been a woman of few words. For some years after our marriage, I was often perplexed to understand her judgement of persons. It frequently happened that on first acquaintance I would form most favorable opinion of the person; and, when I would ask her what she thought of him, she would say, "I don't like him." When asked why, she could give no reason. She knew she was right, but could not tell why. Her knowledge was instinctive; but generally time proved the correctness of her conclusions. It was so with my mother. Her judgment of people was quick, decisive, and generally correct. When a family claimed to have been once rich, though then poor, she always observed whether they had saved any relics as mementoes of former prosperity. If they had not, she doubted their statements.

PURCHASE OF THE STORE — DEATH OF A BURGLAR.

In the spring of 1829 I purchased the stock of goods of Parson Peck at original cost, on eighteen months' credit, for which I gave him my promissory notes. Most of these notes he transferred to his creditors. I was to close up the old business. I built me a log cabin near the store, and moved into it about the same time. Everything went on very smoothly during the year 1829; but in 1830 I found I could not replenish my stock of merchandise, which was so much reduced that I was unable to supply the wants of the locality, and could not well dispose of the remnants I had on hand. Our household furniture was remarkably plain, and our expenses were small.

While I was doing business for myself, I purchased three barrels of old Monongahela whisky, which I retailed out by the pint, quart, and gallon. It was a favorite with those who loved liquor. It took me about three months to retail it out, and during this period I was in the habit of taking a drink in the morning, and occasionally during the day. I was not aware that I loved it until it was all gone. Then I found, to my surprise, that I had acquired a taste for it. I reflected upon the fact, and went into a sort of mathematical calculation under the "single rule of three." I said to myself: "If in three months I have acquired so much love of whisky, how much would I acquire in three years?" The thought alarmed me, and I soon determined that I would abstain entirely, which has been my general practice. As I do everything with all my might, I became satisfied that, if I indulged at all, I would be very apt to do some very tall drinking. Had I not been a married man, and happy as such, I might have fallen into this fatal habit.

While this is no proper place for a long discussion of the question of temperance, I will make a few remarks, suggested by long observation and experience. If we take a hundred men at the age of twenty-one who entirely abstain, there will not be a drunkard among them. If, on the contrary, we select a hundred young men who are moderate drinkers at that age, there will in due time be ten sots out of that number. As no man can tell *in advance* whether he will fall or not, he incurs a risk of ten per cent. in drinking at all. If two young men of anything like equal ability apply to a sound, cautious business man for employment, and one abstains and the other does not, the temperate one is almost sure to be preferred. So, if a young man is extravagant and spends all his income, saving up nothing, he will find it hard to obtain employment. But the young man who does not drink, and who saves up a reasonable portion of his salary, gives *clear proof* that he has a due command over his tastes and appetites — that he has reflection, honesty, and good sense. Such a one can be safely trusted, because he does not need to steal. In the history of embezzlements, very few cases will be found where the party was temperate and saving.

My father never used tobacco in any form; and while I remained with him I had no opportunity and no temptation to use it myself. But in the fall of 1827, while I was in charge of the store for Parson Peck, I one day purchased a hundred home-made cigars, and in the evening invited some young friends to smoke with me. I knew so little of the use of the article and of its effects, that I never once thought of its making me sick. I therefore smoked as long and as much as the others. After they had left the store, I became exceedingly sick. I have had several attacks of fever, and have been seasick at different times; but I never endured sensations so distressing as on this occasion. It seemed as if the hills were rolling over upon me.

But this rash experiment proved in the end a great benefit to me, and I was amply rewarded for my sufferings. It prevented me from ever using tobacco in any form. This was the first and last time I ever smoked.

He is a *very* wise man who profits by the experience of others, without waiting to suffer himself *before* he learns. If I could only place my views in the minds of young men, before they contract the useless, expensive, often offensive, and sometimes positively injurious habit of using tobacco, I should accomplish a great good.

It is our plain duty to give as little pain to our fellow beings as we reasonably can. The man who uses tobacco wastes a considerable sum in the course of a long life, which justly belongs to his family. It is almost impossible for a smoker to avoid giving great pain to others at times. He is sure to smoke at improper times and in wrong places. The danger of using tobacco to excess is so great, that a young man who is known to use it will find it far more difficult to procure employment. The business man who smokes himself would prefer that his clerk should not. The use is undoubtedly injurious to some constitutions, if not to all; and no young man, about to learn the use of tobacco, can tell in advance how much he may be injured. There is, therefore, a *useless* risk incurred, which is not in accordance with good, practical business sense; and the habit, once acquired, is most difficult to correct.

During the time I was retailing liquor above mentioned, in 1830, a melancholy circumstance occurred, which I have long deeply regretted. My stock of goods being very low, and my wife sick with fever, I removed her to her father's house, about a mile distant. Parson Peck had built a neat frame storehouse, which fell to me in the purchase. My brother-in-law, Hardin J. Rogers, often slept at the store, but occasionally no one slept there. One morning, when I went to the store, I found the window-shutter forcibly broken open by the use of some flat instrument, about the size of a two-inch chisel. I lay there myself at night watching for the burglar, until I became so sleepy that I could keep awake no longer. I lay upon the floor behind the counter, with a loaded shot-gun on the counter above me, determined to shoot the burglar if he should come and enter the store. The window-shutter was generally fastened with an iron bolt on the inside. It was not fastened this night, but from the shutter a string extended to the handle of a large tin coffee-pot placed by me on the edge of the counter, so that opening the shutter would at once throw off the pot, the fall of which would necessarily make a great noise. I kept awake until late at night, when I fell asleep. In the morning I found the pot on the floor, but so sound was my slumber that I had not heard it. It had evidently frightened the burglar, so that he did not enter. I then determined I would try another plan. I securely fastened the shutter and placed the shot-gun cocked upon the counter, with a string extending from one end of the yardstick to the shutter, and so arranged that when the shutter was forced open the gun would go off. Next morning, when I went to the store, I found a negro man lying on his back dead, with a mill-pick and a jug by his side. He had broken open the window-shutter with the pick, and the shot and one bullet had entered his forehead and produced instant death. I at once went to Bolivar and told the circumstances as they occurred, and inquired for the coroner. My friend Major John H. Bills told me confidentially that he would advise me not to mention the fact, as it might involve me in penalties; but I told him I must state the truth. An inquest was duly held, and I was called as a witness, but told I was not legally bound to state anything that would tend to criminate myself; but I stated all the facts truly. I was never prosecuted, and the owner of the slave never sued me for damages. It was a clear case of justifiable homicide under the laws of the State. Still, in afterlife, I have deeply regretted the act; and, the older I I become, the more I could wish it had never occurred. The poor negro was fond of liquor, and wanted nothing else. It was a sad case. I had no idea who it could be until he was killed. He was employed at a mill some two miles distant. I am hard to excite, but when fully aroused my natural feelings are desperate. But, thank God, through his mercy, the idea of shedding human blood is now terrible to me. I would rather bear almost any injury than take human life.

RETURN TO MISSOURI — CROCKETT AND HUNTSMAN.

My brother, Glen O. Burnett, two years younger than myself, came to Hardeman County, and married the other daughter of Mr. Rogers, January 6, 1830. In the fall of 1830 Mr. Rogers moved to Clay County, Missouri. I found it impossible for me to continue the mercantile business in that locality; and I decided to close up my business, pay my debts, and study law. My brother Glen determined to return to Clay County, Missouri, where my father had given him a tract of land. I also decided to return thither. It was accordingly arranged between us that my wife and little son should accompany him, while I remained to close up my business. I supposed it would take me a few months. In the mean time Hardin J. Rogers and myself sent to Nashville, by my cousin John M. Hardeman, and purchased a small library of law-books, containing only the elementary works upon the science. We boarded and lodged with an uncle of my wife's, William Hardin, built a little log office, and prosecuted our studies vigorously. I had my old business to wind up, and had to travel about the country a good deal, endeavoring to collect debts due to me, in which effort I had but moderate success. Cotton was low, and times were hard. When my notes became due, they were placed in the hands of Austin Miller, Esq., a lawyer of Bolivar, for collection. I went at once to him and assigned to him all debts due to me, with a few exceptions. He took the assignment, and then placed the debts in my hands for collection. I collected all I could, and paid the amounts collected to him. I would not leave the State without his consent.

In the fall of 1831 new troubles assailed us. I was first attacked with fever, and then Hardin J. Rogers was attacked in turn. I recovered, and he died. Poor fellow! I loved him as a brother, and he was worthy.

After remaining in Tennessee thirteen months, and collecting all I could, there was still a considerable sum due upon my notes. It was useless to remain longer; and, after consultation with Austin Miller, and with his consent, I determined to accompany my wife's uncle, George M. Pirtle, who was then moving from Hardeman County to the southwestern portion of Missouri, as far as the Mississippi River, and there take a steamer bound to St. Louis. This was in March, 1832. We traveled on slowly with wagons and teams, stock and family, until we reached the river; and there we separated. My finances were exceedingly low, and I was dressed in a suit of jeans with my elbows out, as when I arrived at Bolivar five years before. I soon took a cabin passage on a large steamer; and was perhaps the most shabbily dressed man in the cabin. I was evidently considered by the other passengers as quite green, as some of them soon started a report that the small-pox was on board. But I saw, from the glances they gave toward me and the winks they gave their companions, that they were simply aiming to quiz me and other passengers. I said nothing and paid no attention to theirstatements.

We arrived safely at St. Louis, and I at once went up and down the shore of the river to find a steamer up for Liberty Landing; but I could find only one for the Missouri River, and that was the old "Car of Commerce," only bound to Lexington, about thirty-five miles below my point of destination. I had only $15.62 1/2 in my pocket, and the price of a cabin passage was $15; and the boat wouldnot leave for several days. I therefore debated with myself whether I should take a cabin or deck passage, and I determined that I would stand erect as long as possible. I went to the clerk of the boat and told him I would take a cabin passage, provided he would allow me to come on board at once, without the expense of staying at an hotel. To this he at once assented.

We were seven days making the trip to Lexington, and arrived there on Sunday morning. I at once crossed the Missouri River, and went on foot eight miles to Richmond, where I had acquaintances, from whom I hoped to procure a horse. But, it being Sunday, I could find no one at home that I knew; and I continued the journey on foot until near sundown, when I arrived at the house of Winfrey E. Price, about twelve miles from Liberty. I was not much sensible of fatigue until I made an effort to cross the fence around the yard, when I found it was all I could do to throw my right foot over. I had traveled the distance of about twenty-two miles. The next day I made my way to Liberty, riding a portion of the distance on a led horse, bareback. At Liberty I procured a horse and reached the house of Mr. Rogers before night. I found my wife and boy well, after a separation of fourteen months. This long separation was one of the hardest trials of my life, and gave us perhaps more pain than any other; not only because it was long, but because its length was not anticipated by us, and our young and fond hearts were not prepared to meet the severe trial.

There are some singular coincidences in the facts of our acquaintance and marriage. My wife and myself were born in adjoining counties in Tennessee, but our parents never knew or heard of each other. My father moved first to Williamson County, Tennessee, then to Howard, and lastly to Clay County, Missouri. When I was nearly grown, circumstances wholly unforeseen led me to return to Tennessee, and then to go to Bolivar, and from thence to Clear Creek; and it just so happened that Mr. Rogers, who had long lived on the same farm in Wilson County, moved to the Western District, and located in my immediate neighborhood.

While I was in Hardeman County, David Crockett and Adam Huntsman were rival candidates for Congress. Huntsman was elected by a small majority, the race being very close. He was a man of great ability, fully equal to Crockett in native intellect, and much his superior in education and mental training. He was distinguished as a lawyer, statesman, and wit. Possessed of these qualifications, he would have easily beaten Crockett in an old community; but there was much prejudice in the minds of the early settlers against lawyers. This objection was urged against Huntsman; but he met it with great good humor in this way. He wore a wooden leg; and, after readily conceding that there were objections against the profession of the law, he would insist that his was an exceptional and excusable case; "for," said he, "I could not work, to beg I was ashamed, and I could not steal, because they would all know it was Huntsman by his track; and I was thus compelled to be a lawyer." After the election Crockett complained through the newspaper, giving many reasons for his defeat, and charging his opponents with unfair dealing. Huntsman replied, and among other things said that his rival had not given the best reason for his defeat, and that was, he did not obtain votes enough.

This objection is often urged against lawyers when candidates for seats in legislative bodies. A very inferior lawyer was a candidate for the Legislature in some county in Kentucky; and a distinguished old lawyer happened to overhear some citizens say they would not vote for him because he was a lawyer. The old lawyer at once stepped up to them, saying, "if that was their *only* objection, they might safely vote for him, as he was not lawyer enough to hurt him."

In the Presidential canvass of 1828, General Jackson was accused by some of his political opponents of being illiterate. It was alleged that he spelled the words "all correct" thus, "oll korrect." Hence originated the abbreviation "O.K."About the year 1824, a gentleman from Kentucky, aged twenty-five, settled in Clay County, Missouri. While his education was exceedingly limited, he possessed a superior native intellect. He was a splendid judge of human nature, and, although illiterate, expressed his views of men and measures in language clear, concise, and strong. He soon proved to be a very superior business man, and ultimately acquired a very fine estate, which he subsequently lost during our late civil war. When he first arrived in Clay County, he spelled Congress thus, "Kongriss"; but, like the Baptist preacher Casey (whose name is mentioned in another page), his natural ability was such that the people of his district elected him to a seat in the State Senate. While attending his first session of that body, he was asked how low the mercury fell in his locality. He promptly replied, "It run into the ground about a feet." Hence arose the saying, "running it into the ground."

During my stay in Hardeman County, a young man, who was a droll and eccentric genius, was a burlesque candidate for a seat in the Legislature of Tennessee. His speeches were very amusing. In addressing the people, he declared that he could not truly say, as did his honorable competitors, that he was solicited and urged by his friends to become a candidate; that he was not like some animals, whose ears you had to pull off to get them out, and their tails to get them back; but that he became a candidate voluntarily, and was running on his own hook, and without the solicitation of his friends, for he was not aware that he had any. He, or some other person, about that time, gave a very forcible description of a vacillating politician, and applied to him this verse:

"He wabbled in, and wabbled out,
Until he left the mind in doubt
Whether the snake that made the track
Was going South, or coming back."

I had never heard of this verse before, and have not seen or heard it quoted since, and can not say whether it was original with the speaker or not. It made such an impression upon my memory that I never forgot it.

Chapter II.

ACT AS CLERK FOR A TIME — THEN GO INTO THE MERCANTILE BUSINESS WITH OTHERS.

When I arrived at the house of Mr. Rogers, in Clay County, in the month of April, 1832, I had only sixty-two and a half cents left, was some seven hundred dollars in debt, had a wife and one child to support, and was out of employment. I had studied law altogether about six months only, and was not then prepared to make a living at the practice; and I therefore determined to obtain a position in some store as a clerk. I visited Lexington, Missouri, where John Aull then did a large mercantile business, and who was an intimate friend of my father; but he had no vacancy to fill, having all the help he required. I returned to my father-in-law's house at a loss what to do. In a few days thereafter Edward M. Samuel, then in partnership with Samuel Moor in the mercantile business in Liberty, returned from Philadelphia with a new assortment of goods, and sent me word that he wished to see me. I had sent forward by water from Tennessee my little household furniture, and my best clothes. I therefore dressed myself as well as I could, and promptly went to see Messrs. Samuel and Moor. Mr. Samuel was the active partner, and Mr. Moor the capitalist of the firm. Mr. Samuel was pleased with me, and asked me what I would charge them per annum, and find myself. I replied that I had just arrived, and did not know what I ought to ask; but that I had heard that Mr. Bird had a salary of four hundred dollars per annum, he finding himself, and that I thought I could do their business as well as Mr. Bird did that of Mr. Aull. He replied, without hesitation, that they would give me the same salary, and let me have such goods as I might want for myself and family at a price below the ordinary retail price of the store. Mr. Bird had been a schoolmate of mine in old Franklin in 1820.

I at once removed with my family to Liberty, rented a log-house for twenty-five dollars a year, and set to work manfully. Expenses were then light in Liberty. Pork was one dollar and fifty cents per hundred pounds, wood one dollar a cord, flour very cheap, corn meal twenty-five cents a bushel, potatoes twenty cents per bushel, chickens seventy-five cents per dozen, and eggs fifteen cents a dozen.

I remained in the employment of Samuel & Moor fifteen months, and they urged me to remain longer, offering to increase my salary; but, having pretty well paid up my debts, I determined to go into the law. I obtained a license to practice from Judge Tompkins, of the Supreme Court of Missouri, purchased a house and lot in Richmond, Missouri, for the small sum of eighty dollars, repaired the same, and was on the eve of going there to reside and practice my profession, when I received a proposition from James M. and G. L. Hughes to enter into partnership in the mercantile business with them, upon very advantageous terms. They were to furnish a cash capital of eight thousand dollars, while I was not required to contribute any, and each partner was to give his personal services to the business and have one third of the profits.

At that time, the mercantile business was prosperous, while the practice of the law was at a low stage, there being very little litigation in the country. I was still anxious to make a fortune, and this was the best opportunity that offered. We entered into partnership at the beginning of 1834, and received our first supplies in the spring of that year. We did a safe, good business that season, and I went East in the beginning of 1835 to make the annual purchases. In 1836 we took into the firm, as a partner, Colonel John Thornton, one of the wealthiest men of Clay County, who contributed five thousand dollars cash capital; thus making our total cash capital thirteen thousand dollars, which was large for that time and country. We continued this firm until the middle of 1837, when Thornton and myself purchased the interest of James M. and G. L. Hughes; and I went East in the beginning of 1838 to procure a new stock of goods. By the agreement between them and us, we were to occupy the storehouse, which belonged to James M. Hughes, until the first of May, 1838. It was understood between Colonel Thornton and myself that he should erect a storehouse upon a lot he owned in Liberty, and have it ready by the time the lease should expire. I made a very successful trip to Philadelphia, and returned with our new goods about the first of April, but found the storehouse unfinished. The Colonel had employed a man to lay the stone foundation, who did the work so badly that it became necessary to tear it down and rebuild. Our sales were fine during the month of April; but when the first of May arrived, no house on the Public Square could be obtained in which we could open our goods; and we were compelled to box them up in part, and send another portion of them to the country, where we did but a poor business. The new store was finished and occupied in October; but the season for our summer goods had passed, our customers had gone to other houses, and we could not reclaim our lost position. The result was a heavy loss to us. But besides this, the monetary revolution of 1837-'38 had reached us, and a great number of our customers failed, enough to absorb all the profits of the former firm, and more than enough to swallow up those of Thornton & Burnett.

Toward the close of 1834 my brother Glen visited me on one occasion, and told me it was almost impossible for him to make a living on his little farm; and that, as his family bade fair to be large, he did not know what to do. A plan at once occurred to me. Said I, "Will you do as I advise?" He replied "Yes." "Then go home, sell all you have, raise all the money you can, and I will put in as much as you do; and I will bring you out a small stock of goods in the spring, and you have the house ready to receive them when they shall arrive." He at once acted on my suggestion and established the store at Barry, a small place ten miles west from Liberty. Here he did well for a year or two; but, by the advice of others, we engaged in building and running a steam saw-mill and distillery, which entailed upon us a heavy loss. It somehow or other always happened so with me, that whenever I had anything to do with liquor, either in making or selling it, some misfortune would befall me. I have a dread of steam saw-mills, steam distilleries, and the mercantile business generally.

In 1837 William L. Smith, one of my brothers-in-law, came into partnership with Glen and myself; and the new firm borrowed of John Aull the sum of ten thousand dollars, with interest at the rate of ten per cent. per annum, the principal payable in five years after 1838. Mr. Smith and myself became in time the sole partners, my brother Glen having retired. I had myself finally to pay most of the losses of Glen O. Burnett & Co. (Glen O. and Peter H. Burnett), which amounted to some two thousand dollars, the loss mainly caused by that steam saw-mill and distillery. Mr. Smith and myself were equally unfortunate; and, after prosecuting the business five years with unremitting energy, I found myself in debt to the extent of about fifteen thousand dollars.

My partners, Colonel Thornton and Major Smith, were men of capital, and no creditor of either firm lost anything. But I was only the business man, with little or no capital; and I lost five years' time and expenses, and a great deal more besides. I was unable to make up my portion of the partnership losses in the firms of Thornton & Burnett, and Smith & Burnett, or to pay the amount I had used for my support. I lost in both firms.

RETURN TO THE LAW — EMPLOYED BY THE MORMON ELDERS — PROCEEDINGS ON HABEAS CORPUS.

From the latter part of 1833 to the middle of 1838 I had not opened a law-book, and had forgotten much of that which I had learned. In the spring and summer of 1838 I had an attack of sickness, which prevented me from doing any business for several months. After my recovery, foreseeing what might be the result of my mercantile operations, I read the Statutes of Missouri, and studied well the decisions of the Supreme Court of that State, in the fall and winter of 1838-'39.

In the beginning of 1839 I determined once more to try the law, and to bid a final adieu to the mercantile business. Circumstances were favorable. After my arrival in Liberty in April, 1832, I was a member of a debating society, and in 1838 I engaged to some extent in the political contests of that time, and made several stump speeches. I also edited a weekly newspaper, "The Far West," published in Liberty. My services were gratuitous, as I desired improvement, not salary. I had therefore acquired some reputation as a speaker and writer. Besides, the Mormon difficulties of 1838-'39, which led to their final expulsion from Missouri, produced a heavy amount of litigation.

The lawyers with whom I came mainly in competition had been at the bar from eight to fifteen years; and among them were D. R. Atchison, William T. Wood, Amos Rees, A. W. Doniphan, John Gordon, Andrew S. Hughes, and William B. Almond. Austin A. King was then our Circuit Judge. Atchison was a member of the Legislature, and Doniphan had been sick, and was for some months unable to attend to business. These combined circumstances threw into my hands a considerable practice the first year. I remember that among the first suits I brought were several for debt against some of the Mormons in Caldwell County, some thirty miles from Liberty. I had to begin them at once, as the circumstances would not admit of delay. I had no books to refer to, and had to draw up the declarations from memory. I therefore stated the facts substantially, but in a form most untechnical. These declarations caused considerable amusement; but I amended them, and obtained my judgments.

In the beginning of 1839, Amos Rees, A. W. Doniphan, and myself were employed as counsel by Joseph Smith, Jr., Sidney Rigdon, Lyman Wight, and other Mormon leaders, then in Liberty jail, they having been committed by Judge King for treason, arson, and robbery, alleged to have been committed in Davis County. There was no jail in that county, and, as Liberty jail was the nearest secure prison, they were confined there until the meeting of the Circuit Court of Davis County, in March, 1839. An investigation had been had in December, 1838, at Richmond, before Judge King as committing officer, in which I had not participated, though present. The Mormons had been driven from Jackson County in 1833, and had taken refuge in Clay; and, after remaining there a year or two, they had moved to the new prairie county of Caldwell, north of Clay, where they advanced rapidly with their improvements, until interrupted by the difficulties of the fall of 1838.

We had the prisoners out upon a writ of habeas corpus, before the Hon. Joel Turnham, the County Judge of Clay County. In conducting the proceedings before him there was imminent peril. The people were not only incensed against the Mormons, but they thought it was presumption in a County Judge to release a prisoner committed by a Circuit Judge. The law, however, considered all committing magistrates — judges of courts as well as justices of the peace — as equals when acting simply in that inferior capacity. We apprehended that we should be mobbed, the prisoners forcibly seized, and most probably hung. Doniphan and myself argued the case before the County Judge — Mr. Rees, who resided in Richmond, not being present. All of us were intensely opposed to mobs, as destructive of all legitimate government, and as the worst form of *irresponsible* tyranny. We therefore determined inflexibly to do our duty to our clients at all hazards, and to sell our lives as dearly as possible if necessary. We rose above all fear, and felt impressed with the idea that we had a sublime and perilous but sacred duty to perform. We armed ourselves, and had a circle of brave and faithful friends armed around us; and, it being cold weather, the proceedings were conducted in one of the smaller rooms in the second story of the Court-House in Liberty, so that only a limited number, say a hundred persons, could witness the proceedings.

Judge Turnham was not a lawyer, but had been in public life a good deal, and was a man of most excellent sense, very just, fearless, firm, and unflinching in the discharge of his duties. We knew well his moral nerve, and that he would do whatever he determined to do in defiance of all opposition. While he was calm, cool, and courteous, his noble countenance exhibited the highest traits of a fearless and just judge.

I made the opening speech, and was replied to by the District Attorney; and Doniphan made the closing argument. Before he rose to speak, or just as he rose, I whispered to him: "Doniphan! let yourself out, my good fellow; and I will kill the first man that attacks you." And he did let himself out, in one of the most eloquent and withering speeches I ever heard. The maddened crowd foamed and gnashed their teeth, but only to make him more and more intrepid. He faced the terrible storm with the most noble courage. All the time I sat within six feet of him, with my hand upon my pistol, calmly determined to do as I had promised him.

The Judge decided to release Sidney Rigdon, against whom there was no sufficient proof in the record of the evidence taken before Judge King. The other prisoners were remanded to await the action of the grand jury of Davis County. Rigdon was released from the jail at night to avoid the mob.

ORATION BY SIDNEY RIGDON. — SERMON BY JOSEPH SMITH, JR. — BATTLE BETWEEN THE DANITES AND CAPTAIN BOGARD.

If I remember correctly, it was in the spring of 1838 that Smith and Rigdon came from Kirtland, Ohio, to Far West, the county seat of Caldwell County, Missouri. Rigdon delivered an oration on the Fourth of July, 1838, at Far West, in which he assumed some extraordinary positions in reference to the relation the Mormons sustained to the State Government. This discourse gave great offense to the people of the adjoining counties, particularly to those of Ray and Davis. Serious difficulties were evidently brewing.

I well remember the first time I ever saw Joseph Smith, Jr. I arrived at Far West one Saturday evening in June or July, 1838, and found there John McDaniel, a young merchant of Liberty. John was wild, imprudent, and fond of frolics. On Saturday he had openly ridiculed Smith's pretensions to the gift of prophecy, and his remarks had been reported to the prophet. On Sunday John and myself went to hear Smith preach. The church was a large frame building, with seats well arranged and a good pulpit. We were treated with great politeness, and kindly shown to seats that commanded a full view of the whole proceedings. The congregation was large, very orderly, and attentive. There were officers to show people to their seats, who were most polite and efficient in the discharge of their duties.

Two sermons were delivered by other preachers, which were simply plain, practical discourses, and created no emotion. But, when Joseph Smith, Jr., rose to speak, he was full of the most intense excitement. He boldly denounced McDaniel in the most severe terms, saying, in substance, that no man should come to Far West and openly vilify and slander him, and that, if his brethren would not protect him, he would protect himself. I had not heard of the remarks of McDaniel, and was wholly taken by surprise. I watched him as he sat by my side, and he was as pale as a corpse, but did not stir or open his lips. The Mormon audience were deeply moved, but preserved good order. After the services were ended, McDaniel requested me to go with him to see Smith, and we did so. An explanation was made on both sides, and the matter there terminated.

The Mormons extended their settlements into the adjoining county of Davis, at a place called Adam on Diamon, the name being significant of some religious idea which I have forgotten. The people of Davis (who were rather rude and ungovernable, being mostly backwoodsmen) were very much opposed to this, although the Mormons had paid for the lands they occupied. The Mormons insisted on their legal rights as citizens of the State, while the people of Davis determined that they should not vote in that county at the August election of 1838.

When the election came on, the men of Davis County made an effort to prevent the Mormons from voting at that precinct. A fight ensued, in which the Mormons had the best of it. Other difficulties followed, until Lyman Wight, at the head of the Mormon forces, invaded Davis County, most of which he overran, driving all before him. General D. R. Atchison, then commanding the militia in that part of the State, ordered Captain Bogard, of Ray County, to call out his militia company and occupy a position on or near the county line between Ray and Caldwell, and preserve the peace between the people of the two counties. But Captain Bogard was not a very discreet man, and his men were of much the same character. Instead of confining himself and his men within the limits of his own county, he marched one day into the edge of Caldwell, and was not only rather rude to the Mormons residing there, but arrested one or two of them, whom he detained for some little time.

Information of this proceeding was conveyed to Far West that same evening; and Smith at once ordered Captain Patton, with his Danite band, to march that night and attack Bogard. Captain Bogard had retired into the edge of Ray County, and encamped in a narrow bottom on the banks of a creek, among the large scattering oak timber, and behind a slough-bank some four feet high. He apprehended an attack, and had well selected his ground. The wagon-road crossed the stream just below his encampment, and the road ran down the top and point of a long ridge, covered thickly with young hickories, about ten feet high and from one to two inches in diameter at the ground. No one could be seen approaching the encampment until arriving within a short distance of it; but Captain Bogard had placed out a picket-guard on the road some half mile above, at a point where open woods commenced.

I remember well one of the two guards. His name was John Lockhart, a tall East Tennesseean. Just before day the Mormons were seen approaching, and were hailed by the guards; but, receiving no satisfactory answer, the guards fired then fled to the camp. One of the Mormons was killed here, but they fired no shot in return, made no halt, but continued their march in silence and good order, and drew up in line of battle immediately in front of Bogard's position, and about forty yards distant. Not a word was said until the line was formed, and then orders were given to fire. Patton's men, being entirely exposed, suffered severely from the first fire, he himself being mortally wounded, and one or two of his men being killed and others. wounded. He saw at a glance that his men could not stand such a fire, while his enemies were protected by a slough-bank; and he at once ordered his men to charge with their drawn swords. Bogard's men, having no swords, broke their ranks and fled. Several were overtaken in the retreat, and either cut down or captured. Bogard had about sixty and Patton eighty men, and eight or ten on each side were killed or wounded. One Mormon was evidently killed by one of his own companions, as his wound was a sword-cut in the back of his head. He had doubtless charged with more precipitancy than his comrades; and, as there was no difference in the dress of the opposing forces, he was mistaken for a retreating enemy.

MILITIA ORDERED OUT — SURRENDER OF THE MORMONS

John Estes, one of Bogard's men, who was in the fight, escaped and came to Liberty the same day, and gave information to General Atchison. The latter at once ordered the Liberty Blues to march to the battleground, and there await further orders. I was a member of this independent militia company.

We made ready, and were off before night, and marched some ten miles that evening, under General Doniphan. The next day we reached the scene of conflict, and encamped in the edge of the open oak-woods next to the prairie that extended from that point to Far West (the town being in the open prairie), and on the road that Patton had traveled to attack Bogard, and about one mile nearer Far West than Bogard's men, so that we numbered about one hundred. The first night after our encampment was cold and frosty. I remember it well, for I was on guard that night.

Among those who had fallen in with us was a lad of about eighteen, quite tall, green, and awkward. He was dressed in thin clothing, and when put on guard was told by the officer not to let any one take his gun. He said no one would get *his* gun. When the officer went around to relieve the guard, this boy would not permit him to come near, presenting his gun with the most determined face. In vain the officer explained his purpose; the boy was inflexible, and stood guard the remainder of the night, always at his post, and always wide awake. We anticipated no attack this night, as the Mormons, at Far West, were not aware of our approach in time to reach us until the next night, when we did expect an attack.

The next day was warm and beautiful, and was what is called "Indian summer." I went upon the battlefield and examined it carefully. The dead and wounded had all been removed; but the clots of blood upon the leaves where the men had fallen were fresh and plainly to be seen. It looked like the scene of death. Here lay a wool hat, there a tin cup, here an old blanket; in the top of this little tree hung a wallet of provisions; and saddles and bridles, and various articles of clothing, lay around in confusion. The marks of the bullets were seen all around. I remember that a small linden-tree, three or four inches in diameter, that stood behind Patton's men, seemed to have been a target, from the number of shots that had struck it.

The second night was clear moonlight, warm and pleasant. Having been on guard the night before in the cold frost, I slept very soundly. Somewhere about midnight one of the picket-guards, placed some distance out in the prairie, on the road toward Far West, came in, giving information to our commander that a body of armed men was approaching us along that road, and from the direction of Far West. Very soon another guard, from another point, came in and confirmed the statement of the first. An alarm was at once given. The first thing I remember to have heard was the voice of Lieutenant William A. Dunn, close to our camp, calling aloud, "Parade! parade! the Mormons are coming." His voice was remarkably loud and distinct, and rang awfully in my ears. A fearful impulse came over me, such as I had never felt before. I knew that it was most probable that the victorious Danites would be upon us, as they had been upon Bogard. It was what we had every reason to expect. We knew they had about eight hundred men at Far West, and were fully able to subdue us if they determined to do so. I said to myself, "Now we catch it." I at once seized my rifle and fell into the ranks. A few of our men were so alarmed that they mounted their horses and rode to the rear of our encampment. A moment after falling into ranks, I looked up and down the line, and the men were shivering as if with cold, though the night was warm. Their teeth chattered from the effects of alarm. I said, "Boys, it has turned cold very suddenly," which remark produced a feeble laugh.

After waiting a few moments, which seemed to us very long, and no enemy attacking us, Doniphan came around calling for twenty volunteers to go out to reconnoiter and bring on the action. I said to myself, "I am not in that scrape." There was not a word said, and not one volunteered. I reflected upon it until I became ashamed; and I said to Thomas Parish, who stood by my side, "Suppose we go out." He said, "Agreed," and out we went. We were joined by four others, making, with Lieutenant Dunn, seven in all, which number was all we could obtain. We asked Dunn if we should go, and he replied, "Say yourselves." We said, "Go," mounted our horses, and were off in a gallop. As we passed the front line, all the men were down on one knee, rifle in hand. We found the guards at their posts, and passed on rapidly. The sorrel mare that I rode was a very fleet little animal, and, having been often trained and run before I purchased her, she no doubt supposed we were running a race; and to carry my gun in my right hand, and hold her in with my left, I found impossible. I was about twenty yards ahead of my comrades when, sure enough, we saw in the clear moonlight a body of armed men approaching. We galloped on until we reached within some hundred yards, then drew up and hailed them, when, to our great satisfaction, we found it was a body of militia under Colonel Gilliam, from Clinton County, coming to join us. Thus ended this alarm.

During all this hubbub, the boy who had persisted in standing guard the preceding night slept on until some one happened to think of him and ask where he was. He was then awakened and fell into ranks without hesitation or trepidation. All admired his courage, and agreed that an army composed of such material would be hard to defeat.

After remaining a day or two in camp, so as to give time for others to join us, we marched to within half a mile of Far West, around which the Mormons had made a sort of barricade of timbers, not sufficient to offer any serious resistance. Finding themselves overpowered by numbers, the Mormon leaders, Smith, Rigdon, Wight, and others, surrendered. As I understood at the time, a proposition was seriously made and earnestly pressed in a council of officers, to try the prisoners by court martial, and, if found guilty, to execute them. This proposition was firmly and successfully opposed by Doniphan. These men had never belonged to any lawful military organization, and could not, therefore, have violated military law. The law of the soldier could not apply to them, as they had not been soldiers in any legal sense. I remember that I went to Doniphan and assured him that we of Clay County would stand by him. Had it not been for the efforts of Doniphan and others from Clay, I think it most probable that the prisoners would have been summarily tried, condemned, and executed.

PRISONERS BROUGHT BEFORE JUDGE KING — JOSEPH SMITH, JR. — LYMANWIGHT — SIDNEY RIGDON.

The prisoners were turned over to the civil authorities, and sent to Richmond, where they were brought before Judge King, who acted as a committing magistrate. The proceedings occupied some days, as a great number of witnesses were examined, and their testimony was taken down in writing, as the statute required. I witnessed a portion of the proceedings, and remember well that Dr. Alvord (if I mistake not the name) was examined on the part of the prosecution. He was a very eccentric genius, fluent, imaginative, sarcastic, and very quick in replying to questions put by the prisoners' counsel. His testimony was very important, if true; and, as he had lately been himself a Mormon, and was regarded by them as a traitor from selfish motives, his testimony labored under some apparent suspicion. For these reasons he was cross-examined very rigidly.

After the doctor had been upon the witness stand some hours, General Andrew S. Hughes (a great wit) came into the case, as counsel for the prisoners; but the fact was unknown to Alvord. Hughes was seated among the prisoners, and wore a blanket overcoat, and the doctor was wholly unacquainted with him. Other counsel for the prisoners had cross-examined the witness, and he had refused to answer a question put by them. General Hughes said to him, "I will let you know that it is not for you, but for the Court, to determine whether you shall answer the question." The witness turned quickly, looked the General full in the face, and, with a most quizzical expression of mock surprise upon his countenance, said, "Sir, I do not know what relation you sustain to this case. Are you one of the prisoners?" This question produced quite a sensation among the attending crowd, who were greatly amused at the situation of the counsel.

General Hughes was quizzed for the time; but he was not the man to remain long in that unpleasant condition. In a short time he made a motion in the case, and in support of that motion made a speech; and when he had finished his argument he took his seat. The District Attorney rose to reply; and, just as he commenced, General Hughes rose quickly from his seat, saying, in the most droll, sarcastic manner, "If it please your Honor, I will save my friend the District Attorney the trouble of making a speech. I have gained my point, and I withdraw my motion. I only made a speech to influence *public opinion*," at the same time waving his hand over the crowd.When the March (1839) term of the District Court of Davis County came on, the sheriff of Clay removed the prisoners, under a strong guard, from the jail in Liberty to Davis County, to be present at the impaneling of the grand jury. It was apprehended that the prisoners would be mobbed by the irritated people of Davis, and the sheriff of Clay was determined to protect his prisoners if he could. Mr. Rees and myself went to Davis County as their counsel. The courthouse at the county seat having been burned the fall before by Lyman Wight's expedition, the court was held in a rough log school-house, about twenty-five feet square. This house was situated on the side of a lane about a quarter of a mile long. It being immediately after the annual spring thaw, this lane was knee-deep in mud, especially in the vicinity of the court-house.

The people of the county collected in crowds, and were so incensed that we anticipated violence toward the prisoners. In the daytime the Court sat in this house, the prisoners being seated upon a bench in one corner of the room; and they were kept under guard there during the night. In the end of the room farthest from the fire-place there was a bed in which the counsel for the prisoners slept. The floor was almost covered with mud.

The prisoners arrived on Saturday evening, and the Court opened on the following Monday. They were fully aware of their extreme danger. As I slept in the room, I had an opportunity to see much of what passed. The prisoners did not sleep any for several nights. Their situation was too perilous to admit of repose. Smith and Wight talked almost incessantly. Smith would send some one for a bottle of whisky; and, while he kept sober himself, Lyman Wight would become pretty well drunk, and would kindly invite the guards of Davis County (into whose keeping the prisoners were then committed) to drink with him, which invitation was cordially accepted. Some of the guards had been in the combats between the Mormons and the people of Davis County.

The subject of incessant conversation between Wight and these men was the late difficulties, which they discussed with great good nature and frankness. Wight would laughingly say, "At such a place" (mentioning it) "you rather whipped us, but at such a place we licked you." Smith was not in any of the combats, so far as I remember. The guard placed over the prisoners in Davis, after the sheriff of Clay delivered them into the hands of the sheriff of that county, did not abuse them, but protected them from the crowd. By consent of the prisoners, many of the citizens of Davis came into the room, and conversed with them hour after hour during most of the night. Among others, I remember two preachers, who had theo-logical arguments with Smith, and he invariably silenced them sooner or later. They were men of but ordinary capacity, and, being unacquainted with the grounds Smith would take, were not prepared to answer his positions; while Smith himself foresaw the objections they would raise against his theory, and was prepared accordingly.

Joseph Smith, Jr., was at least six feet high, well-formed, and weighed about one hundred and eighty pounds. His appearance was not prepossessing, and his conversational powers were but ordinary. You could see at a glance that his education was very limited. He was an awkward but vehement speaker. In conversation he was slow, and used too many words to express his ideas, and would not generally go directly to a point. But, with all these drawbacks, he was much more than an ordinary man. He possessed the most indomitable perseverance, was a good judge of men, and deemed himself born to command, and he did command. His views were so strange and striking, and his manner was so earnest, and apparently so candid, that you could not but be interested. There was a kind, familiar look about him, that pleased you. He was very courteous in discussion, readily admitting what he did not intend to controvert, and would not oppose you abruptly, but had due deference to your feelings. He had the capacity for discussing a subject in different aspects, and for proposing many original views, even of ordinary matters. His illustrations were his own. He had great influence over others. As an evidence of this I will state that on Thursday, just before I left to return to Liberty, I saw him out among the crowd, conversing freely with every one, and seeming to be perfectly at ease. In the short space of five days he had managed so to mollify his enemies that he could go unprotected among them without the slightest danger. Among the Mormons he had much greater influence than Sidney Rigdon. The latter was a man of superior education, an eloquent speaker, of fine appearance and dignified manners; but he did not possess the native intellect of Smith, and lacked his determined will. Lyman Wight was the military man among them. There were several others of the prisoners whose names I have forgotten.

I remember to have heard of a circumstance which was said to have occurred while the prisoners were under guard in Davis, but I can not vouch for its truth from my own knowledge. Joseph Smith, Jr., was a very stout, athletic man, and was a skillful wrestler. This was known to the men of Davis County, and some of them proposed to Smith that he should wrestle with one of their own men.

He at first courteously objected, alleging substantially that, though he was once in the habit of wrestling, he was now a minister of the gospel, and did not wish to do anything contrary to his duty as such, and that he hoped they would excuse him upon that ground. They kindly replied that they did not desire him to do anything contrary to his calling; that they would not bet anything; that it was nothing but a friendly trial of skill and manhood, for the satifaction of others, and to pass away the time pleasantly; and that they hoped he would, under all the circumstances, comply with their request. He consented; they selected the best wrestler among them, and Smith threw him several times in succession, to the great amusement of the spectators. Though I did not witness this incident, I heard it stated as a matter of fact at the time, and I have no doubt of its truth.

The grand jury having found true bills of indictment against the prisoners, we applied to the Court for a change of venue to some county where the prisoners could have a fair trial. Upon a hearing of the application, the Court changed the venue to Boone County, and committed the prisoners to the sheriff of Davis, with instructions to convey them to the proper county; but the prisoners escaped on the way and safely arrived in the State of Illinois. Thus ended the Mormon troubles in Missouri.

APPOINTED DISTRICT ATTORNEY — QUALIFICATIONS OF A GOOD LAWYER — LABORIOUS PRACTICE.

I continued the practice of my profession; but I had to close up the old mercantile concerns in which I had been a partner, and this labor absorbed a large share of my time and thoughts. I found that my mercantile knowledge was of great benefit to me in my profession of the law, especially in commercial cases. I was almost always employed in cases to wind up partnerships. I made it a rule, when employed with another lawyer in a case, especially with older counsel, to perform all the labor I could, and that he would permit, without regard to any question as to the proper proportion of labor to be performed by each of us. This course in due time made me a preferred associate. I was often employed with Doniphan as assistant counsel in civil cases. In criminal cases we were generally opposed. He knew that nothing would be neglected. I was a good pleader, cautious, energetic, and vigilant in managing a case. It was not often that a demurrer was sustained to a pleading of mine, either in civil or criminal cases.

Some time in the winter of 1839-'40, my friend William T. Wood, then District Attorney for our district, very generously came to me, and voluntarily informed me that he intended to resign, and would recommend me to the Governor of the State for the position. I was appointed; but the district having been subsequently divided, and a new judicial district created, composed of the counties of Clinton, Andrew, Buchanan, Holt, and Platte, and D. R. Atchison appointed Judge, I was appointed District Attorney for the new district.

When I commenced the practice, having but lately read the statutes and the reported decisions of the Supreme Court, I was more familiar with them than most of the other members of the bar, and was thus able in many cases to defeat lawyers much older than myself. I was not afraid of labor, and made it a rule that, when two different modes of reaching an end suggested themselves to my mind, one *certain*, but accompanied with great labor, and the other *uncertain*, but requiring little or no work, I always preferred the certain to the uncertain. I generally avoided being on the wrong side of a case, and made it a rule to get at the true facts, so far as I could obtain them from my client, by a strong cross-examination. If he proposed to bring a suit, and had in my judgment no merits in his case, I candidly advised him not to sue. If he was a defendant, I advised him to settle the difficulty with the plaintiff, with as little delay and costs as possible.

There are two qualities very necessary to a good lawyer, one who is truly an ornament to his noble profession, namely, *judgment and impartiality*. Unless he possesses *both* of these qualities, he will be made to give his efforts to vexatious litigation, to the disgrace of his profession and the subversion of justice. I was never a successful lawyer on the wrong side of a case, but I seldom failed when in the right. I was a very poor defender of guilty men, and was only employed for the defense in a very few criminal cases.

In 1839 I was employed with Doniphan to defend a man of property in Ray County, indicted and tried for a very serious offense. We at the time believed him to be innocent, and defended him successfully. I can not, in my own mind, yet say whether he was guilty or not; but I have long regretted having had anything to do with that melancholy case. A young woman was examined as a witness for the prosecution, who was of good family and character, and whose testimony was positive; and we were forced to impeach her veracity in order to acquit our client. Her conduct was open to apparent objection, but might have been wholly the result of timidity or confusion. I remember that her uncle, a most estimable citizen, wept when he heard his niece's character for truth called in question. I shall never forget his manly tears. It was enough to make him weep, under any view of the question.

I was a vigilant but candid prosecutor. If I became satisfied that the prisoner was innocent, I told the jury so; but, if I thought him guilty, I prosecuted him with all the energy and ability I possessed, and was generally successful. I was District Attorney a little upward of three years, was twice appointed by the Governor of the State, and was once elected by the people of the district, of which Atchison was judge. In this new district there was more criminal business than in any other district of the State, except that of St. Louis. The great Platte Country, the most fertile portion of the State, was annexed to Missouri in the beginning of 1837, and settled up rapidly with every class of people. Besides this fact, the land was open to preëmption claims, though the country was not at first surveyed; and this uncertainty as to titles and boundaries led to much harassing and bitter litigation, which produced an unusual amount of crime. In all my labors since I was grown, though I have seen some hard service at different times, I do not remember to have been so often utterly worn out as I was while District Attorney in Judge Atchison's district. In Platte County, the largest in the district, and the second county in the State in point of population, we generally had from seventy-five to one hundred criminal cases on the docket at each term of the Court. These cases were of every character, from the most trifling to very grave offenses. While they were mainly indictments for gambling at cards, there were commonly from fifteen to twenty cases of a serious character, for which the punishment was generally imprisonment in the Penitentiary.

It was the duty of the District Attorney not only to prosecute the cases before the Court and trial-jury, but to attend the grand jury, give them advice, and draw up all the indictments. During the first week of the term, and while the grand jury were in session, I usually wrote from dark until midnight, commenced again next morning at sunrise, wrote until breakfast, and, after taking a light, hasty meal, wrote until about 9 a.m., when Court met. The criminal had precedence over civil cases on the docket, and were disposed of before the civil cases were reached. In Court, I prosecuted from 9 a.m. until 2 p.m., when the Court adjourned half an hour for dinner, and then met again, and remained in session until sundown. While in Court I was nearly always upon my feet, case after case following in succession. I have often gone into the trial of a case of grand larceny, without knowing anything of the facts except that the prisoner was charged in the indictment with stealing a horse or other personal property of the person whose name was stated in the indictment as the owner. I knew the names of the witnesses on the part of the State, because the names were endorsed upon the back of the indictment. In these cases I had the witnesses called, and, if present, I was ready for trial. I examined them, in general terms, only far enough to make out a *prima facie* case against the accused; and then I turned the witnesses over to the prisoner's counsel, knowing they would bring out all the facts before the Court and jury. After the examination of the first witness, I was able to see the thread of the testimony, and knew how to proceed. I had the criminal law at my tongue's end, and was seldom at a loss for authority to sustain my position, because I would not ask of the Court any decision that I thought incorrect. In my civil practice it was my general rule not to ask a decision of a point in my favor that I was satisfied would not be sustained in the Supreme Court. I liked to practice against prejudiced lawyers, who would insist upon points that were not just. I could always defeat them in the highest Court, and made it a rule to take appeals where I knew I was right.

DIFFICULTY OF ADMINISTERING CRIMINAL JUSTICE — A NOTED CRIMINAL — AN ABLE AND UPRIGHT JUDGE.

The duties of District Attorney in that district were not only laborious, but difficult and extremely responsible upon other accounts. There were five counties in the district, and the Platte country was in the shape of the letter V, bounded on the east by the old State line, on the southwest by the Missouri River, and on the northwest by the then wild prairie lands of Iowa. The remote county of Holt was in the western and narrowest portion; and, being not only remote, but thinly inhabited, it was under the control for a time of thieves and counterfeiters, who, by being upon the trial-juries, defeated the ends of justice. I remember that at one term of the Court there were some thirty indictments and only one or two convictions. I would prove up the case as clearly as possible, and yet the jury, after being out but a few moments, would return into

Court with their verdict, "We, the jury, find the defendant not guilty." In some rare cases, when the punishment was very trifling, they would find the defendant guilty for the sake of appearances.

There was at that time an organized band of criminals, at the head of whom was the notorious Daniel Whiteman. These men and their friends overawed the good citizens of the county. Whiteman said to me, laughingly, "Pete, you can't convict anybody. I manage these juries." I remember that much the same state of things once existed in Jackson County, at an early day, and before I was a member of the bar. Amos Rees was then District Attorney, and I have heard the facts of the case from other lawyers who were present.

A man was indicted and tried for selling whisky to an Indian. A most intelligent and trustworthy witness testified before the trial-jury, that upon a stated day and year, in Jackson County, in the State of Missouri, he saw an Indian come into the defendant's grocery, and put down upon the counter a quarter of a dollar, in silver coin of the United States, at the same time handing the defendant an empty bottle; that he saw the defendant take a gallon measure and draw from a barrel, and out of the contents of the gallon measure fill up the bottle for the Indian, put the quarter into his (defendant's) drawer, and that he then asked the witness to drink out of what remained in the measure from which the bottle had been filled; that witness drank from the measure, and that what he drank was whisky. Colonel William T. Wood, who defended the party, thought the evidence so clear against his client that he was about to give up the case, when one of the jurors asked the witness, "But did you drink out of the bottle itself?" The witness answered, "No; I only drank of the liquid left in the measure after filling the bottle." Upon this state of evidence the jury found the defendant not guilty. Mr. Rees at once sternly told the sheriff that, if he summoned any more such juries, he would move the Court to punish him for contempt.

This state of things continued only for a time. Some one in the adjoining county had Whiteman arrested upon a charge of theft, alleged to have been committed in that county, and he was sent to jail to await his examination before a justice of the peace. In the mean time he was taken out by the people, severely lynched, and then turned loose. He returned to Holt, where he was loud in his threats against Judge Atchison and myself, as he had been informed that we had encouraged his being lynched.

I remember that in the spring of 1843 I was at the county seat of Holt County, where I delivered a public address to the people in reference to Oregon; and I found Whiteman there. He at once took me aside and asked me if I had heard that "they had given him h — l." I told him I had. He then said that he had understood that Judge Atchison and myself had encouraged the people to act as they did. I told him that it was not true as to myself; that I could not, would not, and never did encourage illegal violence; but I would state to him what I said, and which was true. When people asked me why persons indicted and tried in that county could not be convicted, I had told them that it was not my fault, but the fault of the trial-juries, who were under the influence of the criminals of the county.

While I was addressing the people, I observed that Whiteman stood near me all the time, but did not once suspect that he meditated an attack upon me. After I had finished my address, a gentleman whom I knew took me apart from the crowd, and told me that he had overheard Whiteman making threats of personal violence against me, just before I commenced speaking; and that he (my friend) had placed himself by Whiteman's side, ready and determined to shoot him at the first offensive movement he should make. Whiteman asked me several questions about Oregon before I left the stand, which were respectfully put and respectfully answered. A short time after this, as I was informed, he was lynched the second time. He made a desperate resistance, and was almost killed in the struggle. This was the last of that noted culprit, as he soon thereafter left the county.

Judge Atchison was an upright, incorruptible judge, and was a man of fine literary and legal education, and of superior native intellect. He possessed a kind heart, and a noble, generous, manly spirit; but, when first appointed, he seemed to me to err too often in his rulings in favor of the accused. I was always courteous and respectful to any Court before which I consented to appear, and never in the course of my practice had an angry altercation with the Court, or was punished for contempt. I determined, in the proper manner, to correct the supposed errors of the Judge. The Judge decided several cases against me; but, being satisfied that I was right, I took them up to the Supreme Court, and a majority of them came back reversed.

CASE OF WHITTLE — JUDGE AUSTIN A. KING.

As illustrative of the then mixed state of society, I will refer to the following case.

A celebrated counterfeiter of the name of Whittle went from the county in which he resided to an adjoining county, and passed upon a plain farmer some counterfeit gold coin, in payment for a horse. Having been indicted in the proper county, he applied for a change of venue; and the case, upon a proper showing, was sent to Buchanan County.

When the case was called, the prisoner was ready for trial, and I asked the Court to order the sheriff to call the trial-jurors. The moment I heard their names called, I was satisfied that it was mainly a packed jury. I knew that some of them belonged to the band of criminals in that county, or they were unfortunate in reputation and association. I promptly rose and said; "If the Court please, it is now very near dinner time, and I would thank the Court to adjourn until after dinner. I wish a little time to examine this jury list, and I think it very likely that I will dispose of this case without troubling the Court." Judge Atchison seemed to understand what I was driving at, and readily adjourned the Court.

When the Court met again, there was a large crowd present, as it must have been anticipated that some decisive step in the case would be taken. When the case was again called, I said: "With the leave of the Court, I will enter a *nolle prosequi*, and let the prisoner go. I do not mean to make a farce of justice by trying this prisoner before such a jury." The prisoner was wholly taken by surprise, and looked exceedingly mortified. He evidently expected to be tried and acquitted. I intended to have the witnesses again subpoenaed before the grand jury of the proper county, and they would no doubt have found another indictment; and, upon another application for a change of venue, I should have opposed successfully any effort of the defendant to have the case sent again to Buchanan County. But the prisoner was killed in a private quarrel before the next term of the Court.

He was a man of herculean frame, and of desperate character. His death happened in this wise: He forced a quarrel upon a peaceable, awkward, and innocent young man, about the age of twenty-one, for the purpose, most likely, of showing off his bravery and prowess before his friends. At all events, when the young man had hitched his horse to the rack, Whittle went out and cut off the horses's tail, and came into the room where the young man was sitting, and thrust it rudely into his face. Upon the young man's remonstrating, Whittle chased him into the street; and several times afterward during the day he followed him into other places, and forced him hastily to leave. The poor young man became at last desperate, and went and armed himself with a pistol. Whittle again drove him from the house, and was pursuing him in the street, when the young man turned upon him, and shot him through the heart. Though fatally wounded, Whittle picked up a large stone, and threw it at the young man with such prodigious force that had it struck him it would have killed him instantly. After throwing the stone Whittle fell upon his face dead.

I have known of several instances, where persons shot through the heart have lived for some little time. When the shot passes through the left ventricle of the heart, the wound is instantaneously fatal, so that the muscles retain the exact position they had at the very moment the wound was given. For example, if the deceased had a pistol tightly grasped in his hand, he would still after death retain his grasp upon it, as also the very same cast of features. This was the case with General Richardson, killed by Cora in San Francisco in the year 1856. So, whenever a shot seriously wounds the spinal marrow, the person is instantaneously paralyzed. I have never known but one instance where a person was fatally shot through the brain, that he did not drop instantly, however excited he may have been. This exceptional case was that of Joel Turnham, Jr., who was killed in Oregon about the year 1844, while resisting a special constable, who was sent to arrest him for assault and battery. Turnham was one of the stoutest, bravest, most reckless men I ever knew; and, though fatally shot through the brain with a pistol, he turned and walked some twenty feet before he fell.

After becoming familiar with the duties of his position, D. R. Atchison made an admirable judge, and gave general satisfaction. In point of legal acquirements, I do not think he was then quite the equal of Judge Austin A. King, who was an older man; but Judge Atchison was more popular with the members of the bar generally. It was the fault of Judge King, at one time, not to be sufficiently indulgent to young lawyers. I remember his treatment of myself when a new beginner. Being satisfied that he did not extend to me the indulgence that my situation justified, I determined to bide my time and correct this supposed error.

I was, upon one occasion, employed to defend a suit brought by one of the older members of the bar upon a promissory note, which he described in his declaration as bearing date a certain day and year set forth. I put in the plea of *non assumpsit*; and, when the note was offered in evidence, I simply objected. It bore a different date from the note described, and was not therefore the same note. I knew that the objection was a good one, but the plaintiff's counsel declared that my objection was invalid, and then handed the papers to the Judge, who compared the note with the declaration, and at once gave judgment for the plaintiff; and I quietly took my appeal. In five or six months, the case came back reversed; and the Supreme Court expressed surprise that so plain an error should have been committed by the Court below. It so happened that I was afterwards employed in another case of much the same character before the same Judge; and I, as before, simply objected to the introduction of the note as evidence in the case. The Judge this time was very polite, and asked me to state my objections (which he had not done in the former case); and after that I could always be heard. I thought the Judge, on several former occasions, had evinced by his manner an indisposition to hear me when I had a right to be heard.

Young lawyers can not, of course, speak as well as those that are older, and judges are very apt to become impatient when listening to irrelevant remarks. But it always seemed to me that it was not only more generous but more expedient, in most cases, to indulge young lawyers in their errors of inexperience. I have no doubt of the fact that many a noble young man, of fine intellect and heart, has been either driven from the profession, or kept in a grade beneath his real abilities, by the harsh and inconsiderate reproofs of crabbed judges. Tyranny has many modes of exhibiting itself; and a man may be the victim of oppression in many other ways than knocking him down, putting him in prison, or confiscating his property.

Young lawyers are generally sensitive and timid, and their feelings should be spared. One of the noblest objects in the world is a pure and intellectual young man; and a court should lean gently upon his young errors. But I can truly say, in justice to Judge King, that he subsequently became as indulgent to young lawyers as he should have been. I remember that the Judge's course toward a young lawyer, Mr. Hovey, was entirely unexceptionable. Judge

King was not so popular with the bar generally as Judge Atchison, mainly for the reason that King was a religious man, and had not the amount of mirth and gayety that Atchison had. The latter was very companionable, and full of anecdote, in which he was not limited by religious views. Most of our lawyers at that time were not religious, and would naturally be partial to a man like themselves.

CHARACTERISTICS OF LAWYERS — NATURE OF LEGAL INVESTIGATIONS — DIFFICULTY OF SIMPLIFYING THE LAW — CAUSES OF INFIDELITY AMONG LAWYERS.

I remember an incident which occurred in the winter of 1839-'40, at Savannah, the county seat of Andrew County. There were about fifteen lawyers of us, all at the hotel; and one evening, after the court had finally adjourned, a discussion arose among us in regard to the truth of Christianity. There was not a single lawyer present who was a professor of religion, and only one who believed Christianity to be true, and that was Amos Rees. He manfully and earnestly maintained its true and divine origin. The next day we rode together, and I said to him: "Amos, you deserve double damnation; because you know and believe the truth, and will not put it in practice. Now, sir, whenever I am convinced of the truth of Christianity, you will find me acting up to what I believe to be true." I have the pleasure of stating that a majority of the lawyers present at that time have since become professors of religion, myself among the number.

I never had any disposition to enter into mere personal quarrels. Let me be satisfied that a great duty demands my exertions, and then I can face danger. When I was satisfied that another person abused me in words, because he was sincere but mistaken in thinking he had good cause, I could not feel like holding him responsible for a mere error of judgment. Good men ought never to quarrel. There is a natural and immeasurable gulf between the good and the bad — between the candid and the hypocritical.

There is, among lawyers, a noble freedom allowed in debate; and though, in the moment of excited discussion, they may say that of each other which they never would in their cooler moments, a due and fair allowance is made for the circumstances. Besides, lawyers must necessarily associate often together on the same side of a case; so that it is almost impossible to keep alive the enmity. The other members of the bar interpose their kind offices for reconciliation; and they have so much respect for the views and feelings of each other that these kind requests will seldom be disregarded. Among honorable members of the profession, there generally exists the greatest personal kindness, and little or no professional jealousy. Each honorable member of this most distinguished profession ·is content with the practice he justly merits; and, as to those merits, there is a plain and satisfactory mode of determining the question. They practice their profession, not only in the presence of each other, but before crowds of people and a competent Court. If a lawyer be ignorant of the law, his adversary and the Court will tell him so, and thus expose his ignorance. If he has merits, they are made manifest, as a general rule, by a conclusive test. Time and experience soon settle the relative merits of different members of the bar practicing before the same Courts.

When a lawyer finds, upon due trial, that he is not suited to the profession, he can go to something else. Most lawyers who find they can not succeed in the profession betake themselves to editing newspapers, where the same exact and logical mode of discussion is not required, but where each writer addresses himself mainly to a prejudiced audience, who seldom know what is said in reply. Practically, most newspaper discussions are one-sided.

In legal discussions, the positions of the opposite counsel are, in general, correctly stated and fairly met. To misrepresent facts or positions is not only unprofessional, but idle and vain. He who confutes a position never advanced does an idle and vain thing, by throwing away his efforts. To labor for the purpose of exposing your own ignorance or unfairness is not very wise.

The modes of investigation in courts of justice are not only the most decisive of the merits of counsel and judges, but they are, for that reason, the best adapted to improve the reasoning faculties of the mind. Any one who has ever participated in the discussion of important and difficult questions must have learned that there are classes of arguments apparently sound, but which in truth are utterly worthless, and have no real bearing upon the case. When you hear a speaker, even upon a simple occasion, you can generally form a very good estimate of his ability. If he has a clear logical mind, he will go to the *exact* merits of the question and place the matter in a clear light; but, if his powers are merely declamatory, he will deal in unmeaning generality, true in itself, but outside the particular case.

I confess I am partial to the law, and that, of all the secular learned professions, I love that of law most. I am aware of the prejudices existing in the minds of many against the profession; and it must be conceded that a mean lawyer is one of the meanest of men, because he sins against light and example. A pettifogger among lawyers is like a demagogue among statesmen — a most detestable character, weak in mind and unsound in morals, deserving neither respect nor pity.But these complaints against the law and lawyers are not much heeded by them. Ignorance has been for ages complaining of the imperfections of the law, and proposing to make it so plain that all sane men could readily understand it. But it seems never to have occurred to these restless wanderers after perfection that science is vast, and no science more so than that of law; and that to simplify the law to such an extent as to enable every man to be his own lawyer is just as difficult as to simplify land and marine architecture, or any other science which comprehends a multitude of particulars. It requires very little intellect and study to construct an Indian wigwam or a rude canoe; but it takes mind and careful training to build a palace or construct a mighty steamship.

Rabid law-reformers have often been in the different State Legislatures; but, though no doubt sincere and determined in the beginning, they soon discovered some of the real difficulties in their way to simplicity. To know how to improve the code you must first know its defects; and to know these you must understand the code itself. By the time the rash and presumptuous law-reformer gets to that point, he begins to perceive the difficulties which beset his path. When he comes to sit down and draft a code that will stand the test of honest and intelligent time, he will fully need all his imagined capacity.

I remember that, in the Vigilance Committee times of this State in 1856, there was a great hue and cry raised against lawyers. I had retired from the practice myself, yet I loved the noble profession. I had, however, no defense to make, but simply a compromise to propose. I said: "Only give us back the productions of our labors — the Declaration of Independence, the Constitutions of the United States and of every State in the Union, all the codes of law, the judicial decisions and learned treatises upon the science — and *do without them*, and we will consent that the profession may be abolished, and the nation go back to barbarism. But, until you have something better to propose, your denunciation of a theory you can not mend must be idle."

Surprise has often been expressed that there should be so many infidels among lawyers. It can not be owing to the want of capacity to investigate the subject. The Rev. David Nelson, in his work entitled "Cause and Cure of Infidelity," has these remarks:

"I do not know why it is so, but it is the result of eighteen years of experience that lawyers, of all those whom I have examined, exercise the clearest judgment while investigating the evidences of Christianity. It is the business of the physician's life to watch for evidence and indication of disease, sanity, and change; therefore I am unable to account for the fact, yet so it is, that the man of law excels. He has, when examining the evidences of the Bible's inspiration, shown more common sense in weighing proofs and appreciating argument, where argument really existed, than any class of men I have ever observed."

The superiority attributed by the author to the legal fraternity arises mainly from these causes:

1. It requires more natural logical power to be successful at the bar than in the practice of medicine. 2. The mental training is more rigid and thorough. 3. There is a competent and authoritative tribunal to determine controversies among lawyers.

The fact that there are so many infidels among lawyers is not owing either to a want of capacity in them, or a lack of evidence to establish the truth of Christianity, but entirely to other causes.

When a young man is studying law, he finds no time to think of religion; and, after he commences practice, the state of the case is much the same. Logical minds are not prone to take a theory as true without proof; and the proofs of Christianity, though complete and conclusive to a moral certainty, yet require time and careful investigation to be able to understand them in their full and combined force. These evidences consist of a great mass of testimony, both direct and circumstantial. To succeed at the bar requires great capacity and industry. The profession is compared by Lord Coke to a jealous mistress that will not tolerate a rival. The main reason, therefore, why there are so many infidels among the members of the bar, is because they do not investigate the subject, and will not believe without investigation; and the reason why they do not investigate is mainly the incessant and arduous nature of their employments.

But, besides the want of time, there are other causes to prevent investigation. There is a good deal, perhaps an over-proportion, of dissipation among lawyers. Their forensic efforts are often so severe and exhaustive that they resort to the use of stimulants to support them for the time. Others resort to stimulants because the use emboldens them, excites the imagination, and thus enables them to make the greatest display of oratory. It is well known to members of the profession that dissipation wonderfully stimulates and matures the intellect for a time. I have long observed that those lawyers who dissipate soonest arrive at maturity, and soonest go down, as a general rule. They are nearly always the greatest wits and orators among us, but not the best reasoners.

But, besides these facts, there are the many varied scenes occurring in the practice, that continually call off the attention of lawyers from things future to things present. The witty joke, the amusing anecdote, and the ardent discussion of legal questions in and out of court, make their lives one continued round of excitement. Human nature is exhibited in courts of justice in its most vicious, melancholy, and ridiculous aspects. One case is full of the most cunningly devised fraud, another of the most brutal crime, and a third is so full of the ridiculous that all must laugh; and the transition from one class of cases to others is often very rapid. Lawyers but seldom see the best traits of man exhibited in court, for the reason that the best men are not often engaged in lawsuits. For these and other reasons, the path of the lawyer is beset with temptation.

POLITICAL VIEWS.

My father was a Whig, and so were my brothers-in-law. When I was between sixteen and seventeen years of age, I read a paper edited by Duff Green, published in St. Louis, and became a Democrat. But as I grew older, and since I have studied more deeply the science of government, I have seen more cause to doubt the practical result of our republican theory as it now exists. I have always desired, whatever may have been my doubts, to give our theory a full and fair trial; being satisfied that, so long as our theory can be honestly and efficiently administered, it is the best form of government for the greatest number. It is especially adapted to a young people, free from extreme want, and therefore independent and virtuous. But when the population becomes dense, dependent, and suffering, and for that reason more corrupt, then will come the genuine test of our existing theory; and I think, without a thorough and radical amendment, it must fail. The three principles of universal suffrage, elective offices, and short terms, in their combined legitimate operation, will in due time politically demoralize any people in the world. I have given my views, in full, in a pamphlet published in 1861 by D. Appleton & Co. of New York, to which I refer. I am now of the opinion that the masses will never permit a sound conservative amendment of our theory, except by revolution, which I think will occur within the next fifty years. It may require several revolutions in succession. This I think most probable.

Mr. Jefferson was once considered by me as the apostle of liberty and a great statesman. I do not question his sincerity or his patriotism, but I doubt his statesmanship. I am now of the opinion that Alexander Hamilton was a much greater statesman than Jefferson or Madison. Patrick Henry was the orator more than the statesman. I now consider Hamilton to have had the clearest mind and the most logical power, and to have been the greatest statesman of our country. His contributions to the "Federalist" prove this. Chief Justice Marshall was a great man; but Hamilton was before him. The appreciation of Hamilton by Washington was one of the greatest proofs of his most superior good sense. He understood true merit when he found it. Hamilton sacrificed himself to mistaken public opinion — the only serious error he committed.

REMARKS ON DUELING.

I was never engaged in sending, or in bearing, and never received, a challenge to fight a duel. As a humble and steadfast believer in the sublime truths of Christianity, I could not sanction that semi-barbarous code. But, aside from the theological view of the question, I could not approve the practice.

It is claimed by its friends that it operates as a practical check upon the tongues and acts of men; and this no doubt is true as to some persons, but untrue as to others; so that, upon the whole, it is exceedingly doubtful whether it does, in point of fact, operate as a check upon slander and violence. I have reflected much upon this subject, and watched its practical effect with some care. I do not understand all the minute provisions of this code, but only know enough of its main points to justify my conclusions as to its substantial character.

It is insisted by the advocates of this code that the parties are placed as near upon an equality as, in the nature of things, they can be. But is this true? I think not. It is made the duty of the party insulted to send the challenge, and the party challenged has a right to fix the terms upon which they meet; and he, consequently, insists upon those that give him a decided advantage. The skillful use of weapons, especially of the dueling pistol, is an acquired art to a great extent, and requires years of continued practice to fix the art as a *habit*. In fact, a man must grow up accustomed to the use of such arms, to become completely and habitually skillful. Besides, he must possess a natural steadiness of nerve and quick accuracy of sight, to enable him by this long practice to acquire the habitual art to perfection. I suppose that the great majority of men, with all possible training, never could become first-rate shots on the wing with a shot-gun, or with a pistol at a stationary object.

Those who possess the natural capacity and the habitual training have an immense advantage over those who have them not. Habit is second nature, and becomes almost as certain as instinct; so that the habitually good shot will still shoot with his accustomed accuracy, whether alarmed or not, and, *knowing* his advantage, he has less cause to be excited. On the contrary, the party who has not the natural capacity, or lacks the habitual training, though able in a pistol-gallery to shoot with accuracy at an inanimate figure, will generally fail when he comes to face his enemy. His excitement, brave and determined as he may be, will affect him; and he has no fixed habit to save him from the effect. That those not habitually accustomed to the use of the pistol shoot very wildly upon the field of battle, as compared with their previous practice, is conclusively shown by the history of different duels.

To induce a man to acquire the habitual use of the pistol, he must have, in his own estimation, some considerable motive; and when he becomes a first-rate shot he is almost certain to be proud of it, and will very naturally seek to use an art of which he is master. We naturally love most that in which we most excel. I have observed that men who continually wear arms become at last anxious to use them, and thirsty for blood. They seem to think that, after they have carried arms for a long time and not used them, they have done an idle and vain thing. It is a great personal inconvenience to wear arms and keep them always in good order; and he who does so must be continually brooding over scenes of blood, until he becomes at last anxious to get into them himself. He is therefore much more apt to insult others than he would be if the dueling code did not exist. He covets the reputation of the duelist, and seeks an opportunity to insult some one he dislikes. He knows that, if he gives the *first* insult, the party must challenge him, and then he will adjust the terms to suit himself. The world will not inquire who was to blame in the first instance, inasmuch as he has given the insulted party the satisfaction he demanded. He kills his man, and secretly, if not openly, glories in his success. In the future he has only, at intervals, to insult and kill others in the same way. The greater the number he slays, the greater his fame; and, the greater his fame, the greater are his chances of success. True, he may fall at last by a chance shot, but not until he has slain from two to six persons.

Duels are much more numerous among politicians, in proportion to numbers, than among any other class, except perhaps army officers. This arises, in many cases, from rivalship. It becomes desirable to kill off certain aspirants, to get them out of the way. Hence they are insulted. Those well skilled in such matters know how much and what to say to produce a challenge.

As I have before stated, the code prevents some men from saying and doing things they would otherwise say or do; but it has a contrary effect on others. There is, in the minds and hearts of proud men, a sort of glory in defying consequences; and this stimulates many men to say and do offensive things that they would not otherwise say and do; and also prevents them from making a proper explanation after they have done wrong, for fear it will be said that the explanation was the result of cowardice. If public opinion held the practice of bitter language disreputable, this would prevent the use of it more effectually than the dueling code. One thing seems certain, that personal quarrels are most common among those who admit the code.

Duels are not necessarily evidence of *personal*, though they are evidence of the want of true *moral* courage. It is the fear or love of what others may think and say that generally impels the duelist. He has not the moral nerve to face a false public opinion. He flees from moral to physical responsibility, which shows more of the animal than of the intellectual being. The question with him is not so much what is right in itself, as what is considered so. He is for effect, not reality, and prefers the shadow to the substance. He is essentially selfish, and therefore he heeds not the ruin he produces. The cry and distress of the widow and the orphan never reach his dull, cold ear, or affect his stony heart. He is generally the slave of the times and the country in which he lives, and never rises superior to the scorn and contempt of the unwise. Being contemptible himself, he fears contempt. He is not satisfied with simply being in the right, but is content to be considered so, whether right or wrong. He is a being who worships appearances, and is willing to do wrong to save them. His moral being exists in "others' breath." He is never a martyr for truth, but falls a victim to interest or pride. The only man who can with any plausible consistency be a duelist is the man without principle, and who determines to gain the temporary advantages of doing wrong, and at the same time enjoying the reputation of an honorable man. Hence, when detected in a mean action, and told of it, his remedy is to drown the infamy in blood.

When a duelist uses courteous and gentlemanly language, no one can tell whether it is the result of fear or principle. All are uncertain as to what motive to attribute his conduct, as all know he is acting under restraint if the code has any effect in silencing his tongue. On the contrary, if he abuses another, there is still a difficulty in determining whether he is sincere in what he says, or whether he only wishes to show off his courage, or to induce his victim to send him a challenge that he may kill him. The general and legitimate effect of the code is to make hypocrites of those it restrains, and bullies of those it urges on.

I can not understand upon what principle two really good men should fight a duel. If they are willing to kill each other simply for fear of public opinion, they can not be good men. If a man abuses and misrepresents you, and you are satisfied that he is sincere but mistaken, will you seek his life for a mere error of judgment or defect of memory? On the contrary, if you are convinced that he willfully misrepresents you, then you believe he is a liar; and, unless you are a liar yourself, he is not your equal. Why should a gentleman and a man of pure justice put his life against that of a man he regards as destitute of honest principles?

In short, my opinion of men who engage in duels is that most of them are atheists, whose moral conduct depends upon the sliding scale of the times, and who have no strict moral principles independent of public opinion. They can generally have no faith in a future state of rewards and punishments; and hence they do whatever they deem most *successful* in this life. They are slaves to success, not devotees of principle. There are very few duels in communities where they are odious.

I most readily and willingly admit that there are exceptions to these remarks. Men sometimes labor under strange delusions, and lug themselves into the opinion that it is right, in some cases, to do wrong that good may come. This was the case with Alexander Hamilton. He conceded that the practice was wrong in itself, but yielded to a false public opinion, in order that he might be useful to that public; and most grievously did he answer for it. The result of his own act shows how much he was mistaken. Had he dared to do right, his life would have been spared to his country.

But this plea of necessity is always found in the mouths of tyrants and moral culprits of every grade. It is as false as the theory that you can do an unconstitutional act in accordance with the Constitution. Whenever the public require a man to do that which is plainly wrong, in order to gain the privilege of serving it, I must say it is unworthy of his services, and he should leave those with more pliable consciences to serve a vitiated public.

JOIN THE DISCIPLES — ART OF GOVERNING CHILDREN.

In 1840 I became a professor of Christianity, and joined the Disciples, or Campbellites as they were sometimes called. I was in my thirty-third year. I had long reflected much upon the subject, but could not come to the conclusion that Christianity was true. I was a Deist. I could never doubt the existence of God. I saw in the visible creation the plainest possible evidences of design — a perfect adaptation of means to ends. I could not conceive how chance could originate a *system* of any kind; and, even if such a thing were possible, chance could destroy to-day that which it created but yesterday. No one could conceive that such a machine as a clock could be the result of accident; and the wonderful mechanism of man's physical organization far surpasses the most magnificent productions of human genius.

Nor could I understand how this universe could be uncreated, and therefore eternal. That which is uncreated must be infinite; and infinitude admits of no changes, additions, or improvements. The visible creation is subject to change and to come to an end. It is confined within limits, and it admits of additions and improvements. It exists as the production of some superior; and that superior can be nothing but God, who is infinite, and who communicates to inferior beings such natures, powers, and capacities as in His wisdom and goodness He sees fit. "To be eternal is to be without beginning; and to be without beginning is to be independent of any cause or power."

The next step in the logical process is the conclusion that the Creator must govern, in some proper form, His own creation. Matter without properties, brutes without instinct, and rational beings without free will and without law, are logically inconceivable. Pursuing this logical process to an extent that I can not, for want of space, record here, I became thoroughly convinced of the entire truth of Christianity.

In the fall of 1840, I moved to Platte City, the county seat of Platte County. My youngest child, Sallie, was born there in 1841. My son John M. Burnett was born in 1838, and is now a lawyer of good standing in San Francisco.

The true art of governing children is to study their peculiarities, and adapt your government to the disposition of the child. The art of rearing good children is almost as difficult as that of governing a state. Children, so far as they know the facts, are far more competent to draw correct conclusions than most people suppose. Children are naturally truthful; and parents should not violate their own words, either in making promises of reward or threats of punishment. Those who assume to govern ought to be worthy to direct, and should themselves never violate the principles or rules they inculcate or enforce. Perfect truth and consistency should characterize the parents. Then the task of government will be much lighter.

John was a noble and peculiar child, and always obedient when old enough to understand. He was very sensitive, and never would bear scolding, the only punishment we ever inflicted upon him. He cured us of this practice in this way: When he was about four years old, and while we lived in Platte City, he was in the habit of talking a great deal at table. One day I said to him, "John, why do you talk so much at table?" He looked at me with the expression of astonishment in his face, and replied with childlike simplicity and earnestness, "I can not talk by myself," meaning that it was useless to talk unless he had some one to listen. Within a day or two after this, his little tongue was again clattering away while we were at dinner, and his mother scolded him for it. Upon this he was silent, but it was evident that he thought he was badly treated. Just about that time some one commenced blowing a tin trumpet , and the boy's large black eye gleamed with a triumphant expression, and he at once said, "Mother! there's a horn or a woman's voice." After that he was scolded very little. I remember a very acute reply made by a little girl when seven years of age. I was staying at a friend's house in Brooklyn, New York, in 1866, and his daughter Mattie was remarkably fond of her half-grown cat; so much so, that she would take it with her to the dinner-table. Her mother said to her, "Why do you pet your cat so much?" The child, with a serious expression upon her countenance, at once answered, "This cat can't go to heaven," meaning that the cat must be petted *here*, and that was her reason for petting it so much.

Chapter III

***DETERMINE TO GO TO OREGON. — ARRIVE AT THE REN-
DEZVOUS. — REMARKS ON THE NATURE OF THE TRIP.***

In the fall of 1842 I moved to Weston, in Platte County, having purchased an interest in the place. During the winter of 1842-'43 the Congressional report of Senator Appleton in reference to Oregon fell into my hands, and was read by me with great care. This able report contained a very accurate description of that country. At the same time there was a bill pending in Congress, introduced in the Senate by Dr. Linn, one of the Senators from Missouri, which proposed to donate to each immigrant six hundred and forty acres of land for himself, and one hundred and sixty acres for each child. I had a wife and six children, and would therefore be entitled to sixteen hundred acres. There was a fair prospect of the ultimate passage of the bill.

I saw that a great American community would grow up, in the space of a few years, upon the shores of the distant Pacific; and I felt an ardent desire to aid in this most important enterprise. At that time the country was claimed by both Great Britain and the United States; so that the most ready and peaceable way to settle the conflicting and doubtful claims of the two governments was to fill the country with American citizens. If we could only show, by a *practical* test, that American emigrants could safely make their way across the continent to Oregon with their wagons, teams, cattle, and families, then the solution of the question of title to the country was discovered. Of course, Great Britain would not covet a colony settled by American citizens.

The health of Mrs. Burnett had been delicate for some three years, and it was all we could do to keep her alive through the winter in that cold climate. Her physician said the trip would either kill or cure her. I was also largely indebted to my old partners in the mercantile business. I had sold all my property, had lived in a plain style, had worked hard, and paid all I could spare each year; and still the amount of my indebtedness seemed to be reduced very little.

Putting all these considerations together, I determined, with the consent of my old partners, to move to Oregon. I therefore laid all my plans and calculations before them. I said that, if Dr. Linn's bill should pass, the land would ultimately enable me to pay up. There was at least a chance. In staying where I was, I saw no reasonable probability of ever being able to pay my debts. I did a good practice, and was able to pay about a thousand dollars a year; but, with the accumulation of interest, it would require many years' payments, at this rate, to square the account. I was determined not to go without the free consent and advice of my creditors. They all most willingly gave their consent, and said to me, "Take what may be necessary for the trip, leave us what you can spare, and pay us the balance when you become able to do so."

I followed their advice, and set to work most vigorously to organize a wagon company. I visited the surrounding counties, making speeches wherever I could find a sufficient audience, and succeeded even beyond my own expectations. Having completed my arrangements, I left my house in Weston on the 8th day of May, 1843, with two ox wagons, and one small two-horse wagon, four yoke of oxen, two mules, and a fair supply of provisions; and arrived at the rendezvous, some twelve miles west of Independence, and just beyond the line of the State, on the 17th of May.

A trip to Oregon with ox teams was at that time a new experiment, and was exceedingly severe upon the temper and endurance of people. It was one of the most conclusive tests of character, and the very best school in which to study human nature. Before the trip terminated, people acted upon their genuine principles, and threw off all disguises. It was not that the trip was beset with very great perils, for we had no war with the Indians, and no stock stolen by them. But there were ten thousand little vexations continually recurring, which could not be foreseen before they occurred, nor fully remembered when past, but were keenly felt while passing. At one time an ox would be missing, at another time a mule, and then a struggle for the best encampment, and for a supply of wood and water; and, in these struggles, the worst traits of human nature were displayed, and there was no remedy but patient endurance. At the beginning of the journey there were several fisticuff fights in camp; but the emigrants soon abandoned that practice, and thereafter confined themselves to abuse in words only. The man with a black eye and battered face could not well hunt up his cattle or drive his team.

But the subject of the greatest and most painful anxiety to us was the suffering of our poor animals. We could see our faithful oxen dying inch by inch, every day becoming weaker, and some of them giving out, and left in the wilderness to fall a prey to the wolves. In one or two instances they fell dead under the yoke, before they would yield. We found, upon a conclusive trial, that the ox was the noblest of draft-animals upon that trip, and possessed more genuine hardihood and pluck than either mules or horses. When an ox is once broken down, there is no hope of saving him. It requires immense hardship, however, to bring him to that point. He not only gathers his food more rapidly than the horse or mule, but he will climb rocky hills, cross muddy streams, and plunge into swamps and thickets for pasture. He will seek his food in places where other animals will not go. On such a trip as ours one becomes greatly attached to his oxen, for upon them his safety depends.

Our emigrants were placed in a new and trying position, and it was interesting to see the influence of pride and old habits over men. They were often racing with their teams in the early portion of the journey, though they had before them some seventeen hundred miles of travel. No act could have been more inconsiderate than for men, under such circumstances, to injure their teams simply to gratify their ambition. Yet the proper rule in such a case was to allow any and every one to pass you who desired to do so. Our emigrants, on the first portion of the trip, were about as wasteful of their provisions as if they had been at home. When portions of bread were left over, they were thrown away; and, when any one came to their tents, he was invited to eat. I remember well that, for a long time, the five young men I had with me refused to eat any part of the bacon rind, which accordingly fell to my share, in addition to an equal division of the bacon. Finally they asked for and obtained their portion of the bacon rind, their delicate appetites having become ravenous on the trip. Those who were in the habit of inviting every one to eat who stood around at meal-times, ultimately found out that they were feeding a set of loafers, and gave up the practice.

START FROM THE RENDEZVOUS — KILL OUR FIRST BUFFALO — KILL OUR FIRST ANTELOPE — DESCRIPTION OF THE ANTELOPE.

I kept a concise journal of the trip as far as Walla Walla, and have it now before me. On the 18th of May the emigrants at the rendezvous held a meeting, and appointed a committee of seven to inspect wagons, and one of five to draw up rules and regulations for the journey. At this meeting I made the emigrants a speech, an exaggerated report of which was made in 1875, by ex-Senator J. W. Nesmith of Oregon, in his address to the Pioneers of that State. The meeting adjourned to meet at the Big Springs on Saturday, the 20th of May.

On the 20th I attended the meeting at the Big Springs, where I met Colonel John Thornton, Colonel Bartleson, Mr. Rickman, and Dr. Whitman. At this meeting rules and regulations were adopted. Mr. — , who was from high up on Big Pigeon, near Kit Bullard's mill, Tennessee, proposed that we should adopt either the criminal laws of Tennessee or those of Missouri for our government on the route. William Martin and Daniel Matheny were appointed a committee to engage Captain John Gant as our pilot as far as Fort Hall. He was accordingly employed; and it was agreed in camp that we all should start on Monday morning, May 22. We had delayed our departure, because we thought the grass too short to support our stock. The spring of 1843 was very late, and the ice in the Missouri River at Weston only broke up on the 11th of April.

On the 22^{d} of May, 1843, a general start was made from the rendezvous, and we reached Elm Grove, about fifteen miles distant, at about 3 p.m. This grove had but two trees, both elms, and some few dogwood bushes, which we used for fuel. The small elm was most beautiful, in the wild and lonely prairie; and the large one had all its branches trimmed off for firewood. The weather being clear, and the road as good as possible, the day's journey was most delightful. The white-sheeted wagons and the fine teams, moving in the wilderness of green prairie, made the most lovely appearance. The place where we encamped was very beautiful; and no scene appeared to our enthusiastic visions more exquisite than the sight of so many wagons, tents, fires, cattle, and people, as were here collected. At night the sound of joyous music was heard in the tents. Our long journey thus began in sunshine and song, in anecdote and laughter; but these all vanished before we reached its termination.

On the 24th we reached the Walkalusia River, where we let our wagons down the steep bank by ropes. On the 26th we reached the Kansas River, and we finished crossing it on the 31st. At this crossing we met Fathers De Smet and De Vos, missionaries to the Flathead Indians. On the 1st of June we organized our company, by electing Peter H. Burnett as Captain, J. W. Nesmith as Orderly Sergeant, and nine councilmen. On the 6th we met a war party of Kansas and Osage Indians, numbering about ninety warriors. They were all mounted on horses, had their faces painted red, and had with them one Pawnee scalp, with the ears to it, and with the wampum in them. One of them, who spoke English well, said they had fasted three days, and were very hungry. Our guide, Captain Gant, advised us to furnish them with provisions; otherwise, they would steal some of our cattle. We deemed this not only good advice but good humanity, and furnished these starving warriors with enough provisions to satisfy their hunger. They had only killed one Pawnee, but had divided the scalp, making several pieces, some with the ears on, and part with the cheek. Two of this party were wounded, one in the shoulder and the other in some other part of the body.

None of us knew anything about a trip across the Plains, except our pilot Captain Gant, who had made several trips with small parties of hired and therefore disciplined men, who knew how to obey orders. But my company was composed of very different materials; and our pilot had no knowledge that qualified him to give me sound advice. I adopted rules and endeavored to enforce them, but found much practical difficulty and opposition; all of which I at first attributed to the fact that our emigrants were green at the beginning, but comforted myself with the belief that they would improve in due time; but my observation soon satisfied me that matters would grow worse. It became very doubtful whether so large a body of emigrants could be practically kept together on such a journey. These considerations induced me to resign on the 8th of June, and William Martin was elected as my successor.

On the 12th of June we were greatly surprised and delighted to hear that Captain Gant had killed a buffalo. The animal was seen at the distance of a mile from the hunter, who ran upon him with his horse and shot him with a large pistol, several shots being required to kill him. We were all anxious to taste buffalo meat, never having eaten any before; but we found it exceedingly poor and tough. The buffalo was an old bull, left by the herd because he was unable to follow.

On the 15th of June one of our party killed an antelope. This is perhaps the fleetest animal in the world except the gazelle, and possesses the quickest sight excepting the gazelle and the giraffe. The antelope has a large black eye, like those of the gazelle and giraffe, but has no acute sense of smell. For this reason this animal is always found in the prairie, or in very open timber, and will never go into a thicket. He depends upon his superior sight to discern an enemy, and upon his fleetness to escape him. I have heard it said that, when wolves are much pressed with hunger, they hunt the antelope in packs, the wolves placing themselves in different positions. Antelopes, like most wild game, have their limits, within which they range for food and water; and, when chased by the wolves, the antelope will run in something like a circle, confining himself to his accustomed haunts. When the chase commences, the antelope flies off so rapidly that he leaves his pursuers far behind; but the tough and hungry wolf, with his keen scent, follows on his track; and, by the time the antelope has become cool and a little stiff, the wolf is upon him, and he flies from his enemy a second time. This race continues, fresh wolves coming into the chase to relieve those that are tired, until at last the poor antelope, with all his quickness of sight and fleetness of foot, is run down and captured. As soon as he is killed, the wolf that has captured him sets up a loud howl to summon his companions in the chase to the banquet. When all have arrived, they set to eating the carcass, each wolf taking what he can get, there being no fighting, but only some snarling, among the wolves. This statement I do not know to be true of my own knowledge, but think it quite probable. It seems to be characteristic of the dog family, in a wild state, to hunt together and devour the common prey in partnership. Bruce, in his account of his travels in Abyssinia, relates that he saw five or six hyenas all engaged in devouring one carcass; and that he killed four of them at one shot with a blunderbuss, loaded with a large charge of powder and forty bullets.

When an antelope once sees the hunter, it is impossible to stalk the animal. On the trip to Oregon I tried the experiment without success. When I saw the antelope, upon the top of a small hill or mound, looking at me, I would turn and walk away in the opposite direction, until I was out of sight of the animal; then I would make a turn at right angles, until I found some object between me and the antelope, behind which I could approach unseen within rifle-shot; but invariably the wily creature would be found on the top of some higher elevation, looking at me creeping up behind the object that I had supposed concealed me from my coveted prey. The only practical way of deceiving an antelope is to fall flat upon the ground among the grass, and hold up on your ramrod a hat or handkerchief, while you keep yourself concealed from his view. Though exceedingly wary, the curiosity of the animal is so great that he will often slowly and cautiously approach within rifle-shot.

On the 16th of June we saw a splendid race between some of our dogs and an antelope, which ran all the way down the long line of wagons, and about a hundred and fifty yards distant from them. Greyhounds were let loose, but could not catch it. It ran very smoothly, making no long bounds like the deer or horse, but seemed to glide through the air. The gait of the antelope is so peculiar that, if one was running at the top of his speed over a perfectly smooth surface, his body would always be substantially the same distance from the earth.

Lindsey Applegate gave this amusing and somewhat exaggerated account of a race between a very fleet greyhound and an antelope. The antelope was off to the right of the road half a mile distant, and started to cross the road at right angles ahead of the train. The greyhound saw him start in the direction of the road, and ran to meet him, so regulating his pace as to intercept the antelope at the point where he crossed the road. The attention of the antelope being fixed upon the train, he did not see the greyhound until the latter was within twenty feet of him. Then the struggle commenced, each animal running at his utmost speed. The greyhound only ran about a quarter of a mile, when he gave up the race, and looked with seeming astonishment at the animal that beat him, as no other animal had ever done before. Applegate declared, in strong hyperbolical language, that "the antelope ran a mile before you could see the dust rise."

CROSS TO THE GREAT VALLEY OF THE PLATTE — BUFFALO HUNT — DESCRIPTION OF THAT ANIMAL.

Ever since we crossed Kansas River we had been traveling up Blue River, a tributary of the former. On the 17th of June we reached our last encampment on Blue. We here saw a band of Pawnee Indians, returning from a buffalo-hunt. They had quantities of dried buffalo-meat, of which they generously gave us a good supply. They were fine-looking Indians, who did not shave their heads, but cut their hair short like white men.On the 18th of June we crossed from the Blue to the great Platte River, making a journey of from twenty-five to thirty miles, about the greatest distance we ever traveled in a single day. The road was splendid, and we drove some distance into the Platte bottom, and encamped in the open prairie without fuel. Next morning we left very early, without breakfast, having traveled two hundred and seventy-one miles from the rendezvous, according to the estimated distance recorded in my journal.

We traveled up the south bank of the Platte, which, at the point where we struck it, was from a mile to a mile and a half wide. Though not so remarkable as the famed and mysterious Nile (which, from the mouth of the Atbara River to the Mediterranean sea, runs through a desert some twelve hundred miles without receiving a single tributary), the Platte is still a remarkable stream. Like the Nile, it runs hundreds of miles through a desert without receiving any tributaries. Its general course is almost as straight as a direct line. It runs through a formation of sand of equal consistence; and this is the reason its course is so direct.

The valley of the Platte is about twenty miles wide, through the middle of which this wide, shallow, and muddy stream makes its rapid course. Its banks are low, not exceeding five or six feet in height; and the river bottoms on each side seem to the eye a dead level, covered with luxuriant grass. Ten miles from the river you come to the foot of the table-lands, which are also apparently a level sandy plain, elevated some hundred and fifty feet above the river bottoms. On these plains grows the short buffalo-grass, upon which the animal feeds during a portion of the year. As the dry season approaches, the water, which stands in pools on these tablelands, dries up, and the buffaloes are compelled to go to the Platte for water to drink. They start for water about 10 a.m., and always travel in single file, one after the other, and in parallel lines about twenty yards apart, and go in a direct line to the river. They invariably travel the same routes over and over again, until they make a path some ten inches deep and twelve inches wide. These buffalo-paths constituted quite an obstruction to our wagons, which were heavily laden at this point in our journey. Several axles were broken. We had been apprised of the danger in advance, and each wagon was supplied with an extra axle.

In making our monotonous journey up the smooth valley of the Platte, through the warm genial sunshine of summer, the feeling of drowsiness was so great that it was extremely difficult to keep awake during the day. Instances occurred where the drivers went to sleep on the road, sitting in the front of their wagons; and the oxen, being about as sleepy, would stop until the drivers were aroused from their slumber. My small wagon was only used for the family to ride in; and Mrs. Burnett and myself drove and slept alternately during the day.

One great difficulty on this part of the trip was the scarcity of fuel. Sometimes we found dry willows, sometimes we picked up pieces of drift-wood along the way, which we put into our wagons, and hauled them along until we needed them. At many points of the route up the Platte we had to use buffalo-chips. By cutting a trench some ten inches deep, six inches wide, and two feet long, we were enabled to get along with very little fuel. At one or two places the wind was so severe that we were forced to use the trenches in order to make a fire at all.

On the 20th of June we sent out a party of hunters, who returned on the 24th with plenty of fresh buffalo-meat. We thought the flesh of the buffalo the most excellent of all flesh eaten by man. Its flavor is decidedly different from that of beef, and far superior, and the meat more digestible. On a trip like that, in that dry climate, our appetites were excellent; but, even making every reasonable allowance, I still think buffalo the sweetest meat in the world.

The American buffalo is a peculiar animal, remarkably hardy, and much fleeter of foot than any one would suppose from his round short figure. It requires a fleet horse to overtake him. His sense of smell is remarkably acute, while those of sight and hearing are very dull. If the wind blows from the hunter to the buffalo, it is impossible to approach him. I remember that, on one occasion, while we were traveling up the Platte, I saw a band of some forty buffaloes running obliquely toward the river on the other side from us, and some three miles off; and, the moment that their leader struck the stream of tainted atmosphere passing from us to them, he and the rest of the herd turned at right angles from their former course, and fled in the direction of the wind.

On one occasion five of us went out on fleet horses to hunt buffaloes. We soon found nine full-grown animals, feeding near the head of a ravine. The wind blew from them to us, and their keen scent was thus worthless to them, as the smell will only travel with the wind. We rode quietly up the ravine, until we arrived at a point only about one hundred yards distant, when we formed in line, side by side, and the order was given to charge. We put our horses at once to their utmost speed; and the loud clattering of their hoofs over the dry hard ground at once attracted the attention of the buffaloes, which raised their heads and gazed at us for an instant, and then turned and fled. By the time they started we were within fifty yards of them. The race was over a level plain, and we gradually gained upon the fleeing game; but, when we approached within twenty yards of them, we could plainly see that they let out a few more links, and ran much faster. I was riding a fleet Indian pony, and was ahead of all my comrades except Mr. Garrison, who rode a blooded American mare. He dashed in ahead of me, and fired with a large horse-pistol at the largest buffalo, giving the animal a slight wound. The moment the buffalo felt himself wounded, that moment he bore off from the others, they continuing close together, and he running by himself.

I followed the wounded buffalo, and my comrades followed the others. The moment I began to press closely upon the wounded animal, he turned suddenly around, and faced me with his shaggy head, black horns, and gleaming eyes. My pony stopped instantly, and I rode around the old bull to get a shot at his side, knowing that it would be idle to shoot him in the head, as no rifle-ball will penetrate to the brain of a buffalo-bull. But the animal would keep his head toward me. I knew my pony had been trained to stand wherever he was left, and I saw that the wounded bull never charged at the horse. So I determined to dismount, and try to get a shot on foot. I would go a few yards from my horse, and occasionally the buffalo would bound toward me, and then I would dodge behind my pony, which stood like a statue, not exhibiting the slightest fear. For some reason the wounded animal would not attack the pony. Perhaps the buffalo had been before chased by Indians on horseback, and for that reason was afraid of the pony. At last I got a fair opportunity, and shot the buffalo through the lungs. The moment he felt the shot, he turned and fled, and after running a quarter of a mile fell dead. The shot through the lungs is the most fatal to the buffalo, as he soon smothers from the effects of internal hæmorrhage. It is a singular fact that, before a buffalo is wounded, he will never turn and face his pursuer, but will run at his best speed, even until the hunter is by his side; but the moment a buffalo-bull is wounded, even slightly, he will quit the band, and when pressed by the hunter will turn and face him. The animal seems to think that, when wounded, his escape by flight is impossible, and his only chance is in combat.

On the 27th of June our people had halted for lunch at noon, and to rest the teams and allow the oxen to graze. Our wagons were about three hundred yards from the river, and were strung out in line to the distance of one mile. While taking our lunch we saw seven buffalo-bulls on the opposite side of the river, coming toward us, as if they intended to cross the river in the face of our whole caravan. When they arrived on the opposite bank they had a full view of us; and yet they deliberately entered the river, wading a part of the distance, and swimming the remainder. When we saw that they were determined to cross at all hazards, our men took their rifles, formed in line between the wagons and the river, and awaited the approach of the animals. So soon as they rose the bank, they came on in a run, broke boldly through the line of men, and bore to the left of the wagons. Three of them were killed, and most of the others wounded.

CROSS THE SOUTH FORK — ARRIVE AT FORT LARAMIE — CHEYENNE CHIEF — CROSS THE NORTH FORK — DEATHS OF PAINE AND STEVENSON — CROSS GREEN RIVER — ARRIVE AT FORT HALL.

On the 29th of June we arrived at a grove of timber, on the south bank of the South Fork of the Platte. This was the only timber we had seen since we struck the river, except on the islands, which were covered with cottonwoods and willows. From our first camp upon the Platte to this point, we had traveled, according to my estimates recorded in my journal, one hundred and seventy-three miles, in eleven days.

On July 1st we made three boats by covering our wagon-boxes or beds with green buffalo-hides sewed together, stretched tightly over the boxes, flesh side out, and tacked on with large tacks; and the boxes, thus covered, were then turned up to the sun until the hides were thoroughly dry. This process of drying the green hides had to be repeated several times. From July 1st to the 5th, inclusive, we were engaged in crossing the river. On the 7th we arrived at the south bank of the North Fork of the Platte, having traveled a distance of twenty-nine miles from the South Fork. We had not seen any prairie-chickens since we left the Blue. On the 9th we saw three beautiful wild horses. On the 14th we arrived at Fort Laramie, where we remained two days, repairing our wagons. We had traveled from the crossing of South Fork one hundred and forty-one miles in nine days. Prices of articles at this trading post: Coffee, $1.50 a pint; brown sugar, the same; flour, unbolted, 25 cents a pound; powder, $1.50 a pound; lead, 75 cents a pound; percussion-caps, $1.50 a box; calico, very inferior, $1 a yard.

At the Fort we found the Cheyenne chief and some of his people. He was a tall, trim, noble-looking Indian, aged about thirty. The Cheyennes at that time boasted that they had never shed the blood of the white man. He went alone very freely among our people, and I happened to meet him at one of our camps, where there was a foolish, rash young man, who wantonly insulted the chief. Though the chief did not understand the insulting words, he clearly comprehended the insulting tone and gestures. I saw from the expression of his countenance that the chief was most indignant, though perfectly cool and brave. He made no reply in words, but walked away slowly; and, when some twenty feet from the man who had insulted him, he turned around, and solemnly and slowly shook the forefinger of his right hand at the young man several times, as much as to say, "I will attend to your case."

I saw there was trouble coming, and I followed the chief, and by kind earnest gestures made him understand at last that this young man was considered by us all as a half-witted fool, unworthy of the notice of any sensible man; and that we never paid attention to what he said, as we hardly considered him responsible for his language. The moment the chief comprehended my meaning I saw a change come over his countenance, and he went away perfectly satisfied. He was a clear-headed man; and, though unlettered, he understood human nature.

In traveling up the South Fork we saw several Indians, who kept at a distance, and never manifested any disposition to molest us in any way. They saw we were mere travelers through their country, and would only destroy a small amount of their game. Besides, they must have been impressed with a due sense of our power. Our long line of wagons, teams, cattle, and men, on the smooth plains, and under the clear skies of Platte, made a most grand appearance. They had never before seen any spectacle like it. They, no doubt, supposed we had cannon concealed in our wagons. A few years before a military expedition had been sent out from Fort Leavenworth to chastise some of the wild prairie tribes for depredations committed against the whites. General Bennet Riley, then Captain Riley, had command, and had with him some cannon. In a skirmish with the Indians, in the open prairie, he had used his cannon, killing some of the Indians at a distance beyond rifle-shot. This new experience had taught them a genuine dread of big guns.

The Indians always considered the wild game as much their property as they did the country in which it was found. Though breeding and maintaining the game cost them no labor, yet it lived and fattened on their grass and herbage, and was as substantially within the power of these roving people and skillful hunters as the domestic animals of the white man.

On the 24th of July we crossed the North Fork of Platte by ford-ing, without difficulty, having traveled the distance of one hundred and twenty-two miles from Fort Laramie in nine days. On the 27th, we arrived at the Sweetwater, having traveled from the North Fork fifty-five miles in three days. On the 3d of August, while traveling up the Sweetwater, we first came in sight of the eternal snows of the Rocky Mountains. This to us was a grand and magnificent sight. We had never before seen the perpetually snow-clad summit of a mountain. This day William Martin brought into camp the foot of a very rare carnivorous animal, much like the hyena, and with no known name. It was of a dark color, had very large teeth, and was thought to be strong enough to kill a half-grown buffalo.

On the 4th of August Mr. Paine died of fever, and we remained in camp to bury him. We buried him in the wild, shelterless plains, close to the new road we had made, and the funeral scene was most sorrowful and impressive. Mr. Garrison, a Methodist preacher, a plain, humble man, delivered a most touching and beautiful prayer at the lonely grave.

On the 5th, 6th, and 7th we crossed the summit of the Rocky Mountains, and on the evening of the 7th we first drank of the waters that flow into the great Pacific. The first Pacific water we saw was that of a large, pure spring. On the 9th we came to the Big Sandy at noon. This day Stevenson died of fever, and we buried him on the sterile banks of that stream. On the 11th we crossed Green River, so called from its green color. It is a beautiful stream, containing fine fish. On the margins of this stream there are extensive groves of small cottonwood-trees, about nine inches in diameter, with low and brushy tops. These trees are cut down by the hunters and trappers in winter, for the support of their mules and hardy Indian ponies. The animals feed on the tender twigs, and on the bark of the smaller limbs, and in this way manage to live. Large quantities of this timber are thus destroyed annually.

On the 12th of August we were informed that Dr. Whitman had written a letter, stating that the Catholic missionaries had discovered, by the aid of their Flathead Indian pilot, a pass through the mountains by way of Fort Bridger, which was shorter than the old route. We therefore determined to go by the fort. There was a heavy frost with thin ice this morning. On the 14th we arrived at Fort Bridger, situated on Black's Fork of Green River, having traveled from our first camp on the Sweetwater two hundred and nineteen miles in eighteen days. Here we overtook the missionaries. On the 17th we arrived on the banks of Bear River, a clear, beautiful stream, with abundance of good fish and plenty of wild ducks and geese. On the 22[d] we arrived at the great Soda Springs, when we left Bear River for Fort Hall, at which place we arrived on the 27th, having traveled two hundred and thirty-five miles from Fort Bridger in thirteen days.

Fort Hall was then a trading post, belonging to the Hudson's Bay Company, and was under the charge of Mr. Grant, who was exceedingly kind and hospitable. The fort was situated on the south bank of Snake River, in a wide, fertile valley, covered with luxuriant grass, and watered by numerous springs and small streams. This valley had once been a great resort for buffaloes, and their skulls were scattered around in every direction. We saw the skulls of these animals for the last time at Fort Boise, beyond which point they were never seen. The Company had bands of horses and herds of cattle grazing on these rich bottom-lands.

Up to this point the route over which we had passed was perhaps the finest natural road, of the same length, to be found in the world. Only a few loaded wagons had ever made their way to Fort Hall, and were there abandoned. Dr. Whitman in 1836 had taken a wagon as far as Fort Boise, by making a cart on two of the wheels, and placing the axletree and the other two wheels in his cart. (Gray's "Oregon," page 133.)

We here parted with our respected pilot, Captain John Gant. Dr. Marcus Whitman was with us at the fort, and was our pilot from there to the Grande Ronde, where he left us in charge of an Indian pilot, whose name was Stikas, and who proved to be both faithful and competent. The doctor left us to have his gristmill put in order by the time we should reach his mission.

We had now arrived at a most critical period in our most adventurous journey; and we had many misgivings as to our ultimate success in making our way with our wagons, teams, and families. We had yet to accomplish the untried and most difficult portion of our long and exhaustive journey. We could not anticipate at what moment we might be compelled to abandon our wagons in the mountains, pack our scant supplies upon our poor oxen, and make our way on foot through this terribly rough country, as best we could. We fully comprehended the situation; but we never faltered in our inflexible determination to accomplish the trip, if within the limits of possibility, with the resources at our command. Dr. Whitman assured us that we could succeed, and encouraged and aided us with every means in his power. I consulted Mr. Grant as to his opinion of the practicability of taking our wagons through. He replied that, while he would not say it was impossible for us Americans to make the trip with our wagons, he could not himself see how it could be done. He had only traveled the pack-trail, and certainly no wagons could follow that route; but there might be a practical road found by leaving the trail at certain points.

LEAVE FORT HALL — SAGE-BRUSH LANDS — SALMON FALLS — THE SPEAR OF THE INDIAN FISHERMAN — CROSS SNAKE RIVER — KILL A LARGE SALMON.

On the 30th of August we quitted Fort Hall, many of our young men having left us with pack-trains. Our route lay down Snake River for some distance. The road was rocky and rough, except in the dry valleys; and these were covered with a thick growth of sage or wormwood, which was from two to three feet high, and offered a great obstruction to the first five or six wagons passing through it. The soil where this melancholy shrub was found appeared to be too dry and sterile to produce anything else. It was very soft on the surface, and easily worked up into a most disagreeable dust, as fine as ashes or flour.

The taste of the sage is exceedingly bitter; the shrub has a brown somber appearance, and a most disagreeable smell. The stem at the surface of the ground is from one to two inches in diameter, and soon branches, so as to form a thick brushy top. The texture of the stem is peculiar, and unlike that of any other shrub, being all bark and no sap or heart, and appears like the outside bark of the grape-vine. How the sap ascends from the roots to the branches, or whether the shrub draws its nutriment from the air, I am not able to decide. One thing I remember well, that the stems of the green growing sage were good for fuel and burned most readily, and so rapidly that the supply had to be continually renewed; showing that they were not only dry, but of very slight, porous texture. Had the sage been as stout and hard as other shrubbery of the same size, we should have been compelled to cut our wagonway through it, and could never have passed over it as we did, crushing it beneath the feet of our oxen and the wheels of our wagons.

The geographical features of the Pacific coast are Asiatic in their appearance, being composed of mountains and valleys. Our hills swell to mountains, and our valleys are to the eye a dead level, yet they generally descend about nine or ten feet to the mile. We have consequently very little gently undulating land, such as is generally found in the great Mississippi valley. Gibbon, speaking of the route of the army of the Emperor Julian, well but concisely describes the sageplains of this coast: "The country was a plain throughout, as even as the sea, and full of wormwood; and, if any other kind of shrubs or reeds grew there, they had all an aromatic smell, but no trees could be seen." ("Decline and Fall," chapter xxiv., pp. 477-'78.)

Colonel Mercer of Oregon delivered a lecture in the City of New York on April 6, 1878, as appears from the telegram to the "Daily Alta" of the 7th, in which he set forth the wonderful fertility of the sage-brush lands, which until recently had been supposed to be valueless. The sage-brush lands through which we passed in 1843 appeared to be worthless, not only because of the apparent sterility of the soil, but for the want of water. With plentiful irrigation, I think it quite probable that these lands, in most places, might be rendered fruitful. Water is a great fertilizer, and nothing but experiment can actually demonstrate how far these wilderness plains can be redeemed.

On the 7th of September, 1843, we arrived at the Salmon Falls on Snake River, where we purchased from the Snake Indians dried and fresh salmon, giving one ball and one charge of powder for each dried fish. We found several lodges of Indians here, who were very poorly clad, and who made a business of fishing at the falls. The falls were about eight feet perpendicular at that stage of water, with rapids below for some distance. The stream is divided upon the rapids into various narrow channels, through which the waters pass with a very shallow and rapid current, so that the fisherman can wade across them. The salmon are compelled to pass up these channels, and readily fall a prey to the quick, sharp spear of the Indian fisherman. This spear consists of a strong, smooth pole, ten or twelve feet long and an inch and a half in diameter, made of hard, tough wood, upon one end of which there is fastened a piece of sharp-pointed buck-horn, about four inches long. The larger end of this piece of buck-horn is hollowed out to the depth of about three inches, and fastened on the end of the pole, which is tapered to fit into it. To the middle of this buck-horn there is securely fastened a thong or string of sinew, the other end of which is firmly attached to the pole about one foot above the buck-horn, leaving a considerable slack in the string. With this spear the Indian fisherman lies down or sits close to one of these narrow channels, with the point of his spear resting near where the fish must pass. In this position he remains motionless until he sees a fish immediately opposite the point of the spear, as the fish slowly ascends the rapid current; when, with the quick motion of a juggler, he pushes his spear clear through the salmon before this powerful fish can dodge it. The buck-horn at once slips off the end of the pole, on the other side the fish, the first flounce he makes; but he is securely held by the thong attached to the pole. No spear could be more skillfully designed or more effectually used than this.

One of our emigrants, having been informed before he started on the trip that the clear, living waters of the Columbia and its tributaries were full of salmon, had brought all the way from Missouri a three-pronged harpoon, called a gig. The metallic portion of this fishing instrument was securely riveted on the end of a smooth, strong pole, about ten feet long and two inches by a wonderful instinct, ascend to the upper branches, where they can deposit their numerous spawn in a place secure from enemies. The waters of these mountain-streams are so clear as to remind one of Dryden's ·description

"Of shallow brooks, that flowed so clear,
The bottom did the top appear."

In the pebbly bottoms of these tributary streams the female salmon hollows out a cavity of sufficient depth to form an eddy, in which she can deposit her spawn without the danger of their being swept away by the current. The one we killed was doubtless in her nest, which she refused to quit.

From all the information I was able to obtain while residing in Oregon, grown salmon which once leave the ocean never return. This was the opinion of Sir James Douglas, which was confirmed by my own observation. But there seems to be a difference of opinion on the question. I have lately conversed with B. B. Redding upon this subject, and it is his opinion that about ten per cent. return alive to the ocean, as about that proportion are caught in the Sacramento River on the upper side of the gill-nets used by the fishermen. This may be the more correct opinion.

The male salmon is armed with strong, sharp teeth, and they fight and wound each other severely. While the female is making and guarding her nest, her mate remains close by, watching and waiting with the greatest fidelity and patience; and, when any other fish approaches too near, he darts at him with the utmost swiftness and ferocity. The spawn is always deposited in the pebbly bed of the stream, where the water is swift and comparatively shallow, and where other fish are less likely to molest them. The eggs hatch in from forty to forty-five days.

For hours I have watched the efforts of salmon to pass over the Willamette Falls, at Oregon City. For the space of one or two minutes I would not see a fish in the air. Then, all at once, I would see one leap out of the water, followed immediately by great numbers. Some would rise from ten to fifteen feet, while many would not ascend more than four or five; but all seemed equally determined to succeed. They had selected the most practicable point, and approached very near the column of descending water, and rose from the eddy caused by the reflow. Occasionally one would go over; but the great majority pitched with their heads plump against the wall of rock behind the torrent, and fell back, more or less wounded, to try again. There was a shelf in the rock three or four feet below the top, and I have seen salmon catch on this shelf, rest for an instant, then flounce off and fall into the water below. So long as a salmon is alive, its head will be found up stream, and every effort made, though feeble, will be to ascend. Sometimes, when in very shallow water, the fish may descend to a short distance to escape an enemy for the time; but its constant instinct is to go up higher, until it reaches the place to deposit its eggs.

BOILING SPRING — FORT BOISE — BURNT RIVER — THE LONE PINE — THE GRANDE RONDE — THE BLUE MOUNTAINS — ARRIVE AT DR. WHITMAN'S MISSION — ARRIVE AT WALLA WALLA.

On the 14th of September we passed the Boiling Spring. Its water is hot enough to cook an egg. It runs out at three different places, forming a large branch, which runs off smoking and foaming. It rises half a mile from a tall range of hills, covered with basaltic rock; and the plains around are covered with round rocks of the same kind. The water is clear, and rises at the head of a small ravine.

On the 20th of September we arrived at Fort Boise, then in charge of Mr. Payette, having traveled from Fort Hall, two hundred and seventy-three miles, in twenty-one days. Mr. Payette, the manager, was kind and very polite. On the 21st we recrossed the Snake River by fording, which was deep but safe. On the 24th we reached Burnt River, so named from the many fires that have occurred there, destroying considerable portions of timber. It hardly deserves to be called a river, being only a creek of fair size. The road up this stream was then a terrible one, as the latter runs between two ranges of tall mountains, through a narrow valley full of timber, which we had not the force or time to remove.

On the 27th of September we had some rain during the night, and next morning left Burnt River. To-day we saw many of the most beautiful objects in nature. In our rear, on our right and left, were ranges of tall mountains, covered on the sides with magnificent forests of pine, the mountain-tops being dressed in a robe of pure snow; and around their summits the dense masses of black clouds wreathed themselves in fanciful shapes, the sun glancing through the open spaces upon the gleaming mountains. We passed through some most beautiful valleys, and encamped on a branch of the Powder River, at the Lone Pine.

This noble tree stood in the center of a most lovely valley, about ten miles from any other timber. It could be seen, at the distance of many miles, rearing its majestic form above the surrounding plain, and constituted a beautiful landmark for the guidance of the traveler. Many teams had passed on before me; and at intervals, as I drove along, I would raise my head and look at that beautiful green pine. At last, on looking up as usual, the tree was gone. I was perplexed for the moment to know whether I was going in the right direction. There was the plain beaten wagon-road before me, and I drove on until I reached the camp just at dark. That brave old pine, which had withstood the storms and snows of centuries, had fallen at last by the vandal hands of men. Some of our inconsiderate people had cut it down for fuel, but it was too green to burn. It was a useless and most unfortunate act. Had I been there in time, I should have begged those woodmen to "spare that tree."

On the 29th and 30th of September we passed through rich, beautiful valleys, between ranges of snowclad mountains, whose sides were covered with noble pine forests. On October 1st we came into and through Grande Ronde, one of the most beautiful valleys in the world, embosomed among the Blue Mountains, which are covered with magnificent pines. It was estimated to be about a hundred miles in circumference. It was generally rich prairie, covered with luxuriant grass, and having numerous beautiful streams passing through it, most of which rise from springs at the foot of the mountains bordering the valley. In this valley the camasroot abounds, which the Indians dried upon hot rocks. We purchased some from them, and found it quite palatable to our keen appetites.

On the 2^{d} of October we ascended the mountain-ridge at the Grande Ronde, and descended on the other side of the ridge to a creek, where we camped. These hills were terrible. On the 3^{d}, 4th, 5th, and 6th we passed through the Blue Mountains, arriving at their foot on the 6th, and encamping upon a beautiful stream of water. On the morning of the 5th there was a snowstorm on the mountain. During our passage through the Blue Mountains we had great difficulty in finding our cattle, and the road was very rough in many places. Our camp was about three miles from the Indian village, and from the Indians we purchased Indian corn, peas, and Irish potatoes, in any desired quantity. I have never tasted a greater luxury than the potatoes we ate on this occasion. We had been so long without fresh vegetables, that we were almost famished; and consequently we feasted this day excessively. We gave the Indians, in exchange, some articles of clothing, which they were most anxious to purchase. When two parties are both as anxious to barter as were the Indians and ourselves, it is very easy to strike a bargain.

On the 10th of October we arrived within three miles of Dr. Whitman's mission, and remained in camp until the 14th.

The exhausting tedium of such a trip and the attendant vexations have a great effect upon the majority of men, especially upon those of weak minds. Men, under such circumstances, become childish, petulant, and obstinate. I remember that while we were at the mission of Dr. Whitman, who had performed much hard labor for us, and was deserving of our warmest gratitude, he was most ungenerously accused by some of our people of selfish motives in conducting us past his establishment, where we could procure fresh supplies of flour and potatoes. This foolish, false, and ungrateful charge was based upon the fact that he asked us a dollar a bushel for wheat, and forty cents for potatoes. As our people had been accustomed to sell their wheat at from fifty to sixty cents a bushel, and their potatoes at from twenty to twenty-five cents, in the Western States, they thought the prices demanded by the Doctor amounted to something like extortion; not reflecting that he had to pay at least twice as much for his own supplies of merchandise, and could not afford to sell his produce as low as they did theirs at home. They were somewhat like a certain farmer in Missouri, at an early day, who concluded that twenty cents a bushel was a fair price for corn, and that he would not sell for more nor less. But experience soon taught him that when the article was higher than his price he could readily sell, but when it was lower he could not sell at all; and he came to the sensible conclusion that he must avail himself of the rise, in order to compensate him for the fall in prices. So obstinate were some of our people, that they would not purchase of the Doctor. I remember one case particularly, where an intimate friend of mine, whose supplies of food were nearly exhausted, refused to purchase, though urged to do so by me, until the wheat was all sold. The consequence was, that I had to divide provisions with him before we reached the end of our journey.

On the 16th of October we arrived at Fort Walla Walla, then under the charge of Mr. McKinley; having traveled from Fort Boise, two hundred and two miles, in twenty-four days, and from the rendezvous, sixteen hundred and ninety-one miles, between the 22^d of May and the 16th of October, being one hundred and forty-seven days. Average distance per day, eleven and a half miles.

DESCEND THE RIVER TO THE DALLES — LEAVE MY FAMILY THERE — GO TO VANCOUVER AND RETURN — GOVERNOR FREMONT.

A portion of our emigrants left their wagons and cattle at Walla Walla, and descended the Columbia in boats; while another, and the larger portion, made their way with their wagons and teams to the Dalles, whence they descended to the Cascades on rafts, and thence to Fort Vancouver in boats and canoes. William Beagle and I had agreed at the rendezvous not to separate until we reached the end of our journey. We procured from Mr. McKinley, at Walla Walla, an old Hudson's Bay Company's boat, constructed expressly for the navigation of the Columbia and its tributaries. These boats are very light, yet strong. They are open, about forty feet long, five feet wide, and three feet deep, made of light, tough materials, and clinker-built. They are made in this manner so that they may be carried around the falls of the Columbia, and let down over the Cascades. When taken out of the water and carried over the portage, it requires the united exertions of forty or fifty Indians, who take the vessel on their shoulders, amid shouts and hurras, and thus carry it sometimes three fourths of a mile, without once letting it down. At the Cascades it is let down by means of ropes in the hands of the Canadian boatmen.

We employed an Indian pilot, who stood with a stout, long, broad paddle in the bow of the boat, while Beagle stood at the stern, holding a long steering-oar, such as were used upon flat-bottoms and keel-boats in the Western States. I remember that my friend Beagle, before we left Walla Walla, expressed great confidence in his skill in steering, as he had often passed the Ohio rapids at Louisville. But these rapids were nothing to those on the Columbia. I have seen Beagle turn as pale as a corpse when passing through the terrible rapids on this river.

Our Indian pilot was very cool, determined, and intrepid; and Beagle always obeyed him, right or wrong. On one occasion, I remember, we were passing down a terrible rapid, with almost the speed of a race-horse, when a huge rock rose above the water before us, against which the swift and mighty volume of the river furiously dashed in vain, and then suddenly turned to the right, almost at right angles. The Indian told Beagle to hold the bow of the boat directly toward that rock, as if intending to run plump upon it, while the rest of us pulled upon our oars with all our might, so as to give her such a velocity as not to be much affected by the surging waves. The Indian stood calm and motionless in the bow, paddle in hand, with his features set as if prepared to meet immediate death; and, when we were within from twenty to thirty feet of that terrible rock, as quick almost as thought he plunged his long, broad paddle perpendicularly into the water on the left side of the bow, and with it gave a sudden wrench, and the boat instantly turned upon its center to the right, and we passed the rock in safety.

While passing through these dangers I was not much alarmed, but after they were passed I could never think of them without a sense of fear. Three of our emigrants were drowned just above the Dalles, but we reached them in safety, sending our boat through them, while the families walked around them on dry land. These Dalles are a great natural curiosity; but they have been so often described that I deem it unnecessary to attempt any description myself.

When we arrived at the Methodist mission, located at the foot of the Dalles, I saw at once that there must some day grow up a town there, as that was the head of safe steam navigation. From there to the Cascades, a distance of about fifty miles, the river is entirely smooth and without a rapid. At the Cascades there is a portage to be made, but, once below them, and there is nothing but smooth water to the ocean. I determined at once to settle at the Dalles; and, after consultation with Mr. Perkins, the minister in charge, I left my family there and proceeded to Vancouver, where I arrived about the 7th of November, 1843.

At Fort Vancouver I found Governor Fremont, then Lieutenant Fremont, who had been there a few days. He had left his men and animals at the Dalles, and had descended the river to the fort for the purpose of purchasing supplies, to enable him to make the trip overland to California during that winter. The preceding year he had made an exploring trip to the South Pass of the Rocky Mountains; but this was his first journey to Oregon and California.

The Hudson's Bay Company furnished him, on the credit of the United States, all the supplies he required, and sent them up the river in one of their boats, such as I have already described, and three Chinook canoes. These canoes are substantially of the same model as the clipper-ship, and most probably suggested the idea of such a form of marine architecture. They are made out of a solid piece of white-cedar timber, which is usually one quarter of the first cut of a large tree. It is a soft wood, but very tough. This timber grows upon the banks of the Columbia, below Vancouver, to a very large size. It is easily split with wedges. The Indians manage to cut and burn down the tree, and then cut and burn off a part of the trunk, and split it into quarters. Then they hollow out the inside of the canoe, mostly by burning. For this purpose they kindle small fires along the whole length of the canoe, which they keep steadily burning; and, by careful and constant watching, they cause the fires to burn when and how they please. The outside they shape with their tomahawks; and, before these were introduced, they used sharp flint-stones for axes. These canoes are usually about thirty feet long, three feet wide, and two feet deep, and are sharp at both ends, with a gradual taper from near the center. No craft could have a more handsome model, or run more swiftly. They are light, strong, elastic, and durable, and are propelled by paddles. The boat was navigated by Canadian French, and the canoes by Indians.

Dr. McLoughlin and Mr. Douglas, then chief factors at the fort, advised me to go for my family, and settle in the lower portion of Oregon, and kindly offered me a passage up and down on their boat. We left the fort about the 11th of November in the evening, while it was raining. It came down gently but steadily. We reached the foot of the rapids, three miles below the Cascades, before sundown on the third day. We found that the Indians could propel their canoes with paddles much faster than we could our boat with oars. We ascended the river to the distance of about one mile above the foot of the rapids; and just before dark we encamped upon a sand-beach, the only spot where we could do so without ascending higher up the rapids.

The Indians, with the three canoes, had passed on farther up the river; and, although we fired signal shots, they could not be induced to return. They had with them the sugar and tea, and the Indian lodge, composed of buffalo-skins, neatly dressed and sewed together. This lodge was in a conical form, about fourteen feet in diameter at the base and eighteen feet high, with a hole at the base of about two by three feet for a door, and one in the top for the escape of the smoke. A deer-skin formed the door-shutter, and the fire was built in the center, around which we sat with our backs to the lodge; and when we lay down we put our feet to the fire and our heads from it. In this way we could be warm and comfortable, and free from the effects of the wind and rain, without being at all incommoded by the smoke from our small fire, as it rose straight up and passed out through the hole in the top of the lodge. The lodge was supported by long, strong, smooth poles, over which it was tightly stretched. It was far superior to any cloth tent I ever saw.

When we encamped, it was cloudy but not raining, and we were very hungry after our day's hard work; but our bill of fare consisted of salt salmon and cold bread. We knew, from the appearance of the thickening but smooth clouds, that we should most likely have a rainy night. The lower portion of Oregon lies between the tall Cascade range of mountains and the ocean. This range runs almost parallel with the Pacific Ocean, and about a hundred and twenty-five miles from it. The clouds in the rainy season break upon this range; and the Cascades are at the point where the mighty Columbia cuts at right angles through it. We had been told that it rained oftener and harder at the Cascades than at almost any other point in Oregon; and, to our injury, we found it true.

Supper being ended, we laid ourselves down before a large fire. Governor Fremont wrapped himself in his cloak, keeping on all his clothes, and lay down upon a blanket. For myself, I had with me two pairs of large, heavy blankets, one pair of which I put folded under me, and covered myself with the other pair. Soon after we had lain down the rain began to fall gently, but continued steadily to increase. At first, I thought it might rain as much as it pleased, without wetting through my blankets; but before day it came down in torrents, and I found the water running under me, and into the pockets of my pantaloons and the tops of my boots. It was a cold rain, and the fire was extinguished. I could not endure all this, and I sat up during most of the remaining portion of the night upon a log of wood, with one pair of blankets thrown over my head, so as to fall all around me. In this way I managed to keep warm; but the weight of the wet blankets was great, and my neck at last rebelled against the oppression. I finally became so fatigued and sleepy that just before day, when the rain had ceased, I threw myself down across some logs of wood, and in that condition slept until daylight. As for Governor Fremont, he never moved, but lay and slept as well as if in comfortable quarters. My position was in a lower place on the beach than his, and this was the reason why the water ran under me, and not under him.

Next morning we rose fresh and fasting, and ascended to the Indian encampment, where the Governor found our Indians comfortably housed in the lodge, cooking breakfast. He was somewhat vexed, and made them hustle out in short order.

It took us some days to make the portage, it raining nearly all the while. At the head of the Cascades there were several large, projecting rocks, under one side of which the Indians could lie on the clean dry sand, secure from the rain. They would build a fire in front and sit or lie under the projecting rocks; and, as they were at home with their kindred and families, they were in no hurry to go forward, and were not much disposed to go out in bad weather. At the Cascades there is a celebrated salmon fishery, where the Indians then lived in considerable numbers, supporting themselves in the summer upon fresh, and in the winter upon dried salmon.

We were anxious to proceed, as Governor Fremont had still to make the perilous journey to California; but there were only some five to eight whites to several hundred Indians. But the cool, determined, yet prudent Fremont managed to command our Indians, and induce them to work. When nothing else would avail, he would put out their fires. Finding it necessary to work or shiver, they preferred to work.

When we had reloaded our craft, we set forward for the Dalles; and we had not gone more than ten miles before we could see clear out and beyond the clouds, into the pure blue sky. We were almost vexed to think we had been so near to a sunny region all the time we had been suffering so much from the rain. We soon reached a point on the river above where there had been no rain; and from that point to the Dalles we had cold, clear, frosty nights. We arrived at the Dalles in about ten days after leaving Vancouver. I went with the Governor to his camp of about forty men and one hundred animals.

I was with Governor Fremont about ten days. I had never known him personally before this trip. I knew he was on the way; but he traveled usually with his own company, and did not mingle much with the emigrants, as he could not properly do so, his men being under military discipline, and our emigrants not. He was then about thirty years old, modest in appearance, and calm and gentle in manner. His men all loved him intensely. He gave his orders with great mildness and simplicity, but they had to be obeyed. There was no shrinking from duty. He was like a father to those under his command. At that time I thought I could endure as much hardship as most men, especially a small, slender man like Governor Fremont; but I was wholly mistaken. He had a small foot, and wore a thin calf-skin boot; and yet he could endure more cold than I could with heavy boots on. I never traveled with a more pleasant companion than Governor Fremont. His bearing toward me was as kind as that of a brother.

GO WITH MY FAMILY TO VANCOUVER — INDIAN TRADITION — THE TOWN OF LINNTON.

I returned with my family to Fort Vancouver on the 26th of November, 1843; and, as we passed the place of our encampment on the sand-beach below the Cascades, the Canadian boatmen pointed toward it and laughed.

When we arrived at the Cascades on our return voyage, we carried our baggage upon our shoulders three fourths of a mile, when we reloaded and then "jumped" the rapids below. Until we had passed these rapids on our downward voyage I had no adequate conception of the dangers we had passed through on the voyage from Walla Walla to the Dalles. During that perilous passage I was one of the oarsmen, and sat with my back to the bow of the boat, thus having no fair opportunity to observe well. My attention was mainly confined to my own portion of the work, and I had but little time to look up. But, in running the rapids below the Cascades, I had nothing to do but look on. It was almost literal "jumping."

There was then an Indian tradition that about a hundred years before the Cascades did not exist, but that there was a succession of rapids from the Dalles to where the Cascades are now. The whole volume of the Columbia is now confined to a narrow channel, and falls about thirty feet in the distance of a quarter of a mile. This tradition said that the river gradually cut under the mountain, until the projecting mass of huge stones and tough clay slid into the river and dammed up the stream to the height of some thirty feet, thus producing slack water to the Dalles. And I must say that every appearance, to my mind, sustains this view.

The Columbia, like most rivers, has a strip of bottom-land covered with timber, on one side or the other; but at the Cascades this bottom-land is very narrow, and has a very different appearance from the bottoms at places on the river above and below. The mountain on the south side of the river looks precisely as if a vast land-slide had taken place there; and the huge rocks that lift their gray, conical heads above the water at a low stage go to prove that they could not have withstood that terrible current for many centuries. In the winter, when the water is at its lowest stage, immense masses of thick ice come down over these Cascades, and strike with tremendous force against the rocks; and the consequent wearing away must have been too great for those rocks to have been in that position many centuries.

But there is another fact that seems to me to be almost conclusive. As we passed up the river, the water was at a very low stage; and yet for some twenty miles above we could see stumps of various sizes standing as thick beneath the water as trees in a forest. The water was clear, and we had a perfect view of them. They were entirely sound, and were rather sharp in form toward the top. It was evident that the trees had not grown in the water, but it had been backed up over their roots, and the tops and trunks had died and decayed, while the stumps, being under water, had remained substantially sound; and the reason why they were sharp at the top was, that the heart of the timber was more durable than the sap-wood, which had decayed. Another reason for the sharpness of the stumps at the top is, the abrasion caused by the floating masses of ice.

It was the opinion of Governor Fremont that these stumps had been placed in this position by a slide, which took them from their original site into the river. But I must think that opinion erroneous, because the slide could hardly have been so great in length, and the appearance of the adjacent hills does not indicate an event of that magnitude. It is much more rational, I think, to suppose that the slide took place at the Cascades, and that the Indian tradition is true. Another reason is, that the river at the points where these stumps are found is quite wide, showing an increase of width by the backing up of the water over the bottoms.

I procured a room for my family at Vancouver, until I could build a cabin. General M.M. McCarver and myself had agreed that we would select a town site at the head of ship navigation on the Willamette River. The General, having no family with him, arrived at the fort some time before I did, and selected a spot on the Willamette, about five miles above its mouth, at what we then supposed to be the head of ship navigation. Here we laid out a town, calling it Linnton for Dr. Linn. It was a fair site, except for one small reason: it was not at the head of ship navigation, which subsequent experience proved to be at Portland, some miles above. I had a cabin built at Linnton, and lived there with my family from about the middle of January until the first of May, 1844. We performed a considerable amount of labor there, most of which was expended in opening a wagon-road thence to the Tualatin Plains, over a mountain, and through a dense forest of fir, cedar, maple, and other timber. When finished, the road was barely passable with wagons. Our town speculation was a small loss to us, the receipts from the sale of lots not being equal to the expenses.

I soon found that expenses were certain and income nothing, and determined to select what was then called "a claim," and make me a farm. I knew very little about farming, though raised upon a farm in Missouri, and had not performed any manual labor of consequence (until I began to prepare for this trip) for about seventeen years. I had some recollection of farming; but the theory, as practiced in Missouri, would not fully do for Oregon. Mr. Douglas told me that I could not succeed at farming, as there was a great deal of hard work on a farm. I replied that, in my opinion, a sensible and determined man could succeed at almost anything, and I meant to do it. I did succeed well; but I never had my intellect more severely tasked, with a few exceptions. Those who think good farming not an intellectual business are most grievously mistaken.

PURCHASE A CLAIM — CLIMATE AND SCENERY OF OREGON — NUMBER OF OUR IMMIGRANTS — ASSISTANCE RENDERED OUR IMMIGRATION.

Some time in April, 1844, I went to the Tualatin Plains, and purchased a claim in the middle of a circular plain, about three miles in diameter. The claim was entirely destitute of timber, except a few ash-trees which grew along the margin of the swales. The plain was beautiful, and was divided from the plains adjoining by living streams of water flowing from the mountains, the banks of which streams were skirted with fir and white-cedar timber. The surface of this plain was gently undulating, barely sufficient for drainage. I purchased ten acres of splendid fir timber, distant about a mile and a half, for twenty-five dollars. This supply proved ample for a farm of about two hundred and fifty acres.

These swales are peculiar winter drains, from ten to thirty yards wide, and from one to two feet deep. In the winter they are filled with slowly running water; but in summer they are dry, and their flat bottoms become almost as hard as a brick. No vegetation of consequence will grow in these swales; and the only timber along their margins is scattering ash, from six to eight inches in diameter and from twenty to twenty-five feet high, with wide, bushy tops. The land on both sides of these swales being clean prairie, the rows of green ash in summer give the plain a beautiful appearance.

During the five years I remained in Oregon, the rainy season invariably set in between the 18th of October and the 1st of November, and continued until about the middle of April, with occasional showers to July. In 1845 there were showers in August sufficient to sprout wheat in the shock. Always about the 10th of September we had frost sufficient to kill bean and melon vines. The season for sowing wheat and oats extended from the commencement of the rains until the first of May; and the harvest began about the 20th of July. We had snow every winter but one while I was in Oregon. At one time it was from six to eight inches deep, and remained upon the ground about ten days. The Columbia River was then frozen over at Vancouver; but this fact is not a true indication of the degree of cold, as this stream heads in a cold region, and the ice forms above and comes down in floating masses; and, when the tide is rising, there is little or no current in the river, and it then freezes over very easily. During the winter, and most generally in February, there is an interval of fine clear weather, which lasts about twenty days, with a cold wind from the north, and hard frosts.

But during most of the rainy season the rains are almost continuous. Sometimes the sun would not be seen for twenty days in succession. It would generally rain about three days and nights without intermission, then cease for about the same period (still remaining cloudy), and then begin again. These rains were not very heavy, but cold and steady, accompanied with a brisk, driving wind from the south. It required a very stout, determined man to ride all day facing one of these rains. They were far worse than driving snow, as they wet and chilled the rider through. The summers, the latter half of the spring, and the early half of the fall, were the finest in the world, so far as my own experience extends. Though the rainy seasons be long and tedious, they are, upon the whole, a blessing. The copious rains fertilize the soil of the fields, and keep them always fresh and productive. In my own best judgment, Oregon is one of the loveliest and most fertile spots of earth. It is destined to be densely populated and finely cultivated. The scenery of her mountains and valleys is simply magnificent. Her snow-clad mountains, her giant forests, her clear skies in summer, and her green and blooming valleys, constitute a combination of the beautiful that can not be excelled.

When we arrived in Oregon, we more than doubled the resident civilized population of the country. J. W. Nesmith, our orderly sergeant, made a complete roll of the male members of the company capable of bearing arms, including all above the age of sixteen years. This roll he preserved and produced at the Oregon Pioneers' Celebration in June, 1875. I have inspected this roll as published in "The Oregonian," and find it correct, except in the omission of the name of P. B. Reading, who went to California, and including the name of A. L. Lovejoy, who came the year before.

This roll contained 293 names, 267 of whom arrived in Oregon. Of the 26 missing, 6 died on the way, 5 turned back on Platte River, and 15 went to California. He also gives the names of many of the resident male population, and estimates their number at 157. John M. Shively* made a complete list of *all* the emigrants at the crossing of Kansas River, but that list has unfortunately been lost. Judge M. P. Deady, in his address before the Oregon Pioneers in June, 1875, estimated the immigration of 1843, men, women, and children, at nine hundred. My own estimate would not be so high. I have always estimated the number arriving in Oregon as not exceeding eight hundred.

[Note : John M. Shively is an engineer, and a plain, unassuming man, but possessed of much greater genuine ability than most people supposed. Justice has never been done him. He was in Washington City in the winter of 1845-'46, and was the originator of the project of a steamship line from New York to this coast by way of Panama.]

When we arrived in Oregon we were poor, and our teams were so much reduced as to be unfit for service until the next spring. Those of us who came by water from Walla Walla left our cattle there for the winter; and those who came by water from the Dalles left their cattle for the winter at that point. Even if our teams had

been fit for use when we arrived, they would have been of no benefit to us, as we could not bring them to the Willamette Valley until
the spring of 1844. Pork was ten and flour four cents a pound, and
other provisions in proportion. These were high prices considering
our scanty means and extra appetites. Had it not been for the generous kindness of the gentlemen in charge of the business of the Hudson's Bay Company, we should have suffered much greater
privations. The Company furnished many of our immigrants with
provisions, clothing, seed, and other necessaries on credit. This was
done, in many instances, where the purchasers were known to be of
doubtful credit. At that time the Company had most of the provisions and merchandise in the country; and the trade with our people
was, upon the whole, a decided loss, so many failing to pay for
what they had purchased. Many of our immigrants were unworthy
of the favors they received, and only returned abuse for generosity.

I remember an example, related to me by Captain James
Waters, an excellent man, possessed of a kind heart, a truthful
tongue, and a very patient disposition. As before stated, most of our
immigrants passed from the Dalles to the Cascades on rafts made of
dry logs. This was not only slow navigation, but their rafts were
utterly useless after reaching the Cascades; and they were compelled to remain there for some days, before they could descend the
river to the fort. In the mean time their supplies of provisions had
been consumed. Captain Waters was among the first of our immigrants to arrive at Vancouver, having no family with him; and he at
once applied to Dr. McLoughlin for supples of provisions for the
immigrants at the Cascades, but had nothing wherewith to pay. The
Doctor furnished the supplies, and also a boat to take them up, with
the understanding that Captain Waters would navigate the vessel,
and sell the provisions to the immigrants at Vancouver prices. This
was done; but many of the purchasers never paid, contenting themselves with abusing the Doctor and the Captain, accusing them of
wishing to speculate upon the necessities of poor immigrants. The
final result was a considerable loss, which Dr. McLoughlin and
Captain Waters divided equally between them. I met Waters myself
with the boat laden with provisions going up, as I passed down the
river the first time; and there can be no doubt of the truth of his
statement.

DR. JOHN MCLOUGHLIN — JAMES DOUGLAS — POLICY OF THE HUDSON'S BAY COMPANY IN ITS INTERCOURSE WITH THE INDIANS.

Dr. John McLoughlin was one of the greatest and most noble philanthropists I ever knew. He was a man of superior ability, just in all his dealings, and a faithful Christian. I never knew a man of the world who was more admirable. I never heard him utter a vicious sentiment, or applaud a wrongful act. His views and acts were formed upon the model of the Christian gentleman. He was a superior business man, and a profound judge of human nature. He had read a great deal, and had learned much from intercourse with intelligent men. He spoke and wrote French and English equally well, having learned both languages while growing up from childhood.

In his position of chief factor of the Hudson's Bay Company he had grievous responsibilities imposed upon him. He stood between the *absent* directors and stock-holders of the Company and the present suffering immigrants. He witnessed their sufferings; they did not. He was unjustly blamed by many of both parties. It was not the business of the Company to deal upon credit; and the manager of its affairs in Oregon was suddenly thrown into a new and very embarrassing position. How to act, so as to secure the approbation of the directors and stockholders in England, and at the same time not to disregard the most urgent calls of humanity, was indeed the great difficulty. No *possible* line of conduct could have escaped censure.

To be placed in such a position was a misfortune which only a good man could bear in patience. I was assured by Mr. Frank Ermatinger, the manager of the Company's store at Oregon City, as well as by others, that Dr. McLoughlin had sustained a heavy individual loss by his charity to the immigrants. I knew enough myself to be certain that these statements were substantially true. Yet such was the humility of the Doctor that he never, to my knowledge, mentioned or alluded to any particular act of charity performed by him. I was intimate with him, and he never mentioned them to me. When I first saw him in 1843, his hair was white. He had then been in Oregon about twenty years. He was a large, noble-looking old man, of commanding figure and countenance. His manners were courteous but frank; and the stranger at once felt at ease in his presence.

Mr. James Douglas (subsequently Sir James, and Governor of British Columbia) was a younger man than Dr. McLoughlin by some fifteen years. He was a man of very superior intelligence, and a finished Christian gentleman. His course toward us was noble, prudent, and generous. I do not think that at that time he possessed the knowledge of men that the Doctor did, nor was he so great a philanthropist. I regarded him as a just and able man, with a conscience and character above reproach. In his position of Governor of British Columbia, he was censured by Mr. John Nugent of California, as I must think, without sufficient reason. Errors of judgment Governor Douglas may have committed, as almost any man would have done at time in his trying position; but he must have radically changed since I knew him, if he knowingly acted improperly.

It was most fortunate for us that two such noble men were managers of the Company at the time of our arrival. Our own countrymen had it not in their power to aid us efficiently. Many of them were immigrants of the preceding season; others were connected with the missions; and, altogether, they were too few and poor to help us much. The Company could not afford to extend to succeeding immigrations the same credit they did to us. The burden would have been too great. This refusal led many to complain, but without sufficient reason.

From Dr. McLoughlin and others I learned a great deal in reference to the manner in which the business of the Company had been conducted. At the time of the Doctor's arrival in Oregon, and for many years afterward, the principal inhabitants were Indians, divided into various small tribes, speaking different languages. These Indians were mainly found upon the Columbia and its tributaries, and far outnumbered the hired servants of the Company. The task of controlling these wild people was one of great delicacy, requiring a thorough knowledge of human nature and the greatest administrative ability. The Doctor's policy was based upon the fundamental idea that all men, civilized or savage, have an innate love of justice, and will therefore be *ultimately* best satisfied with fair, honest dealing.

The Company had its various trading-posts located at convenient points throughout a vast territory. The Indian population being about stationary as to numbers and pursuits, it was not very difficult to calculate the amount of supplies likely to be required in each year. The Company was in the habit of importing one year's supply in advance; so that if a cargo should be lost, its customers would not suffer. Its goods were all of superior quality, purchased on the best terms, and were sold at prices both uniform and moderate. Of course, prices in the interior were higher than on the seaboard; but they never varied at the same post. The Indians knew nothing of the intricate law of demand and supply, and could not be made to understand why an article of a given size and quality should be worth more at one time than at another in the same place, while the material and labor used and employed in its manufacture were the same. A tariff of prices, once adopted, was never changed. The goods were not only of the best, but of uniform quality. To secure these results the Company had most of its goods manufactured to order. The wants of the Indians being very few, their purchases were confined to a small variety of articles; and consequently they became the very best judges of the quality of the goods they desired to purchase. No one could detect any imperfection in a blanket more readily and conclusively than an Oregon Indian. There was always kept an ample supply at each post; so that the customers of the Company were not driven at any time to deal with rival traders, or do without their usual supplies.

It was evident that no successful competition with the Company could last long under such circumstances. No one could continue to undersell them and make a profit; and the competitor, without profit, must fail. The uniform low prices and the good quality of its articles pleased the Indians, and the Company secured their custom beyond the reach of competition. The Company adopted a system that would work out best in the end, and, of course, was successful.

In the course of time the Company induced the Indians to throw aside the bow and arrow, and to use the gun; and, as the Company had all the guns and ammunition in the country, the Indians became dependent upon it for their supplies of these articles. It was the great object of the Company to preserve the peace among the Indians within the limits of its trading territory, not only from motives of pure humanity, but from mercantile interest; as the destruction of the Indians was the destruction of its customers, and the consequent ruin of its trade.

When the Indians went to war with each other, the Doctor first interposed his mediation, as the common friend and equal of both parties. When all other means failed, he refused to sell them arms and ammunition, saying that it was the business of the Company to sell them these articles to kill game with, not to kill each other. By kindness, justice, and discreet firmness, the Indians were generally kept at peace among themselves. They found it almost impossible to carry on war.

But the task of protecting the servants of the Company against the attacks of the Indians was one of still greater difficulty. The Doctor impressed the Indians with the fact that the Company was simply a mercantile corporation, whose purpose was only trade with the natives; that its intention was only to appropriate to its exclusive use a few sites for its trading-posts and small parcels of adjacent lands, sufficient to produce supplies for its people; thus leaving all the remainder of the country for the use and in the exclusive possession of the Indians; and that this possession of limited amounts of land by the Company would be mutually beneficial. Even savages have the native good sense to discover the mutual benefits of trade. The Indians wanted a market for their furs, and the Company customers for its merchandise.

It was an inflexible rule with the Doctor never to violate his word, whether it was a promise of reward or a threat of punishment. There is no vice more detested by Indians than a failure to keep one's word, which they call lying. If it were a failure to perform a promised act beneficial to the Indians themselves, they would regard it as a fraud akin to theft; and, if a failure to carry out a threat of punishment, they would consider it the result of weakness or cowardice. In either case, the party who broke his pledged word would forfeit their respect, and in the first case would incur their undying resentment.

To guard against the natural jealousy of the Indians, and insure peace between them and the servants of the Company, it became necessary to adopt and enforce the most rigid discipline among the latter. This discipline was founded upon the great principle that, to avoid difficulty with others, we must first do right ourselves. To make this discipline the more efficient, the Doctor adopted such measures as substantially to exclude all intoxicating liquors from the country. When a crime was committed by an Indian, the Doctor made it a rule not to hold the *whole* tribe responsible for the unauthorized acts of individuals, but to inflict punishment upon the culprit himself. In cases of crime by Indians, the Doctor insisted upon just punishment; and, if the culprit escaped for a time, the pursuit was never given up until he was captured. In some cases, several years elapsed between the date of the crime and that of the capture of the fugitive. Certain and just punishment was always inflicted upon the criminal. This the Doctor was able to accomplish through the Company's agents at the different posts, and by negotiation with the leading Indian chiefs, and the offer of rewards for the arrest of the fugitive.

In this manner the Doctor secured and kept the confidence of the Indians. When he first arrived in Oregon, and for some time thereafter, whenever boats were sent up the Columbia with supplies, a guard of sixty armed men was required; but, in due time, only the men necessary to propel the boats were needed. The Indians at the different portages were employed and paid by the Company to assist in making them.

The Indians soon saw that the Company was a mere trading establishment, confined to a small space of land at each post, and was, in point of fact, advantageous to themselves. The few Canadian-French who were located in the Willamette Valley were mostly, if not entirely, connected by marriage with the Indians, the Frenchmen having Indian wives, and were considered to some extent as a part of their own people. But, when we, the American immigrants, came into what the Indians claimed as their own country, we were considerable in numbers; and we came, not to establish trade with the Indians, but to take and settle the country *exclusively* for ourselves. Consequently, we went anywhere we pleased, settled down without any treaty or consultation with the Indians, and occupied our claims without their consent and without compensation. This difference they very soon understood. Every succeeding fall they found the white population about doubled, and our settlements continually extending, and rapidly encroaching more and more upon their pasture and camas grounds. They saw that we fenced in the best lands, excluding their horses from the grass, and our hogs ate up their camas. They instinctively saw annihilation before them.

As illustrative of the difficulties of Dr. McLoughlin's position, I will state the facts of a few cases, as they were related to me substantially by the Doctor himself.

The shore of the Columbia River in front of Fort Vancouver was covered with cobble-stones, which were used by the Company as ballast for its returning ships. The principal chief of the Indians concluded that the Company ought to pay something for these stones; and one day, in the presence of a large crowd of his people (assembled, perhaps, for that purpose), he demanded payment of the Doctor. Of course, the Doctor was taken by surprise, but at once comprehended the situation. He knew, if he consented to pay in this case, there would be no end to exactions in the future. How best to avoid the payment without giving offense was the question. He knew that the Indians possessed a keen sense of the ridiculous; and, after reflecting a moment, he picked up a cobble-stone, and solemnly offered it to the chief, saying, "Eat this." The Indians present at once saw how ridiculous it was to demand payment for that which was of no practical value to them, and set up a loud shout of derisive laughter. The chief was so much ashamed of his silly demand that he walked off in silence, and never after that demanded payment for things of no value to him.

While the Company's ships lay at anchor in the river opposite the fort, the Doctor occasionally granted a written permit to some particular Indian to visit the ships. On one occasion he granted such a permit to an Indian who was seen by other Indians to go on board, but was not seen by them to return, though, in fact, he did so return. Within a day or two thereafter, the brother of this Indian, being unable to find him, and suspecting that he had been enticed on board the ship, and either murdered or forcibly imprisoned for the purpose of abduction, applied to the Doctor for a permit to visit the ship. As the Indian concealed his reason for asking the permit, the Doctor supposed he was influenced by an idle curiosity, and refused the request. The Indian returned again for the same purpose, and was again refused. He came the third time, with the same result. He then concluded that his brother must either be imprisoned on the ship, or had been murdered; and he at once resolved upon revenge. In the evening of the same day, about an hour before sunset, a shot was heard; and the gardener came running into the fort in great terror, with a bullet-hole through the top of his hat, saying that an Indian had fired upon him from behind the garden-fence. The gates of the fort were at once closed, and all hands prepared for defense. Upon subsequent investigation, the body of the missing Indian was found in the bushes, in the rear of the fort. He had evidently fallen down in a fit, and expired where his body was found. No attempt was made to punish the surviving brother, as he had acted under a very natural mistake.

On one occasion the Indians determined to take and sack Fort Vancouver. The plot for this purpose was conceived, and in part executed, with consummate ability.

Two of their most powerful chiefs quietly went from Fort Vancouver to Nesqualy, a trading-post on Puget's Sound, and remained there several days. While there, they made themselves minutely acquainted with everything about the fort. They then speedily returned to Fort Vancouver, and at once sought and obtained an interview with Dr. McLoughlin and his associates. One of the Indians was the speaker, while the other carefully watched to see what impression their statements would make. The Company's interpreter, a very shrewd Canadian, was present during the interview.

The Indians stated that they left Nesqualy at a certain time, which was true; and that the Indians in that vicinity had attacked and captured the fort by surprise, and had slaughtered all the inhabitants, amounting to a certain number of persons, which number they specified truly. The Indians were subjected to a severe cross-examination without betraying the slightest embarassment, and without making any contradictory statements. When asked how many persons were in the fort at the time, what were their several ages, sexes, appearances, employments, and the position that each occupied in the fort, they invariably gave the correct answer. It was impossible to detect any contradictions in their statements. All were perfectly consistent, as the only falsehood was the alleged fact that Fort Nesqualy had been taken and the people killed. The Doctor and his associates were greatly perplexed, and left in much doubt. The Canadian interpreter was asked his opinion, and he replied, "Let me sleep on it one night." Next morning he said he did not believe the story; that the Indians were such liars that he could not beleive them; that they had before deceived them. This view prevailed.

The object of these Indians was to induce the Company to send nearly all its men to Nesqualy to punish the alleged murderers, thus reducing the force at Fort Vancouver to such an extent that it could be readily taken. These Indians knew, from the invariable practice of the Company, that such a crime, if committed, would not escape punishment if practicable. If they could only make the Doctor believe their narrative, he would at once dispatch an ample force to Nesqualy.

The traders in charge of interior trading-posts were often exposed to peril from the Indians. The Company could only keep a few men at each post, and the Indians at times would become discontented. A rude people, depending entirely upon the spontaneous productions of nature for a supply of provisions, must often suffer extreme want. In such a case men become desperate, and are easily excited to rash acts. Mr. McKinley told me that the Indians on one occasion attempted to rob Fort Walla Walla, and were only prevented by the most cool, intrepid courage of the people of the post.

Chapter IV

ROCKY MOUNTAIN TRAPPERS — THEIR PECULIAR CHARACTER — BLACK HARRIS — JOSEPH L. MEEK — O. RUSSELL — ROBERT NEWELL.

When we arrived in Oregon, we found there a number of Rocky Mountain hunters and trappers, who were settled in the Willamette Valley, most of them in the Tualatin Plains. The invention of the silk hat had rendered the trapping of beaver less profitable. Besides, most of these men had married Indian women, and desired to settle down for life. They had been too long accustomed to frontier life to return to their old homes. Oregon offered them the best prospects for the future. Here was plenty of land for nothing, and a fine climate.

These trappers and hunters constituted a very peculiar class of men. They were kind and genial, brave and hospitable, and in regard to serious matters truthful and honest. There was no malice in them. They never made mischief between neighbor and neighbor. But most of them were given to exaggeration when relating their Rocky Mountain adventures. They seemed to claim the privilege of romance and fable when describing these scenes. As exceptions to this rule, I will mention Judge O. Russell, now living in El Dorado County, California, and Robert Newell, now deceased. Their statements could be relied upon implicitly. Having been so long accustomed to the idle life of the Rocky Mountains, they were not at first pleased with the hard work and drudgery of farming. Meek told me that soon after their arrival in Oregon they applied to Dr. McLoughlin to purchase supplies on credit. This application the Doctor refused. They still urged their request most persistently, and finally asked the Doctor what they should do. He replied in a loud voice: "Go to work! go to work! go to work!" Meek said that was just the thing they did not wish to do.

The romancing Rocky Mountain trapper would exercise his inventive talent to its utmost extent in telling the most extraordinary stories of what he claimed he had seen, and he that could form the most extravagant fiction with a spice of plausibility in it was considered the greatest wit among them. The love of fame is inherent in the breast of man; and the first man in a village is just as proud of his position as the first man in a city or in an empire.

I knew in Missouri the celebrated Black Harris, as he was familiarly called, and was frequently in his company. He, perhaps, invented the most extraordinary story of them all, and thenceforward he had no rival. He said that on one occasion he was hunting in the Rocky Mountains alone, and came in sight of what he supposed to be a beautiful grove of green timber; but, when he approached, he found it to be a petrified forest; and *so sudden* had been the process of petrifaction that the green leaves were all petrified, and the very birds that were then singing in the grove were also petrified in the act of singing, because their mouths were still open in their petrified state. This story I did not myself hear from Harris, but I learned it from good authority.From these Rocky Mountain trappers I learned something in regard to that interesting animal, the beaver. Many persons suppose, from the fact that the beaver is always found along the streams, that he lives, like the otter, on fish. This is a mistake. The beaver lives entirely upon vegetable food, and for this reason its flesh is esteemed a great delicacy. The animal feeds mainly upon the bark of the willow-tree, which grows in abundance along the rich, moist margins of the streams, and is a very soft wood, easily cut by the beaver with his large, sharp teeth. In countries where the streams freeze over in winter, the beaver makes his dam across the stream, of mud and brush so intermixed as to make the structure safe and solid. In this work he uses his fore-paws, not his tail, as some have supposed. The tail is used as a propelling and steering power in swimming. The object in damming the stream is to deepen the water so that it will not freeze to the bottom, but leave plenty of room below the ice for the storage of the winter's supply of food. In summer the beaver cuts down the green willows, and divides them into logs of proper length, so that can be readily moved. These logs are deposited at the bottom of the pond, and kept down by mud placed upon them. The willow in its green state is almost as heavy as water, and these logs are easily sunk and confined to the bottom. On one portion of his dam the beaver constructs his house above the water, with an entrance from beneath. This gives him a warm home and safe retreat in winter.

The mode of trapping the beaver is peculiar. The trap itself is never baited The animal has in his body a secretion something like musk. The trapper finds out the home of the beaver, and selects a place on the side of the pond where the water is shallow near the shore; and there, in the edge of the stream, he drives down a stake of hard-seasoned wood, which the beaver can not cut. To this stake he fastens the chain that is attached to the trap, and then sets the trap in water some six inches deep. On the shore, exactly opposite the trap, he places a bait of the secretion. The beaver always swims up the center of the pond; and when he comes immediately opposite the bait he turns at right angles and goes straight toward it, but is caught in the trap while passing over it. So soon as he feels the trap he endeavors to escape, and drags the trap into deep water as far as the chain will permit. The steel trap is so heavy that the beaver can not possibly swim with it, but is confined by its weight to the bottom, and is there drowned, as the beaver, like other amphibious animals, can remain alive under water only for a limited time.

The beaver is easily tamed, and makes a very docile and interesting pet. He is remarkably neat and cleanly in his habits, as much so as the domestic cat, and almost as much so as the ermine, which never permits its snow-white covering to be soiled.

I am not aware that any wild animal, except the glutton, ever preys upon the beaver or otter. Their terrible teeth are most formidable weapons, and few wild animals would venture to attack them. Besides, they are covered with a large, loose skin and thick fur, so that the teeth of another animal can hardly reach a vital part. It is a well-known fact that one otter will vanquish a number of large, brave dogs. Every bite of the otter leaves a large gash, like that made by the huge tusks of the wild boar.

Among the most noted of these trappers was my neighbor and friend, Joseph L. Meek, whose life has been written by Mrs. Victor, of Oregon. Meek was a tall man, of fine appearance — a most genial, kind, and brave spirit. He had in his composition no malice, no envy, and no hatred. I do not remember ever to have heard that he had a personal difficulyt with any one. In relating his Rocky Mountain adventures, he was given, like a majority of his comrades, to exaggeration.

His comrades told a story upon him, which he admitted to me was true. A party of them, while in the Rocky Mountains, were one day stopping to rest, when they saw a band of hostile Indians mounted and charging down upon them, at the distance of a few hundred yards. Meek and his comrades mounted their animals in the hottest haste; but the fine mule Meek was riding became sullen and would not budge. Meek screamed out, at the top of his voice: "Boys, stand your ground! We can whip 'em. Stand your ground, boys!" But his comrades were of a different opinion, and were fleeing from the Indians as fast as possible. However, as the Indians approached, Meek's mule began to comprehend the situation, changed its mind, and set off at its utmost speed in pursuit of its companions. In a short time Meek and his mule were alongside of the fleeing hunters; and very soon Meek passed them, whipping his mule, and crying out most lustily: "Come on, boys! We can't fight 'em! Come on, boys! come on!"

I remember a story Meek told to myself and four others, as we were returning from Oregon City to our homes in the Tualatin Plains. He said that on one occasion he was out hunting by himself, some four hundred miles from Brown's Cove, in the Rocky Mountains, where his company were staying, and that one night his horse escaped, leaving him afoot. He started on foot, with his rifle on his shoulder; but the first day he lost the lock of his gun, so that he could kill no game. The result was, that he walked that long distance, less fifteen miles, in eight days, and without anything to eat except one thistle-root, and that purged him like medicine! He said that toward the end of his trip he would often become blind, fall down, and remain unconscious for some time; then recover, and pursue his painful journey. At last, in this way, he reached a point within fifteen miles of Brown's Cove, where one of his comrades happened to find him, and took him into camp.

I replied: "That was a most extraordinary adventure, Joe; and, while I don't pretend to question your veracity in the least, don't you really think you might safely fall a snake or two in the distance?" He declared it was four hundred miles. "But," said I, "may you not be mistaken in the time?" He insisted he was only eight days in making the trip on foot. "But, Joe," I continued, "don't you think you may be mistaken as to the time in this way? When you had those attacks of blindness, fell down, and then came to again, don't you think you might have mistaken it for a new day?" He said he was not mistaken. "Then," said I, "this thing of walking four hundred miles in eight days, with nothing at all to eat, and being physicked into the bargain, is the most extraordinary feat ever performed by man." He said no man could tell how much he could stand until he was forced to try; and that men were so healthy in the Rocky Mountains, and so used to hard times, that they could perform wonders.

Meek was a droll creature, and at times very slovenly in his dress. One day in summer I called for him, sitting on my horse at his yard-fence. He came to the door and put his head out, but would not come to the fence, because his pantaloons were so torn and ragged. He was then sheriff; and at the next term of our Circuit Court I drew up a fictitious indictment against him, charging him with notorious public indecency; had it endorsed on the back: "People of Oregon *vs.* Joseph L. Meek. Notorious Public Indecency. A true bill"; and quietly placed it among the real indictments. Very soon Meek was looking through the bundle of indictments, and found this one against himself. He, of course, supposed it genuine; and it would have amused an invalid to see the expression of his face. I soon told him it was only a joke, which was apparent upon the face of the indictment, as it had not the signatures of the proper officers.

On one occasion he came to my house, wearing one of the most splendid new white figured-silk vests that I had ever seen, while the remainder of his dress was exceedingly shabby. He was like a man dressed in a magnificent ruffled shirt, broadcloth coat, vest, and pantaloons, and going barefoot.

The second or third year after my arrival in Oregon, and in the month of October, before the rainy season set in, I was about to start to Oregon City with a load of wheat, to secure a winter's supply of flour, when Meek asked me to let him put ten bushels in the wagon, and he would go with me. I said all right — that I would be at his place the next morning early, with my wagon and team, and for him to have his wheat ready. He promised he would. According to my promise, I was at his house by eight next morning; but Meek had to run his wheat through the fan, and put it into the sacks. The result was that I had to help him; and it was ten by the time we were loaded up. In a great hurry, I asked him if he had anything to eat, as I only had some bread in the wagon, the only thing I could bring. I saw he was rather embarrassed, and said, "Have you any meat?" "No!" "Have you any butter?" "No!" "What, then, have you?" "Plenty of squashes." I said, "Roll them in." He soon brought as many squashes as his long arms and big hands could carry, put them into the wagon, and we were off. I drove the team and he rode his horse.

On the way Meek rode ahead of me, and overtook Mr. Pomeroy, going to Oregon City with a wagon loaded with fresh beef. Meek, in a good-humored, bantering way said, "Pomeroy, I have an execution against you, and I can not let you take that beef out of this county." Pomeroy, with equal good humor, replied, "Meek, it is a hard case to stop a man on the way to market, where he can sell his beef, and get the money to pay his debts." "Well," said Meek, it does look a little hard, but I propose a compromise. Burnett and I will have nothing to eat to-night but bread and squashes. Now, if you will let us have beef enough for supper and breakfast, I will let you off." Pomeroy laughed and told Meek to help himself. When we encamped about sundown, some eight miles from the city, Meek did help himself to some choice ribs of beef, and we had a feast. I had had nothing to eat since the morning of that day but bread; and I was hungry after my hard drive. I roasted the squashes, and Meek the beef; and we had a splendid supper. I found this beef almost equal to buffalo-meat. We both ate too much, and Meek complained that his supper had given him "the rotten belches."

I have already mentioned the name of Judge O. Russell as one of the Rocky Mountain men. He is a native of the State of Maine, and came to the mountains when a young man, in pursuit of health. All his comrades agreed that he never lost his virtuous habits, but always remained true to his principles. He was never married. He was at one time one of the Executive Committee of our Provisional Government in Oregon, and most faithfully did he perform his duty. He is a man of education and of refined feelings. After the discovery of gold he came to the mines, and has been engaged in mining in El Dorado County, California, ever since.

When in Oregon, he was occasionally a guest at my house, and would for hours together entertain us with descriptions of mountain life and scenery. His descriptive powers were fine, and he would talk until a late hour at night. My whole family were deeply attentive, and my children yet remember the Judge with great pleasure. He was always a most welcome guest at my house. He did not tell so many extraordinary stories as the average Rocky Mountain trapper and hunter; but those he did tell were true. I remember one instance.

He said that he and a colored man were out hunting together on one occasion, and wounded a large grizzly bear. A grizzly bear, when wounded, will rush upon the hunter if near him; but, if at a distance from the hunter, the animal will retire into thick brush, and there conceal himself as well as possible. In this case, the bear had crept into a small but thick patch of willows, and so concealed himself that the hunters had to approach very near before they could obtain a shot. The Judge and his comrade, with loaded and cocked rifles in hand, separately approached, on different sides, almost to the edge of the thicket, when the grizzly, with a loud, ferocious cry, suddenly sprang to his feet and rushed toward the Judge, and, when within a few feet of him, reared upon his hind legs, with his ears thrown back, his terrible jaws distended, and his eyes gleaming with rage. The Judge said he knew that to retreat was death, and that the only chance was to make a sure shot. With the accuracy and courage of a skillful hunter, he fired as the bear stood up, and gave him a fatal shot through the heart. The bear fell, and the colored man came up as pale as a colored man could be, and exclaimed, "That was a 'roshus animal!"

Robert Newell was a native of the State of Ohio, and came to the Rocky Mountains when a young man. He was of medium height, stout frame, and fine face. He was full of humanity, good will, genial feeling, and frankness. He possessed a remarkable memory; and, though slow of speech, his narrations were most interesting. In his slow, hesitating manner, he would state every minute circumstance in its own proper place; and the hearer was most amply compensated in the end for his time and patience. I knew him well, and have often listened to his simple and graphic description of incidents that came under his own observation while he was in the service of the Missouri Fur Company. I remember a very interesting narration which I heard from him. I can only give the substance.

The hired men of the Company were mostly employed in trapping beaver and otter. A war grew up between the whites and Indians, as usual. It was not desirable to the Company, and its manager made efforts to secure peace. For this purpose he consulted with Newell, and asked him if he would be willing to go as a commissioner to the Crow Indians to treat for peace. Newell consented, upon condition that he should only take with him an interpreter and a cook.

With these two men Newell boldly made his way to the Crow camp. The Indian chiefs assembled in the council-lodge, and the orator on the part of the tribe brought in a bundle of small sticks. He commenced and stated an aggressive wrong against the Crows on the part of the whites, and demanded for that a certain number of .blankets. Having done this, he laid aside one stick, and then proceeded to state another grievance and to lay aside another stick, and so on until the bundle was exhausted. The number of these complaints was great, and the amount of merchandise demanded far exceeded the ability of the Company to pay.

Newell said that, while this process was going on, he felt himself almost overwhelmed. He could not make a detailed statement of wrongs committed by the Indians against the whites sufficient to balance this most formidable account. He had not prepared himself with a mass of charges and a bundle of sticks to refresh his memory. In this emergency he determined to take a bold, frank position, and come directly to the point by a short and comprehensive method. When it came to his turn to speak, he told the council that he was sent as the mere agent of the Company, and was not authorized to enter into any stipulation for payment to either party; that he did not come to count over the wrongs committed in the past; that both parties had done wrong often, and it was difficult to say which party had been oftenest or most to blame; that he came to bury the past and stipulate for peace in the future, and wished to know of them whether they would mutually agree to be friends for the time to come. This was the best possible ground to be taken, and so pleased the assembled chiefs that they entered into a treaty of peace.

But a very short time after this treaty was made, and before Newell and his two men had left, a sad accident occurred that wellnigh cost Newell his life. One night, before bedtime, the cook had hung a small kettle above the fire in Newell's lodge, and had pretty well filled it with choice pieces of fat buffalo-meat, with intent to have a feast. After doing this, the careless cook went out, and the kettle boiled over; and the first thing that Newell saw was the fire blazing out at the top of the lodge. When he first saw it, he was at the lodge of one of the chiefs, a short distance off. In the hurry and confusion of the moment, Newell ran to his lodge, seized the kettle, and gave it a sudden sling, and it happened to strike an Indian in the face and scalded him terribly. The Indian gave a loud scream, which at once aroused all the camp. The excitement was terrific. The act could not be denied, and the injury was palpable and most grievous. It was thought that both the eyes of the Indian had been put out; and his friends and kindred were vehement and loud in their demands for punishment.

The principal chief at once summoned a council to consider the case. The chiefs met in the council-lodge, while the people, including men, women, and children, squatted in front of the door leaving a narrow passage for the prisoner, with his interpreter, to enter the lodge. Newell said that as they passed through this enraged mass of people they exhibited the utmost hatred against him, especially the women, who manifested their intense animosity in every way, by word and gesture. In passing by them, they would lean away and shrink from him, as if his touch was pollution itself.

When he entered the dimly lighted council-lodge, all was grim and profound silence. Not a word was spoken, nor a move made, for some time. Then one of the chiefs commenced howling like a large wolf, the imitation being almost perfect. After he had ceased, there was again profound silence for some moments; and then another chief successfully imitated the fierce cry of the panther; and then, after another pause, a third chief most energetically imitated the loud cry of an enraged grizzly bear. He said that he had never witnessed a scene of terror equal to this. All the chiefs, except the principal one, seemed to be his enemies. He thought his chance of escape exceedingly small.

The head chief was an old man, of superior native intellect, and, though uneducated, he understood human nature. He seemed to comprehend the case well. He could see no malicious motive for the act. He told Newell to state the facts to the council truly, and he thought there might be some hope for him.

Newell, through his interpreter, stated to them all the facts as they occurred; and this just statement and Newell's honest and manly face and frank manner had a great effect upon the principal members of the council. It was also found that the poor Indian had not been so severely hurt as at first supposed, and that his sight was not totally destroyed. The council sat nearly all night, and then decided to postpone the case until time should show the extent of the injury. In the mean time Newell and his companions were not allowed to depart, but were to be detained until the case should be finally decided.

But another painful incident soon occurred, that seriously imperiled their lives.

One day an Indian horseman was seen approaching the camp rapidly; and, when within some hundred yards, he dismounted, rolled up his buffalo-robe, took hold of one end of the roll, and slowly and solemnly swung it around his head several times; then he folded it up, and sat upon it, and brought both his open hands slowly down his face several times in succession. The Indians in camp at once understood the sad significance of these signs. They knew that he was a messenger sent to inform them that the small-pox had broken out at another camp of their tribe. He would not come near, for fear of communicating the disease to them.

Newell said that he had never witnessed such a scene of sorrow as this. The women and children filled the camp with their loud wailings and bitter lamentations; and despair sat upon the countenances of the men. The Indians were now more fiercely hostile than ever, because they believed that this terrible scourge, far worse to them than war itself, had been introduced by the trappers. They knew that this fell disease was never heard of in their country until white men appeared among them. They thronged around Newell and his comrades, and it seemed that they would slaughter them outright.

But the old chief was equal to the occasion. He at once mounted his horse and rode through the camp, saying to all that it was useless to weep and lament, and ordering the people to pack up at once and be off for the Wind River Mountain. This order was instantly obeyed; the cries and lamentations at once ceased; and Newell said he never saw lodges so quickly taken down and packed up as he did on this occasion. In less than one hour the whole camp was on the march to the place mentioned. In due time they arrived safely at the Wind River Mountain, where the sky was clear, the climate cool and healthy, and game abundant. It being in midsummer, the deer had followed up the melting snows to crop the fresh grass as soon as it sprang up just below the snow-line, and to be in a cool atmosphere, where the flies would not torment them. Here the Indians recovered from their alarm and excitement. Not a case of small-pox appeared in camp. All were healthy and had plenty to eat. The poor fellow that was scalded recovered in this healthy locality, and was not so seriously injured as was at first supposed. Newell became popular with the Indians, and they at last let him depart in peace.

THE PROVISIONAL GOVERNMENT.

Soon after my arrival at Linnton, I was consulted as to the right of the people of Oregon to organize a provisional government. At first I gave my opinion against it, thinking we had no such right; but a few weeks' reflection satisfied me that we had such right, and that necessity required us to exercise it. Communities, as well as individuals, have the natural right of self-defense; and it is upon this ground that the right to institute governments among men must ultimately rest. This right of self-preservation is bestowed upon man by his Creator.

We found ourselves placed in a new and very embarrassing position. The right of sovereignty over the country was in dispute between the United States and Great Britain, and neither country could establish any government over us. Our community was composed of American citizens and British subjects, occupying the same country as neighbors, with all their respective national prejudices and attachments, and so distant from the mother-countries as to be a great extent beyond the reach of home influences. We had, therefore, a difficult population to govern; but this fact only rendered government the more necessary.

We also found, by actual experiment, that some political government was a *necessity*. Though political government be imperfect, it is still a blessing, and necessary for the preservation of the race. Without it, the strongest and most reckless characters in the community would be tyrants over the others. The theory of the wandering savage, to leave the kindred of the murdered victim to revenge his death, would not answer for a civilized race of men. The weak and timid, the peaceful and conscientious, and those who had no kindred, could not be protected under such a theory. Without any law but that of individual self-defense, we found it impossible to get along in peace. When a person died, the worst characters could seize upon his estate under some pretense or other, and defeat the just rights of defenseless heirs. So long as these violent, bad men had only to meet and overcome single individuals, they had no fears. It is only when the combined force of a whole community is brought to bear upon these desperadoes that they can be effectually kept in order.

As we could not, with any exact certainty, anticipate the time when the conflicting claims of the two contending governments would be settled, we determined to organize a provisional government for ourselves. In this undertaking our British neighbors ultimately joined us with good will, and did their part most faithfully, as did our American citizens.

I was a member of the "Legislative Committee of Oregon" of 1844. It was composed of nine members elected by the people, and consisted of only one House. The year before, the people of Oregon had substantially organized a provisional government; but the organization was imperfect, as is necessarily the case in the beginning of all human institutions. We improved upon their labors, and our successors improved upon ours.

Our Legislative Committee held two sessions, one in June and the other in December of that year, each session lasting only a few days. In our then condition, we had but little time to devote to public business. Our personal needs were too urgent, and our time too much occupied in making a support for our families. Our legislation, however, was ample for the time. There was then no printing establishment in Oregon. We passed an act in relation to land claims, the first section of which provided that "all persons who have heretofore made, or shall hereafter make permanent improvements upon a place, with a *bona fide* intention of occupying and holding the same for himself, and shall continue to occupy and cultivate the same, shall be entitled to hold six hundred and forty acres, and shall hold only one claim at the same time; *provided*, a man may hold town lots in addition to his claim." The seventh and last section gave all persons complying with the provisions of the act "the remedy of forcible entry and detainer against intruders, and the action of trespass against trespassers." This act was passed June 25, 1844. It will be seen that the remedy against intruders was simple, cheap, quick, and efficient, and well adapted to existing circumstances.

By an act passed June 27, 1844, the executive power was vested in a single person, to be elected at the then next annual election by the people, and at the annual election to be held every two years thereafter, to hold his office for the term of two years, and receive an annual salary of three hundred dollars. By the same act the judicial power was vested in the circuit courts and in justices of the peace; and the act provided that one judge should be elected by the qualified voters at the annual election, who should hold his office for one year, and whose duty it was to hold two terms of the Circuit Court in each county every year; and for his services he should receive an annual salary of five hundred dollars, and also legal fees for probate business. By the same act the legislative power was vested in a House of Representatives, composed of members elected annually by the people.

The first section of the third article of the same act was as follows:

Section 1. All the statute laws of Iowa Territory passed at the first session of the Legislative Assembly of said Territory, and not of a local character, and not incompatible with the condition and circumstances of this country, shall be the law of this government, unless otherwise modified; and the common law of England and principles of equity, not modified by the statutes of Iowa or of this government, and not incompatible with its principles, shall constitute a part of the law of this land.

Article V. was in these words:

Section 1. All officers shall be elected by the people once a year, unless otherwise provided, at a general election to be held in each county on the first Tuesday in June in each year, at such places as shall be designated by the Judge of the Circuit Court.

Sec. 2. As many justices of the peace and constables shall be elected from time to time as shall be deemed necessary by the Circuit Court of each county.

The seventh article fixed the time of holding the terms of the circuit courts in the several counties, and gave the judge the power to designate the several places of holding said terms by giving one month's notice thereof.

We also passed on June 24th an act consisting of eight sections, prohibiting the importation, distillation, sale, and barter of ardent spirits. For every sale or barter the offender was to pay a fine of twenty dollars; and for establishing or carrying on a distillery the offender was subject to be indicted before the Circuit Court as for a nuisance, and, if convicted, to a fine of one hundred dollars; and it was made the duty of the court to issue an order directing the sheriff to seize and destroy the distilling apparatus, which order the sheriff was bound to execute.

On June 22^d an act containing twenty-six sections was passed concerning roads and highways. On December 24th an act was passed allowing the voters of Oregon at the annual election of 1845 to give their votes for or against the call of a convention.

The following act in relation to Indians was passed December 23^d: *Whereas*, The Indians inhabiting this country are rapidly diminishing, being now mere remnants of once powerful tribes, now disorganized, without government, and so situated that no treaty can be regularly made with them; *And whereas*, By an act passed in July, 1843, this government has shown its humane policy to protect the Indians in their rights; *And whereas*, The Indians are not engaged in agriculture, and have no use for or right to any tracts, portions, or parcels of land, not actually occupied or used by them; therefore, *Be it enacted by the Legislative Committee of Oregon as follows*:

Section 1. That the Indians shall be protected in the free use of such pieces of vacant land as they occupy with their villages or other improvements, and such fisheries as they have heretofore used.

Sec. 2. That the executive power be required to see that the laws in regard to Indians be faithfully executed; and that whenever the laws shall be violated, the said Executive shall be empowered to bring suit in the name of Oregon against such wrong-doer in the courts of the country.

An act was passed on June 27th fixing the number of members of the next House of Representatives at thirteen, and apportioning the representation among the then five counties of Oregon.

All necessary local bills were passed, and our little government was put into practical and successful operation. Having adopted the general statutes of Iowa and the common law, we had a provision for every case likely to arise in so small a community.

At first, the great difficulty was to make our little government efficient. Our people honestly differed very much in their views as to our right to institute government. In 1843 there were fifty-two affirmative and fifty negative votes. There were so many of our people who were conscientiously opposed to the organization of any government that we found it a delicate matter to use force against men whose motives we were sure were good. Still, government had to be practically enforced.

Joseph L. Meek was selected in May or July, 1843, for sheriff. He was the very man for the position. He was both as brave and as magnanimous as the lion. Do his duty he would, peacefully if possible, but forcibly if he must. If we had selected a timid or rash man for sheriff, we must have failed for a time. To be a government at all, the laws must be enforced.

Meek soon had his courage fully tested. A stout carpenter named Dawson was engaged in a fight in the winter of 1843-'44, and a warrant was at once issued for his arrest, and placed in Meek's hands to be executed. Dawson was no doubt of opinion that we had no right to organize and enforce our government. Meek went to Dawson's shop, where he was at work at his bench with a jack-plane. Meek walked in, and said laughingly, "Dawson, I came for you." Dawson replied that Meek had come for the wrong man. Meek, still laughing, said again, "I came for you," and was about to lay his hands on Dawson, when the latter drew back with his jack-plane raised to strike. But Meek was not only stout, but active and brave; and, seizing the plane, he wrested it by force from Dawson. Dawson at once turned around and picked up his broad-axe; but the moment he faced Meek, he found a cocked pistol at his breast. Meek, still laughing, said; "Dawson, I came for you. Surrender or die!" Very few men will persist under such circumstances; and Dawson, though as brave as most men, began to cry, threw down his broad-axe, and went with Meek without further objection. Dawson declared that, as *he* had to submit, every other man must; and he was no longer an enemy of our government.

This intrepid performance of his official duty so established Meek's character for true courage in the exercise of his office that he had little or no trouble in the future; and the authority of our little government was thus thoroughly established.

CONDITION OF THE PEOPLE — HARDSHIPS ENDURED BY THE EARLY SETTLERS.

We were a small, thinly-settled community, poor, and isolated from the civilized world. By the time we reached the distant shores of the Pacific, after a slow, wearisome journey of about two thousand miles, our little means were exhausted, and we had to begin life anew, in a new country. The wild game in Oregon was scarce and poor. The few deer that are found there seldom become fat. The wild fowl were plentiful in the winter, but they constituted an uncertain reliance for families settled some distance from their usual places of resort. Besides, we had no time to hunt them, and the weather was generally too wet to admit of it. Had the country contained the same amount and variety of wild game, wild fruits, and honey as were found in the Western States at an early day, our condition would have been better. But the only wild fruits we found were a variety of berries, such as blackberries, raspberries, strawberries, blueberries, and cranberries, which were not only abundant but of excellent quality. We only found one nut in the country, and that was the hazelnut in small quantities. There were no wild grapes or plums, and no honey.

For the first two years after our arrival the great difficulty was to procure provisions. The population being so much increased by each succeeding fall's immigration, provisions were necessarily scarce. Those who had been there for two years had plenty to eat; but after that the great trouble was to procure clothing, there being no raw materials in the country from which domestic manufactures could be made. We had no wool, cotton, or flax.

But, after we had grown wheat and raised pork for sale, we had new difficulties in our way. Our friends were arriving each fall, with jaded teams, just about the time the long rainy season set in. The community was divided into two classes, old settlers and new, whose views and interests clashed very much. Many of the new immigrants were childish, most of them discouraged, and all of them more or less embarrassed. Upon their arrival they found that those of us who preceded them had taken up the choice locations, and they were compelled either to take those that were inferior in quality or go farther from ship navigation. There was necessarily, under the circumstances, a great hurry to select claims; and the new-comers had to travel over the country, in the rainy season, in search of homes. Their animals being poor, they found it difficult to get along as fast as they desired. Many causes combined to make them unhappy for the time being. The long rainy seasons were new to them, and they preferred the snow and frozen ground to the rain and mud. There were no hotels in the country, as there was nothing wherewith to pay the bills. The old settlers had necessarily to throw open their doors to the new immigrants, and entertain them free of charge. Our houses were small log-cabins, and our bedding was scarce. The usual mode of travel was for each one to carry his blankets with him, and sleep upon the puncheon-floor. Our families were often overworked in waiting upon others, and our provisions vanished before the keen appetites of our new guests. "They bred a famine wherever they went."

As illustrative of the then condition of things, I will relate an incident which I had from good authority. An old acquaintance of mine, whom I had known in Missouri, came to Oregon in 1844, and selected a claim on the outskirts of the settlements. He was a man of fair means, and had a large family. His place was upon the mainly traveled route which led to the valleys above and beyond him. The consequence was, that he was overwhelmed with company. He had to travel many miles to secure his supplies, and had to transport them, especially in winter, upon pack-animals. He was a man of very hospitable disposition; but the burden was so great that he concluded he could not bear it. The travelers would eat him out of house and home. He determined, under the severe pressure of these circumstances, to put up an hotel-sign. He went into the woods, cut down a tree, split out a slab some two feet long and one foot wide, shaved it off smooth on both sides with his drawing-knife, and wrote upon it with charcoal, "Entertainment," and swung it upon a pole before his door. The result was, that travelers passed by without stopping, as they had naught wherewith to pay, and were too honest to pretend to be able. My friend said that for two months he had the greatest relief. His stock of provisions lasted much longer, and he was quite easy in his circumstances. But at the end of the two months he began to be lonesome; and by the time the third month had passed he became so lonely that he took down the sign, and after that he had plenty of company.

Our new immigrants not only grumbled much about the country and climate in general, but had also much to say against those of us who had written back to our friends, giving them a description of the country. In the winter of 1843-'44 I had, while at Linnton, written some hundred and twenty-five foolscap pages of manuscript, giving a description of the journey and of the country along the route, as well as of Oregon. I had stated the exact truth, to the best of my knowledge, information, and belief; and my communications were published in the "New York Herald," and were extensively read, especially in the Western States. I therefore came in for my full share of censure. They accused me of misrepresentation.

In a letter I wrote on the Sweetwater, a tributary of the North Fork of the Platte, I stated that, up to that point, the road we had traveled was the finest natural route, perhaps, in the world. Without any regard to the place from which the letter bore date, they construed it as a description of the *entire* route. Consequently, whenever they came to any very bad road, they would most commonly say, "This is more of Burnett's fine road."

In my communications published in the "Herald," I gave as much statistical information as I could well do, giving the prices of most kinds of personal property; and, among other articles mentioned, I stated that feathers were worth 37 1/2 cents a pound. Two or three years afterward, the demand having increased faster than the supply, the price went up to 62 1/2 cents. I was therefore accused of misrepresentation in this case. They would say: "Now, Burnett, here is a plain case. You said feathers were worth 37 1/2 cents, and we find them worth 62 1/2." I would answer: "That seems to be too plain a case even for a lawyer to get around; yet I have this to say, that I did not assume to act the prophet, but only the historian. I told you what the price then was, and not what it would be two or three years later."

I remember that on one occasion, in passing a house late in the fall, I saw that a new immigrant family occupied it, from the fact that it had previously stood vacant; and I determined to call. The lady told me the name of the State from which they came, gave me other particulars in regard to the family, and asked me how long I had been in the country. Finally she inquired for my name; and, when I told her it was Burnett, she said: "We abused you a great deal on the road. I suppose we ought not to have done it, but we did do it." I could not but laugh, there was such perfect frankness in her statement. It was the whole truth, and no more. I said to her: "Madam, that makes no difference. On a trip like that some one must be abused, and it is well to be some one who is not present."

I made it a rule never to become irritated, and never to enter into any heated discussion with them in reference to the country or the journey to it. My usual plan was to listen kindly to their complaints. They often declared that the country was so poor they would return to their former homes. In such cases I would good-humoredly reply that "misery loved company; that we found ourselves in a bad fix, and wanted our friends to come here to comfort us; that, as to their going back, it was out of the question; that, if the country was as poor as they supposed, they would never be able to get back; and, if it was not so bad as they believed, they would not wish to return; and that, anyhow, we had them just where we wanted them to be, and they had better make up their minds to stand it."

At any public gathering, it was easy to distinguish the new from the old settlers.

They were lank, lean, hungry, and tough;
We were ruddy, ragged, and rough.

They were dressed in broadcloth, and wore linen-bosomed shirts and black cravats, while we wore very coarse, patched clothes; for the art of patching was understood to perfection in Oregon. But, while they dressed better than we did, we fed better than they. Of the two, we were rather the more independent. They wanted our provisions, while we wanted their materials for clothing. They, seeing our ragged condition, concluded that if they parted with their jeans, satinets, cottons, and calicoes, they would soon be as destitute as we were; and therefore they desired to purchase our provisions on credit, and keep their materials for future use. This plan did not suit us precisely. We reasoned in this way: that, if they wished to place themselves in our ruddy condition, they should incur the risk of passing into our ragged state — they should take the good and bad together. We therefore insisted upon an exchange. After much grumbling on their part, the parties ultimately came to an agreement. But in many cases the new immigrants had nothing to give in exchange, and we had to sell to them on credit.

I remember that a new immigrant purchased a place in my neighborhood one fall, and in the succeeding month of June came to my house and asked me if I had any wheat in my garner. I told him I had, but I was compelled to purchase some clothing for my family, and my wheat was the only thing I had with which I could pay for the articles we required; that I could not see how we could do without, or how else to obtain them. He said his wife and children were without anything to eat, and that he had a good growing crop, and would give me three bushels after harvest for every bushel I would let him have now. I could not withstand such an appeal, and said I would furnish him with the wheat, and would only require the same quantity after harvest.

But the state of discontent on the part of the new immigrants was temporary, and only lasted during the winter. In the spring, when the thick clouds cleared away, and the grass and flowers sprang up beneath the kindling rays of a bright Oregon sun, their spirits revived with reviving nature; and by the succeeding fall they had themselves become old settlers, and formed a part of us, their views and feelings, in the mean time, having undergone a total change.

It was interesting to observe the influence of new circumstances upon human character. Among the men who went to Oregon the year I did, some were idle, worthless young men, too lazy to work at home, and too genteel to steal; while some others were gamblers, and others were reputed thieves. But when they arrived in Oregon they were compelled to work or starve. It was a dire necessity. There were there no able relatives or indulgent friends upon whom the idle could quarter themselves, and there was little or nothing for the rogues to steal; and, if they could steal, there was no ready way by which they could escape into another community, and they could not conceal themselves in Oregon. I never saw so fine a population, as a whole community, as I saw in Oregon most of the time while I was there. They were all honest, because there was nothing to steal; they were all sober, because there was no liquor to drink; there were no misers, because there was no money to hoard; and they were all industrious, because it was work or starve.

In a community so poor, isolated, and distant, we had each one to depend upon his own individual skill and labor to make a living. My profession was that of the law, but there was nothing in my line worth attending to until some time after my arrival in Oregon. I was therefore compelled to become a farmer. But I had not only to learn how to carry on a farm by my own labor, but I had to learn how to do many other necessary things that were difficult to do. It was most difficult to procure shoes for myself and family. The Hudson's Bay Company imported its supply of shoes from England, but the stock was wholly inadequate to our wants, and we had no money to enable us to pay for them; and as yet there were no tan-yards in operation. One was commenced in my neighborhood in 1844, but the fall supply of leather was only tanned on the outside, leaving a raw streak in the center. It was undressed, not even curried. Out of this material I made shoes for myself, my eldest son, and a young hired man who was then living with me. To keep the shoes soft enough to wear through the day, it was necessary to soak them in water at night.

My father, in the early settlement of Missouri, was accustomed to tan his own leather, and make the shoes for the family. In my younger days he had taught me how to do coarse sewed work. But now I had to take the measure of the foot, make the last, fit the patterns to the last, cut out the leathers, and make the shoe. I had no last to copy from, never made one before, and had no one to show me how. I took the measures of all the family, and made what I supposed to be eight very nice lasts; and upon them I made the shoes, using tanned deer-skin for the females and small boys. The shoes were not beautiful, nor all comfortable, as they were not all good fits.

In the fall of 1846 my brother William came to Oregon, and afterward lived with me about nine months. He was a good mechanical genius, and could do well almost any kind of work. He could make a splendid last and a good boot. One day I showed him my lasts. He was too generous to wound the feelings of his elder brother by criticising his poor work. He said not a word, but in a few days thereafter he made a pair of right and left lasts for himself. I observed how he did it, and the moment the first last was about finished I saw that mine were very poor. They were almost flat, scarcely turning up at the toe at all. I quietly took my lasts and cast them into the fire, and then set to work and made an entire new set; and I never gave up the attempt until I succeeded in making not only a good last, but a good shoe.

In the course of about two years we had other tanyards in successful operation, where we could have hides tanned on shares. I had in the mean time made a trade for a small herd of cattle; and after this I had an ample supply of good leather, and upon that point I was at ease.

The greatest difficulty I had to encounter for the want of shoes was in 1844. I had sown some three acres of wheat about the first of May, and it was absolutely necessary to inclose it by the first of June to make a crop. I did not commence plowing until about the 20th of April. My team was raw, and so was I, and it required several days' trial to enable us to do good work. While I was engaged in making and hauling rails to fence in my wheat, my old boots gave out entirely, and I had no time to look for a substitute. I was worse off than I was when without a hat in Bolivar, Tennessee.

I was determined to save my wheat at any sacrifice, and I therefore went barefoot. During the first week my feet were very sore; but after that there came a shield over them, so that I could work with great ease, and go almost anywhere except among thorns.

But we had another trouble on our hands. By permission of a neighbor of ours, a sincere minister, we were allowed to occupy temporarily the log-cabin then used for a church, upon condition that I would permit him to have services there every Sunday. Our minister was always regular in his attendance, and the congregation consisted of about thirty persons. I could not well absent myself from church, as it was my duty to attend. I therefore quietly took my seat in one corner of the building, where my bare feet would not be much noticed. The congregation collected, and the services went on as usual, with the addition of some church business, which happened to come up on that occasion. The sea-breeze set in early that day, and before the church business was finished it became quite cool. Our minister was a thin, spare man, very sensitive to cold, and requested me to make a fire in the stove. I did not hesitate a moment, but went through the congregation and made the fire. They wore moccasins, and stared at my bare feet as I passed.

There was no money in the country, and the usual currency consisted in orders for merchandise upon the stores, or wheat delivered at specified points. Our community had an ample opportunity to practically learn the value of a sound circulating medium. No one who has not had that practical experience can fully appreciate the true importance of such a medium as a great labor-saving device.

A savage people, who have little or no property to sell, and very few wants to gratify, may get along with a system of barter. An Indian generally has nothing to sell but furs and peltries, and wants nothing in return but arms, ammunition, blankets, tobacco, beads, and paint. All he wants he can find at one place, and all he has to dispose of he can readily bring to the same place. But the property of a civilized race of men is so various in kind, so large in amount, and the ownership and possession change so often, that a good circulating medium is a very great if not an absolute necessity. For example, a farmer may have a pair of oxen for sale, and may want a pair of plow-horses. In case there be no circulating medium, he will have great difficulty in making an exchange. He may find a number of persons who have plow-horses for sale, but none of them may want his oxen. But should he, after much inquiry and loss of time and labor, succeed in finding some one who has a pair of plow-horses to exchange for a pair of oxen, most likely there will be a difference in value; and how shall this difference be adjusted?

In the course of my practice as a lawyer, I had received orders upon an American merchant at Oregon City, until the amount to my credit upon his books was forty-nine dollars. I called upon him to take up the amount in goods; and he said to me: "Judge, my stock is now very low, and I would suggest to you to wait until my new goods shall arrive from Honolulu. I am going there to purchase a new supply, and will return as soon as I can." I readily assented to this suggestion.

After waiting about three months I heard he had returned with his new stock; and Mrs. Burnett and myself set about making out a memorandum of what we wanted. But the great difficulty was to bring our wants within our means. After several trials we made up our memorandum, consisting mostly of dry-goods, and only six pounds of sugar. I went to Oregon City, and at once called upon the merchant. I asked him if he had any satinets? None. Any jeans? Any calico? None. Any brown cottons? None. I then asked what he had. He said tools of various kinds, such as carpenters' implements and others. He said he feared I would think the prices high, as he had to pay high prices, and must make a little profit upon his purchases. This statement no doubt was true. He had purchased in a market where the stocks were limited and prices high.

I then made a selection of several implements that I had not on my memorandum, which amounted in all to about thirteen dollars, and found the prices more than double those at Vancouver. I became tired of paying such prices for articles I could do without for the time, and inquired if he had any brown sugar, and at what price. He said plenty, at 12 1/2 cents a pound. This was the usual price, and I replied at once that I would take the balance in sugar. I went home, knowing that we had sugar enough to last for a long time, and that we could use Oregon tea. There grows among the fir timber of that country a small aromatic vine, which makes a very pleasant tea, about as good as the tea made from the sassafras-root in the Western States.

On another occasion, while I was Judge of the Supreme Court, a young hired man, my son Dwight, and myself had on our last working-shirts. It was in harvest-time, and where or how to procure others I could not tell. Still, I was so accustomed to these things that I was not much perplexed. Within a day or two a young man of my acquaintance wrote me that he desired me to unite him in marriage with a young lady, whose name he stated. I married them, and he gave me an order on a store for five dollars, with which I purchased some blue twilled cotton (the best I could get), out of which my wife made us each a shirt. The material wore well; but, having been colored with logwood, the shirts, until the color faded from them, left our skins quite blue.

I never felt more independent than I did on one occasion, in the fall of 1847. In the streets of Oregon City I met a young man with a new and substantial leather hunting-shirt, brought from the Rocky Mountains, where it had been purchased from the Indians. I said to him, "What will you take for your leather hunting-shirt? He replied, "Seven bushels of wheat." I said at once, "I will take it." I measured him out the grain, and took the article. I knew it would last me for several years. I found it a most excellent article of dress, in clear weather, for rough work. I wore it to the California gold-mines in the fall of 1848, and after my arrival there during most of the winter of 1848-'49. A nephew of mine took it with him to the mines in the spring of 1849, and it was lost to me. I regretted this loss, because I desired to preserve it as a memento of old times. It was made of the best dressed buckskin, with the flesh side out, to which the dust would not adhere; and it was easily kept neat and clean, for that reason.

For the first two years after our arrival in Oregon we were frequently without any meat for weeks at a time, and sometimes without bread, and occasionally without both bread and meat at the same time. On these occasions, if we had milk, butter, and potatoes, we were well content.

I remember, on one occasion, that several gentlemen from Oregon City called at my house in the Plains, and we had no bread. I felt pained on my wife's account, as I supposed she would be greatly mortified But she put on a cheeful smile, and gave them the best dinner she could. Oregon was a fine place for rearing domestic fowls, and we kept our chickens as a sort of reserve fund for emergencies. We had chickens, milk, butter, and potatoes for dinner; and our friends were well pleased, and laughed over the fact of our having no bread.

In May, 1845, we were entirely without anything in the house for dinner. I did not know what to do, when my wife suggested a remedy. The year before we had cultivated a small patch of potatoes, and in digging had left some in the ground, which had sprung up among the young wheat. We dug a mess of these potatoes, which sufficed us for a meal, though not very good. That year I sowed about one acre in turnips, which grew to a large size. The vegetables most easily grown in new countries are lettuce, turnips, potatoes, and squashes.

The country improved rapidly in proportion to our population. The means of education were generally limited to ordinary schools. In the course of three or four years after my arrival in Oregon, our people had so improved their places that we were quite comfortable. There was no aristocracy of wealth and very little vice. I do not think I ever saw a more happy community. We had all passed through trials that had tested and established our patience; and our condition then was so much better than that of the past that we had good cause for our content. Few persons could be found to complain of Oregon.

BECOME A CATHOLIC — MY GENERAL RULE AS TO CHARGES AGAINST ME.

In the fall of 1844 a Baptist preacher settled in my immediate neighborhood, who had the published debate between Campbell and Purcell; and, as the Catholic question was often mentioned, and as I knew so little about it, I borrowed and read the book. I had the utmost confidence in the capacity of Mr. Campbell as an able debater; but, while the attentive reading of the debate did not convince me of the entire truth of the Catholic theory, I was greatly astonished to find that so much could be said in its support. On many points, and those of great importance, it was clear to my mind that Mr. Campbell had been overthrown. Still, there were many objections to the Catholic Church, either not noticed by the Bishop, or not satisfactorily answered; and I arose from the reading of that discussion still a Protestant.

But my thoughts continually recurred to the main positions and arguments on both sides, and, the more I reflected upon the fundamental positions of the Bishop, the more force and power I found them to possess. My own reflections often afforded me answers to difficulties that at first semed insurmountable, until the question arose in my mind whether Mr. Campbell had done full justice to his side of the question. Many of his positions seemed so extreme and ill founded that I could not sanction them. All the prejudices I had, ·if any, were in his favor; but I knew that it was worse than idle to indulge prejudices when investigating any subject whatever. I was determined to be true to myself, and this could only be in finding the exact truth, and following it when known.

My mind was therefore left in a state of restless uncertainty; and I determined to examine the question between Catholics and Protestants thoroughly, so far as my limited opportunities and poor abilities would permit. In the prosecution of this design, I procured all the works on both sides within my reach, and examined them alternately side by side. This investigation occupied all my spare time for about eighteen months.

After an impartial and calm investigation, I became fully convinced of the truth of the Catholic theory, and went to Oregon City in June, 1846, to join the Old Church. There I found the heroic and saintly Father De Vos, who had spent one or more years among the Flathead Indians. He received me into the Church. The reasons for this change are substantially set forth in my work entitled "The Path which led a Protestant Lawyer to the Catholic Church," from the preface to which the foregoing statement is taken.

I was the only Catholic among my numerous living relatives. None of my ancestors on either my paternal or maternal side had been Catholics, so far as I knew. All my personal friends were either Protestants or nonprofessors, except four: Dr. McLoughlin, Dr. Long, and Mr. Pomeroy of Oregon, and Graham L. Hughes of St. Louis. Nine tenths of the people of Oregon were at that time opposed to my religion. Nearly all the Catholics of Oregon were Canadian French, in very humble circumstances, many of them being hired menial servants of the Hudson's Bay Company. I had no reason for the change from a popular to an unpopular religion but the simple love of truth; and, as I have so long borne whatever of censure may have been heaped upon me in consequence of this change, I think I can afford to die in the Old Church.

When I was a young man I was often much concerned as to what others might think of me; and at times I was deeply pained by what others did say of me. In due time, however, and after full consideration and more experience, I came to this final conclusion: that it was my duty to do what was right in itself, and to avoid so far as I could even the *appearance* of evil; and then, if others wrongfully blamed me, it would be their fault, not mine. I saw I could control myself, and was therefore responsible for my own conduct; but I could not control others, and was not responsible for their actions, so long as I did right myself, and avoided all appearance of evil. If I should make myself unhappy because other people erred in their judgment of me, then my happiness would be within their power and in their keeping. I thought it my duty to keep my happiness under my own control so far as I could. I had confidence in the good sense and justice of good men, and was perfectly willing to await their ultimate decision. When I knew I was in the right, I was able and prepared to bear the censure even of the wise and good; but I "did not hanker after it."

I never would engage in newspaper controversies or personal squabbles. If I was unjustly censured, I paid no attention to it, and gave myself no trouble about it. In this way I have mainly led a life of peace with my fellow men. I have very rarely had the sincerity of my motives called in question. The general course of the press toward me has been impartial and just.

I have never claimed to be a *liberal* man, as many people construe that almost indefinable term; but I have scrupulously sought to be just to all men. The character of a just man is enough for me. I esteem and reasonably desire the approbation of good men; but I love the right more. I can do without the first, but not the last.

But I must depart from my usual course to notice certain charges made against me by W.H. Gray in his "History of Oregon." My nephew, George H. Burnett, Esq., of Salem, Oregon, was a guest at my house in San Francisco in January, 1878, and mentioned to me the fact that such charges had been made. I had never seen the work at that time. In May, 1878, I procured and read the book. I notice these charges because they are in the form of *historical* facts or opinions. Had Mr. Gray made these charges verbally or in a newspaper article, I should never have noticed them in any form.

MISSTATEMENTS OF W. H. GRAY.

On pages 374-'5 Mr. Gray, in speaking of the members of the Legislative Committee of 1844, says:

Peter H. Burnett was a lawyer from Missouri, who came to Oregon to seek his fortune, as well as a religion that would pay best and give him the most influence; which in the Legislative Committee was sufficient to induce that body to pay no attention to any organic law or principle laid down for the government of the settlements. In fact, he asserted that there were no constitutional provisions laid down or adopted by the people in general convention at Champoeg the year previous. Mr. Burnett was unquestionably the most intelligent lawyer then in the country. He was a very ambitious man — smooth, deceitful, and insinuating in his manners.

As regards the imputation of improper motives to me in the above extract, if intended as the assertions of fact, such assertions are untrue; and, if intended as expressions of opinions, such opinions are mistaken. These charges are made not only without proof, but against both the evidence and the fact.

I went to Oregon for three purposes:

1. To assist in building up a great American community on the Pacific coast. 2. To restore the health of Mrs. Burnett. 3. To become able to pay my debts.

Before I became a believer in the truth of the Christian religion, I had sought fortune with avidity; but, after that fundamental change in my views, I ceased to pursue riches, and my only *business* object was to make a decent living for my family, and pay what I owed. Considering the large amount of my indebtedness, I could not have been so visionary as to suppose I could accomplish in distant and isolated Oregon more than the three objects mentioned.

As regards my change of religion, and the motives which led to it, I have already stated the simple truth. At the time I joined the Old Church I was independent in my pecuniary circumstances, so far as a *decent living* was concerned. I had a claim of six hundred and forty acres of most excellent land, well improved, and well stocked with domestic animals and fowls. With the industrious and sober habits of myself and family, we were secure of a good living.

As to my influence in the Committee, it could not possibly have arisen from any change of religion, for these simple and conclusive reasons: that I was then a Protestant, without any idea of becoming a Catholic, and every member was opposed to the Catholic religion. My influence arose from the fact of my qualifications and my good character. Waldo, McCarver, Gilmore, and Keizer had traveled with me across the Plains, and had seen me fully tested in that severe school of human nature. Waldo knew me by reputation, and Gilmore personally, in Missouri.

As to the assertion that I was "very ambitious," the fact is not correctly stated. I had a reasonable desire for distinction, but never so great as to induce me to sacrifice my personal independence or compromise my true dignity. I never sought any position under the provisional government of Oregon, and I do not remember to have personally asked any citizen to vote for me. I was elected a member of the legislative body in 1844 and again in 1848, and Judge of the Supreme Court in 1845, without any serious efforts on my part. I have been a candidate before the people six times: once in Missouri, twice in Oregon, and three times in California; and I was successful in every case. I resigned the office of District Attorney in Missouri to go to Oregon in 1843, and my seat in the Legislature of Oregon in 1848 to come to California, and the office of Governor of this State in January, 1851, when the salary was ten thousand dollars per annum. I was appointed on the 14th of August, 1848, by President Polk, one of the Justices of the Supreme Court of the Territory of Oregon. My commission did not reach me until the spring of 1849, in California. This appointment I declined, as I could not accept it and pay my debts. This was done before any movement was made to organize a State government in California, and before I had any expectation of being Governor. I can safely say that the remark of President Jefferson, in regard to the office-holders of his time, that "deaths were few and resignations none," can not justly apply to me.

As to the charge of being deceitful, it is the precise opposite of the truth. No man of decent manners and good character ever called upon me without receiving my candid opinion, where I had any mature judgment upon the question. I am not a disputatious spirit, ready to engage in a wordy quarrel upon any and every subject, however trivial; but in regard to all important subjects, on all proper occasions, I am frank to speak just what I think.

As to the falsity of all these charges, I can refer to all good men who have known me longest and best. I lived in Missouri some twenty-one years, and have resided in California nearly thirty years, and I appeal to all good men who have known me, without regard to their religion or place of nativity.

THE QUESTION WHETHER THERE WERE ANY CONSTITU-TIONAL PROVISIONS IN THE LAWS OF 1843 CONSIDERED.

The Legislative Committee of 1844 did maintain the position that there were no constitutional provisions adopted by the people at their mass meeting, July 5, 1843.

It appears that there were two publications claiming to be copies of these laws: one by Charles Saxton, published in 1846, and the other by the compiler of the "Oregon Archives" in 1853. (Gray's "Oregon," 352.) I shall use the copy given by Mr. Gray, as he ought to know best, and which is found in his history, beginning on page 353.

At a meeting of the people held May 2, 1843, at Champoeg, the proposition to establish a provisional government was put to vote; and, upon a division, there were found to be fifty-two for and fifty against it. (Gray's "Oregon," 279.)

At that meeting, Robert Moore, David Hill, Robert Shortess, Alanson Beers, W.H. Gray, Thomas J. Hubbard, James A. o'Neal, Robert Newell, and William Dougherty were chosen to act as a Legislative Committee, and instructed to make their report on the 5th of July, 1843, at Champoeg. (Gray, 280-'81.)

On the 5th of July, 1843, said Committee made their report, which was adopted at the mass meeting of citizens at Champoeg. The question whether there were any, and, if so, what constitutional provisions in the laws adopted at said meeting, was one that admitted of discussion; but, upon as full a consideration of the subject as our limited time and opportunities allowed, we became satisfied that there were none.In their report the Committee say, "The Legislative Committee recommend that the following *organic laws* be adopted." The term *organic* does not necessarily mean constitutional; because, whether the laws were constitutional or not, they were equally organic. We were aware of the fact that there were no lawyers among the members of the Committee, and that there were then no law-books in the country, except one copy of the Statutes of Iowa; but we knew that the members were Americans, and that all Americans competent to read a newspaper must know that the fundamental laws of the United States and of the several States were called *constitutions*; and hence we supposed that the Committee would surely have used the plain, ordinary, and appropriate term *constitution* to designate their fundamental law, had they intended it as such.

But, besides the want of proper language to designate a constitution, the nature of the laws themselves seemed to show a different intent. From the face of the Code, no one could tell where the constitutional laws ended and the statutory began. It was either all constitution or all statute. All were adopted at the same public meeting, and were recommended by the same Committee. That Committee "recommended that the following *organic laws* be adopted." Now, whatever laws were recommended by them were all of the *same* character, or they failed to distinguish one portion from another. There being no mode of amendment provided, these laws, if constitutional, could only be amended in violation of their own terms; that is, by revolution. If considered as statutory provisions, then there was a plain mode of amendment provided in Article VI., section 2, which enacts that "the legislative power shall be vested in a committee of nine persons, to be elected by the qualified electors at the annual election."

The code goes into the most minute provisions, such as fixing the fees of the Recorder and Treasurer, and for solemnizing marriage. It also contains a militia law, and a law on land claims, and a resolution making the statute laws of Iowa the law of Oregon. Such provisions, in their very nature, are but statutory.

Considering the "organic laws" (so named by the Committee) as composing a constitution, not amendable except by revolution, the Legislative Committee of 1844 had nothing to do worth mentioning. In this view it was a useless body, constituted for an idle and vain purpose. We came to the conclusion that our Legislative Committee had practical legislative power, and that it was our duty to exercise it. While we were not disposed to make useless changes, we were obliged to amend the code in many respects, as will be seen from what follows.

Article VII., section 2 vests "the judicial power in a Supreme Court, consisting of the supreme judge and two justices of the peace, a Probate Court, and Justice Court." If a majority of the persons composing the Supreme Court, under this quaint and original theory, could make the decision, then the two justices of the peace could overrule the Supreme Judge. If, on the contrary, it required the unanimous consent of all three, then there would often be no decision at all.

Our Committee amended this by the act of June 27, 1844. The first section of the second article of that act is as follows: "Section

1. The judicial power shall be vested in the Circuit Courts and as many justices of the peace as shall from time to time be appointed or elected according to law." The second section provides for the election of *one* judge, and makes it his duty to hold two terms of the Circuit Court in each county, at such times and places as shall be directed by law; and the third section fixes the jurisdiction of the Circuit Courts, including probate powers.

The fifth article of section 2 vested the executive power in a committee of three persons. This provision was adopted not because it met the approbation of the Legislative Committee of 1843, but from necessity, as their instructions were against a governor (Gray's "Oregon," 349). We repealed this provision, and vested the executive power in a single person.

Article XVII. All male persons of the age of sixteen years and upward, and all females of the age of fourteen years and upward, shall have the right to marry. When either of the parties shall be under twenty-one years of age, the consent of the parents or guardians of such minors shall be necessary to the validity of such matrimonial engagement. Every ordained minister of the gospel, of any religious denomination, the supreme judge, and all justices of the peace, are hereby authorized to solemize marriage according to law, to have the same recorded, and pay the recorder's fee. The legal fee for marriage shall be one dollar, and for recording fifty cents.

This extreme law made the marriage of persons under the age of twenty-one years without the consent of their parents or guardians *invalid*, and therefore void; thus subjecting the young people to the charge and consequences of living in a state of adultery, and their innocent children to all the consequences of bastardy.

Our Committe passed the following act:

An Act amendatory of the Act regarding Marriage. Section 1. That all males of the age of sixteen years and upward, and all females of the age of twelve and upward, shall be deemed competent to enter into the contract of marriage. Sec. 2. That when either of the parties about to enter into the marriage union shall be minors, the male under the age of twenty-one years, or the female under the age of eighteen, no person authorized to solemnize the rites of matrimony shall do so without the consent of the parent or guardian of such minor; and in case such person shall solemnize such marriage without the consent of the parent or guardian of such minor, he shall be liable to pay such parent or guardian the sum of one hundred dollars, to be recovered by action of debt or assumpsit before the proper court: *Provided*, however, that the want of such consent shall not invalidate such marriage.

Sec. 3. That all acts and parts of acts coming in conflict with this act be and the same are hereby repealed.

The Legislative Committee of 1843 was properly called a *committee*, because its duty was to prepare a code to be submitted to the mass meeting of citizens held on the 5th of July, 1843, for their approval or rejection; the *legislative* power being exercised by the people themselves on that occasion. But, as already stated, the legislative power was vested by the sixth article, section 2, of the laws of 1843, in a committee of nine persons. To call a legislative body a *committee* was a misnomer; and we amended that provision by vesting the legislative power in a House of Representatives composed of members elected annually by the people.

The laws of 1843 made no provision for the support of the government, except putting in circulation a subscription paper as follows:

We, the subscribers, hereby pledge ourselves to pay annually to the Treasurer of Oregon Territory the sum affixed to our respective names, for defraying the expenses of the government: *Provided*, That in all cases each individual subscriber may at any time withdraw his name from said subscription, upon paying up all arrearages and notifying the Treasurer of the colony of such desire to withdraw.

Our Committee were fully satisfied that no government could be practically administered without taxation; and we therefore passed a revenue law containing twelve sections.

The law of 1843 in relation to land claims is as follows:

Article I. Any person now holding or hereafter wishing to establish a claim to land in this Territory, shall designate the extent of his claim by natural boundaries, or by marks at the corners and upon the lines of said claim, recorded in the office of the Territorial Recorder, in a book to be kept by him for that purpose, within twenty days from the of making said claim: *Provided*, That those who shall be already in possession of land shall be allowed one year from the passage of this act, to file a description of their claims in the Recorder's office.

Art. II. All claimants shall, within six months from the time of recording their claims, make permanent improvement upon the same, by building or inclosing, and also become occupant upon said claims within one year of the date of said record.

Art. III. No individual shall be allowed to hold a claim of more than one square mile, or six hundred and forty acres, in a square of oblong form, according to the natural situation of the premises, nor shall any individual be able to hold more than one claim at the same time. Any person complying with the provisions of these ordinances shall be entitled to the same process against trespass as in other cases provided by law.

Art. IV. No person shall be entitled to hold such a claim upon city or town lots, extensive water privileges, or other situations necessary for the transaction of mercantile or manufacturing operations: *Provided*, That nothing in these laws shall be so construed as to affect any claim of any mission of a religious character made prior to this time, of an extent not more than six miles square.

Our Committee passed the following act, June 25, 1844:

An Act in relation to Land Claims.

Section 1. That all persons who have heretofore made, or shall hereafter make, permanent improvements upon a place, with a *bona fide* intention of occupying and holding the same for himself, and shall continue to occupy and cultivate the same, shall be entitled to hold six hundred and forty acres, and shall hold only one claim at the same time: *Provided*, A man may hold town lots in addition to his claim.

Sec. 2. That all claims hereafter made shall be in a square form, if the nature of the ground shall permit; and in case the situation will not permit, shall be in an oblong form.

Sec. 3. That in all cases where claims are already made, and in all cases where there are agreed lines between the parties occupying adjoining tracts, such claims shall be valid to the extent of six hundred and forty acres, although not in a square or oblong form.

Sec. 4. That in all cases where claims shall hereafter be made, such permanent improvements shall be made within two months from the time of taking up such claim, and the first settler or his successor shall be deemed to hold the prior right.

Sec. 5. That no person shall hold a claim under the provisions of this act except free males over the age of eighteen, who would be entitled to vote if of lawful age, and widows: *Provided*, No married man shall be debarred from holding a claim under this act because he is under the age of eighteen.

Sec. 6. That all laws heretofore passed in regard to land claims be and the same are hereby repealed.

Sec. 7. That all persons complying with the provisions of this act shall be deemed in possession to the extent of six hundred and forty acres or less, as the case may be, and shall have the remedy of forcible entry and detainer against intruders, and the action of trespass against trespassers.

On December 24, 1844, we passed the following explanatory and amendatory act:

Section 1. That the word "occupancy," in said act, shall be so construed as to require the claimant to either personally reside upon his claim himself, or to occupy the same by the personal residence of his tenant.

Sec. 2. That any person shall be authorized to take six hundred acres of his claim in the prairie, and forty acres in the timber, and such parts of his claim need not be adjoining to each other.

Sec. 3. That when two persons take up their claims jointly, not exceeding twelve hundred and eighty acres, they may hold the same jointly for the term of one year, by making the improvements required by said act upon any part of said claim, and may hold the same longer than one year if they make the said improvements within the year upon each six hundred and forty acres.

The land law of 1844 dispensed with recording of claims, because, under the then existing condition of the country, it was an onerous burden upon the new immigrant. The great body of the immigration arrived late in the fall, just as the rainy season set in; and to require each locater of a claim to travel from twenty to one hundred miles to the Recorder's office, and return through an Oregon winter, was indeed a harsh condition. Under the land law of .1843 the old settler was allowed one year within which to record his claim, while the new settlers were only allowed twenty days. Besides, recording a claim without a proper survey was of very doubtful utility, as parties would be very apt to include within their lines more than six hundred and forty acres.

By the land law of 1843, as will be seen, *all* persons of every age, sex, or condition, could hold claims. If a man had several sons, he could hold one claim for himself and each of his sons one, though under age; and, as each claimant had six months within which to make his improvements, and one year within which to become an occupant from the date of the record, the act left open the door to speculation and monopoly to a grievous extent. A man, having a number of children, could record one claim in the name of each child one month before the annual arrival of the new immigrants, and that record would hold the land for six months; thus forcing the late comers either to go farther for locations or purchase these claims of his children. Besides, this act did not require the locater to make his improvements with the *bona fide* intention of occupying and holding the claim for himself, but only required the improvements to be made; thus allowing claims to be made for speculative purposes.

But one of the most objectionable provisions of the land law of 1843 was the proviso allowing each mission six miles square, or thirty-six sections of land. From what Mr. Gray says, page 344, it appears that this proviso was adopted to gain the support of those connected with the Methodist and Catholic missions; as, without such support, it was feared the attempt to establish a government at that time would fail. The Committee of 1843, in their short experience, learned one great truth: that civil government is a *practical* science; and that, while a true statesman can adapt his legislation to existing circumstances, he can not create or control them; and for that reason he is often compelled to choose between evils, and to support measures that his individual judgment will not approve. Our Legislative Committee of 1844 were placed in more independent circumstances; and, having no fear of the mission influence, we repealed this proviso.

THE LEGISLATIVE COMMITTEE OF 1844 — MISTAKES OF W. H. GRAY.

On page 383 Mr. Gray, speaking of the Legislative Committee of 1844, says:

"In fact, the whole proceedings seemed only to mix up and confuse the people; so much so that some doubted the existence of any legal authority in the country, and the leading men of the immigration of 1843 denounced the organization as a missionary arrangement to secure the most valuable farming lands in the country."

The writer is correct as to the fact of confusion and opposition among the people, but most sadly mistaken as to the true cause. It was not the measures passed by the Legislative Committee of 1844, but the law of 1843, that caused the confusion and opposition. It is very true that many of "the leading men of the immigration of 1843 denounced the organization as a missionary arrangement to secure the best farming lands in the country." They had much apparentreason for their opposition, and that reason was found in the laws of 1843, especially in the proviso allowing each mission six miles square, and not in the land law of 1844, which repealed this objectionable proviso. Whatever else may be said against the laws of 1844, they were plain, simple, and consistent as a whole, and could not have produced the confusion mentioned.

The first time I was in Oregon City, to the best of my recollection, was when I went there to take my seat in the Legislative Committee in June, 1844. Previous to that time I do not remember to have seen the laws of 1843. After all the examination I could give them, I saw that no regular and efficient government could be sustained without a revenue; that no certain and reliable revenue could be had without taxation; that no system of taxation could be enforced unless the great and overwhelming majority of the people were satisfied with the government, and that such majority would not support the organization unless they believed they were receiving an equivalent in the form of protection for the money they paid in the shape of taxes. Many good men doubted our legal right to organize any government. Our object was to gain the consent of *all* good men; and, to do this, we must make good laws. Of course, the bad would oppose all government.

In consulting upon our then condition, we were for a time much perplexed to know what peaceable course to pursue, in order to secure the consent of all good men to our organization. We knew that Americans were devotedly attached to two things: land and the privilege of voting. Our Committee, therefore, passed an act to provide by taxation the means necessary to support the government, the fourth section of which was as follows: "Sec. 4. That any person refusing to pay tax, as in this act required, shall have no benefit of the laws of Oregon, and shall be disqualified from voting at any election in this country."

By this provision we plainly said to each citizen substantially as follows: "If you are not willing to pay your proportion of the expenses of this government, you can not sue in our courts or vote at our elections, but you must remain an outlaw. If any one should squat or trespass on your claim, or refuse to pay you what he owes, you can have no protection from our organization. If you can do without our assistance, we certainly can do without yours."

This provision very soon had its legitimate effect. As the elections approached, those who had been opposed began to doubt, and finally yielded. The friends of the organization were active, kind, and wise in their course toward those opposed. When one opposed to the government would state that fact, some friend would kindly remind him that his claim was liable to be "jumped," and that he could not alone defend his rights against the violent and unprincipled; and that it was a desolate and painful condition for a citizen, in a civilized community, to be an *outlaw*.

After the laws passed by the Legislative Committee of 1844 became known, there was no serious opposition anywhere. It is my solemn opinion that the organization could not have been kept up under the laws of 1843.

On page 375, Mr. Gray, speaking of the Legislative Committee of 1844, says:

"On motion of Mr. Lovejoy (another lawyer), the several members were excused from producing their credentials."

This statement is true, so far as it goes; but, without the explanatory facts, it might convey a false impression. The laws of 1843 made no provision as to the manner of conducting elections, except by adopting the laws of Iowa; and as there was but one copy in the country, and this was the first election held in Oregon, and as two thirds of the voters were late immigrants, the various officers of the election knew nothing of their duties, and gave no credentials to the members elect; and, of course, they could produce none. We knew that we had been fairly elected, and our respective constituents also knew the fact, and no one was found to dispute it; and, as credentials are only *evidence* of the fact of the election of the person mentioned, we had in this case the next best evidence to prove our election. We did the best we could under the circumstances.

"Such being the composition of the Legislative Committee of Oregon in 1844, it is not surprising that interests of classes and cliques should find advocates, and that the absolute wants of the country should be neglected. The whole time of the session seems to have been taken up in the discussion of personal bills." (Page 378.)

I find it difficult to justly characterize this sweeping misstatement.

The two sessions of the Committee of 1844 occupied together fifteen to seventeen days; and in that time we passed forty-three bills, some of them of considerable length, and most of them of general importance. Among these forty-three acts there were not exceeding eight that could be properly termed personal, viz.: act granting Hugh Burns a right to keep a public ferry; act authorizing Robert Moore to establish and keep a ferry; act to authorize John McLoughlin to construct a canal around the Willamette Falls; act for the relief of John Connor; act appointing Jesse Applegate engineer; act authorizing L. H. Judson and W. H. Wilson to construct a mill-race in Champoeg County; act amending the several acts regulating ferries; act for the relief of J. L. Meek.

These acts were all just in themselves, and some of them of public importance. Public ferries are public conveniences. The act to authorize John McLoughlin to construct a canal enabled him to bring the water to propel his extensive flour-mill, and was of much public benefit. The act for the relief of John Connor was a short act of one section, remitting a fine and restoring him to citizenship. The act appointing Jesse Applegate

engineer authorized him to survey a route for a canal at the expense of J. E. Long, and report the result to the next session of the Legislature. The act authorizing Judson & Wilson to construct a mill-race was of a similar nature to the one in regard to John

McLoughlin. The act to amend the several acts regulating ferries simply fixed the rate of toll of the two ferries across the Willamette River, at Oregon City. The act for the relief of J. L. Meek is a short one, giving him further time to finish the collection of the revenue for the year 1844.

The acts of the Legislative Committee of 1844 will fill some thirty printed pages, while the laws of 1843 only occupy seven pages of Gray's "History." If we spent a part of our time in the discussion of personal bills, we passed but a few of them, and did a large amount of other legislative work.

"The proposed constitutional revision was also strongly recommended by the Executive Committee, and the Legislative Committee went through the farce of calling a convention, and increased the number of representatives, and called it a Legislature." (Page 383.)

The Executive Committee, in their communication to our Committee, dated December 16, 1844, say:

"We would advise that provision be made by this body for the framing and adoption of a constitution for Oregon previous to the next annual election, which may serve as a more thorough guide to her officers and a more firm basis of her laws."

It will be seen that, while the Executive Committee recommended that provision should be made for the framing and adoption of a constitution previous to the then next annual election, they did not suggest the *mode* in which this should be done. Our Legislative Committee thought that a convention, composed of delegates elected by the people for the *sole* and *only* purpose of framing the fundamental law, was the American and the proper mode. When the people come to choose delegates to a constitutional convention, they are very apt to duly appreciate the great importance of the work to be done, and will therefore generally select the best and most competent men for that great purpose. The body that forms a constitution should have but *one* task to accomplish, for the simple and conclusive reason that nothing is more difficult than to frame a good constitution. The greatest statesmen and the mightiest intellects among men have essentially differed as to the true theory of a constitution. The members of a constitutional body should not have their attention distracted by ordinary statutory legislation. A *perfect* constitution has never yet been framed, and, most likely, never will be.

While we could not see the great and immediate *necessity* of a constitution for mere temporary government, we thought that, if the object sought was necessary at all, then the work should be well and thoroughly done, so that our constitution would be an honor to our new country. Believing, as we did, that a constitutional convention was the *only* appropriate and competent body to frame a constitution that would stand the test of fair criticism, and be beneficial in its practical operation, and not seeing any pressing necessity for immediate action, we did *not* go "through the farce of calling a convention," as asserted by the author; but we passed the following act, December 24, 1844:

> Section 1. That the Executive Committee shall, in the manner prescribed by law for notifying elections in Oregon, notify the inhabitants of all the respective counties qualified to vote for members of the Legislature at their next annual election, to give in their votes for or against the call of a convention.
>
> Sec. 2. The said votes shall be in open meeting received, assorted, and counted, and a true return thereof made to the Executive Committee, agreeable to the requisitions of the law regulating elections.
>
> Sec. 3. It shall be the duty of the Executive to lay the result of the said vote before the Legislative Committee for their information.

While we had our doubts as to the necessity of a constitution for a mere temporary government (which we then had every reason to believe would last only a year or two), we thought it but just to submit the question of calling a convention to the people for their decision. It is usual to submit such a question to the people, as was lately done in California.

The treaty of June 15, 1846, between Great Britain and the United States, settled the question of sovereignty over Oregon in favor of our country; and the act of Congress creating a Territorial government was passed August 14, 1848. The treaty was delayed beyond our reasonable expectations; and the creation of a Territorial organization was postponed by the Mexican war, which war was not foreseen by our Committee in December, 1844.

We did increase the number of representatives from nine to thirteen, and we really thought we were moderate in this respect. According to Mr. Gray's estimate, the immigration of 1843 amounted to eight hundred and seventy-five persons, and the whole population at the end of that year to about twelve hundred people. (Pages 360-'61.) If, then, some three hundred and twenty-five persons were entitled, under the laws of 1843, to nine members in the Legislative Committee, how many representatives should twelve hundred have had under the law of 1844? We only increased the number of members from nine to thirteen, when the same ratio of representation to population would have given us twenty-seven. We did call the law-making body of Oregon a Legislature, and left off the word "Committee" for reasons already stated.

Chapter V

THE ACT IN REGARD TO SLAVERY AND FREE NEGROES AND MULATTOES — MISREPRESENTATIONS OF W. H. GRAY.

Mr. Gray, in speaking of the Legislative Committee of 1844, says:

"There was one inhuman act passed by this Legislative Committee, which should stamp the names of its supporters with disgrace and infamy." (Page 378.)

"The principal provisions of this bill were, that in case a colored man was brought to the country by any master of a vessel, he must give bonds to take him away again or be fined; and in case the negro was found, or came here from any quarter, the sheriff was to catch him and flog him forty lashes at a time, till he left the country." (Page 378.)

"The principles of Burnett's bill made it a crime for a white man to bring a negro to the country, and a crime for a negro to come voluntarily; so that in any case, if he were found in the country he was guilty of a crime, and punishment or slavery was his doom." (Page 379.)

"At the adjourned session in December we find the Executive urging the Legislative Committee . . . . to amend their act relative to the corporal punishment of the blacks," etc. (Page 379.)

"To the honor of the country, Peter H. Burnett's negro-whipping law was never enforced in a single instance against a white or black man, as no officer of the provisional government felt it incumbent upon himself to attempt to enforce it." (Page 383.)

This is all the information given by Mr. Gray as to the provisions of this act, and nothing is said as to its amendment. The act is as follows:

An Act *in regard to Slavery and Free Negroes and Mulattoes.*
Be it enacted by the Legislative Committee of Oregon as follows:

> Section 1. That slavery and involuntary servitude shall be
> for ever prohibited in Oregon.

Sec. 2. That in all cases where slaves shall have been, or shall hereafter be, brought into Oregon, the owners of such slaves respectively shall have the term of three years from the introduction of such slaves to remove them out of the country.

Sec. 3. That if such owners of slaves shall neglect or refuse to remove such slaves from the country within the time specified in the preceding section, such slaves shall be free.

Sec. 4. That when any free negro or mulatto shall have come to Oregon, he or she (as the case may be), if of the age of eighteen or upward, shall remove from and leave the country within the term of two years for males and three years for females from the passage of this act; and that if any free negro or mulatto shall hereafter come to Oregon, if of the age aforesaid, he or she shall quit and leave the country within the term of two years for males and three years for females from his or her arrival in the country.

Sec. 5. That if such free negro or mulatto be under the age aforesaid, the terms of time specified in the preceding section shall begin to run when he or she shall arrive at such age.

Sec. 6. That if any such free negro or mulatto shall fail to quit the country as required by this act, he or she may be arrested upon a warrant issued by some justice of the peace, and, if guilty upon trial before such justice, shall receive upon his or her bare back not less than twenty nor more than thirty-nine stripes, to be inflicted by the constable of the proper county.

Sec 7. That if any free negro or mulatto shall fail to quit the country within the term of six months after receiving such stripes, he or she shall again receive the same punishment once in every six months until he or she shall quit the country.

Sec. 8. That when any slave shall obtain his or her freedom, the time specified in the fourth section shall begin to run from the time when such freedom shall be obtained.

United States Of America. State Of Oregon, Secretary's Office. Salem, *June* 10, 1878.

I, S. F. Chadwick, Secretary of the State of Oregon, do hereby certify that I am the custodian of the Great Seal of the State of Oregon. That the foregoing copy of original bill for an act in regard to slavery and free negroes and mulattoes passed the Legislative Committee of the Territory of Oregon June 26, 1844, has been by me compared with the original bill for an act, etc., on file in this office, and said copy is a correct transcript there-from, and of the whole of the said original bill.

Seal. In witness whereof, I have hereto set my hand and affixed the Great Seal of the State of Oregon, the day and year above written.

S. F. Chadwick, Secretary of the State of Oregon. By Thomas B. Jackson, Assistant Secretary of State.

The Executive Committee, in their communication to the Legislative Committee, dated December 16, 1844, made this recommendation:

"We would recommend that the act passed by this Assembly in June last, relative to blacks and mulattoes, be so amended as to exclude corporal punishment, and require bonds for good behavior in its stead." ("Oregon Laws and Archives," 58.)

At the December session I introduced the following bill, which was passed December 19, 1844:

AN ACT *amendatory of an Act passed June 26, 1844, in regard to slavery and for other purposes.*

Be it enacted by the Legislative Committee of Oregon as follows:

Section 1. That the sixth and seventh sections of said act are hereby repealed.

Sec. 2. That if any such free negro or mulatto shall fail to quit and leave the country, as required by the act to which this is amendatory, he or she may be arrested upon a warrant issued by some justice of the peace; and if guilty upon trial before such justice had, the said justice shall issue his order to any officer competent to execute process, directing said officer to give ten days' public notice, by at least four written or printed advertisements, that he will publicly hire out such free negro or mulatto to the lowest bidder, on a day and at a place therein specified. On the day and at the place mentioned in said notice, such officer shall expose such free negro or mulatto to public hiring; and the person who will obligate himself to remove such free negro or mulatto from the country for the shortest term of service, shall enter into a bond with good and sufficient security to Oregon, in a penalty of at least one thousand dollars, binding himself to remove said negro or mulatto out of the country within six months after such service shall expire; which bond shall be filed in the clerk's office in the proper county; and upon failure to perform the conditions of said bond, the attorney prosecuting for Oregon shall commence a suit upon a certified copy of such bond in the circuit court against such delinquent and his sureties.

It will be readily seen how much the *original* act differs from Mr. Gray's statement of its substance.

Not a word is said in the original act about the criminality of the master of a vessel in bringing a colored man into the country. The assertion that "the sheriff was to catch the negro and flog him forty lashes at a time, until he left the country," is not only untrue, but the statement conveys the idea that the sheriff was *himself* to be the sole judge, both as to the guilt of the negro and as to how often the flogging should be repeated. The act, on the contrary, required a judicial trial before a justice of the peace, and that the punishment should only be inflicted in obedience to his order by a constable. The general right of appeal to a higher court existed in these, as in other cases, under section 3, Article II., of the "Act regulating the Judiciary and for other purposes."

The statement that the principles of the original act "made it a crime for a white man to bring a negro to the country" is equally untrue, as will be readily seen. A crime is an offense for which the party may be arrested, tried, convicted, and punished; and there is no provision in the act authorizing the arrest of a white man for any act whatever.

It is perfectly clear that Mr. Gray either willfully misrepresented the original act, or attempted to state its substance from memory; and if the latter be true, he misrepresented the measure, and made it much worse than it really was. There can be no excuse for the misrepresentation of an act by a grave historian, especially one that he condemns in the harshest language, when he has easy access to the act itself.

But he not only essentially misrepresents the original act itself, but entirely ignores the amendatory bill; and does it in such a way as to increase the censure of the Legislative Committee of 1844. There are two modes of falsehood: false statement of fact, and false suppression of the truth. The historian first misrepresents the substance of the original act, then informs the reader that the Executive urged its amendment, and then suppresses the fact that the act was amended. This mode of historical misstatement and suppression left the reader to say to himself, "These men first passed an act containing objectionable provisions, and then obstinately refused to amend, when their attention was urgently called to the error." Throughout his history of this act, he represents it as *unamended* and as in full force according to its own terms; and his last words in regard to it are, that "Burnett's negro-whipping law was never enforced in a single instance, against a white or black man, as no officer of the provisional government felt it incumbent upon himself to attempt to enforce it."

It will be seen, by an inspection of the original act itself, that it was *prospective*, and that not a single case could possibly arise under it until the expiration of *two years after its passage*; and that no officer was required to act until he was commanded to do so by the regular warrant or order of a justice of the peace. In the mean time, and eighteen months *before* a single case could possibly arise under the act, it was amended by the very *same* body that passed the original bill, and at the instance of the very *same* member who introduced it.

An act that is simply prospective, and does not take effect until two years after the date of its passage, is an incomplete measure, liable to be amended at any time before it goes into operation; and, if amended before any one suffers any injury from its erroneous provisions, those provisions are as if they never had been. It is like a bill imperfect when first introduced by a member of a legislative body, and so amended by the author, before its final passage, as to remove its objectionable features. In such case, no sensible man would censure the introducer for mistakes *he himself had corrected.* All that could be said is, that the second sober thought of the member was better than his first hasty thought.

It was substantially so in this case. In the hurry of the June session of 1844 I could not think of any other mode of enforcing the act but the one adopted; but by the December session of 1844 I had found another and less objectionable remedy, and promptly adopted it. This remedy was not the one urged by the Executive Committee, as will easily be seen. Neither myself nor the other members who voted for the original bill are responsible for the objectionable features of the measure because we ourselves corrected the error. I maintain as true this general proposition: that a person who commits a mistake, and then corrects it himself, before any one suffers in consequence of it, deserves commendation rather than censure; because the act of correction shows a love of justice, and a magnanimous willingness to *admit* and *correct* error. All the intense indignation of the historian is, therefore, thrown away upon an imaginary evil, about which he is as much mistaken as the girl that wept over the imaginary death of her imaginary infant.

On page 378 the historian gives, *professedly* from the Journal, the yeas and nays upon the final passage of the original bill, as follows: "Yeas, Burnett, Gilmore, Keizer, Waldo, Newell, and Mr. Speaker McCarver — 6; Nays, Lovejoy and Hill — 2." He then informs us, as already stated, that the Executive urged the amendment of the act at the December session, 1844; and then, on pages 380-'3, gives the communication of the Executive Committee in full. Now, as he had the Journal before him, why did he not follow it up to the short December session, and ascertain what the Legislative Committee had done, if anything, in regard to amending this act?

His history of the proceedings of the Committee of 1844 is very short; but, concise as it is, it is full of flagrant misrepresentations. There was one act, however, that he affirmatively approved; and yet, so great was his prejudice, that he wrongfully imputes a bad motive for a confessedly good act. He says, on page 379, "Mr. Burnett claimed great credit for getting up a prohibitory liquor law, and made several speeches in favor of sustaining it, that being a popular measure among a majority of the citizens."

All our legislation under the provisional government was based upon the settled conviction that Oregon would be the first American State on the Pacific. We considered ourselves as the founders of a new State of the great American Union.

At the time this measure was passed, each State had the constitutional right to determine who should be citizens, and who residents. Any person born on the soil of a State had the natural, moral, and legal right to a residence within that State, while conducting himself properly; because the place of one's birth is an accidental circumstance, over which he can have no control. But, for the very reason that every human being has the right of domicile in the place of his nativity, he is not, *as a matter of right*, entitled to a residence in another community. If that other community denies him the privilege of such residence, it denies him no *right*, natural or acquired, but only refuses a *favor* asked. The territory of a State belongs to its people, as if they constituted one family; and no one not a native has a right to complain that he is not allowed to form one of this family. Although every one, under the broad and enlarged principles of law and justice, has the right to quit his original domicile at his pleasure, he has not the equal right to acquire a new residence in another community against its consent. "The bird has the right to leave its parent-nest," but has not, for that reason, the equal right to occupy the nest of another bird. A man may *demand* his rights, and justly complain when they are denied; but he can not demand *favors*, and can not reasonably complain when they are refused.

The principle is no doubt correct that when a State, for reasons satisfactory to itself, denies the right of suffrage and office to a certain class, it is sometimes the best humanity also to deny the privilege of residence. If the prejudices or the just reasons of a community are so great that they can not or will not trust a certain class with those privileges that are indispensable to the improvement and elevation of such class, it is most consistent, in some cases, to refuse that class a residence. Placed in a degraded and subordinate political and social position, which continually reminds them of their inferiority, and of the utter hopelessness of all attempts to improve their condition as a class, they are left without adequate *motive* to waste their labor for that improvement which, when attained, brings them no reward. To have such a class of men in their midst is injurious to the dominant class itself, as such a degraded and practically defenseless condition offers so many temptations to tyrannical abuse. One of the great objections to the institution of slavery was its bad influence upon the governing race.

Had I foreseen the civil war, and the changes it has produced, I would not have supported such a measure. But at the time I did not suppose such changes could be brought about; and the *fundamental* error was *then* found in the organic laws of Oregon adopted in 1843. Article IV., section 2, of those laws conferred the right to vote and hold office upon every free male descendant of a white man, inhabitant of Oregon Territory, of the age of twenty-one years and upward. (Gray's "Oregon," 354.) While the organic laws of

1843 professedly admitted *all* of the disfranchised class to reside in the Territory, they were so framed as effectually to exclude the *better* portion; for surely every intelligent and independent man of color would have scorned the pitiful boon offered him of a residence under conditions so humiliating.

· For years I had been opposed to slavery, as injurious to both races. While I resided in Tennessee and Missouri, there was no discussion upon the subject of manumitting the slaves in those States. I was not then in circumstances that made it proper to discuss the question. But when I arrived in Oregon, the first opportunity I had, I voted against slavery while a member of the Legislative Committee of 1844. I presided at a public meeting at Sacramento City, January 8, 1849, that unanimously voted for a resolution opposing slavery in California. This was the first public meeting in this country that expressed its opposition to that institution. A public meeting was held in San Francisco, February 17, 1849, which endorsed the resolution against slavery passed at Sacramento. ("Alta California," February 22, 1849.)

As already stated, one of the objects I had in view in coming to this coast was to aid in building up a great American community on the Pacific; and, in the enthusiasm of my nature, I was anxious to aid in founding a State superior in several respects to those east of the Rocky Mountains. I therefore labored to avoid the evils of intoxication and of mixed races, one of which was disfranchised.

W. H. GRAY — CRITICISM UPON THE HISTORY OF OREGON.

It is more charitable to impute Mr. Gray's misrepresentations to inveterate prejudice than to deliberate malice. Some men seem to become the slaves of prejudice from long indulgence, until it grows into a chronic habit; and it is about as easy to make an angel of a goat as an impartial historian of a prejudiced man. His book, in my best judgment, is a bitter, prejudiced, sectarian, controversial work, in the form of history; wherein the author acts as historian, controvertist, and witness.

I readily admit that circumstances may place a good man in this unpleasant position; but, if so, he should fully comprehend the extreme delicacy of the situation, and should rise with the occasion to the dignity of temperate and impartial history. He should make no appeals to prejudice, and should not, in advance, load down with derisive epithets those he in his own opinion is finally compelled to condemn; but should err, if at all, on the side of charity, and not against it.

The great Dr. Samuel Johnson, in speaking of Burnet's "History of his own Times," said: "I do not believe that Burnet intentionally lied; but he was so much prejudiced that he took no pains to find out the truth. He was like a man who resolves to regulate his time by a certain watch, but will not inquire whether the watch is right or not." (Boswell's "Life of Johnson," vol. ii., p. 264.)

I think this opinion applicable to Gray's "History." I *know* he has done myself and the Legislative committee of 1844 great injustice; and I have every reason to believe that he has been equally unjust to others.

For example, the historian gives the letter of Mr. McBean, written at Fort Nez Percés, dated November 30, 1847, and addressed to the Board of Managers of the Hudson's Bay Company at Fort Vancouver, and the letters of Mr. Douglas and Mr. Hinman to Governor Abernethy (pages 519, 524, and 530). I will give so much of these last two letters as may be necessary to the point I make:

Fort Vancouver, December 7, 1847.

George Abernethy, Esq. — Sir: Having received intelligence last night (on the 4ᵗʰ), by special express from Walla Walla, of the destruction of the missionary settlement at Wailatpu by the Cayuse Indians of that place, we hasten to communicate the particulars of that dreadful event, one of the most atrocious which darken the annals of Indian crime.

James Douglas.

Fort Vancouver, December 4, 1847.

Mr. George Abernethy — Dear Sir: A Frenchman from Walla Walla arrived at my place on last Saturday, and informed me that he was on his way to Vancouver, and wished me to assist in procuring him a canoe immediately. I was very inquisitive to know if there was any difficulty above. He said four Frenchmen had died recently, and he wished to get others to occupy their places.

I immediately got him a canoe, and concluded to go in company with him in order to get some medicine for the Indians, as they were dying off with measles and other diseases very fast. I was charged with indifference. They said we were killing in not giving them medicines, and I found, if we were not exposing our lives, we were our peace, and consequently I set out for this place. This side of the Cascades I was made acquainted with the horrible massacre that took place at Wailatpu last Monday.

Alansan Hinman.

The words ("on the 4th") are put into the letter of Mr. Douglas by the historian, to call the attention of his readers to the discrepancy in the dates of the two letters. Upon these two letters he makes the following comments, among others (page 531):

There is one other fact in connection with this transaction that looks dark on the part of Sir James Douglas. It is shown in the dates of the several letters. Mr. Hinman's is dated December 4th; Mr. Douglas's, December 7th, that to the Sandwich Islands, December 9th. Now, between the 4th and 7th are three days. In a case of so much importance and professed sympathy, as expressed in his letter, how is it that three, or even two, days were allowed to pass without sending a dispatch informing Governor Abernethy of what had happened, and of what was expected to take place?

The distance from Wailatpu (Dr. Whitman's mission) to Walla Walla (Fort Nez Percés) was about twenty-five miles, and from Walla Walla to Wascopum (Mr. Hinman's place at the Dalles) about one hundred and forty miles. The massacre took place on the afternoon of Monday, November 29, 1847. Mr. McBean states in his letter, dated Tuesday, the last day of November, 1847, that he was first apprised of the massacre early that morning by Mr. Hall, who arrived half naked and covered with blood. As Mr. Hall started at the outset, his information was not satisfactory; and he (McBean) sent his interpreter and another man to the mission. As the two messengers had to travel twenty-five miles to the mission and the same distance back again, Mr. McBean's letter must have been written late on Tuesday night; and the messenger he sent to Vancouver must have left on Wednesday morning, December 1st. This messenger must have traveled the one hundred and forty miles from Walla Walla to the Dalles on one horse, and could not have reached there before late on Friday, December 3^d. To do this he would have had to travel about forty-six miles a day. To go from the Dalles to Vancouver in a canoe, and be "wind-bound" at Cape Horn (as Mr. Gray states on page 517), in much less time than three days, would be very difficult indeed. No one knew any better than Mr. Gray the distance traveled, and the time it would occupy under the then existing circumstances.

The historian, on page 535, gives the communication of Governor Abernethy to the Legislative Assembly of Oregon, dated December 8, 1847. How, then, could Mr. Hinman be at Vancouver on Saturday, December 4, 1847? And, had he written his letter there on that day, why did it not reach Governor Abernethy two or three days in advance of that of Mr. Douglas, dated December 7th? But there is on the face of Mr. Hinsman's letter itself conclusive evidence that *his* date, *as given*, is an error. He says: "A Frenchman from Walla Walla arrived at my place on last Saturday." Now, if his letter had been *correctly* dated December 4, 1847, then the "last Saturday" mentioned would have been November 27th, two days before the massacre took place. It seems plain that Mr. Hinman and the Frenchman arrived at Vancouver Monday evening, December 6th, and that Mr. Hinman wrote his letter that evening, and Mr. Douglas his next day, as he states. Upon this supposition Mr. Hinman could correctly say, "the horrible massacre that took place at Wailatpu last Monday." It may be that the figure 6 in Mr. Hinman's letter was mistaken for the figure 4; or it may have been a typographical error in publishing the letter; or Mr. Hinman, in the excitement of the moment, may have mistaken the date. That there was a mistake in the date of Mr. Hinman's letter, as given by the historian, is quite certain.

Would an impartial historian have made so gross a mistake as this against any man of respectable standing, whom he accused of the most atrocious crime? Would he have seized upon this discrepancy in dates as evidence, without careful investigation? An impartial historian will put himself on the side of the accused when weighing and scrutinizing testimony, however guilty he may think him to be. He will not form an opinion that the accused is guilty unless he, the impartial historian, thinks the good and legitimate evidence amply sufficient; and therefore, in his view, he need not rely, *even in part*, upon false testimony; and he will be the more cautious and careful, in proportion to the gravity of the crime charged. The massacre being a most noted event, and its date being Monday, November 29th, and Mr. Hinman's letter December 4th, it was easy to see that the latter day was Saturday. But the historian "was so much prejudiced that he took no pains to find out the truth."

It seems that a public meeting was held in Oregon on the 18th of February, 1841, at which a committee of nine persons was chosen "to form a constitution and draft a code of laws"; and that the Rev. F.N. Blanchet was one of this committee. At an adjourned meeting, June 11, 1841, the historian says:

His Jesuitical Reverence, F. N. Blanchet, was excused from serving on the committee, at his own request. The settlers and uninitiated were informed by his reverence that he was unaccustomed to make laws for the people, and did not understand how to proceed; while *divide and conquer*, the policy adopted by the Hudson's Bay Company, was entered into with heart and soul by this *Reverend Father* Blanchet and his associates. (Pages 199, 200, and 202.)

Now, without regard to the question of motive, why should the historian apply derisive epithets to the accused at any stage of the inquiry, and more especially before the author had submitted his proofs? In other words, would any impartial and enlightened historian seek, by the use of such epithets, to prejudice his readers against the accused *in advance*, and before the testimony was submitted? It will be seen that the writer emphasizes the phrase " *His Jesuitical Reverence*," so that the reader might not forget this derisive and bitter expression. A decent respect for the feelings of others, as well as a due regard to the dignity of history, would have restrained the impartial historian from the use of such language at every stage of the investigation. Whenever either a good or a bad motive may be plausibly given for the same act, the historian is very apt to impute the bad motive, as he did in this case. I do not think a single instance can be found in the whole book of 624 pages where the author has erred on the side of charity. He is not one of those noble and exalted natures that would magnanimously state the case more clearly in behalf of the accused than the accused would be able to do himself.

In reference to the act in regard to slavery, free negroes, and mulattoes, I find these entries in the journal of the House of Representatives, July 1 and 3, 1845 ("Oregon Laws and Archives," pages 83 and 85):

Mr. Garrison introduced a bill to repeal the several acts in regard to negroes in Oregon . . . .

The House went into Committee of the Whole, Mr. Straight in the chair.

When the Committee rose, the Chairman reported that the Committee had had under consideration:

The bill to divorce M.J. Rice; The act to repeal the several acts on slavery; An act to fix the time and place of the sittings of the Legislature; An act to divorce F. Hathaway; also, The report of the Committee on Revision, which had been adopted.

Report was received; and the bill to divorce F. Hathaway was read a third time, and passed; also, the bill to divorce M. J. Rice; also, the bill concerning acts on slavery.

Thus, the act which Mr. Gray asserts could not be executed was repealed about one year *before* it could have taken effect in a single case, Mr. Gray being present when the repealing act was passed. The historian seems to have had about as vague a conception of the matter he was treating as a man with a distorted vision would have of the country represented.

ELECTED JUDGE OF THE SUPREME COURT — STRANGE RESOLUTION — JESSE APPLEGATE.

On the 18th of August, 1845, I was elected by the House of Representatives Judge of the Supreme Court of Oregon.

On the 4th of December, 1845, the House, on motion of Mr. Gray, passed this resolution:

Resolved, That the Supreme Judge be called upon to inform this House whether he had examined the laws enacted by the previous Legislature of this Territory; also, to inform the House how many of said laws are incompatible with the organic articles of compact, adopted by the people on the 25th of July 1845, if any there be. ("Oregon Laws and Archives," 127.)

To this strange and singular resolution I made a firm but respectful answer, declining to decide in advance, and before proper cases came up before the Court, whether an entire code of laws was constitutional or not.

On the 12th of December, 1845, the Speaker informed the House that he had communications from the Supreme Judge, which he had been requested to present to the House. The communications were read and referred to the Committee on the Judiciary. On the same day Mr. McCarver, from the Judiciary Committee, reported back the communications from the Supreme Judge, which were then referred to a select committee of five, consisting of Messrs. Gray, Hendrick, Garrison, McClure, and McCarver. ("Oregon Laws and Archives," 140-'41.)

There is no further mention of these communications in the Journal, as no report was ever made by this select committee. There was not a single lawyer among the members of 1845; and it is quite probable that this committee found it very difficult to coerce a Supreme Court to decide questions of law before cases were properly brought before it.

My extracts from the laws of 1844 are taken from "Oregon Laws and Archives, by L. F. Grover, Commissioner," except the act in regard to slavery, and the 4th section of the act on ways and means, which latter is found in Gray's "Oregon," 395, as part of Dr. White's report to the Secretary of War. These two acts are not found in Grover's compilation. The act in regard to slavery, free negroes, and mulattoes is a certified copy from the original on file in the office of the Secretary of State. My references to the Journals of 1844 and 1845 are to the same compilation.

In the summer and early fall of 1846 Jesse Applegate, at his own expense as I then understood, opened a new wagon-road into the Willamette valley at its southern end. He met the emigrants at Fort Hall and induced a portion of them to come by that route. They suffered great hardships before they reached the end of their journey. This was caused mainly by their own mistakes. Though he was much censured by many of them, he was not to blame. He had performed one of the most noble and generous acts, and deserved praise rather than censure. I traveled with him across the Plains in 1843, and I can testify that he was a noble, intellectual, and generous man; and his character was so perfect as to bear any and all tests, under any and all circumstances. The Hon. J. W. Nesmith, in his address before the Oregon Pioneers in June, 1875, paid a glowing tribute to the character of "Uncle Jesse Applegate." I knew him long and well, and shall never cease to love him so long as I live.

I left him in Oregon in 1848. He was then a rich man, for that time and that country. I did not see him again until 1872, a period of nearly twenty-four years. In the mean time he had become a gray-headed old man. He and myself are near the same age, he being about two years the younger. One day, without my knowing that he was in California, he walked into the Pacific Bank in San Francisco. I knew, from the serious expression of his face, that he was an old friend; but, for the moment, I could not place him or call his name. He was so much affected that his eyes filled with tears, and he could not speak. I shook his hand cordially, invited him to sit down, and sat down by him, looking him full in the face one moment, when it came into my mind that he was my old friend, and I exclaimed, "Applegate!" and we embraced like brothers.

We talked about one hour, and in this conversation he gave me his history since I left Oregon. He removed to the Umpqua valley; where for a time he had fine lands, stock, and other property. At length he determined to go into the mercantile business, for which he had little or no capacity. Said he: "To make a long story short, I did business upon this theory. I sold my goods on credit to those who *needed them most*, not to those who were *able to pay*, lost thirty thousand dollars, and quit the business."

Any one knowing Jesse Applegate as I do would at once recognize the truth of this statement. It was just like the man. His fine intellect and his experience in life said no; but his generous heart said yes; and that kind heart of his overruled his better judgment. In his old age his fortune is gone; but his true friends only admire and love him the more in the hour of misfortune.

In starting from Missouri to come to this country in 1843, Mr. Applegate announced to his traveling companions, as we have been credibly informed, that he meant to drive the Hudson's Bay Company from the country. To reach the country independent of them, he had sold or mortgaged his cattle to get supplies at Walla Walla. On arriving at Vancouver, he found Dr. McLoughlin to be much of a gentleman, and disposed to aid him in every way he could. The Doctor advised him to keep his cattle, and gave him employment as a surveyor, and credit for all he required. This kind treatment closed Mr. Applegate's open statements of opposition to the Company, and secured his friendship and his influence to keep his Missouri friends from doing violence to them. He carried this kind feeling for them into the Legislative Committee. (Gray, pages 421-'22.)

As already stated, a portion of the immigrants of 1843 left their cattle at Walla Walla. This they did under an agreement with Mr. McKinlay, then in charge of the fort, that we should have the same number and description of cattle in the Willamette valley, from the herds of the Hudson's Bay Company. When we arrived at Vancouver, Dr. McLoughlin and Mr. Douglas candidly stated to us that our American tame cattle would suit us much better than the cattle of the Company, and they advised us to bring our cattle from Walla Walla during the next spring. The same advice was given to all the immigrants who left their cattle at Walla Walla. We all saw at once that this advice was not only generous but practically sound. Mr. Applegate, as I understood at the time, made the same arrangement with Mr. McKinlay that others of us did. That Mr. Applegate sold or mortgaged his cattle at Walla Walla for supplies must be a mistake. He needed but little if anything in that line; and to have mortgaged so many cattle for so small an amount would have been the greatest of folly. He could not have needed provisions, so far as I can remember, as he must have purchased wheat and potatoes from Dr. Whitman, like most of us.

On arriving at Vancouver, Mr. Applegate, no doubt, found a very different state of things from what he anticipated when starting from Missouri. He did find Dr. McLoughlin and Mr. Douglas to be much of gentlemen; for it was very difficult indeed for any man, who was himself a gentleman, to keep the company of those two men, and not find out that they were both gentlemen in the true sense of that term. Mr. Applegate no doubt concluded that, if these men were really opposed to American immigrants, they took the most extraordinary method of showing it. That Mr. Applegate purchased of the Company at Vancouver some supplies on credit is very probable, because he was amply good for all he engaged to pay. He was honesty personified, and was an admirable worker, both as a farmer and surveyor. He also had a fine band of American cattle; and such cattle were then the most valuable property in Oregon. Jesse Applegate and Daniel Waldo were the owners of more cattle than any other two men in our immigration.

THE ACT TO PROHIBIT THE INTRODUCTION, MANUFACTURE, SALE, AND BARTER OF ARDENT SPIRITS.

I have already mentioned (page 181) the happy condition of society in Oregon, and the causes which produced it. This only continued until the beginning of 1847.

The act of 1844 to prohibit the introduction, manufacture, sale, and barter of ardent spirits was amended by the House of Representatives of 1845. The same body drew up and submitted to the people, for their approval or rejection, a new and amended organic law, which was adopted, and which conferred upon the Legislature the power to pass laws to *regulate* the introduction, manufacture, and sale of ardent spirits. This amendatory bill was reported by W. H. Gray from the Committee on Ways and Means, and was passed December 6, 1845, by the following vote: Yeas, Gray, Garrison, Hendricks, H. Lee, B. Lee, McClure, and McCarver — 7; Nays, Foisy, Hill, Straight, and Newell — 4. On the 8th a motion to reconsider was lost by the following tie vote: Yeas, Hendricks, Hill, B. Lee, Smith, Straight, and Newell; nays, Foisy, Gray, Garrison, H. Lee, McCarver, and McClure. (Gray's "Oregon," page 440.)

The amendatory act is incorrectly given by Mr. Gray on pages 440-41, by omitting the first section entirely. The first section of the original act was amended by inserting the word "give" after the word "barter" in two places; and the second section was amended by inserting the word "give" after the word "barter" in one place, and the word "gift" after the word "barter" in the second place.

Section four of the *original* act was as follows:

> Section 4. That it shall be the duty of all sheriffs, judges, justices of the peace, constables, and other officers, when they have reason to believe that this act has been violated, to give notice thereof to some justice of the peace or judge of a court, who shall immediately issue his warrant and cause the offending party to be arrested; and if such officer has jurisdiction of such case, he shall proceed to try such offender without delay, and give judgment accordingly; but if such officer have no jurisdiction to try such case, he shall, if the party be guilty, bind him over to appear before the next Circuit Court.

This section was stricken out, and the following inserted in its stead:

> Section 4. Whenever it shall come to the knowledge of any officer of this government, or any private citizen, that any kind of spirituous liquors are being distilled or manufactured in Oregon, they are hereby authorized and required to proceed to the place where such illicit manufacture is known to exist, and seize the distilling apparatus, and deliver the same to the nearest district judge or justice of the peace, whose duty it shall be immediately to issue his warrant, and cause the house and premises of the person

against whom such warrant shall be issued to be further
searched; and in case any kind of spirituous liquors are
found in or about said premises, or any implements or
apparatus that have the appearance of having been used or
constructed for the purpose of manufacturing any kind of
spirituous liquors, the officer who shall have been duly
authorized to execute such warrant shall seize all such
apparatus, implements, and spirituous liquors, and deliver
the same to the judge or justice of the peace who issued the
said warrant. Said officershall also arrest the person or persons in or about whose premises such apparatus, implements, or spirituous liquors are found, and conduct him or
them to said judge or justice of the peace, whose duty it
shall be to proceed against said criminal or criminals, and
dispose of the articles seized according to law.

It will be readily seen that these amendments radically changed
the original act, in several most material respects. By the amendment to the second section of the act, it was made a criminal
offense to give away ardent spirits. This would prevent the master
of a ship entering the waters of Oregon from giving his seamen
their usual daily allowance of liquor while the vessel remained
within our jurisdiction. So, a private citizen, without the advice of a
physician, could not give the article to any one, for any purpose, or
under any circumstances.

By the provisions of the fourth section as amended, all officers,
and even private citizens, were not only authorized, but required
(without any warrant having been first issued by a court or judicial
officer) to seize the distilling apparatus; and in such case each
officer and each private citizen was to be himself the judge of both
the fact and law, so far as the duty to seize the apparatus was concerned. This was giving to each individual citizen of Oregon a most
extraordinary power, and making its exercise *obligatory*.

The fifth section of the amendatory act, as given by the historian, was as follows:

Sec. 5. All the fines or penalties recovered under this act
shall go, one half to the informant and witnesses, and the
other half to the officers engaged in arresting and trying the
criminal or criminals; and it shall be the duty of all officers
in whose hands such fines and penalties may come, to pay

over as directed in this section. This was a most unusual and extraordinary provision. To give a portion of the penalty recovered to the informant and arresting officer was not very improper; but to give another portion of such penalty to the *witnesses* and *judges*, thus making them interested in condemning the accused, is indeed most extraordinary; and I apprehend that such a provision never before occurred in the history of legislation among civilized men. The author of this fifth section must have had great confidence in the power of money.

These objectionable features were so great, in the view of Governor Abernethy, that he recommended a revision of the amendatory act, in his message to the House of Representatives, December 4, 1846. (Gray, 442.)

The House of Representatives, at the December session, 1846, passed an act entitled "An Act to regulate the manufacture and sale of wine and distilled spirituous liquors." This act Governor Abernethy returned to the House with his objections, as set forth in his veto message of December 17, 1846. In this message he said, among other things:

The act lying before me is the first act that has in any manner attempted to legalize the manufacture and sale of ardent spirits. At the session of the Legislature in June, 1844, an act was passed entitled "An Act to prevent the introduction, sale, and distillation of ardent spirits in Oregon"; and, as far as my knowledge extends, the passage of that act gave general satisfaction to the great majority of the people throughout the Territory. At the session of December, 1845, several amendments were proposed to the old law, and passed. The new features given to the bill by those amendments did not accord with the views of the people; the insertion of the words "give" and "gift" in the first and second sections of the bill, they thought, was taking away their rights, as it was considered that a man had a right to give away his property if he chose. There were several other objections to the bill, which I set forth to your honorable body in my message. I would therefore recommend that the amendments passed at the December session of 1845 be repealed; and that the law passed on the 24th of June, 1844, with such alterations as will make it agree with the organic law, if it does not agree with it, be again made the law of the land. It is said by many that the Legislature has no right to prohibit the introduction or sale of liquor, and this is probably the strongest argument used in defense of your bill.

The bill was passed over the veto of the Governor by the following vote: Yeas, Messrs. Boon, Hall, Hembree, Lounsdale, Loony, Meek, Summers, Straight, T. Vault, Williams, and the Speaker — 11; Nays, Messrs. Chamberlain, McDonald, Newell, Peers, and Dr. W. F. Tolmie — 5.

Mr. Parker, in a public address to the voters of Clackamas County, in May, 1846, charged that rum was sold at Vancouver contrary to law. This charge was based upon rumor. Mr. Douglas, in a communication to the "Oregon Spectator," published June 11, 1846, among other things says:

If, with reference to these supplies, Mr. Parker had told his hearers that her Majesty's ship Modeste, now stationed at Fort Vancouver, had, with other supplies for ship use from the stores of the Hudson's Bay Company, received several casks of rum; or, if, referring to the company's own ships, he had stated that *a small allowance of spirits is daily served out to the crews of the company's vessels*, and that other classes of the company's servants, according to long-accustomed usage, receive on certain *rare occasions* a similar indulgence, he would have told the *plain and simple truth*, and his statement would not this day have been called in question by me. These acts, which I fully admit, and would on no account attempt to conceal, can not by the fair rules of construction be considered as infringing upon any law recognized by the *compact which we have agreed to support*, in common with the other inhabitants of Oregon. (Gray, 447.)

It seems perfectly plain from Mr. Gray's own history, that the final overthrow of this measure was mainly brought about by the following causes:

1. The extremely harsh and erroneous amendments of 1845.

2. The mistake of the same body in using the word "regulate" instead of "prohibit" in the organic law of that year.

3. The sale of rum to the Modeste by the Hudson's Bay Company.

This last act, however excusable it may be considered under the then existing circumstances, gave the opponents a plausible ground of objection.

That the original act was approved by the people is shown by the following extract from the message of Governor Abernethy, dated February 5, 1849:

The proposed amendments to the organic law will come before you for final action: to amend the oath of office, to make the clerks of the different counties recorders of land claims, etc., and to strike out the word "regulate" and insert the word "prohibit" in the clause relating to the sale of ardent spirits. The last amendment came before the people for a direct vote, and I am happy to say that the people of this Territory decided through the ballot-box, by a majority of the votes given, that the word "prohibit" should be inserted. This makes the question a very easy one for you to decide upon. ("Oregon Laws and Archives," pages 273-'4.)

Jesse Applegate was a member of the House of Representatives in 1845, but his name does not appear as voting upon the final passage of the amendatory bill, he having previously resigned his seat.

TREATY OF JUNE 15, 1846 — POLICY OF THE HUDSON'S BAY COMPANY — H. A. G. LEE — INDIAN CHARACTER.

On the 15th of June, 1846, a treaty was concluded between Great Britain and the United States, which acknowledged the sovereignty of our country over that portion of Oregon lying south of the 49th parallel of north latitude. This was known in Oregon as early as December of that year, as the fact is mentioned in Governor Abernethy's message, dated December 1, 1846. ("Oregon Laws and Archives," 158.)

The final settlement of the conflicting claims of the two governments in this manner did not surprise any sensible man in Oregon, so far as I remember. It was what we had every reason to expect. We knew, to a moral certainty, that the moment we brought our families, cattle, teams, and loaded wagons to the banks of the Columbia River in 1843, the question was practically decided in our favor. Oregon was not only accessible by land from our contiguous territory, but we had any desirable number of brave, hardy people who were fond of adventure, and perfectly at home in the settlement of new countries. We could bring into the country ten immigrants for every colonist Great Britain could induce to settle there. We were masters of the situation, and fully comprehended our position. This the gentlemen of the Company understood as well as we did. In repeated conversations with Dr. McLoughlin, soon after my arrival in Oregon, he assured me that he had for some years been convinced that Oregon was destined soon to be occupied by a civilized people. The reasons for this conclusion were most obvious. The country, with its fertile soil, extensive valleys, magnificent forests, and mild climate, was admirably fitted for a civilized and dense population. Its local position on the shores of the Pacific marked it as a fit abode for a cultivated race of men. Besides, the natives had almost entirely disappeared from the lower section of Oregon. Only a small and diseased remnant was left.

The colonization of the country, either by British or Americans, would equally destroy the fur-trade, the only legitimate business of the Company. No doubt the gentlemen connected with that Company thought the title of their own government to Oregon was superior to ours; while we Americans believed we had the better title. I read carefully the discussion between Mr. Buchanan, our Secretary of State, and the British Minister; and while I thought our country had the better title, neither claim could be properly called a plain indisputable right, because much could be and was said on both sides of the question. But, while our *title* might be disputed, there was no possible doubt as to the main fact, that *we had settled the country.*

When the managers of the Company had arrived at the conclusion that Oregon must be inhabited by a civilized race of men, they undoubtedly determined to do all they could reasonably and justly to colonize it with their own people. These gentlemen were as loyal in their allegiance to their own country as we were to ours, and were prepared to go as far as enlightened love of country would lead them, and no farther. It is very true that the Company, by expending the larger portion if not all of its large capital, could have colonized the country in advance of the Americans. But, what proper inducement had the Company thus to sacrifice the property of its stockholders? Colonization was not its legitimate business. Why, then, should a mere mercantile corporation waste its means and ruin its business to settle Oregon? If the settlement of the country was of national importance to Great Britain, then the expense should have been borne by that government itself, and not by the few subjects who happened to be stockholders of the Company. Any one well acquainted with all the facts and circumstances, and who will carefully and thoroughly examine the subject, must see that the only motive the managers of the Company had to settle

Oregon with British subjects, in preference to American citizens, was one of patriotism or love of country. In a pecuniary point of view, the Company saved more money for its stockholders by the treaty than it could have done had the country fallen to Great Britain.

But while the managers of the Company, as British subjects, preferred to colonize Oregon with their own people, they were not, as enlightened and Christian men, prepared to use criminal means to accomplish that purpose. In the address of John McLoughlin and James Douglas to the citizens of Oregon in March, 1845, they say, among other things:

The Hudson's Bay Company made their settlement at Fort Vancouver under the authority of a license from the British Government, in conformity with the provisions of the treaty between Great Britain and the United States of America, which gives them the right of occupying as much land as they require for the operation of their business. On the faith of that treaty they have made a settlement on the north bank of the Columbia River, they have opened roads and made other improvements at a great outlay of capital; they have held unmolested possession of their improvements for many years, unquestioned by the public officers of either government, who have since the existence of their settlement repeatedly visited it; they have carried on business with manifest advantage to the country; they have given the protection of their influence over the native tribes to every person who required it, without distinction of nation or party; and they have afforded every assistance in their power toward developing the resources of the country and promoting the industry of its inhabitants. . . .

Permit us to assure you, gentlemen, that it is our earnest wish to maintain a good understanding and to live on friendly terms with every person in the country. We entertain the highest respect for the provisional organization; and knowing the great good it has effected, as well as the evil it has prevented, we wish it every success, and hope, as we desire, to continue to live in the exercise and interchange of good offices with the framers of that useful institution.

This address was inclosed with the following letter to the Executive Committee of Oregon:

Vancouver, *March* 18, 1845.

Gentlemen: I am sorry to inform you that Mr. Williamson is surveying a piece of land occupied by the Hudson's Bay Company, alongside of this establishment, with a view of taking it as a claim; and, as he is an American citizen, I feel bound, as a matter of courtesy, to make the same known to you, trusting that you will feel justified in taking measures to have him removed from the Hudson's Bay Company's premises, in order that the unanimity now happily subsisting between the American citizens and British subjects residing in this country may not be disturbed or interrupted. I beg to inclose you a copy of an address to the citizens of Oregon, which will explain to you our situation and the course we are bound to pursue in the event of your declining to interfere.

I am, gentlemen, your obedient, humble servant,

J. Mcloughlin.
William Baily, Osborn Russell, P. G. Stewart, Executive Committee of Oregon.

To this letter, the majority of the Executive Committee of Oregon, acting for the whole, made this reply:

Oregon City, *March* 21, 1845.

Sir: We beg to acknowledge the receipt of your letters — one dated 11th of March, and the other 12th of March — accompanied with an address to the citizens of Oregon.

We regret to hear that unwarranted liberties have been taken by an American citizen upon the Hudson's Bay Company's premises, and it affords us great pleasure to learn that the offender, after due reflection, desisted from the insolent and rash measure.

As American citizens, we beg leave to offer you and your esteemed colleague our most grateful thanks for the kind and candid manner in which you have treated this matter, as we are aware that an infringement on the rights of the Hudson's Bay Company in this country, by an American citizen, is a breach of the laws of the United States, by setting at naught her most solemn treaties with Great Britain.

As representatives of the citizens of Oregon, we beg your acceptance of our sincere acknowledgements of the obligations we are under to yourself and your honorable associate for the high regard you have manifested for the authorities of our provisional government, and the special anxiety you have ever shown for our peace and prosperity; and we assure you that we consider ourselves in duty bound to use every exertion in our power to put down every cause of disturbance, as well as to promote the amicable intercourse and kind feelings hitherto existing between ourselves and the gentlemen of the Hudson's Bay Company, until the United States shall extend its jurisdiction over us, and our authority ceases to exist.

We have the honor to be, sir, your most obedient servants,

Osborn Russell,
John McLoughlin, Esq.   P. G. Stewart.

These papers appear in Gray's "Oregon," pages 409-'11, as a portion of Dr. White's report to the Secretary of War.

This attempt to locate a claim in the vicinity of Vancouver was made by Williamson and Alderman. Williamson was apparently a modest and respectable young man, while Alderman was a most notorious character. He was well known in Oregon from his violent and unprincipled conduct. He was always in trouble with somebody. He came to California in the summer or fall of 1848, and was killed in the latter portion of that year, at Sutter's Fort, under justifiable circumstances.

I have given these extracts from the address to the citizens of Oregon, that the then managers of the Hudson's Bay Company might speak for themselves; and I have given the reply of Messrs. Russell and Stewart, of the Executive Committee, to show the opinion of those intelligent, calm, and faithful American officers upon the general subject.

That the facts stated in the address are true, there can be no reasonable doubt. The facts were all within the personal knowledge of

Dr. McLoughlin and Mr. Douglas, and they could not be mistaken about them. If untrue, then they deliberately and knowingly made false statements. To make statements that could be so readily contradicted by the people of Oregon, if untrue, would have been the greatest folly. Besides, the high characters of those gentleman, especially that of Dr. McLoughlin, forbids such inference. Dr. McLoughlin, during his long and active life, gave such conclusive proofs of the possession of the most exalted virtue, that no man of respectable ability and good character would at this late day question his integrity or doubt his statement of facts within his own knowledge. He voluntarily became, and afterward died, an American citizen.

But the truth of their statements, especially that one which declares that "they had given the protection of their influence over the native tribes to every person who required it, without distinction of nation or party," is shown by the fact that no American immigrant was killed by the Indians in Oregon until late in the fall of 1847 — seventeen months after the treaty between Great Britain and the United States had settled the question of sovereignty over that portion of Oregon south of the 49th parallel of north latitude in our favor, and twelve months after that fact was known in that country, and when the Company could not have had any adequate motive to oppose American immigration to acknowledged American territory.

It is true, some thefts were committed by the Indians upon the immigrants; but I apprehend that these were not more numerous or common than usual with Indians under like circumstances. While it is not my intention to enter at large into the subject, I will give an extract from the long letter of H. A. G. Lee to Dr. E. White, assistant Indian agent, dated Oregon City, March 4, 1845. It is, in my judgment, the most sensible and just description of Indian character I have ever seen in so few words. After stating, among other things, that "avarice is doubtless the ruling passion of most Indians," the writer goes on to say:

The lawless bands along the river, from Fort Walla Walla to the Dalles, are still troublesome to the immigrants; and the immigrants are still very imprudent in breaking off into small parties, just when they should remain united. The Indians are tempted by the unguarded and defenseless state of the immigrants, and avail themselves of the opportunity to gratify their cupidity. Here allow me to suggest a thought. These robbers furnish us a true minature likeness of the whole Indian population, whenever they fail to obtain such things as they wish in exchange for such as they have to give. These are robbers now, because they have nothing to give; all others will be robbers when, with what they have to give, they can not procure what they wish. I am satisfied of the correctness of this conclusion from all that I have witnessed of Indian character, even among the praiseworthy Nez Percés. And should the Government of the United States withhold her protection from her subjects in Oregon, they will be under the necessity of entering into treaty stipulations with the Indians, in violation of the laws of the United States, as preferable to a resort to force of arms.

Hitherto, the immigrants have had no serious difficulty in passing through the territory of these tribes; but that their passage is becoming more and more a subject of interest to the Indians is abundantly manifest. They collect about the road from every part of the country, and have looked on with amazement; but the novelty of the scene is fast losing its power to hold in check their baser passions. The next immigration will, in all probability, call forth developments of Indian character which have been almost denied an existence among these people. Indeed, sir, had you not taken the precaution to conciliate their good feelings and friendship toward the whites just at the time they were meeting each other, it is to be doubted whether there had not been some serious difficulties. Individuals on both sides have been mutually provoked and exasperated during the passage of each immigration, and these cases are constantly multiplying. Much prudence is required on the part of the whites, and unfortunately they have very little by the time they reach the Columbia Valley. Some of the late immigrants, losing their horses and very naturally supposing them stolen by the Indians, went to the bands of horses owned by the Indians and took as many as they wished. You are too well acquainted with Indians to suppose that such a course can be persisted in without producing serious results. (Gray's "Oregon," pages 414-416.)

Governor Abernethy, in his message to the Legislative Assembly of Oregon under date of December 7, 1847, says:

Our relation with the Indians becomes every year more embarrassing. They see the white man occupying their lands, rapidly filling up the country, and they put in a claim for pay. They have been told that a chief would come out from the United States and treat with them for their lands; they have been told this so often that they begin to doubt the truth of it. At all events, they say; "He will not come till we are all dead, and then what good will blankets do us? We want something now." This leads to trouble between the settler and the Indians about him. Some plan should be devised by which a fund can be raised, and presents made to the Indians of sufficient value to keep them quiet, until an agent arrives from the United States. A number of robberies have been committed by the Indians in the upper country upon the emigrants as they were passing through their territory. This should not be allowed to pass. An appropriation should be made by you, sufficient to enable the Superintendent of Indian Affairs to take a small party in the spring, and demand restitution of the property, or its equivalent in horses. Without an appropriation, a sufficient party would not be induced to go up there, as the trip is an expensive one. ("Oregon Laws and Archives," page 210.)

We were delicately situated in Oregon up to near the close of 1846, when news of the treaty between Great Britain and the United States reached us. We knew that under former treaties the citizens and subjects of both governments were privileged to occupy the country jointly; but that joint occupation of the territory did not mean joint occupation of the same tract of land or of the same premises, but the party first in possession was entitled to continue it until the question of sovereignty should be settled. Our community was composed of American citizens and British subjects, intermingled together as neighbors, with all their respective national attachments,manners, and prejudices; and we had our full share of reckless adventurers and other bad men. The extremists and ultras of both sides would have brought us into armed conflict, and perhaps involved the two countries in war, but for the manly good sense of our leading men, supported by the great majority of the people.

It was most fortunate for us that the executive office of our little provisional government was at all times filled, not only by Americans, but by those who were well fitted for that position, both as to capacity and conciliatory firmness. I have already spoken of Osborn Russell and P. G. Stewart, who acted as the Executive Committee during part of the years 1844 and 1845. They were admirable men for that position. They were succeeded by George Abernethy, who filled the position until the provisional organization was superseded by the regular Territorial government, under the act of Congress of August 14, 1848.

Governor Abernethy was precisely fitted for the position in every respect. Though he had no regular legal education, he was a man of admirable good sense, of calm, dispassionate disposition, of amiable, gentle manners, and above the influences of passion and prejudice. He did his duty most faithfully to the utmost of his ability; and his ability was ample for that time and that country. He fully comprehended the exact situation, and acted upon the maxim, "Make haste slowly," believing that such was not only the best policy, but the best justice. Time amply vindicated the wisdom and efficiency of the course he pursued. We attained all our hopes and wishes by peaceful means. "Peace hath her triumphs," greater than those of war, because the triumphs of peace cost so much less. It is a matter of doubt whether, in the settlement of any portion of America by the whites, any greater wisdom, forbearance, and good sense have been shown, except in the celebrated case of William Penn.

MASSACRE OF DR. WHITMAN AND OTHERS — INDIAN WAR — ITS RESULT.

On Monday, November 29, 1847, the horrible massacre of Dr. Marcus Whitman, his lady, and others, by the Cayuse Indians, took place; which event, in the just language of Mr. Douglas, was "one of the most atrocious which darken the annals of Indian crime." Within a few days other peaceful Americans were slaughtered, until the whole number of victims amounted to from twelve to fifteen. This painful event was made known at Oregon City on December 8, 1847, as already stated.

I knew Dr. Whitman well; I first saw him at the rendezvous near the western line of Missouri, in May, 1843; saw him again at Fort Hall; and again at his own mission in the fall of that year, as already stated. I remember that the first I heard of the false and ungrateful charge made by a portion of our immigrants (an account of which I have already given) was from his own lips. I was standing near his house when he came to me with the painful expression of deep concern upon his countenance, and asked me to come with him to his room. I did so, and found one or two other gentlemen there. He was deeply wounded, as he had ample cause to be, by this unjustifiable conduct of some of our people. He stated to us the facts. I again saw him at my home in the Tualatin Plains in 1844. He called at my house, and, finding I was in the woods at work, he came to me there. This was the last time I ever saw him. Our relations were of the most cordial and friendly character, and I had the greatest respect for him.

I consider Dr. Whitman to have been a brave, kind, devoted, and intrepid spirit, without malice and without reproach. In my best judgment, he made greater sacrifices, endured more hardships, and encountered more perils for Oregon than any other one man; and his services were practically more efficient than those of any other, except perhaps those of Dr. Linn, United States Senator from Missouri. I say *perhaps*, for I am in doubt as to which of these two men did more in effect for Oregon.

The news of this bloody event thrilled and roused our people at once; and within a very short time, considering the season and other circumstances, we raised an army of some five hundred brave and hardy men, and marched them into the enemy's country. Several battles were fought, the result of which is well and concisely stated by Governor Abernethy, in his message to the Legislative Assembly of Oregon, under date of February 5, 1849:

I am happy to inform you that, through aid of the Territory to go in pursuit of the murderers and their allies, and of those who contributed so liberally to the support of our fellow citizens in the field, the war has been brought to a successful termination. It is true that the Indians engaged in the massacre were not captured and punished; they were, however, driven from their homes, their country taken possession of, and they made to understand that the power of the white man is far superior to their own. The Indians have a large scope of country to roam over, all of which they were well acquainted with, knew every pass, and by this knowledge could escape the punishment they so justly merited. In view of this the troops were recalled and disbanded early in July last, leaving a small force under the command of Captain Martin to keep possession of the post at Wailatpu, and a few men at Woscopum. Captain Martin remained at Wailatpu until the middle of September, when the time for which his men had enlisted expired. He however, before leaving, sent a party to bring in the last company of emigrants.The appearance of so many armed men among the Indians in their own country had a very salutary effect on them; this is seen by their refusing to unite with the Cayuse Indians, by the safety with which the immigration passed through the Indian country the past season.

Heretofore robberies have been committed and insults offered to Americans as they would pass along, burdened with their families and goods, and worn down with the fatigues of a long journey, and this was on the increase; each successive immigration suffered more than the preceding one. But this year no molestation was offered in any way. On the contrary, every assistance was rendered by the Indians in crossing rivers, for a reasonable compensation.

Having learned the power and ability of the Americans, I trust the necessity of calling on our citizens to punish them hereafter will be obviated. ("Oregon Laws and Archives," page 272.)

This attack of the Indians was attributed by some persons, and especially by Mr. Spaulding, to the instigation of the Catholic missionaries in that country. I thought the charge most unjust, and think so still. The charge was too horrible in its very nature to be believed unless the evidence was conclusive beyond a reasonable doubt. There were most ample grounds upon which to account for the massacre, without accusing these missionaries of that horrible crime. Mr. Spaulding and myself agreed to discuss the matter through the columns of a small semi-monthly newspaper, published by Mr. Griffin, and several numbers were written and published by each of us; but the discovery of the gold mines in California put a stop to the discussion.

Chapter VI

DISCOVERY OF GOLD IN CALIFORNIA — DETERMINE TO GO TO THE MINES — ORGANIZE A WAGON-PARTY.

I had been a member of the Legislative Committee of 1844, had taken a leading part in that little body, and had done what I considered my fair proportion of the work, under all the then existing circumstances. We had adopted a code of laws, which, though imperfect, was ample for that time and that country. I looked forward to the speedy settlement of the question of sovereignty in our favor, and it was so settled within two years thereafter.

As before stated, I went to Oregon to accomplish three purposes. I had already assisted to lay the foundation of a great American community on the shores of the Pacific, and the trip across the Plains had fully restored the health of Mrs. Burnett. There was still one great end to attain — the payment of my debts. I had a family of eight persons to support, and a large amount of old indebtedness to pay. My debts were just, and I believed in the great maxim of the law, that "a man must be just before he is generous." Had the *essential* interest of a large body of my fellow men, in my judgement, required further sacrifices, I would have made them most cheerfully. But, the foundation of a great community on this coast having been laid, all else would naturally follow as a matter of course, as there were others competent to continue the work.

The obligation to support my family and pay my debts was sacred with me; and I therefore gave the larger portion of my time to my own private affairs so long as I remained in Oregon. I did not then foresee the discovery of gold in California; and for this reason my only chance to pay, so far as I could see, was to remain and labor in Oregon. I had not the slightest idea of leaving that country until the summer of 1848. Before I left, I had paid a small portion of my old indebtedness. I always had faith that I should ultimately pay every dollar.

In the month of July, 1848 (if I remember correctly), the news of the discovery of gold in California reached Oregon. It passed from San Francisco to Honolulu, thence to Nesqualy, and thence to Fort Vancouver. At that very time there was a vessel from San Francisco in the Willamette River, loading with flour, the master of which knew the fact but concealed it from our people for speculative reasons, until the news was made public by the gentlemen connected with the Hudson's Bay Company.

This extraordinary news created the most intense excitement throughout Oregon. Scarcely anything else was spoken of. We had vanquished the Indians, and that war for the time was almost forgotten. We did not know of the then late treaty of peace between Mexico and the United States; but we were aware of the fact that our Government had possession of California; and we knew, to a moral certainty, that it would never be given up.

Many of our people at once believed the reported discovery to be true, and speedily left for the gold mines with pack-animals. I think that at least two thirds of the male population of Oregon, capable of bearing arms, started for California in the summer and fall of 1848. The white population of Oregon, including the late immigrants, must have amounted then to from eight to ten thousand people. Before we left, many persons expressed their apprehensions that the Indians might renew hostilities during the absence of so many men. But those of us who went to the mines that fall (leaving our families behind in Oregon) had no fears of any further attacks from the Indians. Time proved that we were right.

These accounts were so new and extraordinary to us at that time, that I had my doubts as to their truth, until I had evidence satisfactory to me. I did not jump to conclusions, like some people; but when I saw a letter which had been written in California by Ex-Governor Lilburn W. Boggs, formerly of Missouri, to his brother-in-law Colonel Boon of Oregon, I was fully satisfied. I had known Governor Boggs since 1821, was familiar with his handwriting, and knew Colonel Boon; and there was no reasonable cause to doubt. This letter I read about the last of August, 1848.

I saw my opportunity, and at once consulted with my wife. I told her I thought that it was our duty to separate again for a time, though we had promised each other, after our long separation of fourteen months during our early married life, that we would not separate again. I said that this was a new and special case, never anticipated by us; that it was the only certain opportunity to get out of debt within a reasonable time, and I thought it my duty to make the effort. She consented, and I came to California, and succeeded beyond my expectations. I paid all my debts, principal and interest, security debts and all. Time conclusively proved the wisdom and justice of my course. I set out to accomplish three important objects; and, thanks be to God, I succeeded in all.

When I had determined to come to California, I at once set to work to prepare for the journey. All who preceded me had gone with pack-animals; but it occurred to me that we might be able to make the trip with wagons. I went at once to see Dr. McLoughlin, and asked his opinion of its practicability. Without hesitation he replied that he thought we could succeed, and recommended old Thomas McKay for pilot. No wagons had ever passed between Oregon and California. Thomas Mckay had made the trip several times with pack-trains, and knew the general nature of the country, and the courses and distances; but he knew of no practicable wagon-route, as he had only traveled with pack-animals.

This was about the first of September, 1848. I at once went into the streets of Oregon City, and proposed the immediate organization of a wagon-company. The proposition was received with decided favor; and in eight days we had organized a company of one hundred and fifty stout, robust, energetic, sober men, and fifty wagons and ox-teams, and were off for the gold mines of California. We had only one family, consisting of the husband, wife, and three of four children. We had fresh teams, strong wagons, an ample supply of provisions for six months, and a good assortment of mining implements. I had two wagons and teams, and two saddle-horses; and I took plank in the bottoms of my wagons, with which I constructed a gold-rocker after we arrived in the mines.

We were not certain that we could go through with our wagons, and thought we might be caught in the mountains, as were the Donner party in 1846. In case we had been snowed in, we had plenty of provisions to live upon during the winter. Besides, we were apprehensive that there might be a great scarcity of provisions in the mines during the winter of 1848-'9. The only article I purchased in the mines was some molasses, having everything else in the way of provisions.

"Advances of outfits were made to such men as Hastings and his party, Burnett, and other prominent men . . . .

"Those who proposed going to California could readily get all the supplies they required of the company by giving their notes payable in California." (Gray's "Oregon," 361.)

This is a mistake, so far as I was concerned. I had plenty of wheat, cattle, and hogs, and did not need advances. My outfit cost very little additional outlay, for the simple reason that I had my own wagons and teams, except one yoke of oxen which I purchased of Pettigrove, in Portland, and paid for at the time. I had the two horses that I took with me, and all the provisions that I required, except a few pounds of tea. I had an ample supply of sugar, for reasons already stated. I had all the clothes required, and plenty of tools, except two picks which I got a blacksmith in Oregon City to make. I do not remember to have purchased a single article on credit.

OFF FOR CALIFORNIA — INCIDENTS OF THE TRIP.

I was elected captain of the wagon-party, and Thomas McKay was employed as pilot. We followed the Applegate route to Klamath Lake, where we left that road and took a southern direction. Thomas McKay, myself, and five others, well armed and mounted, went on in advance of the wagons to discover the best route, leaving the wagons to follow our trail until otherwise notified. We, the road-hunters, took with us plenty of flour, sugar, and tea, and depended upon our guns for meat.

We passed over comparatively smooth prairie for some distance. One evening we encamped at what was then called Goose Lake. It being late in the season, the water in the lake was very low, muddy, and almost putrid. Vast flocks of pelicans were visiting this lake at that time, on their way south. I remember that we killed one on the wing with a rifle.

The water being so bad, we drank very little, and left early next morning. We traveled over prairie some twenty miles toward a heavy body of timber in the distance, then entered a rocky cedar-grove about six miles in width. As our horses were not shod, their feet became sore and tender while passing over this rough road. We then entered a vast forest of beautiful pines. Our pilot told us that, if he was not mistaken, we should find in the pine-timber an Indian trail; and, sure enough, we soon came to a plain horse-path through the open forest. We followed this trail until sunset, and encamped in a small, dry prairie, having traveled all day beneath a hot October sun without water. Our little party were sober, solemn, and silent. No one ate anything except myself, and I only ate a very small piece of cold bread.

We left this dry and desolate camp early next morning. About 10 o'clock one of our party saw a deer, and followed it to a beautiful little stream of water, flowing from the hills into the forest. We spent the remainder of the day on the banks of this clear branch, drinking water and eating a badger. When I first drank the water it had no pleasant taste, but seemed like rain-water; but my natural thirst soon returned, and I found that no luxury was equal to water to a thirsty man. We sent out three of four hunters for game; but they returned about 2 p.m. with a large badger. This was all the meat we had. We dressed and cooked it well; and, to our keen and famished appetites, it was splendid food. The foot of the badger, the tail of the beaver, the ear of the hog, and the foot of the elephant are superior eating. I have myself eaten of all but the last, and can speak from personal knowledge; and, as to the foot of the elephant, I can give Sir Samuel Baker as my authority, in his "Explorations," etc.

We left next morning, thoroughly refreshed and rested; and we had not traveled more than ten miles when we came in sight of Pitt River, a tributary of the Sacramento. It was here but a small creek, with a valley about half a mile wide. When we had approached near the stream, to our utter surprise and astonishment, we found a new wagon-road. Who made this road we could not at first imagine. A considerable number of those coming to California with pack-animals decided to follow our trail, rather than come by the usual pack-route. These packers had overtaken us the preceding evening, and were with us when discovered this new wagon-road. It so happened that one of them had been in California, and knew old Peter Lassen. This man was a sensible fellow, and at once gave it as his opinion that this road had been made by a small party of immigrants whom Lassen had persuaded to come to California by a new route that would enter the great valley of the Sacramento at or near Lassen's rancho. This conjectural explanation proved to be the true one. So soon as these packers found this road, they left us. No amount of argument could induce them to remain with us. They thought our progress too slow. This left our little party of road-hunters alone in a wild Indian country, the wagons being some distance behind.

We followed the new road slowly. One day, while passing through open pine-woods, we saw an Indian, some two hundred yards ahead of us. He was intent on hunting, and did not see us until we were within a hundred yards, charging down upon him with our horses at full speed. He saw that escape by flight was impossible; so he hid under a clump of bushes. We soon came up, and by signs ordered him to come out from his place of concealment. This command he understood and promptly obeyed. He was a stout, active young man, apparently twenty-five years of age, and had a large gray squirrel under his belt, which he had killed with his bow and arrow. He evidently feared that we would take his life; but we treated him kindly, spent some time conversing with him as well as we could by signs, and then left him in peace.

From the point where we struck the Lassen road, it continued down the river in a western direction ten or fifteen miles until the river turned to the south and ran through a cañon, the road ascending the tall hills, and continuing about west for twenty to thirty miles, when it came again to and crossed the river. The same day that we saw the Indian we encamped, after dark, on a high bluff above the river. We had had no water to drink since morning, and had traveled late in the hope of finding a good encampment.

The night was so dark, and the bluff was so steep and rough, that we feared to attempt to go to the river for water, though we could distinctly hear the roar of the stream, as it dashed among the rocks below. At length, one of our men determined to go for water. He took with him a small tin bucket; and, after having been absent a considerable time, he returned with the bucket about one fourth full, having spilt most of the water on his return to camp. The amount for each of us was so small that our thirst increased rather than diminished.

The next morning we left early, and followed the road to the crossing of the river, where we arrived about noon. Here we spent the remainder of that day. The valley at this point was about a mile and a half wide, and without timber; and the descent into it was down a tall hill, which was not only steep, but rocky and heavily timbered. In the middle of this valley there was a solitary ridge about a mile long and a quarter of a mile wide at its base, and some two hundred feet high, covered with rocks of various sizes. We determined to discover, if we could, a new and easier route down the hill. For this purpose we ascended this ridge, from the summit of which we could have an excellent view of the face of the hill, down which our wagons must come.

While we were quietly seated upon the rocks, we saw an Indian emerge from the edge of the timber at the foot of the hill, about three fourths of a mile distant, and start in a brisk run across the intervening prairie toward us. I directed the men to sit perfectly still until the Indian should be hidden from our view, and then to separate, and let him fall into the ambush. We occupied the highest point of this lonely ridge, and we knew he would make for the same spot, for the purpose of overlooking our camp. We waited until he came to the foot of the ridge, from which position he could not see us; and then we divided our men into two parties, each party taking up a different position. Very soon the Indian came within about thirty feet of one of our parties, and suddenly found himself confronted with four rifles pointed at him, with a command by signs to stop. Of course it was a perfect surprise to the poor old Indian. He was about sixty years old, was dressed in buckskin, had long coarse hair and dim eyes, and his teeth were worn down to the gums.

Notwithstanding the suddenness and completeness of the surprise, the old hero was as brave and cool as possible. I had with me only an axe with which to blaze the new and better way, in case we found it, and was at first some little distance from the Indian. As I came toward him with the axe on my shoulder, he made the most vehement motions for me to stop and not come any nearer. I saw he was apprehensive that I would take off his head with the axe, and at once stopped and threw it aside. At first he would allow no one to come near him, but coolly wet his fingers with his tongue, and then deliberately dipped them into the sand at the foot of the rock on which he sat; and, with his trusty bow and arrow in his hands, he looked the men full in the face, as much as to say: "I know you have me in your power; but I wish you to understand that I am prepared to sell my life as dearly as possible." I never saw a greater display of calm, heroic, and determined courage than was shown by this old Indian. He was much braver than the young Indian we had seen the day before.

One of our men, who was a blustering fellow and who was for displaying his courage when there was no danger, proposed that we should kill the old Indian. I at once put a damper upon that cowardly proposition, by stating to the fellow that if he wanted to kill the Indian he could have a chance to do so in a fair and equal single combat with him. This proposition, as I anticipated, he promptly declined. I was satisfied that there was no fight in him.

After some time, we were permitted one at a time to approach him. We offered him the pipe of peace, which he accepted. He would let our men look at his bow and arrows one at a time, never parting with both of them at once. He was evidently suspicious of treachery. We staid with him some time, treating him kindly, and then left him sitting on his rock. This was the last we saw of him. We considered this mode of treating the Indians the most judicious, as it displayed our power and at the same time our magnanimity. We proved that we intended no harm to them, but were mere passers through their country. They evidently appreciated our motives, and the result was, that we had not the slightest difficulty with the Indians.

After crossing the river, the road bore south; it being impossible to follow down the stream, as the mountains came too close to it. Next morning we left our camp and followed the road south about ten miles, when we came to a beautiful grassy valley, covered with scattering pine-timber. This valley was about two miles wide where the road struck it, and ran west, the very direction we wished to go. It seemed a defile passing at right angles through the Sierra Nevada Mountains, as if designed for a level road into the Sacramento valley.

We were much pleased at the prospect, and followed this splendid road rapidly about eight miles, when, to our great mortification, we came to the termination of this lovely valley in front of a tall, steep mountain, which could not be ascended except by some creature that had either wings and claws. Upon examination, we found that old Peter Lassen and his party had marched west along this narrow valley to its abrupt termination, and then had turned about and marched back to near the point where they entered it, thus wasting some ten or fifteen miles of travel. The two portions of the road going into and coming out of this pretty valley were not more than half a mile apart; but this fact was unknown to us until after we had brought up against that impassable mountain.

This was a perplexing and distressing situation. Our own pilot did not like this route, as it was not going in the right direction. How to get out of this line of travel, and get again upon the river, was the question. We spent the greater part of one day in exploring a new route, but found it impracticable. In our explorations, we found a lava-bed some two miles wide. It was clear to us that old Peter Lassen was lost, except as to courses, and was wholly unacquainted with the particular route he was going. Our own pilot knew about as little as Lassen, if not less. Our wagons, we knew, would soon overtake us; and we determined to follow Lassen's road ten or fifteen miles farther, to see if it turned west. Several of us started on foot, and found that the road, after leaving the valley, went south about ten miles, and then turned due west, running through open pine-timber and over good ground. We returned to camp in the night, and decided that we would follow Lassen's road at all hazards. We awaited the arrival of our wagons, and then set forward. We found the road an excellent one, going in the right direction; and we soon found ourselves upon the summit of the Sierra Nevada Mountains.

The summit was almost a dead level, covered with stunted pines. We passed between peaks. The ascent on the eastern side was very gradual and easy. We encamped one evening on the summit near a small lake; and it was so cold that night that ice formed along its margin. This was about the 20th of October, 1848. We knew when we had passed the summit, from the fact that the streams flowed west. Though the beds of the streams were dry at that season of the year, we could tell which way the water had run, from the drift-wood lodged in places.

While on Pitt River, we knew from the camp-fires that Lassen's party had ten wagons; and from all appearances we were pretty sure that they were some thirty days ahead of us.

OVERTAKE PETER LASSEN AND HIS PARTY — ARRIVAL IN THE SACRAMENTO VALLEY.

We pressed on vigorously, and soon reached the wide strip of magnificent pine-timber found on the western side of the Sierra Nevada. We had not proceeded many miles, after entering this body of timber, before I saw a large, newly-blazed pine-tree standing near the road. Approaching I found these words marked in pencil: "Look under a stone below for a letter." It was a stone lying upon the surface of the ground, and partly embedded in it. It had been removed, the letter placed in its bed, and then replaced. No Indian would ever have thought of looking under that stone for anything. I did as directed, and found a letter addressed to me by my old friend and law-partner in Oregon City, A. L. Lovejoy, Esq., one of the packers who had gone ahead of us. The letter stated that they had overtaken old Peter Lassen and a portion of his party, lost in the mountains and half starved. That very evening we overtook Lassen and half of his party in the condition described by Lovejoy. In about eight days after we had first seen Lassen's road, we had overtaken him.

Peter Lassen had met the incoming immigration that fall, and had induced the people belonging to ten wagons to come by his new route. This route he had not previously explored. He only had a correct idea of the courses, and some general knowledge of the country through which they must pass. So long as this small party were traveling through prairies, or open woods, they could make fair progress; but, the moment they came to heavy timber, they had not force enough to open the road. After reaching the wide strip of timber already mentioned, they converted their ten wagons into ten carts, so that they could make short turns, and thus drive around the fallen timber. This they found a slow mode of travel. One half of the party became so incensed against Lassen that his life was in great danger. The whole party had been without any bread for more than a month, and had during that time lived alone on poor beef. They were, indeed, objects of pity. I never saw people so worn down and so emaciated as these poor immigrants.

The people that belonged to five of the carts had abandoned them, packed their poor oxen, and left the other half of the party, a short time before we reached those that remained with the other five carts and with Lassen. We gave them plenty of provisions, and told them to follow us, and we would open the way ourselves. Of course, they greatly rejoiced. How their sunken eyes sparkled with delight! Our pilot, Thomas McKay, overtook an old woman on foot, driving before her a packed ox down a long, steep hill. When he approached near to her, he made a noise that caused her to stop and look back. "Who are you, and where did you come from?" she asked in a loud voice. He informed her that he was one of a party of a hundred and fifty men, who were on their way from Oregon, with wagons and ox-teams, to the California gold mines. "Have you got any flour?" "Yes, madam, plenty." "You are like an angel from Heaven!" And she raised a loud and thrilling shout that rang through that primeval forest.

Lassen and our pilot followed the trail of the packers for some twenty or thirty miles, as it passed over good ground, but through heavy timber. We had from sixty to eighty stout men to open the road, while the others were left to drive the teams. We plied our axes with skill, vigor and success, and opened the route about as fast as the teams could well follow.

At length the pack-trail descended a long, steep hill, to a creek at the bottom of an immense ravine. Old Peter Lassen insisted that our wagons should keep on the top of the ridges, and not go down to the water. When the first portion of the train arrived at this point, they had to stop some time on the summit of the hill. How to get out of this position without descending into the ravine below was a perplexing question. Our pilots had been to the creek, and would not let us go down the hill. In looking around for a way out of this dilemma they discovered a strip of ground, about thirty feet wide, between the heads of two immense and impassable ravines, and connecting the ridge we were compelled to leave with another. It was like an isthmus connecting two continents. Over this narrow natural bridge we passed in safety.

That evening a large portion of our party encamped on the summit of a dry ridge, among the intermixed pine- and oak-timber. They had traveled all day, under a hot October sun, without water. This was the first time those with the wagons were compelled to do without water at night. They chained their oxen to their wagons, as the animals would have gone to water had they been turned out. The ox has a keen scent, and will smell water at the distance of one or two miles. It was another sober, solemn, and silent time. Scarcely a word was spoken, and not a mouthful eaten.

By daybreak next morning we were off, and had only gone about five miles when we came to the edge of the pine-forest. From this elevated point we had a most admirable view. Below us, at the seeming distance of ten, but the real distance of twenty miles, lay the broad and magnificent valley of the Sacramento, gleaming in the bright and genial sunshine; and beyond, and in the dim distance, rose the grand blue outlines of the Coast Range. The scene was most beautiful to us, thirsty as we were. How our hearts leaped for joy! That was our Canaan. Once in that valley, and our serious difficulties, our doubts and fears, would be among the things of the past. But the last of our trials was the most severe. We had still to descend to that desired valley over a very rough road.

From the place where we stood, we could see three tall, narrow, rocky ridges, with deep ravines between, running toward the valley.

Neither our pilots nor any of us knew which of the three ridges to take, and we had no time to explore. We contemplated the scene for a few moments, and then looked down the ridges for a short time, and chose the middle one at a venture, not knowing what obstructions and sufferings were before us. We had in our company two classes. One was eager to enter the valley as early as possible, while the other had no desire for haste. I belonged to the latter class. I had lived and suffered long enough to have acquired some caution.

The last camp before the one where a portion of our people had done without water had plenty of grass, fuel, and water. We had been rapidly descending the western side of the Sierra Nevada for some days before we overtook Lassen and his party; and we knew that we could not be very far from the Sacramento valley. Besides this evidence, we found the red oaks appearing among the pines; and this was a conclusive proof that we were not far from that valley. I saw that there was no necessity that the wagons should follow our pilots so closely. Our true policy would have been to remain where we first found the oak-timber until our pilots had explored and selected the route into the valley. We could have safely remained at that good camp a month longer than we did. But one portion of our people had the gold-fever too badly to be controlled. We who were more patient and cautious were willing that those hasty and ambitious men should go on ahead of us, if they desired to do so. Our two classes were well matched, like the man's oxen, one of which wanted to do all the work, and the other was perfectly willing that he should.

I had directed the men in charge of my wagons and teams to remain at that good camp until they should receive other orders. I then assisted to open the road to the natural bridge mentioned. After that, the road ran through open woods and over good ground to the point where the pines terminated. I determined to leave the foremost wagons at that point and return on foot to the good camp, where I arrived in the evening. Next morning early I took my best horse and started on after the foremost wagons, deciding that my own wagons and teams should remain where they were until I *knew* they could reach the valley by that or some other route. The distance from the point where I left the foremost wagons to the good camp was about fifteen miles. About 10 o'clock a.m.a.m. I arrived at that point, which I had left the morning before; and, looking down toward the valley, I could dimly discern some of the white-sheeted wagons on their dry and rugged way to the valley. I followed them as fast as I could, at a brisk trot. At the distance of about eight miles I came to an immense mass of rock, which completely straddled the narrow ridge and totally obstructed the way. This huge obstacle could not be removed in time, and the wagons had to pass around it. They were let down the left side of the ridge by ropes to a bench, then passed along this bench to a point beyond the rock, and were then drawn up to the top of the ridge again by doubling teams.

I passed on about six miles farther, and came to another huge mass of rock entirely across the top of the ridge. But in this case the sides of the ridge were not so steep, and the wagons had easily passed across the ravine to the ridge on the right. Soon, however, the ridges sank down to the surface, leaving no further difficulties in the way except the loose rocks, which lay thick upon the ground. These rocks were of all sizes, from that of a man's hat to that of a large barrel, and constituted a serious obstruction to loaded wagons. We could avoid the larger rocks, as they were not so many; but not the smaller ones, as they were numerous and lay thick upon the ground. In passing over this part of our route two of the wagons were broken down.

About noon I met one of our party who had been to the valley, and was on his return to the good camp, where his wagons and teams as well as mine were left. He reported to me that the route was practicable; and I sent word to my men to come on the next day.

I arrived at the camp in the valley, near a beautiful stream of water, a little after dark, having traveled that day about thirty-five miles. I could hear the wagons coming down that rough, rocky hill until midnight. Some of the people belonging to the foremost wagons had been without water nearly two days.

Next morning I started on foot to meet my wagons, and found them on the middle ridge, this side the first huge mass of rock, about sundown. They had plenty of water for drinking purposes, and chained up the oxen to the wagons. Next day they came into camp in good time, without suffering and without loss.

ARRIVE AT THE HOUSE OF PETER LASSEN — ORIGIN OF THE TERM "PROSPECTING" — ARRIVAL IN THE MINES — MINING.

We left the first camp in the valley the next morning, and after traveling a distance of eight miles, arrived at the rancho of old Peter Lassen. The old pilot was in the best of spirits, and killed for us a fat beef; and we remained at his place two or three days, feasting and resting. All organization in our company ceased upon our arrival in the Sacramento valley. Each gold-hunter went his own way, to seek his own fortune. They soon after scattered in various directions.

A day or two after we left Lassen's place, we were surprised and very much amused upon learning that the packers who had left us in such a hurry on Pitt River were coming on behind us. As stated, they had descended a long steep hill to a creek at the bottom of an immense ravine. They followed down this stream west for some miles, when they came to an obstruction in their route that they could not possibly pass, and were compelled to return up the stream east until they found a place where they could get out of this ravine on its northern side. They came to the creek on its southern side, and thought their best chance to escape was to be found on its northern bank. In this way they were detained in the mountains three or four days longer than we were. They had plenty of provisions, and had suffered but little. We therefore rallied them heartily, all of which they bore with the best of humor. Our ox-teams had beaten their pack-animals, thus proving that the race is not always to the swift.

In passing down the valley, we encamped one evening near the house of an old settler named Potter. He lived in a very primitive style. His yard, in front of his abode building, was full of strips of fresh beef, hung upon lines to dry. He was very talkative and boastful. He had been in the mines, had employed Indians to work for him, and had grown suddenly rich; and, as his head was naturally light, it had been easily turned. He came to our camp and talked with us until about midnight. It was here that I first heard the word "prospecting" used. At first I could not understand what Potter meant by the term, but I listened patiently to our garrulous guest, until I discovered its meaning. When gold was first discovered in California, and any one went out searching for new placers, they would say, "He has gone to hunt for new gold-diggings." But, as this fact had to be so often repeated, some practical, sensible, economical man called the whole process "prospecting." So perfectly evident was the utility of this new word that it was at once universally adopted.

We arrived in a few days at Captain Sutter's Hock Farm, so called from a small tribe of Indians in that vicinity. I called on the agent, and made some inquiries as to the mines. He replied that there was no material difference between the different mining localities, so far as he knew. Those on the Yuba River he knew to be good.

We forded the Feather River a few miles below Hock Farm, and then took up this stream toward the Yuba, and encamped a little before sundown near the rancho of Michael Nye. Dr. Atkinson, then practicing his profession in the valley, came to our camp. I inquired of him who resided in that house. He replied, "Mr. Nye." "What is his Christian name?" "Michael." I had known Michael Nye in Missouri, and my brother-in-law John P. Rogers (who was with me) and Nye had been intimate friends when they were both young men. We at once called upon Nye at his house. He received us most kindly. He and his brother-in-law William Foster, with their families, were living together.

Next morning we left for the Yuba; and, after traveling some eight or ten miles, we arrived at noon on the brow of the hill overlooking Long's Bar. Below, glowing in the hot sunshine, and in the narrow valley of this lovely and rapid stream, we saw the canvas tents and the cloth shanties of the miners. There was but one log-cabin in the camp. There were about eighty men, three women, and five children at this place. The scene was most beautiful to us. It was the first mining locality we had ever seen, and here we promptly decided to pitch our tent. We drove our wagons and teams across the river into the camp, and turned out our oxen and horses to graze and rest.

We arrived at the mines November 5, 1848; and the remainder of the day I spent looking around the camp. No miner paid the slightest attention to me, or said a word. They were all too busy. At last I ventured to ask one of them, whose appearance please me, whether he could see the particles of gold in the dirt. Though dressed in the garb of a rude miner, he was a gentleman and a scholar. He politely replied that he could; and, taking a handful of dirt, he blew away the fine dust with his breath, and showed me a scale of gold, about as thick as thin paper, and as large as a flax-seed. This was entirely new to me.

In the evening, when the miners had quit work and returned to their tents and shanties, I found a number of old acquaintances, some from Missouri and others from Oregon. Among those from Missouri were Dr. John P. Long and his brother Willis, for whom this bar was named. I had not seen either of them for about six years, though our families were connected by marriage — Dr. Benjamin Long, another brother, having married my youngest sister, Mary Burnett. I was perfectly at home here.

Next day my brother-in-law John P. Rogers, my nephew Horace Burnett (both of whom had come with me from Oregon), and myself purchased a mining location, fronting on the river about twenty feet, and reaching back to the foot of the hill about fifty feet. We bought on credit, and agreed to pay for it three hundred dollars in gold dust, at the rate of sixteen dollars per ounce. We at once unloaded the two wagons, and sent them and the oxen and horses back to Nye's rancho, where we made our headquarters.

As already stated, I had brought from Oregon new and suitable plank for a rocker, in the bottoms of my wagon-beds. The only material we had to purchase for our gold-rocker was one small sheet of zinc. I went to work upon the rocker, which I finished in one day; and then we three set to work on the claim with a will. I dug the dirt, Horace Burnett rocked the rocker, and John P. Rogers threw the water upon the dirt containing the gold. Within about three or four days we were making twenty dollars each daily, and we soon paid for our claim. We rose by daybreak, ate our breakfast by sunrise, worked until noon; then took dinner, went to work again about half-past twelve, quit work at sundown, and slept under a canvas tent on the hard ground.

In the summer months the heat was intense in this deep, narrow, rocky, sandy valley. The mercury would rise at times to 118° in the shade. Dr. John P. Long told me that the sand and rocks became so hot during the day, that a large dog he had with him would suffer for water rather than go to the river for it before night. The pain of burned feet was greater to the poor dog than the pain of thirst. After our arrival the days were not so hot.

This was a new and interesting position to me. After I had been there a few days I could tell, when the miners quit work in the evening, what success they had had during the day. When I met a miner with a silent tongue and downcast look, I knew he had not made more than eight or ten dollars; when I met one with a contented but not excited look, I knew he had made from sixteen to twenty dollars; but when I met one with a glowing countenance, and quick, high, vigorous step, so that the rocks were not much if at all in his way, I knew he had made from twenty to fifty dollars. His tongue was so flexible and glib that he would not permit me to pass in silence, but must stop me and tell of his success. Ordinary hands were paid twelve dollars a day, and boarded and lodged by the employer. I knew one young man who had been paid such wages for some time, but finally became disgusted and declared he would not work for such wages. It cost a dollar each to have shirts washed, and other things in proportion. There was no starch in *that* camp, and shirts were not ironed.

THE DONNER PARTY.

During my stay in the mines I was several times at Nye's house, and on one occasion I was there three days. I became well acquainted with William Foster and his family. Foster, his wife, and Mrs. Nye were of the Donner party, who suffered so much in the winter of 1846-'7.

Mrs. Nye did not talk much, not being a talkative woman, and being younger than Mrs. Foster, her sister. Mrs Foster was then about twenty-three years old. She had a fair education, and possessed the finest narrative powers. I never met with any one, not even excepting Robert Newell of Oregon, who could narrate events as well as she. She was not more accurate and full in her narrative, but a better talker, than Newell. For hour after hour, I would listen in silence to her sad narrative. Her husband was then in good circumstances, and they had no worldly matter to give them pain but their recollections of the past. Foster was a man of excellent common sense, and his intellect had not been affected, like those of many others. His statement was clear, consistent, and intelligible. In the fall of 1849 I became intimately acquainted with William H. Eddy, another member of the party. From these four persons I mainly obtained my information on this melancholy subject. I can not state all the minute circumstances and incidents, but can only give the substance as I remember it; for I write from memory alone.

The Donner party consisted of about eighty immigrants, including men, women, and children. They were so called because the men who bore that name were the leading persons of the party. They decided for themselves to cross the Sierra Nevada by a new road. L. W. Hastings, then residing at Sutter's Fort, went out to meet the incoming immigration of that fall, and advised the Donner party not to attempt to open a new route; but his advice was disregarded. He returned to the fort and reported the fact to Captain Sutter, who sent out two Indians, with five mules packed with provisions, to meet the party.

The party had arrived at a small lake, since called Donner Lake, situated a short distance from the present site of Truckee City, and some fifteen miles from Lake Tahoe, and had erected two log-cabins upon the margin of Donner Lake, when the Indians arrived with the mules and provisions. This was in the month of November, 1846. Up to this time there had been several comparatively light falls of snow. Foster said he proposed to slaughter all the animals, including the fat mules sent out by Captain Sutter, and save their flesh for food. This could readily have been done then, and the people could have subsisted until relieved in the spring. But the immigrants were not in a condition to accept or reject this proposition at once. They were unacquainted with the climate, could not well understand how snow could fall to the depth of twenty or thirty feet, and were so much worn down by the tedium of the long journey, and the absence of fresh meat and vegetables, that they were not prepared to decide wisely or to act promptly. Besides, the idea of living upon the flesh of mules and poor cattle was naturally repugnant to them. It is very probable that many of them considered such food unhealthy, and that, crowded as they were into two cabins, the use of such poor food might produce severe sickness among them, and many would die of disease.

While they were discussing and considering this proposition, a terrible storm came up one evening, and snow fell to the depth of about six feet during the night. The poor animals fled before the driving storm, and all perished; and next morning there was one wide, desolate waste of snow, and not a carcass could be found. The little supply of provisions they had on hand, including that sent by Captain Sutter, they saw could not last them long. They now fully comprehended their dreadful situation. It was a terrible struggle for existence.

It was soon decided to start a party across the mountains, on snow-shoes. This party consisted of ten men, including the two

Indians, five women, and a boy twelve years old, the brother of Mrs. Foster. I once knew the names of the eight white men, but at this time I can only remember those of William H. Eddy and William Foster. The women were Mrs. Foster, Mrs. McCutchin, Mrs. — , then a widow, but subsequently Mrs. Nye, Mrs. Pile, a widow, and Miss Mary — , sister of Mrs. Foster, and subsequently wife of Charles Covillaud, one of the original proprietors of Marysville, so named for her.

This little party left the cabins on snow-shoes, with one suit of clothes each, a few blankets, one axe, one rifle with ammunition, and a small supply of provisions. The summit of the mountain where they crossed it was about fifty miles wide, and was covered with snow to the depth of ten to fifteen feet; and they could only travel from five to eight miles a day. On the summit, and for some distance beyond it, not an animal could be found, as the wild game always instinctively fled before the snows of winter to the foot-hills, where the snows are lighter, and where they could obtain food and escape from their enemies by flight. In the spring the wild grazing animals ascend the mountain as the snows melt, to crop the fresh grass and escape the flies.

For the first few days they made good progress; but while they were comparatively strong they could kill no game, because none could be found, and their provisions were rapidly consumed. When they had reached the western side of the summit, they encamped, as usual, on the top of the snow. They would cut logs of green wood about six feet long, and with them make a platform on the snow, and upon this make their fire of dry wood. Such a foundation would generally last as long as was necessary; but on this occasion it was composed of small logs, as the poor people were too weak from starvation to cut and handle larger ones; and there came up in the evening a driving, blinding snow-storm, which lasted all that night and the next day and night. New snow fell to the depth of several feet. They maintained a good fire for a time, to keep themselves from freezing; but the small foundation-logs were soon burnt nearly through, so that the heat of the fire melted the snow beneath, letting them down gradually toward the ground, while the storm above was falling thick and fast. Toward midnight they found themselves in a circular well in the snow about eight feet deep, with the ice-cold water beginning to rise in the bottom. After the foundation was gone, they kept alive the fire by setting the wood on end and kindling the fire on the top. While they were in this condition, one of the Indians, who had been sitting and nodding next the snow-wall until he was almost frozen, made a sudden and desperate rush for the fire, upsetting and putting it out.

Eddy urged them to quit this well of frozen death, as it was impossible to live where they were, with their feet in ice-water. They all climbed out of the well, spread one blanket on the top of the snow, then seated themselves on this blanket, back to back, and covered their heads with the others. In this painful position they remained the rest of that night, all the next day and night, and until some time after sunrise the last morning. During this time four or five of their number perished, one of whom was the boy. Mrs. Foster spoke of this young hero with the greatest feeling. His patience and resignation were of the martyr type. When they were reduced to half a biscuit each, he insisted that she should eat his portion as well as her own; but this she refused.

From this scene of death the survivors proceeded on their melancholy journey down the western side of the mountain. That evening, after they had encamped and kindled a blazing fire, one of the men, who had borne the day's travel well, suddenly fell down by the fire, where he was warming himself, and expired. The cold, bracing air and the excitement and exertion of travel had kept him alive during the day; but when he became warm his vital energies ceased. This is often the case under like circumstances. I have understood that deaths occurred in this manner among Fremont's men, while making the trip from Oregon to California in the winter of 1843-'44. At this camp another of the men sat down by a pine-tree, leaned himself against it, and died.

The remainder of this suffering party continued their journey. All the other men dropped off one after another, at intervals, except Eddy and Foster. When they had almost reached the point of utter despair, Eddy saw a deer, and made a good shot, killing the animal. This supplied them with food for a few days. After it was consumed, they met with some Indians, who furnished them with a small quantity of provisions.

At length they arrived at the last encampment, and within six or eight miles of Johnson's rancho, on the eastern side of the Sacramento valley. Next morning Foster was unable to continue the journey, and refused to make another effort to walk. Eddy was the stouter man of the two, and he proceeded on his tottering course, leaving Foster and the five women at the camp. It was all Eddy could do to walk; but, most fortunately, he soon found two friendly Indians, who kindly led him to Johnson's place, Eddy walking between them, with one hand on the shoulder of each Indian.

They arrived at Johnson's house in the afternoon. Johnson was then a bachelor, but he had a man and his wife living with him. This lady was an admirable woman, full of humanity, and possessed of excellent sense, firmness, and patience. She knew from Eddy's condition what the poor sufferers needed. There were also several families of late immigrants residing temporarily in that vicinity. About ten men promptly assembled, and started for the camp, taking with them everything that was necessary.

The relief-men were piloted by the two humane Indians, and reached the camp a little after dark. Foster said that, when they heard the men coming through the brush toward the camp, the women began to cry most piteously, saying they were enemies coming to kill them; but Foster comforted and pacified them by declaring that the men coming must be friends. The relief-men soon came up, and were so much affected by the woful spectacle that for some time they said not a word, but only gazed and wept. The poor creatures before them, hovering around that small camp-fire, had been snowed on and rained on, had been lacerated, starved, and worn down, until they were but breathing skeletons. The clothes they wore were nothing but filthy rags, and their faces had not been washed or their heads combed for a month; and the intellectual expression of the human countenance had almost vanished. No case of human suffering could have been more terrible. No wonder that brave and hardy men wept like children.

Of all the physical evils that waylay and beset the thorny path of human life, none can be more appalling than starvation. It is not a sudden and violent assault upon the vital powers, that instinctive and intellectual courage may successfully resist; but it is an inexorable undermining and slow wasting away of the physical and mental energies, inch by inch. No courage, no intellect, no martyr-spirit can possibly withstand this deprivation. When there is an *entire* deprivation of food it is said that the greatest pangs of hunger are felt on the third day. After that, the stomach, being entirely empty, contracts to a very small space, and ceases to beg for food; and the sufferer dies from exhaustion, without any violent pain. But, when there is an insufficient supply of food, the severe pangs of hunger must be prolonged, and the aggregate amount of suffering before death is most probably increased.

The relief-party did everything required for the poor sufferers, and next morning carried them to Johnson's house. The lady in charge was careful to give them at first a limited quantity of food at a time. It required all her firmness and patience to resist their passionate entreaties for more food. When the poor, starved creatures could not persuade they violently abused the good lady because she did not comply with their demands. Eddy said that he himself abused her in harsh terms. All this she bore with the kind patience of a good mother, waiting upon a sick and peevish child.

I expressed my surprise to Eddy and Foster that all the women escaped, while eight out of the ten men perished, saying that I supposed it was owing to the fact that the men, especially at the beginning of the journey, had performed most of the labor. They said that, at the start, the men may have performed a little more labor than the women; but, taken altogether, the women performed more than the men, if there was any difference. After the men had become too weak to carry the gun, it was carried by the women. Women seem to be more hopeful than men in cases of extreme distress; and their organization seems to be superior to that of men. A mother will sit up with and wait upon a sick child much longer than the father could possibly do.

The Eddy party were about thirty days in making the trip. Other parties afterward left the cabins, and made their way into the settlement, after losing a considerable portion of their number on the way. Many died at the cabins from starvation. Forty-four of the Donner party escaped, and thirty-six perished.

A LONELY GRAVE — DEATH OF DAVID RAY — JOHN C. MCPHERSON.

The first Sunday after my arrival in the mines, I was strolling on the side of the hill back of the camp, among the lonely pines, when I came suddenly upon a newlymade grave. At its head there was a rude wooden cross, and from this symbol of Christianity I knew it was the grave of a Catholic. I never learned anything of the history of the deceased. He was, most probably, some obscure and humble person. He had died and was buried before my arrival.

"But the sound of the church-going bell
These valleys and rocks never heard;

Or sighed at the sound of a knell,
Or smiled when a Sabbath appeared."

Another death occurred in camp, and while I was there. It was that of David Ray. He was about thirty-five years of age, and his wife about thirty. They had five children, the eldest a daughter about twelve. They started from the State of Indiana in the spring of 1848, intending to locate in some one of the agricultural valleys of California, not then knowing that gold had been discovered. But when they arrived they determined to stop in the mines for a time, and thus came to Long's Bar, on the Yuba River.

Mr. Ray's business partner, Mr. Wright, was about the same age, unmarried, and sober, honest, industrious, and generous. He assisted Ray to build the only logcabin in the camp, for his wife and children, without charge. This house was a rude structure of one room, about sixteen feet square, with a clapboard roof, wooden chimney, and dirt floor. Yet it was the palace of the camp, and was the only place where one could enjoy a cheerful fire without being annoyed by the smoke. At all the tents and cloth shanties we had to make our fires in the open air.

About two weeks after my arrival Mr. Ray was attacked with fever, and died within a week. Neither he nor his widow had any relatives in California, and all the people of the camp were late acquaintances except Mr. Wright. Our tent was near Mr. Ray's house, and we soon became acquainted. He and his wife were devoted Methodists. She was a small, delicate woman, with a sweet musical voice and an eloquent tongue.

We buried him among the stately pines, in the open woods, where the winds might murmur a solemn and lonely requiem to his memory. All the people of the camp left their work and attended the burial; and I never witnessed a more sorrowful scene. There were no tearless eyes in that assemblage. No clergyman was present; but at the lonely grave of her husband Mrs. Ray made an impromptu address, which affected me so much that I soon wrote out its substance, preserving her own expressions so far as I could remember them. The following is a copy of what I then wrote:

O David! thou art cold and lifeless. Little dost thou know the sorrows thy poor and friendless and sickly wife now suffers. Thou art gone from me and from our children for ever. Thou wert ever kind to me; you loved me from my girlhood. O

*friends! he was a man without reproach, beloved by all who
knew him. He was a just man, honest in all his dealings. He
did unto others as he wished they should do unto him. He
defrauded no one. He was a pious and steady man; a profane
oath had never escaped his lips even from a boy; he was
never found at the grog-shop or the gambling-table. He it
was who lifted the prayerful hands. His creed was peace. He
died in his right mind, with a conscience void of reproach,
and committed his children to my charge. The only thing that
wounded his conscience was the reflection that, on the road
from Indiana to this country, he was compelled to do things
that grieved his righteous soul — he was compelled to labor
on the Sabbath day. But he is gone to a better world, where
his weary spirit will be at rest. Oh! if he had only died in a
Christian land! but the thought of his being buried in this
lonesome and wicked place! He has left me alone in a land of
strangers, a poor, sickly, weakly woman. Who shall now read
to me from the Bible, and wait upon me in my sickness? For
months and years he waited upon his sickly wife, without a
murmur. He was ever a tender husband to me, but he has
gone and left me. Who is there here to sympathize with me?
Ah me, what shall I do?*

*While in the mines I became acquainted with John C.
McPherson, a young, genial spirit from old Scotland. He was
a generous soul, and cared little for wealth. On Christmas
eve he composed a very pretty song, begining "Yuba, dear
Yuba." He has since written many poetical pieces, and many
prose communications for the newspapers. One thing can be
said of genial, kindly McPherson, that there is not a particle
of malice in his composition. No one ever thought of suing
him for libel, for he never wrote a harsh word of any one, living or dead. No one then in the mines except McPherson had
poetic fire enough in his soul to write a song. We spent many
pleasant evenings together, around the camp-fire, at Long's
Bar.*

Chapter VII

I remained in the mines until December 19, 1848. In the mean time I had sold my wagons and teams, and, altogether, had accumulated means enough to defray my expenses for six months. I knew that there must be business in my profession, and I found it would take me many long years to make enough in the mines to pay my debts. I therefore decided to quit the mines, and started with the intent to come to San Francisco; but, upon my arrival at Sutter's Fort, I determined to stop there.

Six of us left the camp at noon in an empty, uncovered wagon, drawn by oxen. It was a beautiful day, and that evening we drove to Johnson's ranch, which was about forty miles from the Fort. Next morning the oxen were missing, and were not found until about two hours before sunset. We at once set forward for Sutter's Fort. The wind commenced blowing hard from the south, and rain began to fall briskly about dark. About midnight the wind suddenly changed to the north, blowing quite hard and cold, and snow fell to the depth of about three inches. We had determined not to stop until we reached the Fort. Each of us took his turn at driving the team; and we thus reached the Fort about 10 o'clock a.m., December 21. Our journey was a most uncomfortable one, as we could neither keep ourselves warm nor sleep. We had traveled forty miles from Johnson's place without food, sleep, or rest.

I found a number of old friends at the Fort; and among them were Major Samuel J. Hensley, Major P. B. Reading, and Dr. William M. Carpenter. Dr. Carpenter had rented a small room in the Fort, and I proposed that we should keep our offices together, each paying half the rent and other expenses. As our professions did not clash, he readily assented to this, and we slept in the same rude bed, made by himself. We boarded at the hotel; and in the morning I cut the wood and made the fire, while the doctor swept out the office and made up the bed. The doctor made about six hundred dollars a week by his practice and from the sale of medicines. He charged sixteen dollars for each dose or vial of medicine, or box of pills.

I had only been at the Fort a few days when John A. Sutter, Jr., in whose name the Sutter grant of eleven leagues then stood, proposed to employ me as his attorney and agent. The terms agreed upon between us were such as his mercantile partner, Major Hensley, thought fair and just. I was to attend to all of his law business of every kind, sell the lots in Sacramento City, and collect the purchase money; and for these services I was to receive one fourth of the gross proceeds arising from the sale of city lots. There was a heavy amount of old business to settle up; and, while the labor was certain, the compensation was speculative, none of us then knowing whether the city would be at Sacramento or at Sutterville, a rival place about three miles below.

The city had been partially surveyed and mapped out by Captain William H. Warner, an army officer, who afterward completed the surveys and maps. Captain John A. Sutter, the original grantee, had conveyed his property, real and personal, to his son John A. Sutter, Jr., in the month of October, 1848. This was done to prevent one creditor, who threatened to attach the property, from sacrificing the estate, to the injury of the other creditors and the useless ruin of Captain Sutter and his family. There was no design to defraud the creditors; but, on the contrary, time proved that the course pursued was the wisest and most just, under the circumstances, toward all the creditors. John A. Sutter, Jr., informed me at once that he was bound, under the agreement with his father, to pay all his just debts at the earliest practicable period. I saw both the justice and expediency of this arrangement, and set myself to work with energy to accomplish the end intended. By the middle of August, 1849, the last debt that ever came to my knowledge had been paid.

The history of the settlement of Captain John A. Sutter in the Sacramento valley is so well known that I shall not enter into the subject at large; but, in justice to that old pioneer, who did so much for California, I will state some facts that have not perhaps been fully given by others. He has lately, I am informed, made and published a statement himself, which I have not seen. What I state is solely from memory; and, should there be any conflict in our recollections, I must yield to his superior knowledge.

Captain Sutter came to California from Missouri (where he resided for a time) with little capital. He procured the grant of his eleven leagues of land from the Mexican authorities, went to the Sandwich Islands, and there purchased a small vessel and an outfit from Mr. William French on credit. With this craft and outfit he returned, and commenced his improvements. He soon purchased of Don Antonio Suñol, of San José, a band of California cattle on time. These two purchases together amounted to some six thousand dollars. Later he purchased the Bodega property on credit. Though he employed Indian labor at a low rate, yet his improvements cost him a large sum in the aggregate; and this heavy expenditure of capital and labor was made long before he could realize any returns. He commenced his improvements in the wilderness, and among wild Indians, against whose apprehended attacks he had to make costly defensive preparations. The expenditure was certain, and necessarily made at the beginning, while the income was uncertain and late.

About the time the veteran pioneer had his rancho well stocked with domestic animals, and his farm fairly under way, and, before he could have possibly paid his debts, the immigrants began to arrive across the plains at his establishment. They came in weary, hungry, and poor. He had all the supplies, and they had all the wants and no money. He was only one, and they were many. They out-talked and out-voted him. He could not see them starve. This no pioneer could stand, and especially a man of his generous nature. He was compelled, from the very nature of the circumstances and the extreme necessities of the case, to supply their wants, and take in exchange their old wagons and broken-down teams, for which he had no profitable use, and which he could not convert into money. Being the father of the settlements in the Sacramento valley, he was also obliged to furnish the other settlers with supplies. Then all the traveling-parties passing through that part of California would call on him for more or less assistance. There was almost an entire failure of crops one year. All things considered, he had a heavy burden to carry.

It is not at all surprising that he could not save up money enough to pay his debts until after the discovery of the gold-mines. I am somewhat of a pioneer and business man myself, and I hesitate not to give it as my decided opinion that no man could, under the exact circumstances in which Captain Sutter was placed, have paid those debts before the discovery of gold.

There were very few people then in the country, nearly all of whom were of one class and very poor, engaged in the same pursuits and exposed to a common danger, and, consequently, their friendships became so warm and devoted that one could not refuse to help another when in need. Property was almost held in common. How could any pioneer refuse to aid a poor comrade who would fight and die for him when occasion required? The circumstances of a new country are so different from those of an old one that a different law of social life must prevail. A pioneer that refused to assist others liberally in the settlement of a new country would be as isolated as Mitchell Gilliam in Oregon, with his tavern-sign hung up before his door, as related in a previous chapter. Men are men, and they can not resist appeals to their kindness under such circumstances. This is the reason why so few pioneers ever become rich, and remain so.

Besides, Captain Sutter had a nobler object in view than the mere accumulation of a fortune for himself. His purpose was to colonize the great valley of the Sacramento. At the time gold was discovered, he had around him and in his immediate vicinity a number of colonists. He had established various industries, such as tanning, spinning and weaving, and cultivating a farm, and was engaged in the erection of a saw-mill. When I took charge of the business, I found, stowed away in a small room in the Fort, two or three looms, with the webs only partly woven, and several spinning-wheels, with the spools on the spindles partly filled, and the wool-rolls on the heads of the wheels unspun. I also found the tan-yard on the bank of the American Fork in ruins, the half-tanned hides having spoiled for want of attention. I did not see the saw-mill until October, 1849, and it evidently had never been finished.

The discovery of gold in California is due to Captain Sutter. I obtained my information on this subject from Mr. Marshall, the actual discoverer, who at the date of the discovery was in the employ of Captain Sutter. The latter was engaged in erecting a saw-mill, to be propelled by water-power, at Coloma, on the South Fork of the American River some forty miles from Sutter's Fort. At the site selected the river makes a considerable bend, forming a peninsula from two to three hundred yards wide at the point where the ditch and tail-race were cut across it. From the river above they cut a ditch about a hundred and fifty yards in length, and there put up the frame of the mill, and put in the flood-gate to let the water upon the wheel. It became necessary to construct what is called a tail-race, to enable the water to escape freely from the mill to the river below. The ground through which the ditch and tail-race were cut had a descent of about a hundred and fifty feet to the mile; and the formation was composed of a stratum of sand on the surface about two feet deep, and beneath this was a stratum of clay. Intermixed with these strata of sand and clay were found rocks of various shapes and sizes, from that of a man's hat to that of a flour-barrel.

The plan adopted by Marshall, the superintendent, was to pry up the stones in the line of the tail-race with crowbars, and put them aside during the day; and in the evening to raise the flood-gate, and let the water run down the tail-race all night. This would wash away the loose clay and sand, but would not remove the rocks. In the morning the water was shut off, and the men again went to work, putting aside the stones in the bed of the tail-race. After two or three days all the sand had disappeared, and the water had washed down to the stratum of clay, upon and in which the gold rested. Marshall, one morning after the water had been shut off, was walking along down the bank of the tail-race, when he discovered several pieces of some very bright metal in a little pool of water in the bottom of the race. It occurred to him at once that it might be gold; and upon gathering it up he was satisfied, from its appearance and weight, that it was gold. This occurred on the 19th of January, 1848.

Thus, this great discovery was owing to the act of Captain Sutter. But for that, the gold might have remained undiscovered for a century to come. No one can tell. We only know the fact that he was the cause of the discovery.

The discovery of gold at once so excited the people that they promptly left everything for the mines, and no other industry but mining was thought of for a time. The spectacle of such a sudden destruction of property and change of pursuit was enough to cause much pain to the old pioneer. Though made rich by the change, he often spoke of it with much feeling, as I was informed upon good authority.

In his treatment of the Indians, Captain Sutter was humane, firm, and just. I remember well that, in the winter of 1848-'49, the Indians would often call at the Fort, and anxiously inquire for him, to protect them from wrong. They evidently had the greatest confidence in his justice. He had been their friend and protector for years; but his power was then gone.

SELLING LOTS IN SACRAMENTO — NECESSITY OF SOME GOVERNMENTAL ORGANIZATION — PUBLIC MEETING AT SACRAMENTO CITY.

When I began to sell lots in Sacramento City for John A. Sutter, Jr., early in January, 1849, all the business was done at the Fort, situated about a mile and a half from the river. There were then only two houses near the *embarcadero*, as the boat-landing was then called. One was a rude log-cabin, in which a drinking saloon was kept; and the other, also a log-cabin, was occupied by an excellent old man named Stewart and his family. Nearly all the first sales were of lots near the Fort; but toward the end of January the lots near the river began to sell most rapidly. The prices for lots in the same locality were fixed and uniform; and I made it an inflexible rule not to lower the prices for speculators, thus preventing a monopoly of the lots. I discouraged the purchase of more than four lots by any one person. I said to those who applied for lots: "You can well afford to buy four lots, and can stand the loss without material injury if the city should fail; but, if it should succeed, you will make enough profit on this number." This moderate and sensible advice satisfied the purchasers, and built up the city. The terms were part cash and part on time, the purchaser giving his note for the deferred payment, and receiving a bond for a warranty deed when the note should be paid.

I had been at the Fort only a few days when the question arose as to some governmental organization. The great majority of the people then in California were within the district of Sacramento. Business was remarkably brisk, and continually increasing. Lots were selling rapidly, and who should take the acknowledgments and record the deeds? The war between the United States and Mexico had terminated by a cession of California to our country; and we were satisfied that the military government, existing during and in consequence of the war, had ceased. We knew nothing of the laws of Mexico, and had no means of learning. They were found in a language we did not understand, and we had no translations, and for some time could have none. In the mean time business must go on. We were of the opinion that we had the right to establish a *de facto* government, to continue until superseded by some legitimate organization. This *de facto* government would essentially rest upon the same basis as the provisional government of Oregon.

We accordingly held a public meeting at Sacramento City early in January, 1849, at which we elected Henry A. Schoolcraft as First Magistrate and Recorder for the District of Sacramento. Our rules were few and simple, and were merely designed to enable the people to go on with their necessary business for the time. This action was sanctioned by the people of the district.

But this anomalous and embarrassing position gave rise to efforts for instituting some regular organization for all California. For this purpose meetings were held in several places, and delegates elected to attend a convention to frame a provisional government. The first meeting was held at San José, December 11, 1848; the second at San Francisco, December 21, 1848; and the third at Sacramento City, January 6 and 8, 1849. The history of these efforts, resulting at last in the formation of the State government, may be mainly found in the "Weekly Alta California" for the year 1849. There is but one complete file in existence, the others having been destroyed by the several fires in San Francisco. The paper was then published by Edward Gilbert, Edward Keemble, and George C. Hubbard. The file now in existence is to be found in the State Library at Sacramento.

"The recent large and unanimous meetings in the Pueblo de San José and in this town, in favor of immediate action for the establishment of a provisional government, are believed to be a fair index of the feeling of the community throughout the Territory. That some steps should be taken to provide a government for the country, in the event that the United States Congress fail to do so at the present session, is obvious; and that the plan proposed by the resolutions of the San Francisco meeting is the most proper and feasible, we think beyond a doubt." (Editorial, "Alta," January 4, 1849.)

It will be seen that San Francisco was then called a "town."

Colonel Thomas H. Benton addressed a letter to the people of California, under date of August 27, 1848, from which I take the following extracts, as found in the "Alta" of January 11, 1849:

The treaty with Mexico makes you citizens of the United States. Congress has not yet passed the laws to give you the blessings of our government, and it may be some time before it does so. In the mean time, while your condition is anomalous and critical, it calls for the exercise of the soundest discretion and the most exalted patriotism on your part. The temporary civil and military government established over you as a right of war is at an end . . . .

Having no lawful government, nor lawful officers, you can have none except by your own act; you can have none that can have authority over you except by your own consent.

The proceedings of the meeting at Sacramento City are found in the "Alta" of January 25, 1849:

Provisional Government — Meeting at Sacramento City.

At a meeting held at Sacramento City, on the 6th day of January, 1849, to take into consideration the necessity and propriety of organizing a Provisional Government for the Territory of California, Peter H. Burnett was chosen President; Frank Bates and M. D. Winship, Vice-Presidents; and Jeremiah Sherwood and George McKinstry, Secretaries.

On motion, a committee of five was appointed by the President to draw up a preamble and resolutions expressive of the sense of this meeting. The committee was composed of Samuel Brannan, John S. Fowler, John Sinclair, P. B. Reading, and Barton Lee. The committee, having retired a few moments, returned, and asked for further time to report; whereupon, on motion, the meeting adjourned to meet again on Monday evening next.

Monday, *January* 8, 1849.

The meeting again assembled pursuant to adjournment. The Secretaries being absent, on motion, Robert Gordon was requested to act as Secretary. The committee appointed at the last meeting for that purpose made its report, which, after undergoing a few slight amendments, was adopted, as follows:

"*Whereas,* The Territory of California having by a treaty of peace been ceded to the United States; and the recommendation of the President to Congress to extend the laws of the United States over this Territory has not been acted upon by that body, and the citizens of this Territory are thus left without any laws for the protection of their lives and property; "*And whereas*, The frequency and impunity with which robberies and murders have of late been committed have deeply impressed us with the necessity of having some regular form of government, with laws and officers to enforce the observance of those laws;

"*And whereas*, The discovery of large quantities of gold has attracted, and in all probability will continue to attract, an immense immigration from all parts of the world, as well as from the United States, thus adding to the present state of confusion, and presenting temptation to crime;

"Therefore — trusting in the sanction of the government and people of the United States for the course to which by the force of circumstances we are now impelled, for our own and for the safety of those now coming to our shores —

"*Resolved*, That in the opinion of this meeting it is not only proper, but the present precarious state of affairs renders it very necessary, that the inhabitants of California should form a Provisional Government to enact laws and appoint officers for the administration of the same, until such time as Congress see fit to extend the laws of the United States over this Territory.

"*Resolved*, that while, as citizens of California, we deeply lament the, to us, unaccountable inactivity toward us by the Federal Congress, as manifested in their neglect of this Territory, yet, as citizens of that great and glorious Republic, we shall in confidence wait for, and when received shall joyfully hail, the welcome intelligence that a proper territorial government has been formed by the Congress of the United States for the Territory of California.

"*Resolved*, That we fully concur in opinion with the meetings held at San José and San Francisco in favor of establishing a Provisional Government, and that we recommend to the inhabitants of California to hold meetings and elect delegates to represent them in the convention to be assembled at San José on Monday, 5th March, 1849, at 10 a.m., for the purpose of drafting and preparing a form of government to be submitted to the people for their sanction.

"*Resolved*, That an election be held by the people of this district, in this room, at 10 a.m. on Monday next, by ballot, for five delegates to represent this district in the proposed convention.

"*Resolved*, That the President appoint a Corresponding Committee of three persons to communicate with the other districts, and otherwise further the object of this meeting.

"*Resolved*, That Messrs. Frank Bates, Barton Lee, and Albert Priest be a committee of three to act as judges of the election of delegates."

The report was unanimously adopted.

On motion of Samuel Brannan, a resolution was offered that our delegates be instructed to oppose slavery in every shape and form in the Territory of California. Adopted.

On motion of Mr. Brannan, it was resolved that, in case of the resignation or death of either of the delegates, the remainder be empowered to elect one to fill the vacancy.

The President, in pursuance of the fifth resolution, appointed Messrs. Frank Bates, P. B. Reading, and John S. Fowler, a Corresponding Committee.

On motion of Samuel Brannan, it was resolved that the proceedings of this meeting be published in the "Alta California."

On motion, the meeting adjourned.

Peper H. Burnett, *Pres't.*

Robert Gordon, *Sec'y.*

Edward Gilbert, James C. Ward, and George Hyde, Corresponding Committee for the district of San Francisco, published a recommendation, dated January 24, 1849, that the meeting of the Convention be postponed from March 5 to May 1, 1849.

A Territorial Government.

Our readers will be assured, on perusing on our first page the article from the New York "Journal of Commerce" headed "Present State of the Question," that it is to the institution of slavery we owe the non-establishment of a Territorial Government in this country. And they will have reason to fear, as we do, that another session of Congress may transpire without giving us the government we so much need, in consequence of the divisions and jealousies likely to grow out of the same subject. (Editorial, "Alta," February 15, 1849.)

RIVALRY BETWEEN SACRAMENTO AND SUTTERVILLE — JOURNEY TO SAN FRANCISCO — WONDERFUL COINCI- DENCES — STATE OF SOCIETY.

In the month of March, 1849, the rivalry between Sacramento City and Sutterville was at its greatest height; and, as the ships from the Eastern States were soon to arrive, full of passengers coming to the gold-mines, it was deemed best for the interests of Sacramento City that I should spend a few weeks in San Francisco. I started for San Francisco about the middle of March on board a small schooner. We had some forty passengers.

On our way, and soon after we left Sacramento City, I was lying in a berth below, when Richard D. Torney came to me and said that, though he was a wicked man himself, he was pained to hear a man on board speak against the Christian religion as he had done, and desired me to go on deck and engage in a discussion with him. This I declined to do. The unbeliever was about fifty years of age, had read much, was a man of considerable ability, and seemed quite sincere in his opinions, and therefore outspoken in his opposition to Christianity.

On our way down the Sacramento River, this gentleman and myself had frequent familiar conversations upon other than religious subjects. I soon learned that he was a native of Tennessee. He gave me a very full history of himself and family; and among other incidents he mentioned the death of his only son. His son was a bright and promising youth of sixteen, had been most carefully educated, and was an admirable scholar for his age, speaking several languages well. I could see that his love for his boy was intense, and all that a father could have for his child.

He said that he was a farmer at the time, and was engaged in inclosing a ten-acre tract of land, with a staked-and-ridered fence. The fence was made of split rails and stakes, and he had put up the rails until the fence was ready to receive the stakes. For the purpose of making my meaning clear, I will assume that the fence ran to the cardinal points, and inclosed a square piece of ground. He was engaged in hauling the stakes in his wagon, and put out two stakes at each corner of the fence. He could haul from seventy to eighty stakes at each load, and had put the stakes along the northern line of the fence, and part of the way down the western line, toward the southwest corner of the field. The stakes he was hauling at the time were found south of the new inclosure; and, as he came along the western line toward the northwest corner of the field, he decided that he would *guess* the corner of the fence where he should put out the first two stakes, so as to have *just the number* to reach the point where he had placed the last stakes of the preceding load. He did not count the number of fence-corners between him and the stakes already placed in position, nor had he counted the number of stakes in his wagon. He commenced and put out two stakes at a certain corner; and, in the very act of doing so, a sudden thought flashed through his mind that, in case the stakes should last him to the other stakes, and none be left over, his son, then in perfect health, would die within a week. To his surprise, he had just stakes enough to fill the gap; and, to his extreme sorrow, his son was taken sick the next day, and died within the week.

These coincidences were, indeed, most wonderful. First, there was one chance in two that there would be an even number of stakes on the wagon. Second, there was about one chance in five that he should have begun at the right corner. Third, there was one chance in many thousands that the thought should have flashed through his brain at the very instant that he threw out the first two stakes. Fourth, there was one chance in two thousand that the death of his son should have followed, as it did, within the time apprehended. Fifth, there was one chance in many millions that all the circumstances should have *concurred*. Take a combination bank-lock with one hundred numbers, and set the combination on four numbers — say, 16, 95, 20, and 7; and a burglar would have one chance in one hundred millions to guess the combination. If the lock were only set on one number, there would be one chance in a hundred, but it is the *combination* of several numbers that diminishes the chances so wonderfully.

These strange coincidences greatly puzzled this unbeliever. He expressed to me his extreme surprise. He had been most fondly attached to his son, and seemed to have set his whole heart upon him. I only state the facts, and leave every one to draw his own conclusions.

I arrived in San Francisco on Friday, March 23^{d}. It was then but a village, containing about one thousand five hundred inhabitants. Of them, fifteen were women, five or six were children, and the remainder were nearly all young men, *very few* being over forty. It was difficult to find a man with gray hair. I had never seen so strange a state of society until I arrived in California, although I had been a pioneer most of my life. To see a community composed almost exclusively of young men engaged in civil pursuits was, indeed, extraordinary. In point of intelligence, energy, and enterprise, they could not be exceeded, if equaled, by the same number found anywhere else. At Sacramento City there was about the same proportion of men, women, and children. Women were then queens, and children angels, in California.

Sunday, March 25, 1849, was a bright, genial, beautiful day; and, as I was standing in Kearney Street, about ten o'clock a.m., I saw, on the opposite side of Portsmouth Square, two little girls, about seven years old, dressed in pure white. They were about the age of my youngest child, Sallie, and they appeared to me the most lovely objects I had ever seen. How beautiful are innocent children! I had not seen my loved ones for more than six months, and this spectacle went to my heart. I had it from good authority that, in the fall of 1849, a beautiful flaxen-haired little girl, about three years old, was often seen playing upon a veranda attached to a house on Clay Street, between Montgomery and Kearney, and that hardy miners might be seen on the opposite side of Clay Street gazing at that lovely child, while manly tears ran down their bronzed cheeks. The sight of that prattling child revived memories of the peaceful, happy homes they had left, to hunt for gold on a distant shore.

In coming from Sacramento to San Francisco in April, 1872, on board a steamer, I made the acquaintance of an intelligent man, who had been a member of the Legislature of California. This gentleman informed me that he came to California in 1849, when sixteen years of age, with an uncle of his, who was as kind to him as a father. They located at a remote mining camp, far in the mountains, and had been there some months when he learned, one evening, that a woman had arrived at another mining locality, some forty miles distant. He said he had not seen a lady for six months, and he went to his uncle and said: "Uncle, I want you to lend me Jack to-morrow." "What do you want with him, my son?" "I have heard that there is a woman at — camp, and I want to go and see her." "Well, my son, you can take the mule, and go and see the lady." Next morning he was off by daybreak, and never stopped until he arrived at the place and saw the lady. She was an excellent married woman, and treated the boy with great kindness, esteeming his visit as a sincere compliment to her sex.

I had seen society in Oregon, without means, without spirituous liquors, and without a medium of exchange; but there was a due proportion of families, and the people rapidly improved in every respect. In California, however, there were few women and children, but plenty of gold, liquors, and merchandise, and almost every man grew comparatively rich for the time; and yet, in the absence of female influence and religion, the men were rapidly going back to barbarism.

SAILING SHIPS ARRIVE WITH GOLD-SEEKERS — THEIR SPECULATIVE CHARACTER — GOLD-WASHING MACHINES — CLIMATE OF SAN FRANCISCO.

Within a few days after my arrival in San Francisco the sailing ships from the East began to arrive, full of gold-seekers, who were well provided with outfits, consisting of clothing, towels, brushes, and other articles, many of which were not much used in the mines. Many of them had much greater supplies than they required, and others were destitute of the means to pay their expenses to the mines. As large objects appear small in the distance, most of these people supposed when they left home that their journey would about end at San Francisco. In this they found themselves mistaken. They had many miles yet to travel, and the expenses of travel in California were much greater in proportion to distance than at home. These people would congregate in and around Portsmouth Square, and you could see many auctions going on at the same time. The owner of the articles to be disposed of would turn up a barrel on end, and from his trunks alongside he would draw out his goods, and sell them to the highest bidder for gold dust at sixteen dollars per ounce, there being little or no coin in the country.

One of the greatest proofs of the speculative character of the gold-seekers was found in the various gold-washing machines brought to California. When the discovery of gold was fully believed in the States east of the Rocky Mountains, many inventive minds set to work to construct machines for washing out the gold. It was interesting and very amusing to see the number and variety of these most useless things. They had been brought in many cases across the Isthmus of Darien, at great expense and labor, and upon arrival were only fit for fuel. Many of the owners of these machines would not believe the statements of those who had been in the mines, but carried them to Sacramento City, where they were compelled at last to abandon them on the bank of the river. Some few of these machines were brought across the plains in wagons.

I knew a tinsmith named Coleman in Weston, Missouri, who invented and constructed an iron gold-washer weighing from ten to twelve hundred pounds, and sold it to another man I knew well in the same place, named Murphy, a hotel-keeper, who was a sound business man, and well off. He purchased an extra wagon and ox-team for that machine. When he arrived within four days' travel of Sacramento City, in the fall of 1849, he left the men in charge of his two wagons and teams, and came on in advance of them on horse-back. By some means his acquaintances had heard that he was bringing this machine overland, and they inquired of him whether it was true. He stoutly denied it, intending to return and meet his wagons before they could arrive at the City, and secretly put out the machine in the night by the wayside. But he miscalculated the time it would take the wagons and teams to arrive; and, the first thing he knew, they were in the City. "The boys" at once surrounded and searched his wagons; and in the bottom of one of them, well concealed, they found the machine. Perhaps no man was ever more thoroughly quizzed than Murphy. He was a man who boasted of his shrewd sagacity. The thing was thrown out in the rear of my office on J Street in Sacramento, where I saw it many times, and where no doubt it lies buried to this day.

For days and days I would stand on Kearney Street, in front of Naglee's Bank, near the Square, and talk to the newly arrived. I had been in the mines myself, had "seen the elephant," and could give them any information they desired. The simple absurdity of many of their questions severly tested my risible faculties; but I restrained my laughter, remembering that I had been green myself, and answered all their various questions kindly and truthfully. I have seen them, on their way to Sacramento City, take their spades and pans, shovel up the sand on the bank of the Sacramento River, and wash it out in their pans; and, when they had discovered a scale of mica, it was most interesting to watch the ardent expression of their faces, until they found that all that glitters is not gold.

I will not attempt a lengthy description of the young and great city of San Francisco. I have seen it rise from the rough, irregular sand-hills and ridges of the original site, to the paved streets and magnificent buildings of a city of three hundred thousand people, from every considerable clime and kingdom of the earth. I have seen the events of several generations crowded into one.

No climate, so far as I know, is superior to that of San Francisco, taken as a whole. It is never too cold nor too warm for outdoor work in this city. For ten months in the average year building and other outdoor work can go on most successfully. For eight months in the year we can know, with reasonable certainty, what kind of weather we are to have. If we have a picnic or other occasion to attend, we know there will be no disappointment in consequence of bad weather. We know how to estimate correctly, in advance, what we can accomplish within a time stated. The fact that so little time is lost in consequence of bad weather is one great cause of the city's rapid improvement. Men can do more outdoor work here than elsewhere in a year. A fine frame or brick building can be commenced after the rainy season has passed, and securely covered in before any rain falls to injure or impede the work.

UNSATISFACTORY CONDITION OF THE GOVERNMENT OF THE DISTRICT OF SAN FRANCISCO.

I had not been in San Francisco more than ten days before I became fully aware of the unsatisfactory condition of the government of this district. The alleged facts are concisely and clearly stated in the editorial of the "Alta California" of March 29, 1849, from which I make the following extracts:

In August, 1847, Governor Mason, by reason of many complaints against the ill-defined powers and assumptions of the Alcalde, authorized the election of six citizens to constitute a Town Council. This body continued in existence until the 31st of December, 1848, when it expired by limitation. They passed a law authorizing a new election on December 27th for seven members of a new council to succeed them. This election was duly held, but a majority of the old council was not satisfied with the result, and declared the election nugatory because fraudulent votes were polled thereat, and ordered a new one. Four fifths of the citizens thought that this was an unwarrantable assumption of power on the part of the council, and they would not attend a new election. An election was held, however, by the factionists, and we then had the spectacle of three town councils in existence at one and the same time. The old council finally voted itself out of existence on the 15th of January, 1849, and the other two kept up a cross-fire of counter enactments for a few weeks longer. Despairing of ever being able to establish public justice upon a proper basis so long as the people were at the mercy of this officer, a convention of the people of this district was then called, at which it was resolved to elect a legislative assembly of fifteen members, who should have power to make such laws as might be deemed necessary, "provided they did not conflict with the Constitution of the United States, nor the common law thereof."

The legislative body, to correct these abuses, and inasmuch as the people had elected three justices of the peace, fixed a day upon which the office of Alcalde should cease, and ordered him to hand over his books and papers to Myron Norton, Esq., a newly elected justice.

The proceedings of the meeting of citizens mentioned in the preceding remarks are published in the "Alta California" of February 15, 1849, as follows:

Public Meeting. A public meeting of the citizens of the town and district of San Francisco was held in the Public Square on Monday afternoon, the 12th instant, in accordance with previous notice.

The meeting was organized by calling M. Norton to preside, and T. W. Perkins to act as secretary. The chairman, after reading the call of the meeting, opened it more fully by lucidly but succinctly stating its objects; when Mr. Hyde, on being invited, after some preliminary remarks, submitted the following plan of organization or government for the district of San Francisco:

"*Whereas*, We, the people of the district of San Francisco, perceiving the necessity of having some better defined and more permanent civil regulations for our general security than the vague, unlimited, and irresponsible authority that now exists, do, in general convention assembled, hereby establish and ordain:

"Article I. "Section 1. That there shall be elected by ballot a Legislative Assembly for the district of San Francisco, consisting of fifteen members, citizens of the district, eight of whom shall constitute a quorum for the transaction of business, and whose power, duty, and office shall be to make such laws as they, in their wisdom, may deem essential to promote the happiness of the people, provided they shall not conflict with the Constitution of the United States, nor be repugnant to the common law thereof.

"Sec. 2. Every bill which shall have passed the Legislative Assembly shall, before it becomes a law, be signed by the Speaker and the Recording Clerk.

"Sec. 3. It shall keep a journal of its proceedings, and determine its own rules.

"Sec. 4. The members of the Legislative Assembly shall enter upon the duties of their office on the first Monday of March.

"Article II. "Sec. 1. That, for the purpose of securing to the people a more efficient administration of justice, there shall be elected by ballot three justices of the peace, of equal though separate jurisdiction, who shall be empowered by their commission of office to hear and adjudicate all civil and criminal issues in this district, according to the common law, as recognized by the Constitution of the United States, under which we live.

"Sec. 2. That there shall be an election held, and the same is hereby ordered, at the Public Institute, in the town of San Francisco, on Wednesday, the twenty-first day of February, 1849, between the hours of eight a.m. and five p.m., for fifteen members of the Legislative Assembly for the district of San Francisco, and three justices of the peace, as hereinbefore prescribed.

"Sec. 3. That the members of the said Legislative Assembly, and the three justices of the peace elected as hereinbefore prescribed, shall hold their office for the term of one year from the date of their commissions, unless sooner superseded by the competent authority from the United States Government, or by the action of the Provisional Government now invoked by the people of this Territory, or by the action of the people of this district.

"Sec. 4. Members of the Legislature and justices of the peace shall, before entering on the duties of their respective offices, take and subscribe the following oath:

"'I do solemnly swear that I will support the Constitution of the United States, and government of this district, and that I will faithfully discharge the duties of the office of — according to the best of my ability.'"

Mr. Harris moved the adoption of the entire plan, which was seconded . . . . and was carried almost unanimously . . . .

On motion of Mr. Roach, it was

"*Resolved*, That the persons who were elected on the 27th day of December last, to serve as a Town Council for the year 1849, and those who were elected for the same purpose on the 15th of January, 1849, be and are hereby requested to tender their resignations to a committee selected by this meeting to receive the same."

Messrs. Ellis, Swasey, Long, Buckalew, and Hyde were elected such committee.

On motion, it was

"*Resolved*, That these proceedings be published in the 'Alta California.'"

Myron Norton, *Pres't.*

T. W. Perkins, *Sec'y.* I have omitted some unimportant portions of the proceedings.

It appears that the military authorities pronounced the action of the Legislative Assembly null and void, and that the Alcalde had refused to deliver up the papers of his office to the person designated by the Assembly. This brought up the question as to the right of the people of California to organize a provisional Government.

General Mason was military Governor of California during the war with Mexico, and was succeeded by General Riley. At the time I was in San Francisco on my first visit, General Persifer F. Smith was in command temporarily as the superior officer of General Riley. I remember that I had a friendly conference with General Smith in regard to our civil government. He was a most admirable man — kind, candid, courteous, and dignified. He seemed to regret very much the unsatisfactory condition of governmental affairs in California, but still thought there was no remedy by the action of our people. I differed with him in opinion, and about the 20th of April, 1849, sent to the "Alta California" the following communication, which appeared in the number of that paper issued April 26, 1849:

COMMUNICATION TO THE "ALTA CALIFORNIA" — FAILURE OF THE ATTEMPT TO HOLD A CONVENTION TO FRAME A PROVISIONAL GOVERNMENT.

The Rights Of The People. Mr. Editor:

Have the people of California any rights? If so, what is their extent? Have they not certain rights, founded, based, and implanted in man's very nature — that belong to them as men, as human beings — rights that derive no force from human legislation, but trace their origin up through nature to nature's God? Are not these great principles of liberty and justice, that produced the American Revolutionary war, promulgated in the immortal Declaration of Independence, and are now embodied in the American Constitutions, State and Federal, the birthright of every American citizen? I must answer emphatically, they are yet ours, as much so as they were the rights of our ancestors. We have inherited them by direct, clear, and unquestionable lineal descent.

The Federal Government is a government of limited powers — limited by a written Constitution, published to the world, and placed among the enduring and solemn records of the country. The Constitution of the United States not only limits the powers of the Federal Government, but these powers are distributed among three separate and independent departments, the legislative, executive, and judicial. To these departments are assigned different functions, and they were intended by the framers of the instrument to operate as checks upon each other. No one department has any right to assume the powers or discharge the duties assigned to the others. The President is armed with the veto power, to protect his department from the encroachments of the Legislature, and the judiciary has the right to declare the acts of Congress and of the President unconstitutional, null, and void from the beginning. The President is a mere executive officer.

He possesses no legislative or judicial power. He can make no law, and construe no law except so far as his mere executive action is concerned.

The question whether the people of California under existing circumstances have the right to exercise that power inherent in human nature — the power to institute government for the protection of life, liberty, and the right of property — is a question that does not rightfully belong to the executive department of the government to determine; much less does it come within the province of a subordinate military commander. Neither does it belong to any military officer, in time of peace, to decide what code of civil law is in force in this or any other community; nor does he have the right to determine what judicial office is or is not in existence, nor whether this or that individual is rightfully a judicial officer. These are powers foreign to the military office, and not conferred by the Constitution and laws of our country.

Has the President of the United States distinctly and clearly advanced the astounding proposition that, so long as Congress may choose to abandon and, for the time being, abdicate the right of government here, and refuse to extend over us the laws of our country — that so long the most unfortunate and miserable people of California (not having forfeited their rights by crimes against God and their country) have not the liberty to organize a mere temporary government for their protection? Does the President, or any other American statesman, mean to say that, while the people of Oregon had the right to and did organize a provisional government, recognized by Congress itself, the people of California have no such right? I do not understand the President or the Secretary of State as intending to advance any such idea. I know Colonel Benton distinctly advised the people of California to organize such government. The President has not, as I understand, decided that we have no right to institute a temporary government, and that we must submit to the mere de facto government under the military authority; and, had he so decided, he would have done so in derogation of the Constitution and laws of our country. The idea that he has so decided is simply an inference from language that will not, I apprehend, warrant such a conclusion.

What are, in fact, the opinions of the President in reference to the existing state of things in California? In his late message he says: "Upon the exchange of the ratifications of the treaty of peace with Mexico, on the thirteenth day of May last, the temporary governments which had been established over New Mexico and California by our military and naval commanders, by virtue of the rights of war, ceased to derive any obligatory force from that source of authority." I have italicized a part of the above extract for the purpose of more distinctly showing that, in the President's opinion, whatever government existed after the establishment of peace did not so exist "in virtue of the rights of war," and derived no obligatory force from that source of authority.

The President, after speaking of the adjournment of Congress without making any provision for the government of the inhabitants of New Mexico and California, goes on to say: "Since that time, the limited power possessed by the Executive has been exercised to preserve and protect them from the inevitable consequences of a state of anarchy. The only government that remained was that established by the military authority during the war. Regarding this to be a de facto government, and that, by the presumed consent of the inhabitants, it might be continued temporarily, they were advised to conform and submit to it for a short intervening period, before Congress would again assemble, and could legislate on the subject."

All governments, rightfully instituted, must derive their powers from some source. These powers are derivative, not original. The Declaration of Independence assumes the clear and distinct principle that "governments instituted among men derive their just powers from the consent of the gov-

erned." Now, according to the above extract, from what "source of authority" did the temporary governments continued after the war derive their powers? Not from the "rights of war." They had ceased. Nor yet from the legislation of Congress, for that body adjourned without any action upon the subject. What then was the source of power? The President says the "consent of the inhabitants." Nor can the President or any one else "presume" this "consent" to be given contrary to the fact and the truth, and does the President mean to say so? Surely not. If the President has the right to "presume" this consent to be given, in direct and positive contradiction to the express acts and declarations of the inhabitants, has he not the right to continue such military government without the "consent" of the inhabitants at all, either actual or presumed?

What is the difference between no consent and "presumed consent" contrary to the truth? Can the President, or any man living, presume away the liberties of the people? Never. If we have no power to dissent, we have no power to consent. We are not free, but mere passive instruments. Suppose a despot should say to a certain people, "I will not exercise despotic power over you without your consent, but I will presume such consent against your express declarations to the contrary." Is it possible that the President of the United States intended to say, in substance, to his fellow citizens of California, "Gentlemen, I will not continue the temporary government established during the war without your consent, but I will presume your consent against your express acts and declarations to the contrary, and, if you attempt to organize a mere temporary government to 'protect you from the inevitable consequences of a state of anarchy,' I will put you down by military power, and treat you as traitors and enemies of your country"?

That our military commanders had a right to establish a temporary government "in virtue of the rights of war," to continue during the existence of the war, might readily be admitted; and that the President had the right to continue such government after peace was established, by the "consent of the inhabitants," might be true; and that such consent might fairly be presumed, so long as they submitted to such government, and organized no other, might also be admitted, though doubtful. But to say that the President, a mere executive officer, could continue such government without any actual consent of the inhabitants, and could presume such consent in a manner so violent as utterly to destroy all power of dissent in the neglected people of California, and all power to "protect themselves from the inevitable consequences of anarchy," is to assert a proposition giving to the President a power over his fellow citizens equal to that of a despot.

The opinion of President Polk and that of his distinguished Secretary of State are entitled to the utmost respect, not only upon account of the high and responsible stations they filled, but more especially for the reason that they are both profound jurists and statesmen. But I do not understand them as laying down these two distinct positions — 1. That the government continued in California after the war could only exist by the "consent" of the inhabitants; and 2. That the President has the right to presume such consent to be given although it be expressly withheld. Now, both these positions must be sustained before the right can be denied to the people of California to organize a mere temporary government "to protect them," in the beautiful language of the President, "from the inevitable consequences of a state of anarchy."

Mr. Starkie, in his learned treatise on the "Law of Evidence," gives this definition of a presumption: "A presumption may be defined to be an inference as to the existence of one fact from the existence of some other fact, founded upon a previous experience of their connection." After some other remarks not necessary to illustrate the position I am seeking to establish, the author says: "It also follows from the above definition that the inference may be either certain or not cer-

tain, but merely probable, and therefore capable of being rebutted by proof to the contrary." (Part IV., p. 1235.)

Now, whether the inhabitants gave, and still continue to give, their consent to the continuance of the military government after the cessation of war, is simply a question of fact. So long as the people of the country submitted to such government, organized no other, and made no objection, by their acts they made that government their own, and their consent might be presumed. But I take it that such presumption is not of that kind called by Mr. Starkie "certain," but only "probable," and "therefore capable of being rebutted by proof to the contrary."

All that I understand the President as intending to advance is, that he had the limited power to continue the de facto government by the consent of the inhabitants; and that so long as they submitted, and did not object to such continuance, nor organize any different government, such consent might be presumed; and for this reason he "advised" the inhabitants to "conform and submit to it for a short intervening period, before Congress would again assemble, and could legislate on the subject." He "advised" (not ordered) the inhabitants to submit. The law commands, and does not advise. And, had the President believed that he had the lawful authority to continue the de facto government against our consent, it would have been his duty to speak "as one having authority," and not merely to give advice.

I have thus, Mr. Editor, spoken my candid sentiments in language, I hope, intelligible and plain. I have done so without intending the slightest disrespect to those of my fellow citizens who may differ with me in opinion. I have only sought to discuss most vital principles, and not to make the slightest personal reflection upon any one. I may or may not trouble you again.

P.

The following is an extract from a letter of James Buchanan, Secretary of State of the United States, to William V. Voorhies, dated October 7, 1848:

The President deeply regrets that Congress did not, at their late session, establish a territorial government for California. It would now be vain to enter into the reasons for this omission. Whatever these may have been, he is firmly convinced that Congress feels a deep interest in California and its people, and will at an early period of the next session provide for them a Territorial Government suited to their wants. ("Alta," March 15, 1849.)

But the next session passed without any legislation by Congress in regard to California, except to extend the revenue laws of the United States over us. In the "Alta" of June 2, 1849, will be found an editorial in reference to this treatment of us headed "A Legal Outrage," in which occurs the expression, "thus passing a law to tax California without giving it a representative or even a government."

It will be remembered that the meetings held at San José and San Francisco in December, 1848, and that at Sacramento in January, 1849, recommended the people of California to elect delegates to attend a Convention to be held at San José, March 5, 1849, to frame a provisional government for this Territory. Delegates were accordingly elected, and corresponding committees appointed; but that attempt at organization failed, in consequence of a difference of opinion as to the time when the Convention should meet. The time mentioned was found to be too short to allow the lower districts to be represented. Edward Gilbert, James C. Ward, and George Hyde, Corresponding Committee of San Francisco, published a recommendation, dated January 24, 1849, that the meeting of the Convention be postponed from March 5th to May 1st. ("Alta," January 25, 1849.) Messrs. John Sinclair and Charles E. Pickett, delegates elect to the Convention from Sacramento district, protested against the change of time. ("Alta," March 1, 1849.)

In the "Alta" of March 22, 1849, a communication was published — signed by W. M. Steuart, Myron Norton, and Francis J. Lippitt, delegates from San Francisco; Charles T. Botts, delegate from Monterey; J. D. Stevenson, from Los Angeles; R. Semple, from Benicia; John B. Frisbie and M. G. Vallejo, from Sonoma; S. Brannan, J. A. Sutter, Samuel J. Hensley, and P. B. Reading, from Sacramento — recommending the holding of a Convention for framing a provisional government at Monterey, on the first Monday of August, 1849, in case no act of Congress should be passed to create a territorial government for California, and resigning their positions as delegates.

Congress adjourned March 3, 1849, and President Taylor was inaugurated on the 5th, the 4th being Sunday; but, at the date of the above recommendation, March 22[d], the non-action of Congress in regard to a territorial organization for California was not known here. This recommendation was not acted upon by the people.

Chapter VIII.

RETURN TO SACRAMENTO — COME A SECOND TIME TO SAN FRANCISCO — BECOME A MEMBER OF THE LEGISLATIVE ASSEMBLY — EXTRACTS FROM THE ADDRESS OF THAT BODY TO THE PEOPLE OF CALIFORNIA — EXTRACTS FROM GENERALRILEY'S PROCLAMATION — ADDRESS OF THE COMMITTEE OF FIVE.

About the 21st of April, 1849, I left San Francisco on my return to Sacramento, where I arrived about the 28th of that month. About the middle of May my family arrived in San Francisco from Oregon; and I came the second time to San Francisco, arriving about the 1st of June. I became a member of the Legislative Assembly of SanFrancisco, and took a leading part in its proceedings. This Assembly published an "Address to the People of California," which appears in the "Alta" of June 14, 1849. Though there is no date to the address as published, it was adopted some time before, and was written by me, in entire ignorance of General Riley's intended proclamation to the people of California, which bears date at Monterey, June 3, 1849, but was unknown in San Francisco until Saturday, June 9th. The following are extracts from this address: The Committee appointed by the Speaker, under a resolution of this House, to draw up and submit an address to the people of California, beg leave respectfully to submit the within for the consideration of this body. . . .

The discovery of the rich and exhaustless gold-mines of California has, in and of itself, produced a strange and singular state of things in this community, unparalleled, perhaps, in the annals of mankind. We have here in our midst a mixed mass of human beings from every part of the wide earth, of different habits, manners, customs, and opinions — *all*,however, impelled onward by the same feverish desire of fortune-making. But, perfectly anomalous as may be the state of our population, the state of our government is still more unprecedented and alarming. *We are in fact without government* — a commercial, civilized, and wealthy people, without law, order, or system, to protect and secure them in the peaceful enjoyment of those rights and privileges inestimable, bestowed upon them by their Creator, and holden, by the fundamental principles of our country, to be *inalienable and absolute*.

For the first time in the history of the "model Republic," and perhaps in that of any civilized government in the world, the Congress of the United States, representing a great nation of more than twenty millions of freemen, have assumed the right, not only to *tax us without representation*, but to *tax us without giving us any government at all* — thus making us feel, endure, and bear all the Burthens of government, without giving us even a distant glimpse of its Benefits. A special and separate act was introduced in the House of Representatives, at the late session of Congress, by the Committee on Commerce, and subsequently passed by both Houses, extending the revenue laws of the United States over California, and leaving the bill to organize a territorial government for this neglected people to perish at the close of the session.

Under these pressing circumstances, and impressed with the urgent necessity of some efficient action on the part of the people of California, the Legislative Assembly of the district of San Franciscohave believed it to be their duty to earnestly recommend to their fellow citizens the propriety of electing twelve delegates from each district to attend a general Convention, to be held at the Pueblo de San José on the third Monday of August next, for the purpose of organizing a government for the whole Territory of California. We would recommend that the delegates be intrusted with enlarged discretion to deliberate upon the best measures to be taken; and to form, if they upon mature consideration should deem it advisable, a State Constitution, to be submitted to the people for their ratification or rejection by a direct vote at the polls.

The present state of a great and harassing political question in the United States must certainly defeat, for several coming sessions, any attempts at an organization of a territorial government for this country by Congress. In the Senate of the United States the parties stand precisely equal, there being fifteen free and fifteen slave States represented in that body. Until one or the other gain the ascendancy, we can have no territorial organization by act of Congress. All parties in both Houses of Congress admit, however, that the people of California can and ought to settle the vexed question of slavery in their State Constitution. From the best information, both parties in Congress are anxious that this should be done; and there can exist no doubt of the fact that the present perplexing state of the question at Washington would insure the admission of California at once. *We have that question to settle for ourselves; and the sooner we do it, the better.*

The following editorial, in reference to this address, appeared in the "Alta" of June 14th:

It is important and proper that we should remark, in this connection, that the Legislative Address was prepared and adopted before the publication of General Riley's proclamation in this place, and that it therefore has no reference to, or necessary connection with, that document.

In the same number of the "Alta" will be found a long editorial, of which the following is the beginning:

A Revolution — its Progress

This town was thrown into a state of intense excitement on Saturday morning last, by the publication of the "Proclamation to the People of the District of San Francisco," which is this day given in our colmns. The publication at the same time of a "Proclamation to the People of California," which we also insert to-day, did not detract from the intense excitement of the day.

A meeting was held on Tuesday, June 12th, of the proceedings of which the following correct account will be found in the "Alta" of June 14th: *Large and Enthusiastic Mass Meeting of the Citizens of San Francisco in Favor of a Convention for forming a State Government.*

The mass meeting of the citizens, called for the purpose of considering the propriety of electing delegates to a convention for the formation of a government for California, took place on Tuesday, June 12th, in Portsmouth Square.

At 3 o'clock p.m. the meeting was called to order by Peter H. Burnett, Esq., who proposed to the meeting the following list of officers, which was unanimously adopted: President, William M. Steuart; Vice-Presidents, William D. M. Howard, E. H. Harrison, C. V. Gillespie, Robert A. Parker, Myron Norton, Francis J. Lippitt, J. H. Merrill, George Hyde, William Hooper, Hiram Grimes, John A. Patterson, C. H. Johnson, William H. Davis, Alfred Ellis, Edward Gilbert, John Townsend; Secretaries, E. Gould Buffom, J. R. Per Lee, W. C. Parker.

The object of the meeting having been briefly stated by the President, Peter H. Burnett, Esq., addressed the people assembled, and concluded his remarks by presenting the Hon. Thomas Butler King of Georgia, who responded to the call with his accustomed eloquence and ability. The meeting was further addressed by Dr. W. M. Gwin and William A. Buffom, Esq., when the following resolutions were offered by Myron Norton, Esq.:

> "*Resolved*, That, the Congress of the United States having failed to pass any law for the government of this country, the people of California have the undoubted right to organize a government for their own protection.

> "*Resolved*, That the people of California are called upon by an imperative sense of duty to assemble in their sovereign capacity, and elect delegates to a convention to form a constitution for a State government, that the great and growing interests of California may be represented in the next Congress of the United States, and the people of this country may have the necessary protection of law.

> "*Resolved*, That we earnestly invite our fellow citizens at large to unite with us in our efforts to establish a government in accordance with the Constitution of our beloved country, and that a committee of five persons be appointed by the President of this meeting to correspond with the other districts, and fix an early day for the election of delegates and the meeting of the convention, and also to determine the number of delegates which should be elected from this district."

Major Barry opposed the resolutions. General Morse proposed an amendment to the last resolution, to the effect that the meeting adopt for the time the days appointed by General Riley.

Colonel J.D. Stevenson opposed the amendment.

After some little discussion, the amendment was rejected, and, the vote being taken upon the original resolutions, they were adopted.

The Chairman, in accordance with the last resolution, then appointed the following committee: Peter H. Burnett, W.D.M. Howard, Myron Norton, E. Gould Buffom, Edward Gilbert.

The meeting was then addressed by Edward Gilbert.

On motion, the meeting adjourned *sine die*.

William M. Steuart, *President*.

E. Gould Buffom, J. R. Per Lee, W. C. Parker, *Secretaries.* General Riley's "Proclamation to the People of California," as already stated, bore date at Monterey, June 3, 1849, but was not known in San Francisco until Saturday, June 9th. The following extracts are from this proclamation:

In order to complete this organization with the least possible delay, the undersigned, in virtue of power in him vested, does hereby appoint the first day of August next as the day for holding a special election for delegates to a general convention, and for filling the offices of judges of the Superior Court, prefects and sub-prefects, and all vacancies in the offices of first alcaldes (or judges of first instance), alcaldes, justices of the peace, and town councils. The judges of the Superior Court and district prefects are by law executive appointments; but, being desirous that the wishes of the people should be fully consulted, the Governor will appoint such persons as may receive the plurality of votes in their respective districts, provided they are competent and eligible to the office. Each district will therefore elect a prefect and two sub-prefects, and fill the vacancies in the offices of first alcalde (or judge of first instance) and of alcalde. One judge of the Superior Court will be elected in the districts of San Diego, Los Angeles, and Santa Barbara; one in the districts of San Luis Obispo and Monterey; one in the districts of San José and San Francisco; and one in the districts of Sonoma, Sacramento, and San Joaquin. The salaries of the judges of the Superior Court, the prefects, and judges of first instance are regulated by the Governor, but can not exceed for the first $4,000 per annum, for the second $2,500, and for the third $1,500. These salaries will be paid out of the civil fund which has been formed from the proceeds of the customs, provided no instructions to the contrary are received from Washington . . . .

The method here indicated to attain what is desired by all, viz., a more perfect political organization, is deemed the most direct and safe that can be adopted, and one fully authorized by law. It is the course advised by the President, and by the Secretaries of State and of War of the United States, and is calculated to avoid the innumerable evils which must necessarily result from any illegal local legislation. It is therefore hoped that it will meet with the approbation of the people of California, and that all good citizens will unite in carrying it into execution.

On the 4th of June General Riley issued a proclamation addressed "To the People of the District of San Francisco," in which he declares that the "body of men styling themselves the Legislative Assembly of San Francisco has usurped powers which are vested only in the Congress of the United States," etc. This was made known in San Francisco, June 9th. The time appointed by General Riley for the meeting of the Convention was September 1, 1849, and the place Monterey. The Legislative Assembly of San Francisco issued an "Address to the People of California," in answer to the two proclamations of General Riley. This address was reported by a committee of which I was a member, and was drawn up by me. It may be found at length in the "Alta" under the dates of July 19, 26, and August 9, 1849.

The following was published by the committee of five:

To the Public. The undersigned, composing a committee appointed at a mass meeting of the people of the district of San Francisco, held on the 12th day of June, 1849, to correspond with the other districts, and to fix an early day for the election of delegates and the assembling of the convention, and also to determine the number of delegates which should be elected from this district, have given the subject that attention which their limited time and means would permit. The time being a matter, not of principle, but of mere expediency, the committee, being duly impressed with the urgent necessity of success in the main object desired by all parties, have not deemed it their duty or right, under the circumstances, to do any act that might endanger the ultimate success of the great project of holding the convention. The committee, not recognizing the least power, as matter of right, in Brevet Brigadier General Riley, to " appoint" a time and place for the election of delegates and the assembling of the convention; yet, as these matters are subordinate, and as the people of San José have, in public meeting, expressed their satisfaction with the times mentioned by General Riley, and as we are informed the people below will accede to the same, and as it is of the first importance that there be unanimity of action among the people of California in reference to the great leading object — the attempt to form *a government for ourselves — we recommend to our fellow citizens of California the propriety, under the existing circumstances, of acceding to the time and place mentioned by General Riley in his proclamation, and acceded to by the people of some other districts. The committee would recommend their fellow citizens of the district of San Francisco to elect five delegates to the convention. And they can not but express the opinion that their fellow citizens of the two great mining districts of Sacramento and San Joaquin have not had anything like justice done them, by the apportionment of General Riley; that they are justly entitled to a greater proportion of delegates to the convention than the number mentioned in General Riley's proclamation; and the committee, believing their fellow citizens of the mining districts to have equal rights, in proportion to numbers, with the people of other districts, would recommend them to elect such increased number of delegates as they in their judgment shall think just and right.*

Peter H. Burnett. William D.M. Howard. Myron Norton. E. Gould Buffom. Edward Gilbert. *June 18, 1849.*

EXTRACTS FROM MY SECOND COMMUNICATION TO THE "ALTA CALIFORNIA" — GROUNDS OF GENERAL RILEY'S VIEWS AS TO THE RIGHT OF THE PEOPLE OF CALIFORNIA TO ORGANIZE A PROVISIONAL GOVERNMENT — GROUNDS OF THOSE WHO CLAIMED THAT RIGHT — THE CONTROVERSY MOST FORTUNATE FOR CALIFORNIA — ALL THINGS HAPPILY TENDED TO PRODUCE THE MAIN RESULT DESIRED BY US ALL.

About the 5th of July I sent a communication to the "Alta," which appeared in the number of July 12, 1849. The following are extracts:

But it seems from a late communication in your paper, under the signature of General Riley, that new instructions have been received, which, he says, sustain the views expressed in his proclamation. He says: "It may not be improper here to remark that the instructions from Washington, received by the steamer Panama since the issuing of the proclamation, fully confirm the views there set forth; and it is distinctly said in these instructions that ' *the plan of establishing an independent government in California can not be sanctioned, no matter from what source it may come.*'"

If these instructions do confirm the views of the proclamation, I must say that the General has been unfortunate in his quotation. Although this most solemn and threatening extract from the instructions is put in italics to give it greater point, and introduced in such a connection as to be endorsed as *true* by General Riley, it contains nothing that touches the question, and only puts forth a libel upon the people of California. As a citizen of the United States, attached to the Government of my country by all the ties of duty, kindred, admiration, and love, as a citizen of California, and as a man, I must express my sincere regret and mortification.

What is meant by the phrase "independent government"? Did the intelligent officer who drew up these instructions mean to say that a mere temporary provisional government, merely regulating our domestic affairs, and that only while Congress neglected and refused to do so themselves — not conflicting with any rights of the General Government, not absolving the inhabitants from their allegiance to the United States, not declaring us *independent*, but expressly admitting our *dependence* — in short, such a government as was organized by the people of Oregon and sanctioned by the home Government — I ask in candor, did the writer mean to call this an "independent government" that could not be sanctioned? I can not believe it. The writer knows too well the use of terms. What is an "independent government"? Undoubtedly such a government as was proclaimed by the Declaration of Independence, which declared the colonies to be "free and independent States," and the people to be absolved from all allegiance to the British Crown . . . .Now, Mr. Editor, let me inquire what single individual in California, not to speak of any considerable portion of this community, ever did propose, or dream of proposing, a "plan of establishing an independent government in California"? Is it true that such a plan was proposed? If so, who proposed it? For one, I am not informed of such a thing.

The idea of establishing an independent government here — thus cutting us off from the Union and from all protection of the mother country, and erecting a mere petty state to be the sport and play of all the great powers of the world, that might think it their *interest* or *whim* to insult and plunder us — certainly never was contemplated by our people here. Why, then, are we charged with such an absurd and criminal attempt? Have the authorities at Washington been deceived as to the true state of things here? How have they come to be so mistaken? There is a great mistake somewhere. Who is to blame we can not tell. All we know with unerring certainty is, that we are the doomed sufferers. The officers here shelter themselves behind the impenetrable shield called "instructions," and the authorities at home are ignorant of our condition. Is our country or our brethren in the States to be blamed for this? Certainly not. They will do us justice. The time is coming when California can have her equal station among the States of the Union, and when her servants can be heard, and her voice regarded. P.

An editorial in the "Alta" for July 19, 1849, refers to this charge as follows: "For two years and a half that we have resided in California, we have never heard the idea seriously uttered, that California should become an independent government."

The denial by General Riley of the alleged right of the people of California to form a temporary provisional government was substantially based upon these grounds: That, under the law of nations, the civil laws of the ceded territory remain in force until superseded by those of the government to which the cession is made; that, as Congress possessed the sole power to legislate, but had passed no act creating a territorial government for California, the civil laws of Mexico remained in force; that one of the provisions of that law was that, in case of a vacancy in the office of Governor, the military commander should fill the office for the time being; that there was such a vacancy in the office of Governor of California, and that he, General Riley, was simply *ex officio* Governor; that, in point of fact, the people of California were not living under a military government, but under one of civil law; that, in his capacity of civil Governor, he administered the civil law, as any other Governor would be bound to do; that the condition of the people of California was not similar to that of the people of Oregon when they organized their provisional government, as they were without any law whatever, while we had a code of civil law in full force; and that, consequently, the assumed exercise of legislative power by the body calling itself the Legislative Assembly of San Francisco was a usurpation of powers vested solely in Congress. On the contrary, our claim was substantially based upon these positions: That, conceding the general principle to be true, that under the law of nations the civil laws of the ceded territory continue in force until super-seded by those of the government to which the cession is made, still, in the peculiar case of California, the Mexican civil law had been so superseded; that, the moment the treaty took effect, the Constitution of the United States, and all the great leading princi-ples upon which our American institutions are based, were at once extended over the acquired territory; that the power to legislate was primarily vested in Congress, but that, while that body neglected and refused to exercise such power, it was no usurpation in the peo-ple of California to exercise it temporarily, and in strict subordina-tion to the admitted right of Congress; that usurpation of power is the assumed use of it by an illegal body, when, at the same time, it is claimed and exercised by the rightful authority; that under the theory of our Government the executive office of Governor can not be filled by a subordinate military officer, as the two capacities are incompatible with each other and with our American theory; that, in point of practical effect, the people of California were in the same condition as had been the people of Oregon; that nine tenths of the people of California were American citizens, lately arrived from the States east of the Rocky Mountains, wholly unacquainted with the civil laws of Mexico, and with the language in which they were written and published; that, such being the case, it was not practical good sense or justice to require these nine tenths of the people of California to learn the laws of Mexico for the short period to elapse before the new order of things was morally certain to take place; that imposing this labor and confusion upon these nine tenths would not benefit the native citizens to any extent whatever, as they would still have to learn the laws of the new State when organized; that, as at least nine tenths of the officers charged with the adminis-tration of Mexican law would be Americans, ignorant of the law they were required to administer, and without time to learn it, the law actually enforced would be an inconsistent mixture of Mexican and American law, so confused as not to be understood; and finally, that the temporary exercise of legislative power by the people of California was based upon the original and natural right of society to protect itself by law, and that such exercise by our people was in no true sense a violation of the law of nations; but that the people of California possessed the legal and just right to supersede the civil laws of Mexico in force in California at the date of the treaty, and that this right was also based upon the theory of our American governments, properly extended and applied to the new and extraordinary circumstances of our condition.

The question as to the legal and just right of the people of California, under all the circumstances then existing, to form for themselves a temporary government, was one admitting of discussion and difference of opinion. Among the lawyers then in California, who had been here long enough to understand the true merits of the controversy, there was almost an entire unanimity in the opinion that only a *de facto* government could exist in the country, based upon the consent of the people. This was the view of three fourths of the inhabitants. It seems clear that this was the view of President Polk and Mr. Secretary Buchanan. But it seems equally clear that President Taylor and the secretaries of State and of War under him entertained the opposite view.

But, aside from the true merits of the controversy, it was *most* fortunate for California that it arose, for it resulted in the early formation of the State government, and thus settled the question in a manner most satisfactory to us all. Had General Riley conceded the right of the people of California to organize a provisional government for themselves, then they would most probably have been content with their condition for some time to come; and, had the people quietly submitted to his government, the organization of the State would have been, most likely, delayed for an indefinite time. The slave and free States then had an equal representation in the Senate of the United States, and no act for a territorial organization, and none authorizing the people of California to form a State constitution, could have been passed by Congress.

All things happily combined to bring about the result we all so much desired. The people had suffered so much from the bad administration of laws unknown to them, and were so unused to live under what they held to be a military government, that, in San Francisco especially, they were deeply and grievously excited. So soon as I became a member of the Legislative Assembly of San Francisco, my ardent efforts were mainly directed toward the formation of a State constitution, as the only safe and peaceful mode of settlingn. So far as I and a large majority of that body were concerned, we were opposed to any and all forcible conflicts with General Riley's government. While we were satisfied that our position was right, we preferred patient and peaceful means to attain a satisfactory solution of the difficulty. The resolutions passed at the large and enthusiastic meeting in San Francisco on June 12, 1849, were prepared in advance, and after full consultation, and with a view to secure ultimate unanimity. We had our doubts whether the people would, under the then excited state of public feeling against the rule of General Riley, sanction *at once* the times appointed by him, and we therefore thought it best to have a committee of five appointed to fix the times for the election of delegates, and for the assembling of the convention, and to designate the number of delegates from San Francisco. This would give us an opportunity to consult the people of other districts, and allow time for the excitement to cool in this city, which had been so long and so grievously misgoverned. Our committee, most likely, had the power to defeat General Riley's proclamation by recommending other days, but we were not governed by feelings of opposition or of revenge. We all agreed as to the main purpose, and our committee determined not to disagree about subordinate matters.

There was not the slightest ground for the charge that the people of California desired to establish an independent government; and I can only believe that it was made through mistaken information, based solely on suspicion in the minds of General Riley's informants. I knew that old and tried soldier in Missouri, years before either of us came to California, and had always entertained for him the greatest respect. I bear a willing testimony to his integrity and patriotism. I afterward met him in September, 1849, at Monterey during the sitting of the Convention, and had several friendly interviews with him. In one of these he said to me very frankly: "Burnett, you may be correct in your views in regard to the legal right of the people of California to form a provisional government. I am no lawyer, but only a soldier, and I know how to obey orders; and, when my superior officer commands me to do a thing, I am going to do it." There was no occasion to argue against this conclusion; and, had there been such an occasion, it would have been idle to contest the determination of that honest and brave old man.

RETURN TO SACREMENTO CITY — ITS RAPID IMPROVEMENT — JAMES S. THOMAS.

About the 3^d of July, 1849, I was informed that John A. Sutter, Jr., had reconveyed the property to his father, and that the latter had selected another person as his agent. On the 5th I left San Francisco for Sacramento, and arrived at the latter place on the evening of the 11th. During my absence of six weeks the population of Sacramento had greatly increased; and, although there was not a singlebrick and but few wooden houses in the city, it had become an active business place, teeming with people, who mainly lived and did business in canvastents and cloth shanties.

My friend Dr. William M. Carpenter had just finished a cloth shanty on his lot at the corner of Second and K Streets. It was twenty feet long and twelve wide, with a cloth partition in the center. In the rear room he kept his office and medicines, and I had my office in the front apartment. The shanty was constructed by putting up six strong posts, made from the trunks of small trees, and flattened on two sides with an axe, one of which was put at each corner, and one in each center of the two ends of the structure. Between these posts were placed smaller posts flattened on one side, and placed some two feet apart, and on the tops of these posts were placed flattened pieces of timber, extending along each side of the shanty, and securely nailed into the tops of the posts, the lower ends of which were well let into the ground. On the tops of the two higher posts in the centers of the ends was placed a ridge-pole, nailed with large nails; and fromthis ribs about two feet apart were extended to the sides. The whole frame was then covered with yardwide brown cotton cloth, tacked on with cut tacks. The floor was the earth made smooth, and my writingtable was a large empty dry-goods box.

I was very busily engaged until July 24th in making an amicablesettlement with Captain Sutter. The weather was very warm, and our thin cotton covering afforded very imperfect protection against the scorching rays of a midsummer sun.

About the last of July the immigrants across the Plains began to arrive, and among them was James S. Thomas, from Platte City, Missouri. I had known him for about three years before I left that State for Oregon in the spring of 1843. He was then a poor young lawyer of admirable character, and was most highly esteemed by all who knew him. He was a tall, thin, spare man. I had not seen him for more than six years, and in the mean time his appearance had so changed that I did not at first recognize him. I was very busily employed writing in my office about 8 o'clock one morning, when I observed some tall person standing before me. I raised my eyes and looked at him, but he said nothing, and I continued my writing.

Several minutes passed, and he still remained silent. I raised my eyes and looked at him the second time, when I was greeted with a kind laugh, and then I recognized him. Our meeting was most cordial. Said I: "Sit down and I will give you half an hour's time. That is all I can spare you now."

I at once inquired the time of his arrival, and he informed me that it was the previous evening. He said he was *very* anxious to be at work. I at once asked him what he had, and he replied some mules and a wagon. I said: "Go sell everything and then come to me, and I will do the best I can for you." That day he sold everything, and came to my office next morning. I said to him: "We are to elect a magistrate to-morrow, and I will attend a meeting of citizens called for this evening to make a nomination, and will procure your selection if I can. In case you are selected, my brother-in-law, John P. Rogers, my son, D. J. Burnett, and myself will close our office, and give you one day's electioneering."

I attended the meeting, and made an earnest, vigorous speech for Thomas, and he received the nomination. Next day we had a warm contest at the polls, as his competitor was well known in the city. Many objected to Thomas upon the ground of his profession. To this objection I replied that, while I had nothing to say in defense of lawyers as a class, I would say that Thomas was among the best of his profession. He was elected, and I then said to him: "Take the official oath as early as you can, and then come to me and I will give you something to do." The next day the result was declared, and he took the necessary oath, and came to my office in the evening; and I told him to be at the office next morning at sunrise.

An auctioneer named Scovey had been sent from San Francisco to Sacramento City a few days previously to sell several Sacramento City lots, in subdivisions, to the highest bidder for cash. He had completed the sale, and then came to me to draw up the deeds. There were from twenty to thirty deeds to be written out (there being then no printed blanks), for which I was to be paid ten dollars each. A full list of the property sold, with names of the purchasers and prices paid, was furnished by Scovey. I told Thomas that we would each write as many deeds as we could, and each receive pay for those he wrote; and that, in addition, he could write out and take the acknowledgements, the fee for each being two dollars and a half.

On the morning appointed he was promptly on hand at sunrise, and we commenced our work with a will. I never saw a poor lawyer work with more zeal. It was truly amusing to see him wield that pen. To use a cant but expressive phrase, "I did my level best," and so did he. From sunrise to sunset we scarcely lost a moment, except at twelve to take a hasty lunch. That day Thomas made more than one hundred dollars, and that was his beginning in California.

When I arrived at Sacramento City, I found melons in market. An old man of the name of Swartz cultivated several acres in melons that year, on the west bank of the Sacramento River, at a point some five miles below the city. These melons he sold readily at from one to three dollars each, according to size. From the sale of melons he realized that year some thirty thousand dollars. I mention these cases as illustrative of those times. Such times, I think, were never seen before, and will hardly be seen again.

I have seen a whole community, for a time, substantially living under the theory of an equal division of property. In California, during the years 1848 and 1849, all men had about an even start, and all grew comparatively rich. At least, they were all *equally* secure of a good living, except those who were unable to work. But within a year or two thereafter the usual inequalities in the financial conditions of men began to appear. Nothing more clearly and concisely shows what would be the legitimate result of communism, than the replies of a witty Irishman, who was ironically advocating an equal and forcible division of property among men. "But what would you do, Patrick, with your share?" "Faith," said he, "I would live like a prince." "But you would soon spend it all, and then what would you do?" "And faith, I would go for another division."

APPOINTED TO A SEAT IN THE SUPERIOR TRIBUNAL — SICKNESS OF ONE OF MY DAUGHTERS — REMOVE TO SAN JOSÉ — ADMINISTRATION OF JUSTICE IN CALIFORNIA DURING 1849 — STATE OF SOCIETY — THE QUACK.

I left Sacramento City on my return to San Francisco on the 3^{d} of August, 1849, and arrived in the latter city about the 10th. During my absence of some five weeks, many stirring events had transpired in San Francisco.

On the 10th of July, Francis J. Lippitt, Esq., Speaker of the Legislative Assembly of the district of San Francisco, resigned his seat. A vote of the people had been taken as to whether that body should continue to act. The affirmative vote was 167, the negative, 7. The smallness of the vote polled proved conclusively that a large majority of the people did not deem it necessary to vote at all. The fact that General Riley had substantially allowed the people to choose their own officers, and especially the certain prospect that the convention would soon meet and form a State constitution, and thus give us all the relief we asked, satisfied the good sense of our people that no further controversy was proper or desirable. Thus the Legislative Assembly of the district of San Francisco came to an end. ("Alta," July 12 and 19, 1849.)

On Sunday night, July 14th, the "Hounds" attacked and robbed several Chilian tents in San Francisco. As this occurred during my absence at Sacramento City, I can give no account of it from my own knowledge, but must refer to the "Alta" of August 4th and succeeding numbers for a full account of that most daring crime.

Upon my return to San Francisco, I found that during my absence, and without my knowledge, my name had been used as a candidate for a seat in the Superior Tribunal, and that I had received 1,298 votes, and Mr. Dimmick 212. My commission is in the words and figures following:

Know all men by these Presents, that I, Bennet Riley, Brevet Brigadier General U. S. Army, and Governor of California, by virtue of authority in me vested, do hereby appoint and commission Peter H. Burnett Judge or Minister of the Superior Tribunal of California, to date from the 1st day of August, 1849.

Seal. Given under my hand and seal at Monterey, California, this 13th day of August, A. D. 1849.

B. Riley,

Bt. Brigd. Genl. U. S. A., and Governor of California.

Official.

H. W. Halleck,

Bt. Capt. and Secty. of State.

Before my family left Oregon in May, my eldest daughter, then sixteen, was attacked with what her physician afterward decided to be consumption. The voyage by sea gave her temporary relief, but the cold winds of San Francisco soon increased the serious character of the case. When I returned from Sacramento City, I found her very ill. Her physician told me very frankly that he could do no more for her, as she was in the last stage of consumption.

I at once determined that she should take no more medicine, and should at least die in peace. I remembered that our physician in Missouri, Dr. Ware S. May, had told me that patients were sometimes starved to death, and that he had known of such cases. Mr. Moffat, an assayer of San Francisco, mentioned to me a case within his own knowledge, where the life of the patient was saved by eating a little beefsteak. The medicines taken by my daughter had so deranged the tone of her stomach that she could retain nothing that she ate, and had not the least appetite, but a great aversion for food of every kind. I persuaded her to eat a mouthful of broiled steak, which she at once threw up; but I immediately urged her to try again, and this morsel she was able to retain. From that time she rapidly improved. Believing that the climate of San Francisco was injurious to her health, I decided to leave the city. I could only *then* go to Sacramento City or to San José. In the former place I could procure no shelter except a canvas tent or a cloth shanty; so I went to San José for the first time about the 20th of August, and purchased a house and lot in that city. On the 28th my daughter had so far recovered that she could endure the trip, and we arrived in San José the next day. In two months she was well. She was married in January, 1851, is still living, and is the mother of several living children.

As illustrative of those times, I will relate two occurrences.

I employed a man named Wistman, with a large spring-wagon, to remove us to San José, for which service I paid him one hundred and fifty dollars. It took him two days.

I was the owner of a number of lots in Sacramento City; and one day in August a gentleman of my acquaintance came to my little office in San Francisco, and said to me: "Mr. — and myself will give you fifty thousand dollars in gold-dust for one undivided half of your Sacramento City property — one half cash, and the other half by the first of January next; and we want an answer by ten tomorrow morning." I promptly replied that I would give an answer at the time mentioned. I at once consulted Mrs. Burnett, and we decided that we would accept the offer, with certain reservations. Next morning the gentleman was at my office at the precise hour for an answer. I told him I would accept the offer, with the exception of a few lots that I mentioned. He at once replied, "All right." There happened to be present a mutual friend from Sacramento City, a man about fifty years of age; and this gentleman at once rose from his seat, and, seizing the hand of the first gentleman, he warmly congratulated him upon the splendid purchase he and his partner had made, saying there was a large fortune in the property. During this long-continued burst of enthusiasm I sat perfectly quiet; but, so soon as I could be heard, I said: "Gentlemen, I am glad to learn that I am a much richer man than I supposed I was. If these gentlemen can make a fortune out of the undivided half they have purchased, what do you think I can make out of my half, and the fifty thousand dollars to begin with?" This view of the case rather cooled their enthusiasm.

During the year 1848 there were very few, if any, thefts committed in California. The honest miners kept their sacks of gold-dust in their tents, without fear of loss. Men were then too well off to steal. Toward the close of that year some few murders and robberies were committed. But in 1849 crimes multiplied rapidly. The immigrants from Australia consisted in part of very bad characters, called "Sydney Ducks." These men soon began to steal gold-dust from the miners, and the latter showed them no mercy. In most mining camps they had an alcalde, whose decisions were prompt and final, and whose punishments were severe and most rigidly inflicted.

On one occasion, in the fall of 1849, a tall, handsome young fellow , dressed in a suit of fine broadcloth, and mounted upon a splendid horse, stole a purse of gold-dust from an honest miner, and fled from the camp. The thief took the plain wagon-road that led around a tall mountain, while his pursuers took a shorter route across, reached a mining camp where there was an alcalde in advance of the thief, and quietly awaited his arrival. In due time the thief appeared, mounted upon his splendid steed, and was at once arrested, and promptly tried before the alcalde. After hearing all the testimony, the alcalde said to the prisoner: "The Court thinks it right that you should return that purse of gold to its owner." To this the culprit readily assented, and handed over the purse. The alcalde then informed him that the Court also thought he ought to pay the costs of the proceedings. To this the culprit made not the slightest objection (thinking he was very fortunate to escape so easily), but inquired the amount of the costs. The alcalde informed him that the costs amounted to two ounces of gold-dust. This the prisoner cheerfully paid. "Now," said the alcalde, "there is another part of the sentence of this Court that has not been mentioned yet; and that is, that you receive thirty-nine lashes on your bare back, well laid on." The punishment was promptly inflicted, and, of course, the transgressor thought his way hard. He could only boast that he was "whipped and cleared."

[Note : The origin of this phrase was as follows: In the early days of Missouri, Thomas — — was arrested, indicted, tried, and convicted of grand larceny in stealing a horse, and was sentenced by the Court to receive thirty-nine lashes on his bare back. After he was whipped and discharged, he met an acquaintance who inquired how he came out. He promptly replied: "First-rate. Whipped and cleared."]

In the fall of 1849 William B. Almond, then late of Missouri, became the Judge of the Court of First Instance, in civil cases, for the district of San Francisco. There are proper times and places for all proper things; and no sensible man would approve of Yankee Doodle at a funeral or of Old Hundred at a ball. There are *right* things to be done, and proper *modes* of doing them. Judge Almond was a man of fair legal attainments, and had been one of the early settlers of the Platte Purchase in Missouri, and he well comprehended the situation of California. Perhaps substantial justicewas never so promptly administered anywhere as it was by him in San Francisco. His Court was thronged with cases, and he knew that delay would be ruin to the parties, and a complete practical denial of justice. He saw that more than one half the witnesses were fresh arrivals, on their way to the mines, and that they were too eager to see the regions of gold to be detained more than two or three days. Besides, the ordinary wages of common laborers were twelve dollars a day, and parties could not afford to pay their witnesses enough to induce them to remain; and, once in the mines, no depositions could be taken, and no witness induced to return. He accordingly allowed each lawyer appearing before him to speak five minutes, and no more. If a lawyer insisted upon further time, the Judge would good-humoredly say that he would allow the additional time upon condition that the Court should decide the case against his client. Of course, the attorney submitted the case upon his speech of five minutes. At first the members of the bar were much displeased with this concise and summary administration of justice; but in due time they saw it was the only sensible, practical, and just mode of conducting judicial proceedings under the then extraordinary condition of society in California. They found that, while Judge Almond made mistakes of law as well as other judges, his decisions were generally correct and *always* prompt; and that their clients had, at least, no reason to complain of "the law's most villainous delay." Parties litigant obtained decisions at once, and were let go on their way to the mines.

The state of society in California in 1849 was indeed extraordinary. There were so few families, so few old men, and so many young and middle-aged adventurers, all so eager in search of riches, that a state of things then existed which perhaps has no parallel. Young men just from college, arriving in San Francisco, and never having been accustomed to manual labor, would hire themselves out as porters, journeymen carpenters, and draymen. One young man, who barely knew how to use a hand-saw well, hired himself to a boss carpenter. After working a day or two, he was paid off and discharged, and then went to another and another, repeating the same trick. When all were strangers to each other, all stood upon the same basis as to character and qualifications.

As illustrative of those times, I will relate the following incident:

Before leaving Weston, Missouri, for Oregon, in May, 1843, I was well acquainted with Thomas — — . He was then about thirty years of age, was of poor but honest parentage, could scarcely read or write, and had then never worn any but homespun clothes. He was a very skillful ox-driver and a good fiddler, and this was the extent of his capacity. Because of his skill in managing oxen, I employed him to drive one of my teams for a day or two, until my oxen were trained.

I left him in Missouri in 1843; but, when I arrived at Sutter's Fort in December, 1848, I found him and his family residing in the vicinity. His wife was a plain, good, domestic woman, and Tom himself was considered a *clever* fellow, in the American sense of that term. During the early spring of 1849 I sold him several lots in Sacramento City, upon the resale of which in the fall of that year he realized a net profit of twenty-five thousand dollars. Flushed with this sudden and extraordinary success, he dressed himself in the finest suit of clothes he could procure. He possessed a tall, straight, trim figure, and when thus attired was a very handsome man. Taking advantage of the circumstances, he commenced the practice of medicine. A carpenter named Stincen, who had known Tom well in Weston, came to Sacramento City in the fall of 1849, and soon met Tom arrayed in his splendid apparel. Stincen was a man of excellent sense, and possessed a keen perception of the ridiculous. "How are you, Tom?" said he. "First rate." "How are you getting alone?" "Splendid." "What are you doing?" "Come and see." He took Stincen a short distance, and showed him a splendid mule, rigged up in superb style, with new saddle, bridle, and martingales. Across the saddle was thrown a pair of new medical saddle-bags. Tom raised up the flap of one end, and, pointing to several rows of vials full of liquid medicines, said, "Look at that." "What does all this mean?" asked Stincen. "I am practicing medicine." "But what do you know about the practice of medicine, Tom?" "Well, not much; but I get all I can do, and I kill just as few as any of them. I never give them anything to hurt them."

Stincen himself related this interview to me, and it is no doubt true.

VISIT MONTEREY — ANNOUNCE MYSELF A CANDIDATE FOR GOVERNOR — ELECTED — INAUGURAL ADDRESS.

About the 13th of September I left San José for Monterey, to assist in holding a term of the Superior Tribunal. Four persons had been nominated by the people at the election held August 1st, who were subsequently appointed and commissioned by General Riley. These were José M. Covarubias, Pacificus Ord, Lewis Dent, and Peter H. Burnett. The last-named was chosen Chief Justice by the other Judges. The business before the Court was very small. No appeals had been taken; they were not common in those days.

I remained in Monterey until about the last of September. The proceedings of the Convention, which assembled on the first of that month, had progressed favorably, so far as to leave no reasonable doubt as to the final result, and I then announced myself a candidate for Governor. I arrived in San José about the 5th of October, and left there, to make the canvass, about the 20th. I reached San Francisco on the evening of the same day, and remained there three days. When I left the city about six weeks before, I knew a large portion of the people of the place; but, upon my return, I did not know one in ten, such had been the rapid increase in the population.

I was surprised to find myself so much of a stranger, and I said to myself, "This is rather a poor prospect for Governor."

One of my opponents, Winfield Scott Sherwood, Esq., proposed that we should submit our claims to a committee of mutual friends, and let them decide which of us should withdraw. I declined this proposition, and at once set out to speak to the people. I left San Francisco about the 23^d of October for Sacramento City, on board a very small steamer, the second one that ever ascended the Sacramento River. It was full of passengers, and was so small that they were frequently ordered to trim the boat.

On my arrival at Sacramento City, I addressed a large meeting of the people. From that city I went to Mormon Island on the American River, and made a speech. From there I passed to Coloma, the point where gold was first discovered, and addressed the people at that place; and then to Placerville, where I again addressed a large meeting. From Placerville I returned to Sacramento City on the 29th of October. On my way I spent the night of the 28th at Mud Springs, in an hotel kept in a large canvas tent. They gave me a very fine bed to sleep in, and treated me most kindly.

During the day the wind commenced blowing briskly from the south. After we had all retired to bed, the rain began to fall heavily, and the storm became so severe that the fastenings of the tent gave way,and nothin was left of the frame but the main upright pole, about thirty feet high, that stood in the center, to the top of which the canvas was securely fastened, while it hung flapping around the pole at the bottom. The rain came down in torrents, and the only way we could keep dry was to stand around and hug the lower end of the pole until daylight. This was the first hard rain of that most rainy season of 1849-'50. I never passed a more cheerless and uncomfortable night than this. I was very tired and sleepy, and frequently found myself asleep on my feet, and in the act of sinking down with my arms around the pole.

I remained in Sacramento City until the 5th of November, when the majestic steamer Senator arrived for the first time. The banks of the river, on Front Street, were thronged with people to witness her approach. She was to us a most beautiful object. I came down on board of her, and paid thirty dollars for my passage, and two dollars in addition for my dinner.

I passed through San Francisco, and arrived at San José about the 8th of November. After making a speech to the people of that city, I went again to San Francisco, where I spoke to an immense assemblage in Portsmouth Square. A platform about six feet high, and large enough to seat about a hundred persons, was made of rough boards and scantling. The main audience stood in front, on the ground. In the midst of my address the platform gave way and fell to the ground, except a small portion where I was standing. I paused only for a moment, and then went on with my speech, remarking that, though others might fall, I would be sure to stand.

I was in the city until the 13th of November, the day of the general election, at which the State constitution was ratified, and the principal State officers, Senators, members of the Assembly, and Congressmen were elected. The vote for Governor was as follows: Peter H. Burnett, 6,716; W. Scott Sherwood, 3,188; John A. Sutter, 2,201; J. W. Geary, 1,475; William M. Steuart, 619.

Both Houses of the Legislature assembled on Saturday, December 15, 1849, as required by the constitution. The Governor elect was inaugurated at one o'clock p.m. on Thursday, December 20th, and took the following oath:

"I, Peter H. Burnett, do solemnly swear that I will support the Constitution of the United States and the constitution of the State of California, and with faithfully discharge the duties of the office of Governor of the State of California, according to the best of my ability."

After taking this oath, I delivered the following address:

Gentlemen of the Senate and Assembly: I have been chosen by a majority of my fellow citizens of the State of California to be her first Executive. For this proof of their partiality and confidence I shall ever retain a most grateful sense. To be chosen Chief Magistrate of California at this period of her history, when the eyes of the whole world are turned toward her, is a high and distinguished honor, and I shall do all in my power to merit this distinction by an ardent, sincere, and energetic discharge of the weighty and responsible duties incident to the position I occupy.

Nature, in her kindness and beneficence, has distinguished California by great and decided natural advantages; and these great natural resources will make her either a very great or a very sordid and petty State. She can take no middle course. She will either be distinguished among her sister States as one of the leading Stars of the Union, or she will sink into comparative insignificance. She has many dangers to encounter, many perils to meet. In all those countries where rich and extensive mines of the precious metals have been heretofore discovered, the people have become indolent, careless, and stupid. This enervating influence operates silently, steadily, and continually, and requires counteracting causes, or great and continued energy of character in a people to successfully resist it. How far this influence may mold the character of the future population of California, time alone can determine. If she should withstand and overcome this great peril, she will constitute a bright exception to the fate that has attended other States similarly situated.

But I anticipate for her a proud and happy destiny. If she had only her gold-mines, the danger would be imminent; but she has still greater and more commanding interests than this — interests that seldom or never enervate or stultify a people, but on the contrary tend, in their very nature, to excite and nourish industry, enterprise, and virtue. I mean her agricultural and commercial advantages. While our mines will supply us with ample capital, and our fine agricultural lands will furnish us with provisions, our great and decided commercial facilities and position will give full and active employment to the energies and enterprise of our people, and will prevent them from sinking into that state of apathy and indifference which can not exist in a commercial and active community.

Our new State will soon take her equal station among the other States of the Union. When admitted a member of that great sisterhood, she will occupy an important position, imposing upon her new and great responsibilities. She can never forget what is due to herself, much less can she forget what is due to the whole Union. Her destiny will be united with that of her sister States, and she will form one of the links of that bright chain that binds together the happy millions of the American people.

How wide and extended is our expanding country! With only thirteen States and three millions of inhabitants originally, we have grown in the short space of three quarters of a century to be one of the greatest nations of the earth. With a Federal Government to manage and control our external relations with the world at large, and State governments to regulate our internal and business relations with each other, our system is peculiarly adapted for extension over a wide field, without danger of becoming unwieldy and impracticable. We have now more than twenty millions of inhabitants, and thirty States, with others knocking at the door of the Union for admittance. Our States and cities have the eastern coast of North America facing Europe, and our country extends across the entire continent to the shores of the Pacific, facing the millions of Asia. We have commanding military and commercial positions on both oceans, and nothing can retard our onward march to greatness but our own errors and our own follies. California has her part to act in this great march of improvement, and whether she acts well her part or not depends much upon her early legislation.

With the most ardent desire to do my duty fully and frankly toward our new and rising State, I pledge you my most cordial coöperation in your efforts to promote the happiness of California and the Union. For the principles that will govern me in my administration of the executive department of the State, I beg leave to refer you to my forthcoming message.

I thank you, gentlemen, for the kindness and courtesy you have shown me, and hope that your labors may redound to your own honor and the happiness of your constituents.

THE CHINESE — REASONS FOR THEIR EXCLUSION— THE BURLINGAME TREATY

In the view of many most humane and devoted people, our country should be thrown open to all the world, with the right not only of domicile, but of citizenship. Regarding, as I do myself, all mankind as of the same origin, these persons seem to think that the population of the globe should be left, like water, to find its own level. But this comprehensive and apparently just view is too liberal for practical statesmanship. The *practical* result would be, that the Mongolian race (the most numerous of the families of mankind) would in due time possess the country on this coast, to the ultimate exclusion of the white man.

The Chinese Empire is one of vast extent, everywhere under the same compact government. It contains four hundred millions of people, about equal to one third the population of the world. These people esteem their country (and with much apparent reason) as the oldest, wealthiest, and grandest empire upon this earth. No other people are so proud of their country, or so inveterately attached to it, as are the Chinese. But, while they regard their country with so much admiration and affection as not to desire a *permanent* allegiance to any other government, they would doubtless be willing to extend its limits by the colonization and addition of other territory.

Their policy of isolation, continued for a long series of centuries, has made their people peaceable, economical, loyal, and industrious; and, in the general absence of foreign and domestic wars, the population has increased, under the legitimate effects of this policy, to such enormous proportions as to become suffering and corrupt.

For thousands of years the Chinese have been accustomed to live upon as little as would possibly support human life. For ages upon ages their inventive faculties seem to have lain dormant. Their rulers and statesmen have, during long periods in the past, opposed all labor-saving inventions, for the simple reason that their labor-market was overstocked. They seldom or never change the style or character of their manufactured articles, or their fashions of dress, because such changes would violate their most rigid rules of economy. The style of dress for the laboring classes is the simplest and cheapest possible, consistent with ease and comfort. A Chinese laborer will provide himself with a bamboo hat, costing twenty-five cents, that will last him a lifetime. His shoes are made of cheap but durable materials, with broad, thick, flat bottoms, that wear away slowly and never slip; and his shoes never produce corns on his feet. A Chinese merchant makes all his mathematical calculations upon a plain little wooden box, twelve inches long, six inches wide, and two inches deep, with parallel wires passing lengthwise through it, and one inch apart, upon which are placed a number of small wooden balls. This little instrument will cost fifty cents, last for hundreds of years, and save several hundred dollars a year in stationery to a large establishment.

Their merchants are very intelligent men in their line of business. I was well acquainted with Fung Tang, the Chinese orator and merchant. He was a cultivated man, well read in the history of the world, spoke four or five different languages fluently, including English, and was a most agreeable gentleman, of easy and pleasing manners.

When the Chinese merchants first arrived in San Francisco, and for a time thereafter, they made all their purchases of our merchants for cash. Within a short period they learned that, according to our mercantile usages, cash sales meant payment on steamer-day; and, as these days were semi-monthly, they readily availed themselves of the credit they could thus obtain. A little later they purchased on thirty, forty, and sixty days' time. In short, they learned all our usages that promised them any advantages, except the three days' grace on promissory notes and bills of exchange. That provision no Chinese merchant ever learned; so that, if a Chinaman made his note payable on the first day of June, he would pay on that day, though legally entitled to wait till the fourth. There is something so inconsistent in the position that, although a note by its *express* terms was made payable on the first of June, yet in law it was payable on the fourth, that Chinese acuteness never comprehended it.

While they are perfectly willing themselves to purchase on credit, they decline to sell to our people on time. One of our leading merchants, on one occasion, determined to monopolize all the rice in San Francisco. To carry out this purpose, he went to a large wholesale Chinese rice-house, and said to the owner, "Suppose I should wish to purchase two thousand bags of rice, could you supply me with that number?" "Yes, me sell you that number." After quietly talking some time, the American merchant again asked, "Could you sell me four thousand?" "Yes, me sell you four thousand." The American merchant continued the conversation about other matters for some time, and then quietly said, "Suppose I should conclude to take six thousand, could you supply that number?" "Yes, me sell you six thousand." "Would you give me any time?" "Me know you one very rich Melican merchant. Me give you time. You pay me one half when the rice is weighed, and the other half when it is on the dray."

Born and nursed in poverty, and early trained in the severe schools of unremitting toil and extreme economy, the Chinaman is more than a match for the white man in the struggle for existence. The white man can do as much work, and as skillfully, as the Chinaman; but he *can not live so cheaply*. It would require many centuries of inexorable training to bring the white man down to the low level of the Chinese mode of living. Were Chinamen permitted to settle in our country at their pleasure, and were they granted all the rights and privileges of the whites, and the laws were then impartially and efficiently administered, so that the two races would stand *precisely* and *practically* equal in *all* respects, in one centry the Chinese would own all the property on this coast. This result they would accomplish by their greater numbers and superior economy.

We have not yet had a full and fair opportunity to study Chinese character, as those among us are, by circumstances, put upon their very best behavior. The same number of Americans placed in China would prove very peaceable and industrious. This would necessarily be so. Small bodies of men living in a foreign country, perfectly defenseless, and with full knowledge that they are at the mercy of the natives, will be very apt to act most prudently. In comparing the Chinese with our own people, a fair and just allowance should be made for the difference in their respective positions.

If two equally poor young men of the same capacity and health should start in life together at the age of twenty-one, and obtain the same compensation and continue so for ten years, and one should be a good economist and save up a portion of his income each year, and the other should spend all his as fast as received, at the end of the ten years the first would be in independent circumstances, while the other would be as poor as at the beginning, and would have lost ten years of his business life. Such are the effects of economy even for short periods of time. But extend this practice of saving for a hundred years, and the effects will be surprising.

It is painful to the thoughtful and reflective to see a proscribed class of men in any community. It is more especially so in a republic, where every citizen is a sovereign, where the laws are practically made by the majority, and where the officers charged with the execution of the same are elected by this majority. Under such a theory of government, no unpopular law can be fairly enforced. You may speak, write, and publish all that can be said upon the subject, and still the laws can not be practically and efficiently administered for the protection of an unpopular class of men. Modes of evasion will be successfully resorted to. We see this fully exemplified here in San Francisco. While parents will not very often openly assault Chinamen in the streets of the city, they can manage to show their hostility through their children. The young are natural tyrants, and, when they find victims upon whom they can practice this tyranny with impunity, they never fail to do it. It is very difficult, if not impossible, for the police and other officers of the law to prevent this violence in children, when they are not restrained, but rather encouraged, by their parents and a majority of the voters. The worst effect of the presence of the Chinese among us is the fact that it is making *tyrants and lawless ruffians of our boys*. It is true, the poor Chinamen suffer from this violence, but still their situation in California is better than their former half-starved condition at home. Here they are well fed, housed, and clothed.

I have long been opposed to the residence of the Chinese among us, except for purposes of trade. This opposition is not based upon any prejudice against the race, for I am not conscious of prejudices against any race of men. I believe, with St. Paul, in the unity of the human race, as expressed in the twenty-sixth verse of the seventeenth chapter of Acts. But, while I am opposed to the residence of Chinese laborers among us, I am equally opposed to all illegal methods of preventing the settlement of other Chinamen in our country, or for expelling those that are now resident here. The only legal, loyal, and just mode of preventing and removing the evil is, to begin at the beginning, and correct the first error by amending the treaty.

The Burlingame treaty should have been so framed as to allow the *merchants* of each country a residence within the limits of the other for purposes of trade and commerce only. The treaty, as it now exists, very plausibly assumes to put the people of the two nations upon about equal terms; but in practical effect it is very far from working equally. It is like the fable of the fox and the stork. The fox invited the stork to dinner, which consisted of thin soup served up in shallow dishes. While the fox, with his flexible tongue, readily licked up all the soup, the poor stork, with his long, inflexible bill, could not swallow a drop. All the calm, cunning, but mock politeness of the fox in urging the stork to help himself could not better his condition, and he went without his dinner. So it is with our people. Their condition is such that they can not go to China to reside and make a living, but the Chinese can well come here, and improve their condition by doing so.

The Chinese Empire will not probably sustain for the future the same relative position toward the other nations of the world that it has done for many ages past. The civilized nations found the Chinese isolated from the other peoples of the earth, and brought such influences to bear upon their Government as to induce a departure, at least in part, from the former policy. This is only the beginning of an entire change. The rulers and statesmen of that country will soon learn, especially from the ambassadors they are now sending abroad, that all the intellect of mankind is not to be found in China; that other nations excel them in many decisive respects; and that their Government must adopt all the great improvements of other nations, in order to protect its own rights. These rulers and statesmen will, in due time, come to understand the great fact that the Chinese Empire, by adopting the improvements of other nations, can readily become the greatest power in the world. All that Government has to do, in order to attain the foremost position among the nations of the earth, is to employ its almost unlimited resources to the best advantage. It could readily spare one hundred of the four hundred millions of its population, without impairing its effective strength; and the condition of the remaining three hundred millions would be improved by the change. China could organize and support an army of such numbers as, when well disciplined and ably commanded, would be perfectly irresistible in most portions of Asia. Nothing is more probable than that China within the next century will fully learn and use her mighty power. Then she may give England more trouble in India than England has any reason to fear from Russia. England, some years ago, forced China to admit the importation of opium, and she may not forget or forgive this act. Nations often live long enough to punish their enemies. There being no supernal existence for nations, they can only be punished in this world; and they never learn except through suffering.

Chapter IX.

GENERAL RILEY — JUDGE THOMAS — VARIABLE PRICES — MONOPOLIES.

On the 22^d of December, 1849, I sent the following message, with accompanying documents, to the Legislature:

San José, December 22, 1849.

Gentlemen Of The Senate And Assembly:

I take pleasure in placing before you the two accompanying proclamations issued by the late Governor Riley, and respectfully suggest that a convenient number be printed for distribution.

It has been my happiness to have long known Governor Riley, and I can say, in all sincerity and candor, that there does not exist, in my opinion, a more ardent and devoted friend of his country, or one who has served her more faithfully; and I desire to put on record this humble testimony to the character and services of one who has done so much for the people of California, and enjoys so fully their confidence and esteem.

Peter H. Burnett.

Proclamation. To the People of California. It having been ascertained by the official canvass that the Constitution submitted to the people on the 13th day of November was ratified by the almost unanimous vote of the electors of this State:

Now, therefore, I, Bennet Riley, Brevet Brigadier General U.S. Army, and Governor of California, do hereby proclaim

and declare the said Constitution to be ordained and estab-
lished as the Constitution of the State of California.

Given at Monterey, California, this 12th day of December,
1849.

(Signed) B. Riley,
Bt. Brig. Gen. U.S.A. and Governor of California. By the Governor.

H. W. Halleck, Bt. Capt. and Secretary of State.

On March 30, 1850, the Convention of both Houses unanimously elected James S. Thomas Judge of the Sixth Judicial District of California, which district included Sacramento City. He
returned to Missouri within a year or two thereafter, married, and
then took up his residence in St. Louis, where I saw him in the fall
of 1856. He was then far gone in consumption, and died there in
1857 or 1858. He was an excellent man.

The rainy season of 1849-'50 set in on the night of October 28,
1849, and terminated March 22, 1850. It was one of our wettest
seasons. The rainfall that season, as shown by the rain-gauge kept
by Dr. Logan at Sacramento City, was upward of thirty-six inches.

The first session of our Legislature was one of the best we have
ever had. The members were honest, indefatigable workers. The
long-continued rainy season and the want of facilities for dispatch-
ing business were great obstacles in their way. Besides, they had to
begin at the beginning, and create an entire new code of statute law,
with but very few authorities to consult. The Convention that
framed our Constitution and the first session of our Legislature
were placed in the same position in this respect. Under the circumstances, their labors were most creditable to them. They had not
only few authorities to consult, but their time was short. At the
close of the session, the bills came into my hands so rapidly that it
was a physical impossibility to read them all myself within the time
allowed me. I was, therefore, compelled to refer some to the Secretary of State, and others to my Private Secretary, and approve them
after a single reading upon their recommendation. I had to do this,
or let the State government go on with a mutilated code of statutory
law, or call an extra session.

During the winter of 1849-'50 the prices of provisions were
most exorbitant. This was owing to monopolies and the great cost

of transportation over bad roads. In many mining localities flour was sold at from fifty cents to one dollar a pound. At San José flour was sold for twenty-five cents a pound, sugar fifty cents, and coffee seventy-five.

For some years California was subject to extremely low and high markets. Everything was imported, and nothing made. We were so distant from the sources of supply, and our communication with New York so infrequent, being by monthly steamers, that speculators often monopolized all of certain articles. One large operator purchased all the flour, and others different articles of prime necessity. On one occasion one man went around San Francisco and bought up all the cut tacks in the city, and then put up the price to a high figure. At one time the country would be over-stocked, and then prices would recede to so low a figure that importations into the State would cease for a time. The article of shot in the summer of 1849 was worth only one dollar and twenty-five cents per bag of twenty-five pounds, and in the following winter readily brought ten dollars per bag. Iron at one time was scarcely worth the storage. So of mining implements and many other supplies. Speculators would at such times monopolize these articles and put up the prices.

AGRICULTURAL CHARACTER OF THE STATE — NATIVE GRASSES ANNUAL NOT PERENNIAL — NATIVE CLOVER.

Our agriculture may be said to have fairly started in the spring of 1850. Before that time cultivation in California was very limited. The few people residing in the country before gold was discovered found rearing stock far more profitable than agriculture. Land was very cheap, and pasturage was most ample; and no people will undergo the drudgery of farming when they can do better with less hard work.

At the time I delivered my inaugural address in December, 1849, very few, if any, believed with me that our agricultural and commercial interests were greater and more commanding than our mineral resources; but time has shown the correctness of the opinion then expressed. For some years after the organization of the State government, the members of the Senate and Assembly from the mining counties constituted a large majority in the Legislature, and controlled the action of that body. But time has essentially changed this state of things, and has given the control to the agricultural counties and the manufacturing and commercial cities.

As heretofore stated, the western side of the continent of North America is Asiatic in its main geographical features, and differs very much from the gently undulating country east of the Rocky Mountains. It is a country of mountains and valleys. Our hills generally swell into tall mountains, and our valleys appear to the eye to be substantially dead smooth levels; but they descend about nine to ten feet to the mile. The formation of these valleys is very different from that of the agricultural lands east.

For the sake of illustration, I will take the valley of San José, to which I can almost apply the beautiful and ardent language of Moore: "There is not in the wide world a valley so sweet." This valley has an average width of about ten miles, and a length of about seventy. On the surface there is a stratum of clay, varying in thickness from ten to fifteen feet. Beneath this is a stratum of gravel about five feet thick, beneath that another stratum of clay, and then other alternate strata of clay and gravel. On each side of this long valley there is a range of tall mountains, and from the edges of this valley to the summits of these mountains the distance is from ten to twenty miles. The rainfall in the mountains is double that in the valley. There are two outlets from the valley to the ocean, one through the Bay of San Francisco, and the other through the Bay of Monterey. The length of the streams after they reach the valley is from fiften to twenty miles, and their banks are from six to eight feet high. In the winter the supply of water from the mountains is so great that the beds of the streams in the valley are full, often to overflowing; but in the summer and fall many of their beds are dry, except where the water is found in pools.

During our long dry season, the various living streams from the mountains pour their treasures of water into the valley, but in most cases the water runs but a short distance after entering the valley, being soon swallowed up by the various strata of gravel, through which it percolates slowly, and passes underground into the bays. As there is a descent of about nine or ten feet to the mile, and as the banks of these streams in the valley are only from six to eight feet high, it will be readily seen that, one mile below the point where the water from the mountains enters the strata of gravel, the surface of the valley will be upon a level with the point mentioned; and two miles below that point the surface will be from ten to twelve feet below it. As you go farther down the valley, the surface will be correspondingly lower. As the water percolates slowly through these strata of gravel, the pressure to rise to the surface becomes so strong that the strata of clay above are kept wet even in the dry season; so that, while the moisture necessary to mature the crops east of the Rocky Mountains comes down from above in the shape of rain, in California it comes up by pressure from below. When the surface is well cultivated, and the ground kept perfectly pulverized, evaporation is almost prevented. These are the main reasons why we can produce bountiful crops of grain and grass in California during the long dry season.

But, besides these facts, our mild winter climate aids us very materially. If grain be sown before or soon after the fall rains set in, it will attain a considerable growth during the winter, which substantially ends by the first of February. By the time the rains cease in March, the grain will have attained a height of from six to ten inches, forming an impenetrable green sward, through which the sun's rays can not penetrate to the earth. For about six weeks after the cessation of the main rainy season the dews fall heavily, and this moisture sinks into the ground. As the evaporation is very little until the wheat begins to head, there is enough moisture left with the aid of that which comes from below, to mature the crops of grain.

All our native grasses, with a very few exceptions in rare localities, are annual and not perennial, as they are in most other countries. The seeds of the various native grasses ripen in June, and fall to the ground and into the small crevices produced by the drying of the surface. When the fall rains set in, these seeds begin to sprout; and, although their growth during the winter is slow, it is fast enough to keep the stock alive in many cases. In other cases they have to be fed for a little while. Grasses that are elsewhere grown for hay are never cultivated in California, as the most productive hay-crop is either barley or the smooth-head wheat.

We have a peculiar native clover which produces a rich seed. In each small, prickly, spiral burr there are from five to seven flat, yellow seeds, about as large as the yellow mustard-seed of commerce. During the growing season there are other native grasses which are preferred by animals, and this clover is permitted to mature its bountiful crop of hay and seed untouched. As all the native grasses ripen in the dry season, they make good hay, upon which the animals live for a time. When this hay is consumed, then the animals resort to the clover hay and seed. A stranger will be surprised at first to see the fat cattle with their heads to the dry and apparently bare ground, as if they were feeding upon the dust of the earth; while they are, in fact, eating the seed of this clover, which they gather in with their long, flexible tongues.

Bountiful crops of Indian corn are grown in certain localities without any rain whatever, as the corn is planted after the rains cease. The cultivator of this grain selects a rich soil in a valley and near some mountain, from which the moisture comes underground steadily during the growing season. This water percolates strata of gravel, and rises slowly to the surface of the ground.

The observations I have made apply to the ordinary seasons in California. At intervals we have a famine year, when there is almost an entire failure of crops in three fourths of the State. Our average annual rainfall at Sacramento (which may be regarded as an average point for the agricultural valleys of the country) is about twenty inches. With fifteen inches of rain we can make good crops. In the winters of 1850-'51, 1863-'64, and 1876-'77, our rainfall was about seven inches. The summers of 1851, 1864, and 1877 were our driest seasons since I have been in California; and they were just thirteen years apart. Between these extremely dry seasons there were seasons comparatively dry when the annual rainfall would vary from eight to thirteen inches. Once in five years, upon an average, there has been to little rain for a fair crop.

THE SQUIRRELS OF CALIFORNIA — THEIR PECULIAR CHARACTERISTICS — SPECULATIVE CHARACTER OF OUR FARMERS — UNCERTAINTY OF WEALTH IN THIS STATE — INCIDENTS.

One of the greatest obstacles agriculture has had to meet in California was caused by the millions of squirrels. Our squirrel is of a dirty-gray color, very much resembling that of dry grass, and is about twice as heavy as the gray squirrel of the Mississippi valley, but not so active and beautiful. These creatures live in communities, like the prairie-dogs of the plains. They select the highest and driest localities in the valleys, so as to escape the floods of winter, and there make their homes by burrowing in the ground.

Before the country was inhabited by Americans, these pests were not very troublesome, because cultivation was then so limited, and their excessive increase was prevented by the coyotes (small wolves) and snakes, then very numerous. But, when our people came to the country, they soon destroyed the coyotes by poison and the rifle, and killed the snakes; and, as the squirrels, like other little animals, multiply rapidly, they soon became so numerous as to destroy whole fields of growing grain, even before the berries had formed in the heads.

These animals, which are almost as sensitive to cold as the alligator, lay up a sufficient store of provisions in summer, and confine themselves to their homes during winter. Even in summer they generally do not make their appearance until after sunrise. When they become too numerous in one locality they emigrate to another, most generally in the night-time. In their villages they seem to have sentinels out, as the moment one sees an enemy approaching he sets up a loud cry that brings all to their holes instantly. They can not be driven from their homes. If a village be drowned out by water, the squirrels will not leave and seek safety in other places of refuge. They seem to think that there is no safety anywhere else. If driven by the water from their holes at one entrance they will, in the presence of men or dogs, run to another opening and plunge in. If a grainfield be some distance from their village, they will construct temporary retreats between it and the field, and into these holes they will escape for the time.

The best way to destroy them in the valleys is to cultivate by deep plowing the sites of their villages. By keeping the ground well pulverized upon the surface, the water in our very rainy winters will penetrate to their beds and destroy the squirrels, as they can not exist except in dry and warm homes. The water also destroys their stock of provisions. In some localities the streams are turned out in the winter, and made to overflow large tracts of level land. Vast numbers have been thus destroyed. When their holes are full of water, they will come out wet, sit on the tops of the little hills formed by the earth thrown out from the holes, and, if not disturbed, remain there until they perish with cold.

By poison and other means of destruction, these little pests have been generally destroyed in the fertile valleys; but in the foothills, and other localities that can not be cultivated, they are still most destructive. They feed upon the young green plants as well as upon the ripened grain.

Farming in California, like most other pursuits, has been speculative. A man would come from the mines with say ten thousand dollars, and would lease from one to two hundred acres of good wheat-land. With his own money he could purchase his seed-grain, and pay for a part of his hired labor. He would purchase his farming implements, harness, and work-animals on credit, and draw upon his commission merchant for provisions and other supplies. If the season proved propitious, and the price of grain high, he would net from twenty to thirty thousand dollars on his first crop, and then probably lose it the next or some subsequent year. If he failed, he would be off to the mines again.

Before the production of grain in California and Oregon was equal to the home demand, the prices were high. So soon as there was a surplus for exportation, the home price was governed by the foreign demand, without regard to the quantity grown on this coast. Our farmers commenced with high prices for grain, and paid high wages for labor. But the prices of grain receded in many instances faster than the rates of wages. A farmer in Alameda County employed an honest, industrious, sober, and careful Irishman for five years at the monthly wages of fifty dollars, the employer furnishing board, lodging, washing, and mending. At the end of that time he said to the Irishman: "I can not afford to pay you the wages I have been paying. It is true, I own my farm and stock, and I am not in debt. You have saved up a good sum of money, and I have saved nothing. You have made all the money, and, if things go on in this way, you will soon own my farm, and then what shall I do?" "Well," answered the Irishman, "I will hire you to work for me, and you will get your farm back again." In California it has frequently happened that the teamster in time became the owner of the team, and in turn employed the former owner to drive it. There never was, perhaps, a country in which the mutations of fortune have been greater in time of peace than in California. It has been the country in which a fortune was most easily made and most speedily lost.

When I took up my residence in San José in 1849, Grove C. Cook, then aged about fifty, was one of the wealthy men of that city. He had lived some years in the Rocky Mountains as a trapper or trader, but came to San José some years before the discovery of gold, and had acquired a considerable amount of real estate, the enhanced value of which made him comparatively a rich man. He was generous, kind-hearted, and witty. Soon after the State organization, the population of San José rapidly increased; and, as hotels and boarding-houses were few, the young lawyers and others about the city, who were "too proud to work and too genteel to steal," induced Cook to open a boarding-house. After he had been running this new establishment for some months, he found it a ruinous business to him, and said to some of his friends, "I have the most extraordinary set of boarders in the world. They never miss a meal or pay a dime."

Such cases were very common in California. A man kept a boarding-house at a mining camp, and his boarders did not pay. He called them up and informed them that he could not afford to keep them without pay, and asked them what they would advise him to do. They replied that, if he could not afford to keep them without pay, they would advise him to sell out to some one who could.

A lawyer about thirty-five years of age induced Cook to endorse for him to the amount of one thousand dollars, and Cook had to pay the note. There was a political convention held in San José in the summer of 1851, and Cook and myself among others were spectators. This lawyer was an eloquent man and a most ready debater, and appeared before the convention as an aspirant for a nomination. He made a most admirable speech, and when he had resumed his seat Cook most promptly addressed the president as follows: "Mr. President, I really wish you would give Mr. — some office. He owes me a thousand dollars, and I want my money." This proposition was so clear and so much to the point that our ready and most voluble lawyer could make no reply, and was for once silent. Were I allowed to make a distinction, and to mark it with a new term coined in this city by an obscure person, I should say that a man who devotes most of his time to politics, and yet pays his honest debts, is properly called a politician, but a man who devotes most of his time to politics, and does not pay his honest debts, should be called a "politicioner."

By going upon the official bonds and endorsing the notes of others, Cook soon lost most of his property. "He had his joke, and they had his estate."

For some years after the discovery of gold in California it was dangerous for a man of property to be absent from the State even for a few months, as others were almost certain to administer upon his estate during his absence in some form or other. If he appointed an agent, the owner would be very likely to find upon his return that his agent had sold his property and absconded with the proceeds. If he left no agent, he found his real estate in possession of squatters.

In some cases regular letters of administration were taken out. Mr. — was County Recorder in one of our best counties for two years. He acquired some valuable real estate, and then went upon a visit to his native State, and was absent between two and three years. Upon his return to California, he was astonished and hugely disgusted to find that during his absence regular letters of administration had been granted, and the administrator was in possession of the estate. Although he was a man of fine manners and of good education, he was noted for his homely features; and upon this occasion his personal beauty was not improved.

INCREDULITY OF THE PEOPLE EAST AS TO THE TRUE FACTS IN REGARD TO CALIFORNIA — SCURVY — ADMISSION OF CALIFORNIA INTO THE UNION — STAGE RACE — CHOLERA

The productions of California are so different from those of the States east of the Rocky Mountains that the people of the older States would not for some years believe the truth, though stated by the most worthy and reliable persons. As illustrative of this state of incredulity, I will relate the following incidents:

Cary Peebles (now a resident of Santa Clara County) and myself were schoolmates in old Franklin, Missouri, as early as 1820. When gold was discovered in California, he resided in Lafayette, one of the best counties in Missouri, where he kept a country store. Late in the fall of 1848 he received a long letter from a trustworthy friend in California, giving a fair and truthful description of our gold-mines. A large crowd assembled at the store to hear this letter read. Peebles had not proceeded far with the reading when some one in the crowd gave a loud, shrill whistle, and then exclaimed, "Isn't that a whopper!" This was followed by a universal roar of laughter, as loud as stout lungs and large throats could utter. When the tumult at length ceased, Peebles continued his reading, and was several times greeted with the same derisive laughter. Had he been the author of the letter, he would have been laughed to silence and to scorn.

Page, Bacon & Co. were extensive bankers in St. Louis; and in the latter part of 1849, or the beginning of 1850, they established two branches of their house in California — one in San Francisco, and the other in Sacramento City. The senior partner, "old man Page," commenced business in St. Louis in early manhood as a baker, prospered in that line for a time, and then commenced banking, and still prospered. The branch in San Francisco was managed by Judge Chambers and Henry Haight, and that in Sacramento City by Frank Page, son of the senior partner. In 1852 Frank returned to St. Louis on a visit; and one day at dinner, at his father's house, they had some onions on the table. Frank remarked that those were very small onions. His father replied that they were the largest to be had in the market. Frank very innocently and thoughtlessly said that in California we grew onions almost as large as a man's hat-crown. Upon this the fifteen or twenty guests at table threw themselves back in their seats and laughed most immoderately. Frank was deeply mortified, because he was perfectly alone and entirely helpless. He had always been truthful; and, while they were too polite to say in words that they did not believe him, they plainly said so by their actions. During the remainder of his visit, whenever, in answer to inquiries, he would state any fact in regard to California that exceeded their Missouri experience, his father would take off his hat, run his thumb slowly around the crown, and look slyly at Frank, as much as to say, "Another onion story, my son." Frank became so unhappy from this quizzing that he hastened his return to California sooner than he otherwise would have done.

In the fall of 1853 the old gentleman himself came to California for the first time. Frank had not forgotten the treatment he received in St. Louis, and, when his father came to Sacramento City, quietly invited him to take a walk. He took his father around the city, and, after showing him various establishments, brought him to a large agricultural warehouse, where he showed him large beets, squashes, melons, and potatoes. Finally stopping in front of some sacks containing large onions, he said, "Father, look there," and then took off his hat and slowly ran his thumb around the crown as his father had done, and slyly asked his father what he thought of those onions. The old man gazed with surprise at the onions, his face flushed, and after a time he said, "Frank, I give up. I never could have believed that onions so large could be grown anywhere, had I not seen them with my own eyes."

On one occasion, one of our people was returning east upon a visit, and took with him one of our large potatoes, carefully put up in whisky to prevent shrinkage. One day, in a large concourse of people in New York, the conversation turned upon the size of California vegetables. He said that he had seen potatoes weighing so much each. His statement being disputed, he put them to silence by producing his potato.

There are very good reasons why our vegetables are so large. First, the soil is very rich; secondly, there is an ample and uniform supply of moisture by irrigation; third, the growing season is very long. These facts fully account for the large size of our vegetables.

Before the production of a sufficient supply of vegetables in California, those working in the mines were often afflicted with scurvy. These attacks ceased with ample supplies of fresh meats and vegetables.

The State of California was admitted into the Union September 9, 1850. It so happened that I arrived in San Francisco, on my return from Sacramento City, the same day of the arrival of the steamer from Panama bringing the welcome intelligence of this event. We had a large and enthusiastic meeting in Portsmouth Square that evening. Next morning I left for San José on one of Crandall's stages. He was one of the celebrated stage-men of California, like Foss and Monk. He was a most excellent man, and a cool, kind, but determined and skillful driver. On this occasion he drove himself, and I occupied the top front seat beside him. There were then two rival stage-lines to San José, and this was the time to test their speed. After passing over the sandy road to the Mission, there was some of the most rapid driving that I ever witnessed. The distance was some fifty miles, most of the route being over smooth, dry, hard prairie; and the drivers put their mustang teams to the utmost of their speed. As we flew past on our rapid course, the people flocked to the road to see what caused our fast driving and loud shouting, and, without slackening our speed in the slightest degree, we took off our hats, waved them around our heads, and shouted at the tops of our voices, "California is admitted into the Union!" Upon this announcement the people along the road cheered as loudly and heartily as possible. I never witnessed a scene more exciting, and never felt more enthusiastic. I never can forget Crandall's race. He beat his competitor only a few moments. Poor fellow! When he became old and stiff, he was thrown from his seat while driving his stage, by one of the wheels suddenly dropping into a deep hole, and fell upon the dry, hard earth with such violence that he never recovered. A celebrated stage-driver over the mountainous roads in the State of Nevada, who was beloved by all who knew him, on his death-bed a few years ago, after his sight had vanished, mournfully remarked, "I can't get my foot on the brakes."

In November, 1850, the cholera prevailed in California to a fearful extent. The loss in Sacramento City, according to the best estimate I am able to make, was about fifteen per cent. of the population; in San José, ten per cent.; and in San Francisco, five per cent.

EXTRACTS FROM MY SECOND ANNUAL MESSAGE — RESIGNATION OF THE OFFICE OF GOVERNOR.

The admission of California into the Union settled all questions as to the legality of our State Government, but did not remove the difficulties incident to our peculiar condition. The following extracts are taken from my second annual message:

The attempt to administer the State Government during the past year has been attended by many difficulties. To start a new system under ordinary circumstances is no easy task, but no new State has ever been encompassed with so many embarrassments as California. Our people formed a mixed and multitudinous host from all sections of our widely extended country, and from almost every clime and nation in the world, with all their discordant views, feelings, prejudices, and opinions, and, thrown together like the sudden assemblage of a mighty army, they had no time to compare notes or interchange opinions. Besides this, a majority considered themselves only temporary residents, and had therefore no permanent interest in sustaining the State Government. Serious resistance to the execution of the laws was threatened in some instances, and a very unfortunate disturbance occurred at Sacramento City, in reference to which it would be improper to express an opinion, as the facts of the case will be inquired into by the competent judicial tribunals.

The first session of the Legislature had more difficulties to meet than perhaps the Legislature of any other State. That body had no beaten road to travel, no safe precedents to follow. California required a *new* system, adapted to her new and anomalous condition. What that new system should be, time and experience could alone determine. With the experience of the past year before us, we may be enabled to make some useful and necessary amendments. I have suggested such as have appeared to me the most important. It will be doubtless necessary to amend the acts of the last session in many respects, but I would respectfully suggest the propriety of making no amendments except where manifestly required. The people have now become accustomed to the laws as they are, and by making but few amendments a heavy amount of expense may be saved to the State.

On the 9th day of January, 1851, I sent to both Houses my resignation as Governor of the State in the following words:

Gentlemen Of The Senate And Assembly:

Circumstances entirely unexpected and unforeseen by me, and over which I could have no control, render it indispensable that I should devote all my time and attention to my private affairs. I therefore tender to both Houses of the Legislature my resignation as Governor of the State.

I leave the high office to which I was called by the voluntary voice of my countrymen with but one regret — that my feeble abilities have allowed me to accomplish so little for the State. In the humble sphere of a private citizen, I shall still cherish for her that ardent attachment she so justly merits. Within her serene and sunny limits I intend to spend the remainder of my days, many or few; and, should an unfortunate crisis ever arise when such a sacrifice might be available and necessary for her safety, my limited fortune and fame, and my life, will be at her disposal. Peter H. Burnett.

San José, January 8, 1851.

This resignation was accepted, and my connection with the State as her Governor thus terminated.

RESUME THE PRACTICE OF THE LAW — DEATH OF JUDGE JONES — PASSENGERS OF THE MARGARET — A FAITHFUL SON.

After resigning the office of Governor, I resumed the practice of the law in partnership with C. T. Ryland and William T. Wallace. We had a good practice; but a large portion of my own time was given to my private affairs, as they needed my prompt attention.

In December, 1851, Judge Jones died in San José, and I copy the account of that sad event as I find it recorded by myself, within a few day thereafter, except the day of the month, which I afterward ascertained and filled the blank I had left.

The Hon. James M. Jones, Judge of the United States District Court for the Southern District of California, died at San José on the 15th day of December, 1851.

I can not in justice to the deceased, as well as to my own feelings, refrain from putting on record the substance of a long private interview I had with this gifted and accomplished young judge the day before his death. I first knew the deceased, while he attended as a member of the Convention at Monterey, in September, 1849. He was then about twenty-seven years old, a good and ripe scholar in the Spanish, French, and English languages, which, I am informed, he wrote and spoke with ease and elegance, and that he also had a considerable knowledge of the German and Italian. At the period when I first knew him, I resided at San José with my family; and, immediately after the adjournment of the Convention, he came to that place, and established himself in the practice of the law. His indefatigable perseverance, his eminent knowledge of his profession, and his chaste, earnest, and beautiful style of elocution, soon procured him a most lucrative practice. While I filled the position of Governor of the State, in the beginning of 1850, I had frequent conversations with him upon legal questions, and he was frequently a visitor at my house. In reference to his own aims and prospects in life he maintained a great reserve, never obtruding his private affairs upon the public. He pursued any object he had in view with great earnestness and energy; and to excessive application to his laborious profession his early and untimely death is doubtless in part to be attributed. I knew nothing of his early history, except what I learned during the interview before mentioned.

I visited him on Sunday evening. It was a warm, bright, and lovely day. I found him in the last stage of consumption, wasted away to a skeleton, but in the full possession of his senses, entirely convinced of the near approach of death, and perfectly collected and resigned. After saluting me and asking me to be seated, he held up in his thin, pale, and bloodless fingers a cross which he had suspended from his neck, and in the most feeling manner said: "Governor! this is the image of our most holy Catholic Faith — the representative of that cross upon which Jesus died. You have doubtless heard that I had joined the venerable old Catholic Church. I have never been an infidel. I had examined the positive evidences for Christianity, and they greatly preponderated in favor of its truth; and, taken in connection with its appropriate fitness to man's wants and nature, it was, as a lawyer would say, a plain case upon the face of the papers. But, although a believer in religion, I deferred embracing it, because it required me to give up pleasures that I then looked upon with affection, but which I now regard as of no moment. I had also spent most of my time in new countries, in the midst of the exciting and confused scenes incident to a new and unsettled state of society; and my peculiar cast of mind had thrown me into relations and business with others that called away my attention from God, my Maker. Had I been a permanent resident of an old and regular community, I think I should have been an early member of the Church. I also looked upon our faith as peculiarly hard and exacting; but, oh! if I were only well and able, it would be a pleasure, instead of a labor, to me to enter into the house of God with His children, and there spend every moment I could possibly spare in His service. But I have deferred it so long. I have prayed to Jesus for the pardon of my sins. The greatest sin I have ever committed — that which has given me more pain, and that which I deplore more, than all others — is the fact that I deferred repentance to near the end of my existence — until my last sickness. Oh that I had given God my early days! I have repented of it most bitterly. It is all that I could do. I know that death-bed repentances are not generally entitled to much confidence; but I am sure that, were I to recover, I should henceforward lead a different life. The world may say that my repentance is forced and not sincere; but the world may say what it pleases, it will not alter the fact. I know that I am sincere, and I can well spare the shadow if I can get the substance. If I can only get to heaven, I will be content. I trust in the merits of Christ. I look to His mercy for pardon.

"And now, Governor, if I may be allowed to turn from heavenly to earthly subjects, I wish to mention a few things to you. My father has been dead many years, and my mother was twice married. I was a child by the first marriage. There are two children living, the issue of the second marriage — one a son of eleven years of age, and the other a daughter of thirteen. My brother is an innocent, prattling boy, of modest and quiet demeanor, and he loved me much. My sister is a kind and amiable girl. The great object I had in view in all my exertions to accumulate property was to make these children happy and comfortable. For this end I denied myself most of the luxuries and many of the comforts of life. I have often thought with pleasure, when refraining from some object I was tempted to purchase, that by doing so I might render these children happy for six months. This was the great object for which I toiled — the object" (laying his hand upon his breast) "dearest to my heart. It was to me as a green leaf in a desert. I have not sought fame; I cared but little for the opinions of men.

"I wished also to make my mother happy in her old age. *And such a mother!* She loved me under all circumstances. She could love more than I. She had such a depth of affection — such a pure fountain of love. She loved all her children; but there was so great a disparity in our ages that she loved me much the longest. She died not long since, and of the same disease that I have now. We were both of us sick at the same time, but so distant that neither could go to the other. Her death crushed me — gave me the last fatal blow. Since that time I have not seen a happy moment. The only happiness I have since enjoyed was mere freedom from pain. I had desired that my mother should spend her last days with me in California. I wished to make her last days happy. But I have been disappointed. God has taken her away. He has chastened me for my good. It has been to me a severe but just chastisement.

"I wish, Governor, to make one request of you. I have made my will, and left Mr. Melone my executor. I wish you to render him what assistance you can in closing up the business of my estate. But I make this request with this distinct condition, that, if you can do more justice to your family by taking claims for collection against my estate, I wish you by all means to do so. We are commanded to love our neighbors as ourselves; but a man's family are his nearest neighbors, and especially such a family as yours."

During this most affecting interview I could not but often weep. When he saw me weeping he said, "Governor, you are a good Christian."

By his will he left his property in equal portions to his brother and sister, except that ten per cent. of the amount of his estate was to be appropriated in the erection of a tomb for his mother.

Peter H. Burnett.

Among the other successful lawyers whom I have known in California, and who came here in 1849, was a young man who told me in after years the cause of his coming to this country. His father and mother, brothers and sisters, had resided in the old homestead for many years. It was situated in a town in one of the New England States. It had descended to his father from his grandfather, and had been possessed by the family for one or more centuries. Some time before he left for California, his father endorsed for a friend, and the old place had been sold to pay the debt. From a competency and a good home, they had come to poverty. This had caused the family much sorrow. His parents were too old to begin life anew successfully. He himself was just setting out in life. Under these painful circumstances, he said, he determined with himself that he would come to California, and, if brains and honest industry would succeed, he would accumulate enough means to repurchase the old family mansion, and make his old parents comfortable the remainder of their lives. He was successful; and within a few years he returned with ample funds, repurchased the ancestral domicile, and placed his parents within the pleasant old home in which he himself was born. During their remaining days they were well provided for by this faithful son.

But, while a portion of those who came early to California to improve their condition succeeded well, much the larger number utterly failed. Many came to premature deaths by violence, accidents, and sickness caused by excessive hardships and privations. I should think that about thirty per cent. of the early immigrants perished in this manner. I was told that a party of about thirty miners from Texas lost one half of their number in personal conflicts.

As illustrative of the sad fates of so many in early life, I will quote the following lines, composed by B. L. d'Aumaile while a prisoner in San Francisco, and first published in the latter part of 1856 or the beginning of 1857. There was reason to believe that the author was not guilty of the crime alleged against him. The first graveyard in San Francisco was on Russian Hill, so named from the fact that the first person buried there was a native of Russia. Though the fates of the passengers of the Margaret were exceptionally sad, they are still illustrative of the conditions of the early gold-seekers.

I stood on the barren summit
Of the lonely Russian Hill,
With a grass-grown grave beside me,
On a Sabbath morning still,
And sighed for my old companions,
Scattered through every zone,
Who sailed in the Margaret with me
But seven short years agone.
Yes, seven brief summers only
Have rolled past since that day;
'twas a balmy, soft June evening
When we anchored in the bay.
Of the sixteen buoyant spirits
Enrolled in our companie,
Twelve lie the green sod under,
And three are lost for aye.
The first at my feet was lying,
Far from his native home;
I had watched by his bedside dying,
Slain by the curse of rum.
In the dark and rocky cañon,
Where the Fresno's waters flow,
The mangled corpse of the second
Was buried long ago.
Three entered the wild Sierra
To search for the golden ore,
But back from their quest of lucre
To our camp they came no more.
We sought them long and vainly,
But what their sad fate had been
We never could tell, but only
They never again were seen.
On the hills of the Mariposa,
Where the dead of '50 sleep,
On the bank-side by the ravine,
Where its sluggish waters creep,

Two mounds, with long grass tangled —
There moldering, side by side,
Are the gambler and his victim,
The unshriven suicide.
In the green vale of the Nuuanu,
On the fair isle of Oahu,
Consumption demanded the youngest,
Most gallant, most gentle, most true.
The graveyard of Yerba Buena
Claimeth another; alone,
Far from his friends and his kindred,
Stands his monument stone.
One died in the Independence,
Another on Chagres' shore;
One launched on the Pacific
His bark, and returned no more.
"Mourn not the dead!" the living yet —
Alas! there are but four
Who sailed on the good brig Margaret —
Better their doom deplore.
In the valleys of Nukahiva,
Gem of the Southern Sea,
The soul of our band, if living,
Hath fixed his destiny.
Gladly he went into exile,
Self-banished from his kind;
The stern world's wrong and oppression
Made wreck of his noble mind.
From the dungeons of San Quentin
Ascendeth for evermore
The wail of a convict, sighing
For the days that are past and o'er.
His life to the law was forfeit,
For the blood his hand had shed,
But a cruel mercy spared him,
To be 'mongst the living dead.
The last and saddest of any,
A sister she was to us all,

In the bloom of her girlish beauty,
Was lured by a fiend to her fall;
On the banks of the Sacramento,
She leadeth a life of shame;
For her there is no redemption —
Forgotten be ever her name.
The gifted and brave had perished,
The beautiful and the young;
All trace of their footsteps vanished
The paths of men from among;
While I, as the sole survivor,
Was left to make my moan;
On the shores of the broad Pacific
I was standing all alone.

DEFECTIVE ADMINISTRATION OF CRIMINAL LAW IN CALIFORNIA — ILLUSTRATIONS — PAY THE LAST OF MY OLD DEBTS.

For some eight or ten years after the organization of our State government, the administration of the criminal laws was exceedingly defective and inefficient. This arose mainly from the following causes: 1. Defective laws and imperfect organization of the Courts; 2. The incompetency of the district attorneys, who were generally young men without an adequate knowledge of the law; 3. The want of secure county prisons, there being no penitentiary during most of that time; 4. The great expense of keeping prisoners and convicts in the county jails; 5. The difficulty of enforcing the attendance of witnesses; 6. The difficulty of securing good jurymen, there being so large a proportion of reckless, sour, disappointed, and unprincipled men then in the country; 7. The unsettled state of our land-titles, which first induced so many men to squat upon the lands of the grantees of Spain and Mexico, and then to steal their cattle to live upon.

As illustrative, I will mention the following cases, omitting names for obvious reasons:

A middle-aged native Californian, belonging to one of the richest and most respectable old families of the country, was the owner of an extensive and fertile rancho, bordering upon the navigable waters of the State. He owned a large herd of California cattle, running on his place. Near the rancho there was a small village, between which and San Francisco there was regular communication by a small steamer. Numbers of persons soon engaged in stealing his calves, having the carcasses dressed by their own butcher in the village, the veal shipped to San Francisco by the little steamer, and there sold. They were doing quite a thriving and profitable business. A man some forty-five years of age, residing in the vicinity with his family, seeing the ease and impunity with which this thieving traffic was carried on, concluded that he would go into it himself. The first thing he did in that line was to steal six calves. But in the mean time the Californian, having seen his herd rapidly diminishing, had become very vigilant and watchful, and our new beginner in theft was caught in the act and arrested. Upon being confronted by the witnesses and questioned, he confessed. His case was brought before the grand jury, and he was indicted for grand larceny.

His case excited great sympathy in the neighborhood, and, about the time it was coming on for trial, one of the leading men of the vicinity came to engage me to defend the prisoner. I asked this person whether the prisoner was guilty. With a sorrowful expression of face he said he thought he was, as he had confessed it. This person then went into a long history of the prisoner. He said it was one of the saddest cases he had ever known; that the prisoner had heretofore borne a most excellent character — had undoubtedly been honest all his life up to this time — had a most estimable wife and several most amiable daughters, one or two of whom were grown; that respectable young men were visiting his family; that the prisoner's relatives were excellent people; and that he and his innocent family would be ruined should he be convicted. After talking in this strain for about an hour, my informant seemed to have forgotten his admission made in the beginning of his statement, and closed by saying with great earnestness: "Governor, I wish you would do your best to clear him. He is a good, honest fellow." I replied, "This thing of being a good, honest fellow, and stealing six calves, is what forty Philadelphia lawyers can not put together." This reply startled him for a moment; but he soon rallied, and hastily said: "But he didn't mean any harm by it. It was almost a universal thing in the neighborhood." I told him to go to another lawyer.

On the day of trial the prisoner came into court handsomely dressed in broadcloth, and was a fine-looking man. He appeared as little like a thief as any prisoner I have ever seen in court. The District Attorney, being young and inexperienced, relied solely upon the prisoner's confession for a conviction, and had neglected to subpoena the witnesses to the other facts. This testimony, most likely, would have been sufficient without the confession. The result was, that the prisoner's attorney objected to the confession, on the ground that it was not voluntary, but made under the influence of hope or fear. The court, upon investigation, sustained the objection, the confession was not permitted to go before the jury, and, there being no testimony against the prisoner, he was at once acquitted. This trial took place in 1851. I have lately learned that this person has conducted himself as an honest man and a good citizen ever since that time. There can be no reasonable doubt of the fact that he had been led to commit one theft under the peculiar circumstances mentioned, and that this has been the only criminal act of his life.

The other case was related to me by the lawyer who successfully defended the prisoner, and the facts are unquestionably true. The trial occurred about 1852.

The prisoner was a man of education, about thirty years old, and lived in one of the finest agricultural counties in the State. For some time before the act was committed, the people in the vicinity had lost several fine, fat American cattle, and secretly set a watch to catch the thief. The watchmen secreted themselves, and, after waiting some time, heard the report of a rifle, and saw a fat cow fall, and the prisoner rush up to the animal and cut her throat with a butcher's knife. While in the very act, and before he had removed the carcass, the culprit was arrested.

His case was brought before the grand jury, and he was indicted for grand larceny in stealing this cow. Upon the trial all the facts were fully proven. The theory of the defense was, that the prisoner intended to shoot a dangerous bull; that the cow stood almost in a line between him and the bull, and that he accidentally hit the cow. While the prisoner's counsel was arguing the case before the trial-jury, the District Attorney interrupted him, and asked him how he reconciled the fact that the prisoner cut the cow's throat with the theory of accidental shooting? Without a moment's hesitation the counsel for the prisoner replied: "That is easily answered. When the prisoner saw that he had accidentally killed the cow, he knew it was best for all parties concerned to bleed the animal properly, so that the carcass would be good beef, and thus make the loss as small as possible." When the Judge came to charge the jury, the counsel for the prisoner offered an instruction directing the jury to find the prisoner not guilty, as the facts proven showed that the offense charged in the indictment had not been committed. He took the ground that, to constitute the crime of larceny as charged, there must be *both* a taking and carrying away of the property described in the indictment, with the felonious intent to steal the same. The Court was compelled to give the instruction, and the prisoner was acquitted. That he killed the cow with intent to steal was clear; but that, under the statute, did not constitute the completed crime of grand larceny, as the prisoner had not removed the carcass.

This man continued to reside in the same vicinity during the remainder of his life. Six or eight years after the trial the county was divided by act of the Legislature, and a new county organized, which included this man's residence, and which is one of the richest counties in the State. Twelve or fifteen years after his acquittal he was elected County Judge of this county.

While he held this office, the lawyer who had successfully defended him went to the county seat to attend to some professional business, and while there walked into the court-house, and found the Judge just about to pass sentence upon a prisoner who had been indicted, tried, and convicted in his court for grand larceny. As the scene was novel and most interesting, the lawyer took a seat and listened to the sentence pronounced by his Honor. The Judge went on, in a solemn and eloquent manner, to depict at length the atrocity of the crime of grand larceny, and sentenced the prisoner to a long term in the penitentiary.

It was the extremely defective administration of criminal justice in California for some years that led to the organization of so many vigilance committees, and filled the courts of Judge Lynch with so many cases.

In the early portion of 1852 I finally succeeded in paying the last dollar of my old debts. The total sum paid amounted to twenty-eight thousand seven hundred and forty dollars. I was henceforward a free man. I had been engaged so long in paying old debts that it became almost habitual, and for a time I felt somewhat lost because I owed no man anything. It was a totally new position to me. Our family learn slowly, but they learn well, and they practice on what they know. Since then I have not been pecuniarily embarrassed for a moment, and I owe nothing now. I paid the larger portion of these old debts in the year 1850. During a portion of that year I was in great doubt whether I should be able to accomplish the object of so many years' labor. The flood of the winter of 1849-'50 at Sacramento City not only caused the prices of property and rents to decline heavily, but increased the taxation for city purposes enormously. The rate of taxation that year for State, county, and city purposes, at Sacramento City, amounted to ten per cent. of the assessed value of the property. This extra tax was required to construct the first levee.

GREAT FIRE IN SACRAMENTO CITY — ASSIST IN REBUILDING THE CITY — RANCHO OF SAMUEL NORRIS — COURSING THE JACK-RABBIT.

On the evening of November 2, 1852, the great fire occurred at Sacramento City, which swept off two thirds of the town. Improvements that cost me about twenty-five thousand dollars were consumed in half an hour. When I arrived in the city on the 5th, the business portion of the place, with the exception of here and there a solitary brick house, was one waste of dark desolation. The streets could scarcely be distinguished from the blocks. Notwithstanding this great and severe loss, that indomitable people were not at all discouraged or unhappy. They even seemed inspirited. You would meet with no downcast looks. No people that I ever met can compare with those of Sacramento City in patience, energy, and unconquerable courage. In San Francisco they had two large and terrible fires in 1851, but they had no floods. In Sacramento City they had a succession of both fires and floods; and yet, at this date, Sacramento is the most prosperous city in the State. *All honor to that noble people*! On the 10th of November the regular rainy season set in.

There have been four overflows of Sacramento City. The first occurred in the winter of 1849-'50, the second in March, 1852, the third in the winter of 1852-'53, and the fourth and last in the winter of 1861-'62. The second passed away so soon as to inflict but little injury comparatively, but the others were much longer in duration and far more serious in their effects. Nothing could be done during the floods, nor for about two months after the waters subsided.

I moved to Sacramento City early in December, 1852, to assist in rebuilding it. A proposition was made by the people of Grass Valley to construct a plank-road from that place either to Marysville or Sacramento. The distance to Marysville is about half of that to Sacramento City. The people of Grass Valley would be governed in their choice of a terminus of the road by the amount contributed by each of the two competing cities. The road to Marysville would cost less, but that to Sacramento would terminate at the better point. A large public meeting was held at Grass Valley in the month of February, 1853, and delegates were present from Sacramento and Marysville to represent the people of those cities. At the meeting they out-talked and out-voted us, and we returned rather cast down; but we quietly laid it up in our inmost hearts to rely solely upon ourselves, and rebuild Sacramento City before the people of Grass Valley and Marysville could construct the road agreed upon. We went to work as soon as possible, and with a will; and by the last of July we had the main streets partly graded and newly planked, and by the middle of August a new levee well under way. I never saw the people of any city work with more energy. I was elected a member of the City Council, and I never toiled more earnestly, except on the road to Oregon in 1843, and for a time after I arrived there to keep from starvation, and in the gold-mines in 1848. My first visit to the beautiful town of Grass Valley was as one of the delegates from Sacramento upon the occasion mentioned. He who relies upon himself knows the man he trusts. So it is with a people who rely upon themselves. Self-reliance is the only sure path to success in life. Depend upon yourself, and you will not be apt to suffer from divided counsels.

While at Sacramento City, in the fall of 1853 and the succeeding winter, I was several times at the rancho of Samuel Norris. This place is about six miles from the city, and lies upon the north bank of the American River. As all our work in rebuilding the city had been successfully finished, and the place put in the best condition, I had a little time and inclination for some amusement. Norris had four well-trained dogs. The first was an old dog he called "Old Bull," a cross between the cur and bull-dog. The others were greyhounds. The first of these was about five years old; the other two, about two years old, were brother and sister. The slut was jet-black in color, and was one of the most beautiful animals I ever saw. She was a little fleeter than her brother, and the fleetest of the pack. Nothing could exceed the ease and grace of her movements. The greyhounds were shut up during the night before the chase and kept without food, because if fed they could not catch the game.

One evening Norris told me how he had exterminated the numerous coyotes in his vicinity. He said that, mounted on a good horse, he would go out with his four dogs, and when the greyhounds came in sight of a coyote, in the prairie or in open woods, they immediately gave chase. When they had overtaken the wolf, the foremost hound would run full tilt against him and knock him over; and, if the wolf attempted to run again, the hound would overthrow him the second time. The coyote soon found that there was no chance to escape by flight, and would then stand and snarl, and thus keep the hounds at bay. They would circle around him, but never attack him with their teeth until Old Bull came up. In the mean time that brave old dog was advancing at a slow and steady pace, and when he arrived he made not the slightest stop, but laid hold of the poor wolf despite his quick, sharp, and terrible snaps; then the hounds pitched in, and the defenseless coyote had not the slightest chance for his life, but was strung out full length and speedily dispatched.

Next morning, after an early breakfast, mounted on fleet but gentle horses, Norris and myself set out to run down the large jackrabbits then plentiful in that vicinity. One of these rabbits will weigh as much as two or three of the cotton-tail rabbits of the Western States; and, although their gait in running seems to be very awkward, they are so swift that it requires the fleetest greyhound to catch them. Indeed it is very doubtful whether any single greyhound could catch one of these rabbits, as the animal would dodge the dog, and thus widen the distance between them.

Norris had a smooth, open, and gently undulating stubble-field, about a mile long and three fourths of a mile wide. Although the stubble had been so closely pastured that we could apparently see an animal of that size at the distance of fifty yards, yet the rabbit would fold his long ears to his body, and then lie so close to the ground (which he much resembled in color) that we never in a single instance could see him until he started to run, although often within eight or ten yards of him.

The old greyhound, though about as fleet as the rabbit, was not so fast as either of the other hounds, but he was active, vigilant, and tough, and always started the game. He would run hither and thither, searching in every place, while the two young hounds trotted along at their ease twenty feet or so behind him, never looking for the rabbit, but keeping their attention fixed on the old hound.

The first thing we would know, up would start the rabbit not more than eight or ten feet ahead of the old hound, and then the race began, the rabbit and the hounds running at the top of their speed. It was a most exciting chase. Gradually the slut would overtake the other hounds, and we could see her gain upon them inch by inch until she passed them, and then as gradually gain upon the rabbit. When she approached within about four feet of the rabbit, her brother being about a length behind her, the animal would suddenly turn at right angles to the left or right, and the two foremost hounds would run over a little before they could stop, and, by the time they could turn and start again, the rabbit would be fifteen or twenty feet ahead. But the old hound was on the watch, and, the moment he saw the rabbit double, he would turn and cut across, so as to run to a point that would be about as close to the rabbit as he was at the start. In the mean time the two young hounds were straining every muscle to regain their lost position, and soon the slut would again be close behind the rabbit, when he would double the second time. About the third time the rabbit doubled, the young hound would catch him. The slut invariably caused the rabbit to double, but her brother as invariably caught him.

The hounds would catch the first rabbit in running half a mile, and the second one in running a mile, and the third would outrun them and make his escape. I observed that, in running down an incline, the hounds would run comparatively faster and the rabbit more slowly; but, in going up an incline, the rabbit would run correspondingly faster. When the speed of two animals is the same on level ground, the larger one will run faster than the smaller in descending an incline, but more slowly in ascending.

In these races, the only thing that Old Bull did was to come up as soon as he could after the death, and, like the lion in the fable, appropriate all the game to himself. The hounds never objected, as they knew his power and courage too well to contest his pretensions.

Norris said he had seen the speed of his greyhounds conclusively tested with that of the antelope. On one occasion he was out with his horse and dogs, when he saw a band of some forty antelopes grazing in open woods. He quietly approached as near as he could, and, when the antelopes started to run, he and the hounds pursued them at full speed. The attention of the fleeing animals seemed to have been fixed on him, and they measured their pace so as to keep about a hundred yards ahead. In this way the two fleetest hounds were permitted to approach within about twenty yards of the hindmost antelopes, the foremost ones being about forty yards ahead of them. Then the slut made a sudden and tremendous dash at the nearest antelopes, but they let out a few more links, and were very soon up with the foremost ones, and they all so increased their speed as to leave the slut far behind. They beat her with ease, and yet she was one of the fleetest of her race. The exquisite gazelle of Africa, "the child of the desert," and perhaps the fleetest animal in the world, as it is the most beautiful, belongs to the antelope family. There has never been, so far as I am advised, any conclusive test of the speed of the gazelle as compared with that of the Arab steed.

THE VIGILANCE COMMITTEE OF 1856 — MY FIRST VOYAGE AT SEA — INCIDENTS.

In the month of March, 1854, I returned to my home in Santa Clara County. At that time I had a large interest in the town of Alviso, situated at the southern extremity of the Bay of San Francisco, where I had erected a large frame dwelling-house in 1850. This building was constructed of the best eastern pine lumber, except the frame, was two stories high, was twenty-nine by forty-eight feet, and contained ten or twelve rooms. I employed the remainder of 1854 in removing this house from Alviso to San José, about nine miles distant. To remove it, we took it all apart, piece by piece, without injuring any of the materials, except the shingles, and put it together again, each plank in its proper place. I worked hard at it myself, as did my two sons, John and Armstead, then about grown. I employed Stincen, the carpenter of Sacramento, whose name has already been mentioned in connection with Tom the quack.

My first residence in San José cost me six thousand dollars, and it was afterward sold for one thousand. My second residence cost me ten thousand, and afterward sold for two thousand. These instances will indicate the shrinkage in value of real estate in San José. It is but justice to say that the prices mentioned would not at present be a fair criterion of the value of real estate in that city, which would rule neither so high nor so low as the rates mentioned.

During the years 1855 and 1856 I had no business employment, having quit the practice of my profession early in 1854, and devoted my time to reading. In the early part of August, 1856, I was attacked for the first time with neuralgia; and from that date until May, 1861, I had at intervals a succession of attacks, so that I was sick two thirds of the time during that period.

In 1856 the Vigilance Committee of San Francisco was in full and successful operation. I opposed this organization on the ground of principle, as I considered it incipient rebellion and a fatal precedent. It is very true that the good people of San Francisco had great reason to be dissatisfied with the administration of criminal justice. So many of the then residents of the city considered themselves but sojourners; while they, and many who regarded themselves as permanent settlers, were so eager in the pursuit of wealth that they could not be induced to serve on juries, that that duty thus devolved upon those unworthy of the trust. The consequence was that the guilty escaped, and crime continued unrestrained, until the situation became almost intolerable. I made two most vigorous speeches against the Committee. These were my last speeches. It is not my purpose to go fully into that exciting event, as it is a matter of history accessible to all.

In August and September, 1856, I made my first sea-voyage. My son-in-law, C. T. Ryland, and myself left San Francisco, on the 20th of August, on board the steamship John L. Stephens, for Panama. Supposing myself to be very susceptible to sea-sickness, I dreaded a voyage, thinking I should suffer severely. I had been suffering from a slight attack of neuralgia for some days, and I remembered the medical maxim that the human system will not generally tolerate more than one disease at the same time, and that the principal one will banish all the others. When the ship had passed the heads and was at sea, I became sea-sick, and I never once thought of the neuralgia for some days. But, as soon as I had entirely recovered from the sea-sickness, the neuralgia came limping back by slow degrees. My own experience therefore proved the truth of that medical maxim. On my return from New York, on board the steamship bound to Aspinwall, I became acquainted with a most intelligent gentleman who was far gone with consumption, and was on his way to South America in the hope that the change might restore him to health. While most of the passengers were sea-sick, he was not at all affected. This fact, he sorrowfully told me, he regarded as an indication of approaching death. From the best estimate I can make, after having made three trips between San Francisco and New York by sea, about seven per cent. of the passengers escape sea-sickness entirely, three per cent. are sick the entire voyage, and ninety per cent. are sick from one to five days.

At Aspinwall we went on board the steamship George Law, bound for New York. We came by Havana, but the yellow fever was then prevailing there to such an extent that our commander, Captain Herndon, deemed it best not to enter the harbor, but to take in a supply of coal at Key West. We left Key West about two hours before sunset. The weather was calm and the sky clear. The evening was most lovely, and the chaste moonlight danced upon the waves of the restless sea. Ryland, myself, and a young man named Twillager, occupied the same cabin. I slept in the upper, Ryland in the middle, and Twillager in the lower berth.

The moon set that night about 10 p.m., and we had all been asleep some hours when, about three o'clock a.m., I was awakened by Ryland's entering the cabin door. He was more wakeful than we were, had heard some stir on deck, had quietly left his berth, gone above, learned the cause, and returned. I at once asked him what was the matter. He solemnly replied, "We are aground." The ship had run in too close to the shore, and had reached a position upon a coral reef, on the eastern coast of Florida, from which she could not then retreat.

This was about the 9th of September, and the equinoctial storm was just before us. I at once comprehended the terrible situation. We had on board about one thousand passengers. I hastily dressed myself, went on deck, and took a calm survey; and I thought that I could discern through the darkness the dim outlines of a low bushy shore to our left. The ship was beating upon the reef. When a large wave rolled under her she rose, and when it receded she came down upon the rocky bottom with a melancholy thump. The human ear never heard a sound more terrible than that made by a great ship thumping upon a rock. It is a dead, dull sound, ominous of death. The ship struck at about full tide, and when the tide went down she was as still as a house on shore.

After remaining on deck a short time, I went below, and found all the passengers up. No one could sleep in our situation. I never saw a more solemn assemblage of people. Every one seemed to have a clear perception of our extremely critical situation. There were no jests, no smiles, no witticisms. Those who were professors of religion seemed resigned, those who were confirmed infidels seemed indifferent, while dread sat upon the countenances of those who were halting between two opinions. We were a little world to ourselves, and our little world seemed near its end.

The darkness was so great that nothing could be done until daylight. When day returned, the shore was in plain view about five miles distant. The water was so shallow and so clear that we could see the bottom of the ocean as plainly as one can see the carpet on the floor. At the distance of some two miles to our right we could see the deep, blue water, while around the ship the water was apparently green, owing to its being so shallow. The day was calm and beautiful.

Captain Herndon ordered a large portion of the coal to be thrown overboard, and the passengers went to work with a will to lighten the ship. There were among our passengers two experienced navigators, who had before this been engaged in commanding whaling-vessels, and were brave, hardy, and skillful seamen. They gave their utmost assistance. Captain Herndon was going all the time. I did not see him stop to eat or drink. No man could possibly have done more. The two sea-captains put on cheerful faces, went among the lady passengers, and assured them there was no danger; but they would tell me confidentially that our peril was great, as we were at the mercy of the first gale, and that the calm, beautiful weather was but the prelude to the dread equinoctial storm.

Toward noon several wreckers came in sight, and soon sailed all around and close to us. Soon afterward a large Spanish clipper-ship hove in sight, and, seeing our signals of distress, came as near to us as it was safe for her to do. Captain Herndon went out in a small row-boat to meet her, and made arrangements with her master to take on board a portion of our passengers. When he returned he announced to the passengers that a certain number could go aboard the clipper, and took down the names of those who were willing to go. Ryland and I decided to go.

In the mean time large quantities of coal had been thrown into the sea, a heavy anchor attached to an immense hawser had been thrown forward some distance, and the men were hauling upon it with all the force they could apply to the capstan. The tide had risen to its full height, the wheels of the ship were put in motion, and, just as we, with our carpet-bags in our hands, were about to descend into the small boats to go to the clipper, the steamship glided off the reef as easily as the sea-bird rises from the summit of the wave. As already stated, the ship had run in too close to the shore, and, when its dim outlines had been discovered by the man on the watch, her wheels were reversed; but, in the attempt to regain the deep water, she ran upon a bump in the reef, and stuck fast. The water gradually deepened from the shore to the blue water, as we could readily perceive from the difference in its apparent color.

As we slowly passed toward the anchor, Captain Herndon ordered the hawser to be cut, which was promptly done by one of the sailors. It was about three o'clock in the afternoon of that beautiful day, and all the passengers were on deck. Many efforts of the same kind had been previously made to haul off the ship, but all had failed, and when at last we succeeded we were utterly surprised. The head of the ship was turned toward the deep, blue water, and she moved at a slow and cautious rate toward it. We could plainly see the bottom, apparently gliding beneath and past the ship, as we passed over it. During this slow progress from our perilous situation to one of comparative safety, not a word was said. Every feature was set and every eye fixed. We did not know how soon the ship might strike upon another bump. At last we reached the deep sea, and then such a shout rose from our passengers as I never heard before, and never expect to hear again in this world. It rang and rang again. One lady, the wife of a physician, who had borne the danger with unmoved and heroic courage, swooned with joy.

Soon after the shouts had ceased, I met Captain Herndon on deck, when he threw his arms around my neck, wept, and said, "Governor, my heart was almost broken." I remember him with feelings of the most tender regard. He was a noble man, and an honor to his race. One year after that time, while still in command of the same steamship (though her name had been changed to that of the Central America), his vessel went down at sea in an equinoctial storm off Cape Hatteras, and he and most of his passengers perished.

The ship was so little injured that in due time we arrived safely in the port of New York. Next morning I read in the daily papers an account of the voyage and arrival of the George Law, but not one word was said about our having been aground upon a coral reef on the coast of Florida.

Chapter X

**APPOINTED A JUSTICE OF THE SUPREME COURT — PAIN-
FUL INCIDENT — ANTICIPATED OUR CIVIL WAR — MY
VIEWS UPON THAT SUBJECT.**

From New York I went West as far as Platte County, Missouri,
visited the scenes and friends of my early days, and returned to California about the 2^d day of December. I was appointed a Justice of
the Supreme Court of California by Governor J. Neely Johnson,
and my commission bears date January 13, 1857. This position I
held until my term expired early in October, 1858.

While occupying a seat on the Supreme Bench, a remarkable
circumstance occurred, which I felt more intensely than I can
describe. My brother, Glen O. Burnett (two years younger than
myself), then resided in Oregon. He had been an invalid for two or
three years, and I expected to hear of his death. One day in 1857 an
old acquaintance of both of us came to me in Sacramento City, and
informed me that he had just received a letter from his father-in-
law, in which it was stated that my brother died the day previous to
the date of the letter. As the writer lived in Oregon, only about
twelve miles from my brother, I had not the slightest doubt of the
fact. About three months had passed, and I was sure my brother
was dead, when, one evening, after I had closed my judicial labors
for the day, and while I was descending the outside iron stairs that
led from the court chambers above to the sidewalk, I observed a
venerable old gentleman standing below, evidently waiting for
some one. I could only see the top of his head and his long gray hair
as it extended below his hat; but when I reached the sidewalk, and
saw his face, I found he was my brother. My feelings can be better
imagined than described. He was like one risen from the dead. How
the mistake originated, I never knew.

I spent the month of December, 1859, and the month of January, and a small portion of February, 1860, in the city of New York.
During that time I attentively read all the most important Congressional debates. Early in March, 1860, I returned to California, and

told my friends that there would be civil war in case the Republican candidate should be elected President of the United States. No one agreed with me in this opinion. I thought that I saw, form the tone, temper, and matter of the speeches of the Southern members and Senators, that they had generally determined upon war in the contingency mentioned. It required only about one fourth of the population of the United States to produce civil war. As in such a contest there can practically exist only one party in the rebellious division, it required only a decisive majority of the Southern people to bring on the war. The minority would have not only to submit, but to aid and assist.

I was born and reared in the slave section of the United States, and most of my relatives resided there. I knew well the sincerity and courage of the Southern people; but it was a question of principle, and not of feeling. The unity and perpetuity of this great nation were a cardinal object with me. I could not fight against the grand old flag. If an intelligent stranger from another planet were to visit this earth, and were the flags of all the nations of this world placed before him, he would unhesitatingly select the Stars and Stripes as the most brilliant and magnificent of them all. No one can ever look upon that flag and forget it. Besides, it is the symbol of the first great nation that ever established political and religious liberty in its fullness and perfection. Whatever defects may exist in our theory of government can be corrected, even at the expense of revolution; *but the unity and integrity of the nation can never be destroyed*. The day of weak, defenseless States has passed away for ever. Only great governments can succeed, now or hereafter. If our country should err for a time, and commit temporary injustice, we must trust her still, and patiently and lovingly wait for her returning sense of justice, as a dutiful son would for that of his father or mother. He who trusts the *ultimate* justice of his country will seldom be disappointed.

During the war I was called upon publicly to express my opinion in regard to it. My answer was published at the time, but, as usual with me, I preserved no copy. As already stated, I published a pamphlet of more than one hundred printed pages, in which I gave my views in full. I voted for Abraham Lincoln for his second term.

DETERMINE TO ENGAGE IN BANKING — ELECTED PRESIDENT OF THE PACIFIC ACCUMULATION LOAN COMPANY — THE INSTITUTION PUT IN PRACTICAL OPERATION — DIFFICULTIES IN OUR WAY — CHANGE THE NAME TO "PACIFIC BANK."

When I had finished my work, "The Path which led a Protestant Lawyer to the Catholic Church," which appeared early in 1860, and the pamphlet just mentioned, which was published in the summer of 1861, I had a period of leisure. I had given up the practice of the law, and did not intend to resume it. I was not in debt, and had an income sufficient for a plain, decent support. All my children were married and settled for life, except my son John M. Burnett. For about two years I had time to read, but I could not see how I could make my knowledge useful. I maturely reflected upon my condition, and came to the conclusion that, as my health had been in a measure restored, it was my clear duty to make my personal services useful in some form. I thought it the duty of all persons, who are able, to work. It is the proper condition of man.

But what business to engage in was the question. I had always been unsuccessful in mercantile pursuits, and was determined never to engage in them again. I was too old to go back to the farm. In considering the matter fully, it occurred to me that banking would suit me better than any other occupation. It was an honest business, in which the temptation to do wrong was really less than in almost any other secular pursuit. We had in California a gold currency, and that which we lent was of full quantity, of pure quality, and of fixed value. All we asked of our debtors was to return to us the same amount of gold coin they had borrowed, with the addition of the interest, which was at the lowest market rates. We did not lend money (like some individual money-lenders) with the view of ultimately becoming the owners of the mortgaged property, as no bank would wish to own real estate, except its banking-house.

Furthermore, it was not only an honest business, but one very useful to all parties concerned. While the income upon the capital was only moderate, and not speculative or exorbitant, a sound, well-conducted bank was a most beneficial institution to the community generally. A bank that never fails affords a safe place of deposit for the money of others. This is a great convenience and a great benefit to the depositors. Besides, a good bank has it in its power to aid its worthy customers in various ways. The successful manager of a bank must necessarily be a first-class business man; must know what kinds of business are safe, and what doubtful; and should supply his customers, not only with judicious loans, but with the soundest advice. Many a business man is saved by good counsel. So many banks had failed in San Francisco, to the injury of many and the utter ruin of some of their depositors, that a good institution that would be just and yet firm to all, I thought, would be a great benefit to its own customers, and, by its successful example, to the public in general.

Therefore, after calm and full deliberation, I came to the fixed conclusion that I would go into the business of banking when a fair opportunity should offer. I was then, as now, fully aware of the prejudices existing in the minds of many persons against the business. But I am one of those independent men who rely upon their own judgment in regard to their own business. I do not follow the opinions of others, unless they agree with my own. My business is *my* affair and not theirs.

I had not capital enough to engage in the business alone, and I could find no one desirous of going into it, who could put up the same amount that I could. Being determined not to endanger the competency I had already acquired, so far as I could reasonably avoid it, I had to bide my time.In the spring of 1863 I was consulted by some of the officers of the "Pacific Accumulation Loan Company" in regard to the framing of its by-laws, and gave my views promptly. I was then residing in San José. This institution had been incorporated early in February, 1863, with a capital stock of five millions of dollars, divided into fifty thousand shares of the par value of one hundred dollars each, and its principal place of business was in the city of San Francisco. On the 3^{d} of June, 1863, I was notified by the Secretary that I had been chosen President, to fill the vacancy occasioned by the resignation of Mr. Samuel Brannan, and came at once to San Francisco. I found several defects in the charter and by-laws, some of which I did not approve. First, I did not like the name. Second, the capital was too large. Third, the by-laws provided that the Board of Directors could only demand payments upon the stock subscribed for in monthly installments, not exceeding two per cent. The first thing was to obtain subscriptions for the capital stock, and then it would require four years and two months to call in the amount subscribed. I saw before me the work of a lifetime; yet, as I had a basis to stand upon, I deliberately determined to undertake the enterprise of ultimately establishing the soundest and most reliable bank in the city. I had no special knowledge of the business, as I had never been trained in this most difficult of all secular pursuits. Circumstances had thrown me into different kinds of business during my varied experience, but I had made it a general rule not to engage in more than one business at the same time, and to devote my whole attention for the time being to the work I had in hand, and to learn it as early as possible.

Books of subscription for the capital stock of the institution had not been opened, and I set to work vigorously to get the stock taken. Mr. Brannan, myself, and some others subscribed, but I found that most of the very men who were the original incorporators either refused to take any stock or subscribed for mere nominal amounts. I labored hard at the task for some three months, but my success was not satisfactory. About the 1st of September I had another attack of neuralgia, and returned to San José, believing that our banking enterprise must fail. I had been at home about two weeks when I received a communication from the Secretary, stating that such arrangements had been made as would put the bank into practical operation within a few days.

Upon my return to the city, I was informed that Mr. Brannan had positively declared that the enterprise *must* and *should* succeed, and had largely increased his subscription. One other gentleman had subscribed for one thousand shares, four others for two hundred and fifty shares each, and others for various amounts. I also increased my subscription. We quietly but resolutely laid it up in our hearts that the enterprise should succeed.

It is but simple justice to Samuel Brannan to state that he is the father of the bank. Without his determined action, it would never have gone into successful operation. He was the first man in California, so far as I am informed, that spoke out in public against the introduction of slavery into this country. With all his faults, he has many noble qualities, and has done much for California.

When we opened the bank, on the 8th of October, 1863, we had less than twenty thousand dollars capital paid in. We had about seven hundred thousand dollars subscribed, but it would require fifty months to call it in. It was a small beginning, and a long, slow race, but we did not flinch or falter. The most durable timber is of slow growth, and the very best fruits do not ripen first. Our officers gave their services without compensation for the first fifteen months. The current rate of interest was then two per cent. a month.

About the end of the year 1863 I found to my surprise that all the directors except myself were in favor of paying a dividend early in 1864. I wished to accumulate a surplus fund, but they outvoted me, and for the time I was compelled to submit. In 1864 we paid dividends upon the capital paid in, at the rate of two per cent. a month. In 1865 they were reduced to one and a half and one and a quarter, and in 1866 to one and one fifteenth per cent. a month. Dividends were then paid semiannually, on the first days of January and July.

As I had foreseen, in the summer and fall of 1866 the bank sustained losses to such an extent as to compel the suspension of dividends for fifteen months. When we were about to resume, I introduced a resolution that the bank would pay monthly dividends at the rate of ten per cent. per annum, until the further order of the Board. I was the only one who voted for this resolution. The dividends were put at one per cent. a month, payable monthly. In the summer of 1871 the bank again sustained losses which compelled a second suspension of dividends. The last monthly dividend was paid September 1, 1871.

In the mean time we had amended the by-laws in several respects, and, by authority of a special act of the State Legislature, we changed the name of the institution to "Pacific Bank," its present corporate title. Later still we reduced the capital stock to one million dollars, United States gold coin, divided into ten thousand shares of the par value of one hundred dollars each. The stock of the bank never sold for less than eighty-five dollars per share for full-paid stock, but during the suspension of dividends it ruled from eighty-five dollars to par. According to the report in the "Alta California," the market value of the full-paid stock of the Bank of California to-day, September 26, 1878, is $80 bid and $82 asked; that of the First National, $89 bid and $90 asked; that of the National Gold Bank, $79 bid and $80 asked; and that of the Pacific, $115 bid, and $116 asked.

After the second suspension of dividends, September 1, 1871, and before we could resume, the majority of the stock fell into the hands of sound, safe, conservative men, who understood banking, and who agreed with me not to resume the payment of dividends until January, 1877. In the mean time we accumulated, in the space of five years and four months, a surplus fund of more than half a million dollars. Our capital of one million is now full-paid, and we have a handsome surplus.

WILD BANKS — SPECULATIVE CHARACTER OF OUR PEOPLE — INCIDENT.

I think I can safely say that no sound bank was ever established under greater difficulties than the Pacific. I am sure that I was never engaged in any business enterprise that required so much thought, judgment, labor, firmness, and perseverance. We had not only to overcome the great difficulties in our charter and by-laws, and the serious errors of our governing stockholders, but we had for long years to compete with the wildest banks, wielding immense amounts of capital, and enjoying almost unbounded credit. I was reminded at times, by some of our own directors, that the managers of these fast and flashy institutions were fine business men; but I firmly resisted such a conclusion. At an early day I did not approve of their mode of business, and then took a stand, almost "solitary and alone," that honest and intelligent time has conclusively shown to have been correct.

About two years after our little bank opened its doors for business, one of the leading capitalists of San Francisco, and one of the original incorporators who refused to subscribe for any of the stock, upon hearing some one speak of the Pacific Accumulation Loan Company, asked, "Is that thing going yet?" About 1873 I met an officer of one of the large banks in the city, then in the full tide of success (as was generally supposed), who twittingly remarked to me, "Governor, the signs upon your bank windows are quite pretentious. They completely take us down." I made no reply. There was ample opportunity for "patience to have her perfect work."

Before the suspension of the largest banks in this city, August 26, 1875, the market value of our stock was less than that of any respectable bank in the city; but when that event occurred, and the wild banks went down to the level of their intrinsic demerits, our stock went up to the head of the list, except that of one other bank. The stock of this *void* concern was still quoted in the public financial reports as worth $125 a share, when its intrinsic value was not one cent. Finally, however, in the fall of 1877, that bank failed, and left the stock of the Pacific Bank at the head of the list.

But we had not only to overcome these great difficulties, but to encounter others equally embarrassing. The people of California, in proportion to numbers, have been, and are yet, the most speculative in America, if not in the world. At least one half of the men who came to this country were full of the most eager desire to make fortunes. A good, reasonable competency would not satisfy their magnificent expectations.

Speculation first ran wild in real estate, then in water-ditches, and for the last fifteen years in mining stocks. In no city on earth is it so difficult to ascertain the true financial condition of men as in San Francisco. With all due care, the average losses of a bank in this city, taking a series of ten years together, will run from two to four per cent. per annum upon the amount loaned. Nothing but the current high rate of interest enabled us to make a decent profit.

All must concede that mining is one of the leading interests of this coast, and that permanent investments in mines are a legitimate business, though exposed to more risks than most other avocations. The investor in a mine has two risks to encounter: first, the character of the mine itself; second, the character of its management, which is the greater risk of the two. If the mine be poor, it can not be made to pay even by the best management. If it be rich, those who practically control its management are very apt to depreciate the market value of the stock, by working for a time the poor ores, or by other devices, and thus compel the board of directors to levy and collect a series of assessments. This process will be continued until the weaker stockholders are forced to sell their stock; and the unprincipled managers, through their agents, buy it in, having the certificates issued in the name of some person as trustee.

But investing in the legitimate business of mining is one thing, and speculating in mining stocks is another and a very different thing. The first is useful and honest, because it develops and adds to the wealth of the country, while the second does not develop or add to its wealth or morals in any form whatever. All the necessaries and comforts of life are the products of labor and skill honestly applied. But the speculator and gambler are leeches upon society, and the worst of all speculators is the speculator in mining stocks. It is the most deplorably demoralizing of all occupations dignified by the name of business. It speedily corrupts crowds of people, and keeps them idle ever afterward; because the man who has once experienced the wild excitement and tasted the insane luxury of a successful speculation in mining stocks is, as a general rule, for ever totally unfitted for any useful occupation. What sound business man would ever employ as a clerk a young man who had been once successful in mining-stock speculations? What is such a being fit for during the remainder of his life? If unsuccessful in his first effort, he is peculiarly fortunate, for then he may be saved from that worse than gambling pursuit. But it is just about as difficult to cure the once successful speculator as to reform the confirmed drunkard.

For one or two years before the late rise in the market value of mining stocks, crowds of men in the prime of life could be seen standing on the streets idle. Their listless faces and seedy, dilapidated appearance indicated extreme laziness and destitution. But since the rise they appear jubilant. They are now seen on the streets with clean-shaven faces, neatly combed hair, new clothes, new hats, and new boots nicely polished. They seem as much revived as withered grass after a plenteous fall of rain.

It is well known to all intelligent men, who have been in business in this city for any considerable time, that mining speculators will readily sacrifice their best friends, *because they can*. The old adage, "A long stitch for a friend," is most applicable to this character of swindling. When you hear one of these men say he has a confidential "point," as it is called, in regard to a certain mine, you may justly conclude that he has his stock in the hands of a broker for sale. So, if you hear a man puffing a certain stock, and saying he would invest if he only had the money, you had better conclude that he is anxious to sell. The only possible way in which these gamblers in mining stocks can deceive a sensible man is by telling the truth. That would be such a singular case as to deceive any fallible being.

A man who had once been in the habit of lending on mining stocks as collateral told me an incident within his own knowledge. He lent a man a sum of money, and took from the borrower what is called an "ironclad note," secured by the pledge of a certain number of shares of a certain mining company. The note was payable one day after date, and contained a clause stipulating that the borrower should keep up the margin on the stock. If it should depreciate in its market value, the borrower was to put up more stock, or reduce the debt by a proportionate payment in money. In this case the stock was declining in value, and the lender was continually calling upon the borrower to keep good the margin. This the lender did several times, and the margin was made good by the borrower putting up more stock. The lender urged the speculator to sell, but he refused, insisting that the depression was only temporary. But the stock still continued to decline, and the lender as continually called for more stock, and urged the borrower to sell, saying to him, "I can not spare you. In case of a speculation you would get all the profit, and you must take all the risk. The chance of profit and the risk of loss must go together."

The borrower at last had no more stock to put up, and no money to reduce the debt. He concluded to go to a large stock-speculator, and ask *his* opinion about the mine. This stock-sharp at once replied that it was a good mine, and that the depreciation of the stock in the market was a bear movement, and that it would soon go up again. "But," said the borrower, "I have borrowed money on my stock, and I am called upon by the lender to put up more stock, but I can not do it." "Well," said the sharp, "I will lend you the stock. How many shares do you lack?" and, upon being informed of the number, he at once handed over to the borrower the stock required. At that very time this large operator was selling out that very stock as rapidly as he could. He lent this parcel of stock to keep it from being thrown upon the market. But the stock still declined, and the lender gave orders to his broker to sell every share that very day. The stock was sold accordingly, and by this prompt sale the borrower was saved several thousand dollars, as the stock continued to decline until it went much lower.

MERCHANTS AND OTHER BUSINESS MEN OFTEN SECRETLY ENGAGE IN STOCK-SPECULATIONS — ILLUSTRATIVE CASES OF SPECULATION — FAILURES SOMETIMES FALSELY ATTRIBUTED TO SPECULATION IN MINING STOCKS.

Men engaged in mercantile and other kinds of business in this city are often secretly concerned in speculating in mining stocks. If the firm has a temporary surplus of money, one of the younger partners is very apt to propose to invest that surplus, and no more, in mining stocks. Each speculator pays himself the vain compliment to think that, by watching the market carefully, *he* can know when to buy and sell or that *he* is born to good luck. If the firm should succeed in the first attempt, then all the partners become so elated that they can not condescend to attend to the dull routine of regular business, in which there appears to them nothing worthy of their genius or enterprise, the amount made required so little time and labor. So they go in deeper and deeper. When they sustain losses they are plucky, and act upon the sharp's maxim, "Seek your money where you lost it." They forget the true and sober maxim, "Never be deceived twice in the same way," and never stop in their wild career until they are forced to do so by utter insolvency.

On the contrary, if a firm be embarrassed pecuniarily, then the partners are tempted to engage in speculations in mining stocks as a measure of relief. If successful (as in some *rare* cases may happen), they get out of their difficulties for a time, but hardly ever remain so permanently.

These men fraudulently hold themselves out to the business world as *only* engaged in regular and useful business. Their stock operations are profoundly secret. The certificates of stock are adroitly put in the name of some man as trustee, and endorsed by him in blank on the back, and thus pass from hand to hand like a note endorsed in blank or a bond payable to bearer. You may examine the books of *all* the numerous companies in this city, and you will never find any stock standing in the names of these men. Not a share. The first thing known is the failure of the house. Men above the age of fifty, and who have been sound, safe, and reasonably successful for years, occasionally go into this wild gambling, and are ruined. In fact, age and experience seem no sufficient protection against this infatuation. Lamentable cases often occur. Some are ludicrous, and some are too serious to be so, though equally stupid. Women are often seen crying in the streets, because they have been gambling in mining stocks, and have lost all.

Another difficulty in the way of commercial banking in this city was the absence of good collaterals. Very few of our business men had invested in United States bonds, because the rate of interest was too low, and our State bonds had been mostly absorbed by the State School Fund, while our best county bonds had gone to the East and to Europe. The only abundant collaterals were mining stocks, and these were not reliable, with all the "iron-clad" notes that could be taken. We were, therefore, compelled to lend on names, and to a large extent upon single names. Hence the great losses sustained, and the very moderate net profits realized. Besides, the amount of bank deposits in San Francisco is much less in proportion to bank capital than in other commercial cities.

In Illustration, I will mention a few cases.

A millionaire came from the East to spend the winter in California, and brought letters of introduction to me. We had many conversations about business, and I urged him not to touch mining stocks. But in a month or two the yellow fever of speculation obtained the mastery over him. He was about sixty years of age, and his annual income was about one hundred thousand dollars. He said to me at last that he had concluded to risk fifty thousand dollars in mining stocks, as he desired some excitement, and could readily stand the loss of that amount. I said no more to him, but left him to himself. The next spring he sold out his stocks, and had made about twenty thousand dollars net profit. He was much gratified, and no doubt thought himself more than a match for the San Francisco sharps. I had carefully explained to him the process by which they would ultimately catch him, but he had not yet comprehended it. The succeeding fall he again came to spend the winter in California, and again went into speculations in mining stocks. As he kept his cash accounty with the Pacific Bank, I often saw him; but he said nothing to me, nor I to him, on the subject. But, when he came to close out the second spring, he wore an extremely long face. I observed his downcast looks, and asked him how he was getting along. He replied, "Governor, I feel very blue. I have lost thirty-two thousand dollars in mining stocks." This was a ludicrous case, in regard to which I could afford to laugh heartily.

One of our leading capitalists informed me that on one occasion he determined to engage in speculation in mining stocks. He said his practice was to purchase when they were highest, for fear they would go higher, and to sell when they were lowest, for fear they would go lower. He soon found that he had sustained losses to the amount of more than eight thousand dollars. He also said that the most amusing feature in his case was the fact that his losses occurred while he was dealing in the stock of a mine of which he was president. His experience proved that no man can see beyond the point of the pick.

A gentleman of my acquaintance told me that one evening in 1878 he was riding in a street-car in this city, and that there sat opposite to him a neatly but not extravagantly dressed married lady, some twenty-five years old. She was evidently a woman of education. Soon a gentleman, who appeared to be an acquaintance of herself and husband, entered the car, and took a seat beside her. She was a loud, fluent talker, and at once commenced, and soon explained to him their present as compared with their former condition. She said they had been rich, but had lost all in mining stocks; that they had given up their fine residence, splendid furniture, and magnificent horses and carriage; that they had dismissed their numerous servants, and had taken a small, neat, but comfortable cottage; that she rose early and prepared breakfast, then went out and taught a class in music, returned and cooked dinner and supper; and, in fact, that she did all her house-work herself, and never was so busy or more healthy. At the end of her narrative she paused for a moment, and then exclaimed, with increased emphasis, " *But we had a grand time while it lasted.*"

The same gentleman informed me that he knew a merchant in one of the interior cities of California who was a partner in a most respectable mercantile firm, which for years had done a safe, prosperous, and honorable business. This man was considered an exemplary member of society in his city, but he became tired of his position, sold out his interest in an excellent business, and went into speculations in mining stocks. My informant said he had not seen this man for several years, when he met him in the streets of San Francisco in 1878, and inquired how he was progressing. The man replied, "You know I was at one time worth one hundred and twenty-five thousand dollars in cash; but I have lost it all. I would not have regarded the loss of the money so much, had I not lost it on a *sure thing.*" The melancholy truth was, the man had not alone lost his money, but he had lost his capacity for all useful business, and also his moral principles. This is one of the sad cases.

On one occasion a well-dressed lady came to the bank and engaged in a long conversation with our cashier. On passing through his department several times, I observed the lady frequently weeping. After she had left, I inquired of the cashier as to the subject of the interview. He stated substantially that she came to sell him an elegant copy of Audubon's "Birds of America," and had explained to him the reasons for offering it for sale. She said that she was then living with her second husband; that her first husband, who was much older than herself, had died and left her a fortune; that her second husband was of suitable age for her; that she had married him some eight months before, and soon after his return from Europe, whither he had gone to complete his education; that he was a finely educated gentleman; that they had been some months in San Francisco on a visit; that they had invested all her money in mining-stock speculations, and had lost all; and that they were upon the verge of actual want, and were compelled to sell everything they could spare to procure the mere necessaries of life. It was evident that her second marriage was a love-match; and that, while her second husband was an accomplished gentleman, he was but a child in business. This case was too sad to laugh at.

When I arrived in San Francisco in March, 1849, I found an old settler residing here with his family. He was a man of means, and left the city about 1855, and settled in one of the States east of the Rocky Mountains. About 1873 he sent a telegram to his banker in this city to this purport: "Buy mining stocks for me when they are lowest, and sell when they are highest." He no doubt thought his fortune was certain, as in his opinion this process could not fail. If his banker would only obey orders, how could there be a failure? But he was no doubt greatly surprised when his banker replied that they could not do that kind of business. When stocks were lowest or highest, no man could tell.

But I have every reason to believe that failures are sometimes falsely attributed to speculations in mining stocks. This pretense is resorted to in order to swindle creditors.

For example, a firm composed of two or more partners, finding business dull and expenses and losses greater than gains, deliberately determine to cheat their creditors, and in this way to make a handsome profit. How to do so successfully, and with the least possible delay and disgrace, is the question with them. Bankruptcy they know to be not only a slow but an uncertain mode; and, to save anything, they must hide their money, commit perjury, and incur a stain upon their business honor that will stick to them as long as they live. They therefore adopt the common plan of compromising with their creditors. But to do this successfully they must make out what claims to be a full and true statement of their assets and liabilities, and must be prepared to satisfy their creditors that this statement is true. Perhaps only six months before they had made a statement in full to the mercantile agencies, or to some of their creditors, showing the firm to have been then in a fair condition. But, when they make out a statement for a compromise, showing so great a difference, how are they to account for the discrepancy between the two statements? Every sensible business man will at once see that such extraordinary losses, if truly such, must have been produced by unusual causes. Some creditor will be certain to ask this question: "What caused these heavy losses in so short a time?" This home question must be answered satisfactorily, or the proposition for a compromise, upon the payment of a fraction on the dollar, can not succeed. If they give an explanation, the falsity of which from its nature can be shown by investigation, the fraudulent attempt must fail. The partners, fully comprehending the situation, will of course come prepared to answer that some one of the firm had been speculating in mining stocks, and had secretly used the partnership name to borrow money, which had been lost. The moment this answer is given, the creditors are at fault. That region of darkness can not be penetrated. All possible inquiries can not expose the falsity of the answer. His broker is pledged to secrecy, the stocks stand in the name of some one as trustee, the certificates were endorsed in blank, and it is impossible to trace him. The partners have either agreed among themselves which one of them should bear the odium, or have settled it by lot. The creditors will naturally sympathize with the apparently innocent partner; and, for his sake and that of his family, they agree to the proposition. Having discharged one partner, they legally discharge the other. The firm, having been thus released from their debts upon the payment of a fraction of them, start anew, with a fine capital and no liabilities.

TRUE RULE AS TO BANK CONTRIBUTIONS — BANKING A TRYING BUSINESS — THE INFALLIBLE BANKER — FIVE MAIN POINTS TO CONSIDER IN MAKING LOANS — DEVICES TO OBTAIN CREDIT.

Soon after our little bank went into practical operation, we were called upon to contribute from the corporate funds for various charitable purposes. This bank, being the first incorporated commercial institution in this city, had to take a just stand upon this subject and maintain it. Up to this period all the commercial banks in San Francisco were mere partnerships, and of course could legally and justly give away the partnership funds by the consent of all the partners. But incorporated banks were placed in a new and totally different position, though this difference was not apparent for a time to those who asked for contributions. Our charter did not allow the officers of the bank to give away the money of the stockholders; and, had the officers done so, they would have been individually liable. Besides, it was an unjust principle to ask the bank to give in its corporate capacity, and then go to each stockholder and ask him to give as an individual. This would have been a double burden. Our stockholders claimed the undoubted right to bestow their charities upon such objects as their judgment approved, and in such amounts as they, in their own opinion, could reasonably spare.

It is a wise and salutary feature in the charter of incorporated banks, that no power is conferred upon the officers to give away the funds of the institution. An individual banker or a partnership can well do so, as they bestow only their own money, and not that of others. Most bank officers have but a small amount of stock in the institution, and, if allowed to give away its means, could acquire a splendid reputation for generosity with very little, if any, cost to themselves. The principal officer would receive all the praise, while the stockholders would sustain all the loss. He would find any number of people who would give him unmerited praise for solid gold, without caring whose money it was.

I soon saw what the ultimate result must be, should we act upon a false theory; and I took the stand that, *as a bank*, we would give nothing except to celebrate the fourth of July, and in some other extraordinary cases, approved by all. In this position I was sustained by the stockholders, who were people in every condition of life, and of different political and religious views. On this point we heard no complaints from the stockholders. Each of us gave individually to such objects as he approved, and in such amounts as he pleased.

As already stated, I had had no special training as a banker. I possessed, as I thought, a fair amount of general business knowledge. In my business transactions, I acted upon Lord Chesterfield's rule of politeness — "softness in the manner, but firmness in the execution"; and I found this an admirable rule for a banker. My first care in my new position was to comprehend the true situation. I had engaged in a trying and perilous business, that required for its successful management not only a comprehensive knowledge of business in general, but a superior judgment of men — the highest order of business capacity. I was often forcibly reminded of that profound couplet of Pope:.

"The good must merit God's peculiar care;
But who, but God, can tell us who they are?"

I soon found that a banker would be called either a hard man or a fool. If he lent the money of the bank carefully and successfully, they would call him a hard man, an old fogy, and an old fossil. On the contrary, if he lent the money of the institution carelessly, and ultimately lost it, he would be justly called a fool. He would be judged by ultimate results. A banker must make up his mind as to which reputation he prefers. I never do an idle and vain thing, if I know it. When I undertake any business, I mean to succeed, if I can do so by fair and just means; and, if I can not attain success by such a course, I quit the business.

A banker is exposed to every *possible* test, as he meets every class of men, in all their various conditions and moods. If he is avaricious, they will be very apt to overcome him with presents and commissions. If he is vain and has a lust of praise, they will flatter him to his heart's content. If he is indolent and good-natured, they will pleasantly induce him to make bad loans. If he is too kind-hearted, they will overcome his sympathies. If he is timid, they will bully him. If he is excitable, they will worry and confuse him. If he is not clear-headed, they will out-talk and persuade him. In short, he has to encounter *every* class of men: the good, safe business man, with whom it is a pleasure to deal; the partially insane and abusive man, when pecuniarily embarrassed; the vain, conceited man, who thinks he knows it all, and piles up his advice; the eager, visionary, financial dreamer, full of "hopes and schemes"; the bold, reckless, and unprincipled speculator; the cheat, the forger, the thief. Each one comes with his speech prepared in advance. A banker will in due time find out that the best talkers are generally "men of words and not of deeds." They talk remarkably well, but do not generally pay. The chronic borrower, from long practice, understands borrowing as a science. He will use very few words, but will ask, in a very simple, pleasant way, "Mr. President, are you discounting any first-class paper to-day?" "Yes, sir." "I have a note of that class to offer." Upon the note being declined, he retires with the same ease and grace with which he entered.

A banker may for a time gain the reputation of possessing an *infallible* judgment of men, if he will only adopt the bold plan of quickly and promptly saying yes or no to all applications for loans. If a good man comes and asks for a loan, and it is instantly granted, he, *knowing* that he is good, goes away, saying to himself, "What a splendid judge of human nature!" If the visionary comes, and as promptly obtains a loan, he, *thinking* himself good, goes away admiring the wonderful instinct of the banker. So of all other classes of borrowers who *succeed* in obtaining loans. As all receive what they asked for, they are all pleased, and all equally filled with admiration. The good talkers among the successful borrowers will fill the city with their loud and oftrepeated praises of the wonderful qualifications of this most prompt banker. Those he as promptly refuses are men notoriously in bad credit, and they, too, admire the banker's off-hand sagacity in understanding them so quickly. The reputation of the banker lasts until time, with its absolute veto, puts him down to his proper level. Then men begin to learn that hasty loans too often end in large losses.

In considering a proposed loan, there are five main points of inquiry:

1. Is the proposed borrower thoroughly honest?
2. Has he an adequate capital?
3. Is his business a reasonably safe one?
4. Does he manage it well?
5. Is he a good economist in his living?

All these should concur to make a loan a fair business risk.

We are often forced to form a judgment of men from very trifling circumstances; but these are keys to the position. Men may successfully conceal their real characters in important matters, but will reveal them in little things. If a man borrows money, and at the same time is found insuring his life for the benefit of his family, or improving a homestead, or living above his means, or driving fine horses, or doing any other thing incompatible with the condition of an honest debtor, those who lend him money will be very apt to receive a notice to attend a meeting of creditors.

It is surprising how many devices (most of them old, but some of them new) unprincipled and extravagant men will resort to in order to obtain money.

For example, a speculator will purchase and pay for a valuable and productive parcel of real estate, which he will *never* encumber. Upon the credit of this property, say worth fifty thousand dollars, he will borrow various sums from different parties, at intervals running through several years, always paying his notes punctually. The lenders keep their own business to themselves, each one thinking the borrower owes nobody but him. This process will be continued, the sum total of borrowed money increasing about in proportion to the interest paid, until at last he sells the property for cash, and his creditors find nothing whereon to levy.

Another speculator sets out in his early manhood to speculate in produce, say cotton or grain, and he deliberately adopts a theory, either originated by himself or suggested to him by some older head. He determines to conduct the business as carefully as he can, but upon borrowed capital and at the risk of others. If he should succeed, he will pocket all the profits; if he should fail, his creditors must bear all the loss. He will be liberal in his charities and in his contributions to public objects, as his generosity costs *him* nothing, and he receives great praise without merit. He will be a generous patron of the fine arts, and be called a man of fine taste. In the course of time he suspends, and compromises with his creditors at a fraction on the dollar, giving them a verbal promise (not binding in law) that he will in time pay every dollar of his old debts, without interest. At this, his first suspension, we will assume for the sake of illustration that his total assets amount to five hundred thousand dollars, and his liabilities to the same amount, which he discharges with two hundred and fifty thousand, thus netting that sum by the compromise. He now has a handsome capital, and commences business again, and for a time he succeeds well. He now borrows still more largely, and out of this *borrowed* money he pays his old debts in installments. His old creditors are full of gratitude, and are loud in sounding his praises on all sides. At the payment of each installment of his old indebtedness, his credit grows better, until, when all are paid, it rises to its summit, and he uses it as fully as possible.

In the mean time he marries and rears a family in splendor and in the enjoyment of all the luxuries of the world. In the course of time, however, he overreaches himself in his expenses and speculations, and suspends a second time, calls his creditors together again, and proposes another compromise upon the old basis. He assures them that he will pay every dollar in the future, as he did in the past, if they will only discharge him. His creditors remember well his former noble act, as they consider it, and easily agree to release him upon the terms proposed. In the second suspension he makes a much larger profit than in the first. He starts again with increased capital to run the same career. But at his death it will be found that his life had been insured to a large amount for the benefit of his family, not of his creditors, although *their* money paid the premiums upon the policies. His friends, who are generally the best of talkers, will attribute his losses to the nature of his business, and not to his extravagance. They never seem to understand the fact that extravagant family expenses, continued for a series of years together, will ruin any business, as a general rule. Had he lived in a decent and honorable simplicity, as all men should who owe others, then he could have paid his debts with ease.

Whenever any man lives extravagantly, and at the same time owes any considerable amount of money, his credit in bank should be very low, whatever may be his *apparent* wealth. No loans should be made him except upon unquestionable security. A man that owes nothing has the right to live in splendor; but, when a man has to borrow money to pay family expenses, his condition is bad, and his credit should be so too.

I have lately seen a letter from a man twenty-four years old, who is a student at college, to his father, from which I am permitted to take the following extract: " *The moment a man spends too much on himself, he is to be watched.* Now, I mean whether his income is one hundred dollars a year or five hundred dollars a year. This rule applies whether he has or has not vices, is or is not honest, a Christian or not one. You must not understand me as meaning the old proverb, *If a man spends more than he earns, he will wind up in the poor-house or penitentiary.* He may save three fourths of what he earns; that does not make much difference with my rule. I mean, if he indulges himself in any way, say by overeating, studying, staying up of nights, or excesses of any kind."

There is a depth of sound practical judgment shown in this extract, which is remarkable as coming from one so young and inexperienced.

Natural and reasonable wants are few and limited, while artificial and unreasonable wants are many and unlimited. When, therefore, a man *begins* to expend money to gratify these wants, he starts upon a dangerous and downward path; and, whatever may be his income to-day, he may, and very probably will, soon exceed it. The banker can not rely upon the discretion of such a borrower. He may confine his expenditures within his income for a short time; but his want of judgment, his extreme selfishness, and his insatiable desire to gratify whimsical and inordinate wants, will be very apt to cause his ruin sooner or later, and no one can tell when this may occur.

And I lay down this rule as *generally* true: If a man *once* goes through insolvency or bankruptcy, or compromises with his creditors, or indulges in unreasonable expenses, he is unworthy of credit.

I say *generally* true, as there may be about one exception in ten cases.

A GOOD BANKER MAY OFTEN SAVE HIS CUSTOMERS FROM LOSSES AGAINST THEIR WILL — INCIDENTS OF THE SUSPENSION OF CERTAIN BANKS IN 1875 — DIFFICULTY OF OBTAINING FAITHFUL EMPLOYEES.

Sometimes the greatest good a sound banker can do his customers, and the one for which he receives at the time the fewest thanks and the most censure, is to check their extreme eagerness to grow rich quickly. Impatience ruins multitudes of business men. In their great anxiety to advance rapidly, and to rival older business houses, they are tempted to go too far. This is generally the error of young men, and especially of those who succeed their fathers in business. The ambitious, bold, and inexperienced youngster is easily flattered, and thinks he can excel his father. He is very apt to think the sum left him inexhaustible, and his credit unbounded; while every competent banker knows that most young men in our country, who inherit fortunes from their parents or others, go to ruin. If a firm, for example, be Smith's Sons, a judicious banker will be very apt to decline their paper, though they be rich when it is made. It is, as a general rule, only a question of time when the firm will fail.

Other young business men, who have had no fortune left them, will be very anxious to make a fortune speedily, so that they can enjoy it before they become old. When they come to their banker with paper for discount, these ardent customers are nearly always certain to consider *their* paper first-class, and are much surprised, and often offended, because the paper is declined. If they are about to enter into some outside enterprise, or make a purchase in their proper line of business, but much too large for their capital, they see the great anticipated profits, while the sound, conservative banker can only see probable losses. He therefore refuses to lend them the money, much to their disappointment; but he saves them from ruin against their will and their most persistent importunities.

About a month and a half before the suspension of certain large banks in this city in August, 1875, a customer of ours rushed into our bank one day, and said to me, "I wish to borrow twenty-five thousand dollars for sixty days, and I have first-class collaterals to give." I quietly asked him to let me see his collaterals, and they proved to be one hundred shares of the stock of a certain bank, and the same number of shares of the stock of a certain other bank. After listening to him about twenty minutes, I declined the loan. He was a splendid talker, and argued his case remarkably well. When he found he could not obtain the loan, he said he would go and sell every share of the stock, which he did promptly, at about one hundred and twenty-five dollars a share. When these banks and one other suspended, he was not in the city, but returned in a few days in the best possible humor. I had saved him, against his will, between fifteen and sixteen thousand dollars.

Another service a banker may do his customers, especially young business men, is to require them to pay their notes punctually at maturity. This practice keeps them active, vigilant, and firm in making collections from their own customers. If unduly indulged themselves by their bankers, they in turn become too indulgent, and ultimate ruin is the legitimate result.

I remember a case wherein I erred myself, to the injury of our customer as well as our own, by being too indulgent. He kept a good balance in the bank, and we had loaned him, upon his own name, the sum of four thousand dollars. He was a man of mature age, steady habits, good character, and fair capital. The loan ran on for several years, and was renewed from time to time, the interest being always punctually paid. Finally, this staid, industrious old gentleman went into speculations in mining stocks, and, as usual, lost all. The first I knew of his failure was from his own melancholy letter informing me of the fact. I sent for him, and we had a free conference, in the course of which he said, "I wish to God you had called upon me to pay that note. I could have paid it any day, and there would have been that much saved."

When the run on the banks occurred in 1875, we knew nothing of it until it commenced. We were then told that there was a run on a certain bank, and in half an hour afterward that bank closed its doors. In a panic the crowd of depositors seem to have an infallible instinct. They will be certain to first run on the weakest bank, and then on others in proportion to their want of strength. This run on the banks conclusively proved the truth and reason of the Scripture command, "Be ye always ready."

We at once stopped all loans, and required those who were not depositors with the bank to pay their notes as they fell due; otherwise they would go to protest. We were compelled, for our own protection, to adopt and inflexibly enforce this peremptory rule. They urged us to permit the endorsers to waive demand and protest. I saw that, if we did this in one case, we must in many, and would thus be compelled to carry the customers of other banks through the crisis. I said, "Pay or be protested. The rule is as inflexible as the laws of the Medes and Persians."

One man had two notes falling due on the same day, and he urged me to let them go over, upon a waiver of demand and protest, as he could not possibly pay them when due. I said, "You must pay or be protested." He urged and urged again and again; and about half an hour before the bank closed for the day he went out, declaring the notes must go to protest. But about fifteen minutes later he came into my office, flaunting the notes in my face, and saying he wanted to quarrel with me. I told him to sit down and I would hear him. He complained and grumbled about my harshness, and said I had hurt his feelings. After he had finished, I said to him quietly and good-humoredly: "I have my money now, and I think I can stand your grumbling." At this he laughed heartily, and went away. A day or two afterward I mentioned the circumstance to the endorser of the notes, and he at once said, "Why, he had already provided for those notes." The truth was, the maker had other notes falling due within a few days, and was not *certain* that he could meet them unless he could induce us to permit these two notes to pass without protest. If he could only postpone the payment of these two notes, he would have ample means to pay the others.

In many cases I was very sorry for the parties whose notes we were compelled to protest. I remember the case of a most admirable man, whose hair was gray, and who was evidently a gentleman in every sense of the term. I had never seen him before, because he had never before asked indulgence on a note of his. He assured me that his note had never gone to protest in a single case; and it was so hard, at this period of his life, to have his note protested. He exhibited the truest financial feeling and honor, and told me that he would pay the note within two days if I would permit the endorser to waive. I assured him of my kindest feeling toward him, and of my fullest confidence in his good faith; but the rule of the bank was inflexible and must be carried out. He went away sorrowful, and left me so. I knew he was a true man. The note went to protest, and he paid it within two days thereafter. I then said to him, "Do not let this protest give you any pain. In such a crisis as this, the notes of the best men go to protest. Under all the circumstances, your credit is not impaired at all; and, if you should want any money, come to me and I will lend it to you." He went away consoled and satisfied.

The suspension occurred on Thursday, and on the Tuesday following a gentleman of my acquaintance, who was an officer of an interior bank, came into my office smiling, and inquired whether I thought any money could be borrowed in San Francisco on United States bonds as collateral. I laughed, and told him I *rather* thought not. He then informed me of the fact that his institution, five years before, had purchased United States bonds amounting to ninety-two thousand dollars, and had held them ever since for this very crisis; and now they were not worth anything for the purpose intended. This city is so distant from the great financial cities of the world that for some time money could not be borrowed upon any collaterals whatever. We were offered a loan, secured by a pledge of United States bonds, at two per cent. a month, which we were compelled to decline. The only loans we made for three weeks were small amounts to our good depositors, to save them from protest.

One of the greatest difficulties in conducting a bank is to obtain faithful and competent officers and other assistants. This is especially so in California, as so few young men are natives, whose families are well known here.

The discipline in a bank must be as rigid as that in an army. If an employee willfully and deliberately disobeys orders, he should be discharged. If, when caught in making a mistake, he manifests no feeling, no regret, but takes it coolly and indifferently, it shows that he has deliberately trained his feelings to bear reproof, and he is not to be trusted. If he shirks his duty, and throws an unfair proportion of the work upon others, he exhibits an unjust disposition, and should be discharged. If he is late in coming to the bank, so as just to save his time, he had better be watched. If he is too fond of display, and carries a little cane for show, you had better conclude,

"Little cane,Little brain;

Little work,

And big shirk."

He will spend too much time on the streets to show himself. If he is a fast young man in *any way*, he is unworthy. If he expends all his salary and saves up nothing, as a general rule he is unfit. It will do him no good to increase his salary, because he will be just as poor at the end of the year as he was at the beginning. In fact, an increase of compensation is a positive injury to him, because it increases his fast habits in proportion.

But a young man of good habits, pleasant manners, fair health, and good temper, who saves up a portion of his income, may be safely trusted. To bear the continual strain of good economy is a clear proof of integrity, good, sound, practical common sense, and self-control. Such a man soon becomes independent in his circumstances, and does not need to steal. Occasionally a young man may be found who is competent, sober, economical, and industrious, and who will yet steal from sheer avarice; but such cases are remarkably rare. An inordinate love of pleasure is the ruin of very many young men in our day. Extravagance in dress and living is the great besetting sin of the times, in almost every portion of the world.

EXTREME WEALTH NOT THE HAPPIEST CONDITION IN LIFE — REASONS FOR THIS CONCLUSION.

Since the fundamental change in my religious views, I have not sought to accumulate a large fortune, nor desired to become a millionaire. I understood myself, whether others understood me or not. I do not consider it the happiest state of life. Far from it. The poor need money to supply their wants, while the extremely rich desire more wants to absorb their wealth. Extreme wealth and extreme poverty are two *opposites*, neither of which is at all desirable. When a man has reached the point of independence, where he is secure of the necessaries of life with reasonable effort, he is as rich as any one, if he only knew it. There are but three legitimate and just purposes for which a competency is desirable: first, the privilege of being independent; second, the power to be just; third, the ability to be more charitable. All beyond these purposes becomes a burden, which costs more than it is worth.

As a general rule, it is very difficult to acquire a *large* fortune in any honest, regular, useful business, without resorting to measures that can not be approved by conscientious men; such, for example, as monopolies of provisions, fraudulent combinations to unduly depress or put up the price of stocks, sharp tricks in starting or spreading false rumors, and the many other modes of overreaching one's neighbor.

Before a man can engage in these evil practices, he must first expel from his bosom all genuine love for his race. He must first make his selfish thirst for wealth the absorbing passion of his life, and to the same extent crush or smother every feeling of his better nature. He must first destroy his *capacity* for the enjoyment of the purest and most enduring pleasures of life before he can hope to succeed. He begins with a demoralized nature, goes on through life in the same condition, "then dies the same."

But, when he attains his position as millionaire by these unjust means, he is not at the summit of human happiness. There are thousands of vexations in his path. His wealth is almost certain to be overestimated five to one; and, while such a false estimate may flatter his vanity, he is expected to give in charity or otherwise an amount in proportion to this overestimate. If he fails to do this, then he is severely censured by his fellow men; and if he does comply with these expectations he soon ceases to be rich. He is forced by circumstances to become to a great extent an isolated being, and must limit his friendships to a very small circle. In fact, he can scarcely know the happiness of disinterested friendship, or of devoted love for his children. If he mingles freely in society, and is kind and cordial in his manners, many of those he meets will seek to take advantage of these circumstances to ask for pecuniary favors. Committees of both men and women call on him for contributions for charitable and other purposes, and will bring every influence to bear upon him. If he responds, the amount will hardly equal their expectations, or secure their genuine respect. He can not go through the streets of a city like other men. If he attempts it, he must dash along at a rapid rate, to avoid importunity on the way. If he gives or lends at all, he is beset so often and so persistently that he enjoys no privacy and no peace. If he gives nothing, then he is reproached very justly. He is compelled to go through the streets in his carriage, and to have his regular office-hours for seeing people, and his home in the country, where he can not be seen; or he must spend much of his time abroad, to escape the incessant importunities of friends and relatives, who desire loans they are likely never to return. If he is vain, they will flatter him to any desirable extent. If he receives any favors, he will often be expected to return about ten to one. Like the president of a large bank, who received a present of a fine Durham calf from an applicant for a large loan, he is very certain to become a victim if he consents to accept presents. In short, he is forced to become a being unlike others. To his condition the lines of Pope are most applicable:

"Painful preëminence! yourself to view,
Above life's weakness, and its comforts too."

But the most deplorable feature in the condition of a million-aire, whose fortune has been acquired by unjust means, is the unhappy effect it generally has upon his own descendants, and upon a large proportion of his relatives. Is is not the *practical* way to found, but to extirpate, a family. How few of the chidren and relatives of such men ever become good and happy members of society! This is particularly true in our country, where the law of entail does not exist. When a rich American dies, his property speedily goes into the hands of his heirs or legatees, or into the pockets of the lawyers; and, in nine cases out of ten, those who share his estate become poor before they die. It is well known that rich men make the most complex and silly wills of any class of people in our country. His children are reared in idleness and luxury. They may have a fair classical education, but no knowledge of business or of economy. The father is generally too busy and too selfish, and the mother too fond of travel and display, to teach the children any practical ideas of the serious business of life. When the large fortune is divided among a number of children, the portion that falls to each one is not sufficient long to maintain his expensive habits, because he is ignorant of the cardinal principles of practical business. Every true business man knows that it requires more sound business knowledge to *retain* than to acquire property.

Even if the parents use all reasonable measures properly to rear and educate their children, they will have a most difficult task to accomplish. They will find it impossible to conceal from their children the fact that the parents are rich; and it is exceedingly difficult, when they are once in the possession of this knowledge, to make the young people understand the *absolute* necessity of labor and economy. Everywhere they go, they hear people talk of their father's wealth, and how he ought to spend it, and how his children should enjoy life. These false ideas are incessantly inculcated by multitudes of people. The children are naturally led to conclude that the majority of voices is right, rather than the minority; when the truth is that, in business matters, the majority of people are almost certain to be in the wrong. Most of the sons, like the great majority of mankind, have no natural capacity for business; and how can good business men be made of such material?

The result is, the children half obey their parents while they *must*, be at the same time resolve in their own minds to show their parents, in due time, how to enjoy a fortune. Nine out of ten of the children of rich parents ultimately become poor, sour, unhappy, and worthless members of society. They generally make bad matches. The reason is obvious. Their inferiors in fortune are far more obsequious, deferential, and attentive than their equals. Poor young men who have *just* intellect enough to become well skilled in the usages and amusements of society, and fluent and accomplished in the ordinary topics of fashionable conversation, will be most apt to win the affections of young women who have nothing else to do but seek for pleasure. Rich young men never see young women except in fashionable life, and become enamored with some pretty, poor, and extravagant belle, possessed of more beauty than good common sense.

But the effect upon the other relatives is generally most injurious. If one of a number of brothers becomes very rich (and especially if such riches be acquired by improper means), then some of them will become agrarians, and urge a division. Some of them will be ambitious to rival the rich brother, and will plunge into wild speculations and fail. One portion of them will refuse to do anything they are competent to do, and others will run wild. Most of them will be extremely envious of the rich brother. When he assists one, he must aid all the others, or they will complain bitterly among the kin, and often among strangers. To aid so many in comparative idleness and wild speculations is a huge task. The largest fortune will soon vanish under such exorbitant demands. Each one thinks he ought to live as well as the rich brother; and they will do their utmost practically to carry out their views. If they do not administer upon his estate during his life, they are very apt to succeed after his death. The ultimate general result will be, that not one member of the family, remote or near, not even the rich man himself, will be really and substantially benefited by his riches. He has only accumulated this large fortune for others to waste, to their own material injury.

It is exceedingly difficult for a rich man to protect himself against the countless devices of those who seek his wealth. In large commercial cities especially, they will beset him with every possible plea. Many of the cases will be meritorious, as the world is full of real misery; while many will be false, as the world is full of vice.

To protect himself effectually, the rich man must be armed with the quills of the porcupine, or covered with the hide of the rhinoceros.

Not long since a man came to a rich old acquaintance in San Francisco, and asked for the loan of about one hundred and twenty-five dollars, to pay his passage to New York. He told a most plausible story, and intimated very plainly that he would commit suicide in case he failed to obtain relief. The rich man was deeply concerned, and came to me for advice. It seemed as if the man's life would be lost by his own criminal act in case he could not obtain the sum desired. If the rich man refused the request, then he might, to some extent, be answerable for the life of a fellow creature. If he advanced the money, he might do so to an unworthy man, and be thus encouraging vice by rewarding it. While we were considering the question, we ascertained that this man had drawn from a bank, only two or three days before, about one hundred and seventy-fivedollars. The request was refused; and within a day or two thereafter the man came into the office of the rich man, and boastfully showed him the amount of money he had applied for, alleging that he had obtained it from another person.

The *general* result is as I have stated. Of course, there are exceptions enough to prove the truth of the general rule. All the close observations of a long and active life have satisfied me, beyond a doubt, of the wisdom and truth of the sentiment written some thousands of years ago, and found in the grand old Bible:

" *Give me neither poverty nor riches.. "*

WIVES SHOULD BE CONSULTED ABOUT ALL IMPORTANT AFFAIRS — DAUGHTERS SHOULD BE TAUGHT A KNOWLEDGE OF BUSINESS — CONCLUSION.

The late Colonel John Thornton, then the most distinguished man of Clay County, Missouri, when considering a serious business proposition I submitted to him in 1835, made a remark to me that at once arrested my attention, and met my hearty approbation, it seemed to me to be so sensible and so just. He said: "Burnett, your proposition strikes me favorably; but before I decide upon it I must go home and consult my wife. It is a rule with me to consult her upon all important matters."

I adopted it myself, and have only violated it once or twice, and was justly punished when I did. I have for many years kept my wife well informed of the true state of my business affairs; and we both have taught our sons and daughters to understand business. She and myself have divided the labors and duties of life between us. For example, when we came to live in San Francisco in 1863, I said to her, "Wife, I have to run the bank, and you must run the house." She replied, "All right. You furnish me the money, and I will attend to the house."

As we were well advanced in life, and as we had a private residence in San José, and as I could use all my little capital under my own supervision, we decided to occupy a rented house, and we have been tenants ever since. We both agree upon the house to be leased, and all the bills for rent, fuel, and gas are paid by me. As to all other requirements, except my own clothes, she purchases and pays for them. I have about as little trouble keeping house as an ordinary boarder. The only things that I have purchased for the house since we came to the city were a few small articles during her temporary absence. I never inquire what we shall have to eat, and never know until I enter the diningroom. I follow St. Paul's recommendation and eat what is set before me, asking no questions. She purchases that which pleases her, and I do the same for myself. I have not the slightest concern as to how she will expend the money, knowing that she will apply it more judiciously than I could. I keep an account of all I pay into her hands, as well as of the sums I expend for my own apparel, so that I may know how my finances are running. We contract no debts, except for meats fuel, gas, and rent, and these are all paid at short intervals.

In the course of my long and busy life, I have known many rich widows, and about three fourths of them lost all or most of their estates for want of business knowledge. Their parents and husbands taught them nothing about business, and, when they became widows, they readily fell victims to the wiles of others. We men are engaged in business all our lives, and we never learn too much about it; and it is not at all surprising that women who have never been taught business, and never had any practical knowledge of it, should be overreached and cheated by the numerous and plausible sharpers that are sure to encounter them.

I knew a rich widow, who lent all the money of the estate in the month of May to a smooth, pleasant, plausible talker, without security, and lost it of course. This loan was made contrary to the advice of her lawyers. The result was, that in the month of December following she was forced to borrow money, at two per cent. a month interest, with which to pay the taxes upon the property of the estate. In the final result, the loss, including principal and interest, must have amounted to some twenty thousand dollars. This lady finally learned business by sad experience, and saved the larger portion of the estate.

My wife and myself have now (September 26, 1878) lived together more than fifty years. We have lived happy lives, and I trust we may die happy deaths. Our two sons and two daughters are well married. The two sons and one daughter reside in this city, and the other daughter in San José and we can see all the children and grandchildren within three hours. Our children are all that we could reasonably wish them to be; and our grandchildren, so far, have given us no pain, but have been a great source of pleasure to us in our old age. We have been greatly blest, for which we can not be too thankful to our Heavenly Father. Although

"Time's defacing waves
Long have quenched the radiance of our brows,"

our affection for each other is as warm and devoted as it ever was.

"The heart that once truly loves never forgets, But as truly
loves on to the close; As the sunflower turns on her god when
he sets The same look that she turn'd when he rose."
We have put our house in order. Our labors are about ended.
We know not the future; but we abide God's holy will with faith,
resignation, and hope. Charles Carroll of Carrollton said, in
his ninety-sixth year, that nothing gave him so much satisfac-
tion as the fact that he had regularly discharged his religious
duties. It is so with us.
"Though we are living now, 'twill soon be o'er;
Adown the West
Life's sun is setting, and we see the shore
Where we shall rest."

The End

THE NARRATIVE PRESS
TRUE FIRST-PERSON HISTORICAL ACCOUNTS

THE HISTORICAL ADVENTURE AND EXPLORATION SERIES

The *Historical Adventure and Exploration Series* from The Narrative Press are all first-hand reports written by the explorers, pioneers, scientists, mountain men, prospectors, spies, lawmen, and fortune hunters themselves.

Most of these adventures are classics, about people and places now long gone. They take place all over the world – in Africa, South America, the Arctic and Antarctic, in America (in the Old West and before), on islands, and on the open seas.

Some of our authors are famous – Ernest Shackleton, Kit Carson, Henry Stanley, David Livingston, William Bligh, John Muir, Richard Burton, Elizabeth Custer, Teddy Roosevelt, Charles Darwin, Osborne Russell, John Fremont, Joshua Slocum, William Manley, Tom Horn, Philip St. George Cooke, Apsley Cherry-Garrard, Richard Henry Dana, Jack London, and Buffalo Bill, to name a few.

One thread binds all of our books: every one is historically important, and every one of them is fascinating.

Visit our website today. You can also call or write to us for a free copy of our printed catalogue.

THE NARRATIVE PRESS
P.O. BOX 2487
SANTA BARBARA, CALIFORNIA 93120 U.S.A.
(800) 315-9005
www.narrativepress.com